MOTIVATION IN LEARNING CONTEXTS
THEORETICAL ADVANCES AND METHODOLOGICAL IMPLICATIONS

ADVANCES IN LEARNING AND INSTRUCTION SERIES

Series Editors:
Andreas Demetriou, Erik De Corte, Stella Vosniadou and Heinz Mandl

Published

VAN SOMEREN, REIMANN, BOSHUIZEN AND DE JONG
Learning with Multiple Representations

DILLENBOURG
Collaborative Learning: Cognitive and Computational Approaches

BLISS, SÄLJÖ AND LIGHT
Learning Sites: Social and Technological Resources for Learning

KAYSER AND VOSNIADOU
Modelling Changes in Understanding

SCHNOTZ, VOSNIADOU AND CARRETERO
New Perspectives on Conceptual Change

KOZULIN AND RAND
Experience of Mediated Learning

ROUET, LEVONEN AND BIARDEAU
Multimedia Learning: Cognitive and Instructional Issues

GARRISON AND ARCHER
A Transactional Perspective on Teaching and Learning

COWIE AND AALSVOORT
Social Interaction in Learning and Instruction

Forthcoming Titles

BROMME AND STAHL
Hypertext Writing

Related journals — sample copies available online from:
http://www.elsevier.com

Learning and Instruction
International Journal of Educational Research
Computers and Education
Computers and Human Behavior

MOTIVATION IN LEARNING CONTEXTS

THEORETICAL ADVANCES AND METHODOLOGICAL IMPLICATIONS

EDITED BY

SIMONE VOLET

School of Education, Murdoch University, Western Australia

SANNA JÄRVELÄ

Department of Education, University of Oulu, Finland

2001

Pergamon
An Imprint of Elsevier Science

Amsterdam – London – New York – Oxford – Paris – Shannon – Tokyo

ELSEVIER SCIENCE Ltd
The Boulevard, Langford Lane
Kidlington, Oxford OX5 1GB, UK

First edition 2001 by Pergamon (an imprint of Elsevier Science Ltd) in association with the European Association for Research on Learning (EARLI)

Library of Congress Cataloging in Publication Data
A catalog record from the Library of Congress has been applied for

British Library Cataloguing in Publication Data
A catalog record from the Library of Congress has been applied for

ISBN: 0-08-043990-X

Contents

110602

Contributors

Editors

Simone Volet   Associate Prof. Simone Volet
                        School of Education
                        Murdoch University
                        Murdoch 6150, Western Australia

Sanna Järvelä   Dr Sanna Järvelä
                        University of Oulu
                        Dept. of Educational Sciences and Teacher Education
                        P.O. Box 2000
                        FIN-90014 Oulu, Finland

NOTE: until the end of June 2001, Dr Järvelä is a Visiting academic at
                        King's College, London
                        School of Education
                        Franklin-Wilkins Building
                        King's College
                        Waterloo Road
                        London SE1 8WA

All authors and co-authors email contacts

Andreas.Krapp@rz.unibw-muenchen.de
Boekaert@FSW.LeidenUniv.nl
jean-luc.gurtner@unifr.ch
pintrich@umich.edu
Dhickey@coe.uga.edu
efklides@psy.auth.gr
joaols@mail.telepac.pt
turner.37@nd.edu
Peter.Opteynde@ped.kuleuven.ac.be
willy.lens@psy.kuleuven.ac.be
sjarvela@ktk.oulu.fi
marja.vauras@utu.fi
volet@murdoch.edu.au
wosnitza@zepf.uni-landau.de

All contributors' full contact addresses

Ch 1

Sanna Järvelä
(Note : co-editor of the book and also co-author of Ch 6)
Dr Sanna Järvelä
University of Oulu
Dept. of Educational Sciences and Teacher Education
P.O. Box 2000
FIN-90014 Oulu, Finland

Ch 2

Monique Boekaerts
Leiden University
P.O. Box 9555
2300 RB Leiden
The Netherlands

Ch 3

Daniel T. Hickey
Department of Educational Psychology
Learning & Performance Support Laboratory
University of Georgia
Athens, Georgia 30602
USA

Mary McCaslin
Department of Educational Psychology
The University of Arizona
Tucson, AZ 85721-0069
USA

Ch 4

Simone Volet
Associate Prof. Simone Volet
School of Education
Murdoch University
Murdoch 6150, Western Australia

Ch 5

Julianne C. Turner
Institute for Educational Initiatives and Department
of Psychology
University of Notre Dame
Notre Dame
Indiana 46556, USA

Ch 6

Sanna Jarvela
University of Oulu
Dept. of Educational Sciences and Teacher Education
P.O. Box 2000

Markku Niemivirta
Department of Education
P.O.Box 39
00014 University of Helsinki, Finland

Ch 7
Marina Lemos   Faculdade de Psicologia e de Ciências da Educaçào da
Universidade do Porto
R. do. Campo Alegre 1055
4150 Porto, Portugal

Ch 8
Peter Op't Eynde   Center for Instructional Psychology and Technology
(CIP & T)
University of Leuven
Veseliusstraat 2
B-3000 Leuven, Belgium

Erik De Corte   Center for Instructional Psychology and Technology
(CIP&T)
Department of Educational Sciences
University of Leuven
Vesaliusstraat 2
B-3000 Leuven, Belgium

Dr Lieven Verschaffel   Center for Instructional Psychology and Technology
(CIP&T)
Department of Educational Sciences
University of Leuven
Vesaliusstraat 2
B-3000 Leuven, Belgium

Ch 9
Marold Wosnitza   Centre for Educational Research, University of
Koblenz-Landau at Landau (Germany)
Friedrich-Ebert-Str. 12
D-76829 Landau, Germany

Peter Nenniger   Centre for Educational Research, University of
Koblenz-Landau at Landau (Germany)
Friedrich-Ebert-Str. 12
D-76829 Landau

Ch 10
Jean-Luc Gurtner   Institut de Pedagogie
Universite de Fribourg
Faucigny 2
1700 Fribourg/Switzerland

Isabelle Monnard   Department of Education
University of Fribourg
Faucigny 2
Switzerland

Philippe Genoud

Department of Education
University of Fribourg
Faucigny 2
Switzerland

Ch 11
Andreas Krapp

Universität der Bundeswehr Müchen
Institut für Psychologie und Erziehungswissenschaft
Fakultät für Sozialwissenschaften
85577 Neubiberg
Germany

Doris Lewalter

Universität der Bundeswehr Müchen
Fakultät für Sozialwissenschaften
85577 Neubiberg
Germany

Ch 12
Willy Lens

University of Leuven
Department of Psychology
Tiensestraat 102, B-3000
Leuven, Belgium
Belgium

Joke Simons

University of Leuven
Department of Psychology
Tiensestraat 102
B-3000 Leuven
Belgium

Siegfried Dewitte

University of Leuven
Department of Psychology
Tiensestraat 102
B-3000 Leuven
Belgium

Ch 13
Elizabeth Linnenbrink

Combined Program in Education and Psychology
The University of Michigan
Ann Arbor, MI 48109-1259 USA

Paul Pintrich

Associate Dean for Research, School of Education
Professor and Acting Chair,
Combined Program in Education and Psychology
The University of Michigan
Ann Arbor, MI 48109-1259 USA

Ch 14
Irini Dermitzaki

Ifigenias 14,
543 52 Thessaloniki, Greece

Anastasia Efklides
School of Psychology
Aristotle University of Thessaloniki
T.K. 540 06, Thessaloniki, Greece

Ch 15
Marja Vauras
Department of Teacher Education and Centre for
Learning Research
University of Turku
FIN-20014 Turku, Finland

Erno Lehtinen
Department of Teacher Education
University of Turku
FIN-20014 Turku, Finland

Pekka Salonen
Department of Teacher Education in Rauma and Centre
for Learning Research
Seminaarinkatu 1
FIN-26100 Rauma

Janne Lepola
Department of Teacher Education and Centre for
Learning Research
University of Turku
FIN-20014 Turku

Ch 16
Simone Volet
School of Education
Murdoch University
Murdoch 6150, Western Australia

Contacts of the two referees for the book

*Professor
Noel Entwistle*
Department of Higher and Further Education
The University of Edinburgh
Paterson's Land
Holyrood Road
Edinburgh EH8 8AQ
email: *Noel.Entwistle@ed.ac.uk*

*Professor
Wilbert J Mckeachie*
Combined Program in Education and Psychology
1406 SEB
The University of Michigan
Ann Arbor, MI 48109 USA
email: *billmck@umich.edu*

Part I

Introduction

Chapter 1

Shifting Research on Motivation and Cognition to an Integrated Approach on Learning and Motivation in Context

Sanna Järvelä

The research on motivation in learning has been prolific during the past decades. More research has meant more evidence that human learning is a complex phenomenon and motivation is an essential part of it. This assumption has not always been a joint consensus of opinion, but a lively discussion, even a debate, about how cognitive processes and motivation interact as elements of human learning (Sorrentino & Higgins, 1986). Most of the early research on motivation was associated with the consequential behavior of animals, human beings being considered too complex for researchers to study directly. The applications of such research to education, developed by educational psychologists, focused mainly on specific influences and actions that would result in a change of behavior (Weiner, 1990).

In the 1960s and 1970s motivation was seen as an alternative explanation for a cognitive process. As Sorrentino & Higgins (1986) describe in their review of a history of research on motivation and cognition, rather than studying the interaction of motivational and cognitive processes, a battle developed regarding which of the two, motivation or cognition, was a better explanation of the phenomenon of learning. Motivational aspects of learning were covered with alternative explanations coming from cognitive theory. For example, problems in behavior and learning were often seen to be due to information processing errors and cognitive limitations (e.g. Nisbett & Ross, 1980). In the 1980s much of the research was based on competence values and motivation was determined by what you expected to get and the likelihood of getting it (Ames & Ames, 1989). Motivating activities were considered to influence such emotions as pride, shame, guilt, and a general self-concept of the ability to achieve specific goals (Bandura, 1986). Taking into account these differences in assumptions of knowing and learning (Hickey & McCaslin, this issue) and the role of motivation in human learning, it is not surprising that "hot" and "cold" waves of discussion on motivation in learning have been billowing during the past century, depending on whether cognition or motivation was seen as the more relevant explanatory factor for human learning and behavior. Just as "hot cognitions" (stressing the interplay of motivation, cognition and social behavior) were insufficient explanations of information processing and perceptual processes; so, too, was the "cold approach" (stressing the cognitive

Motivation in Learning Contexts: Theoretical Advances and Methodological Implications, pages 3–14.
Copyright © 2001 by Elsevier Science Ltd.
All rights of reproduction in any form reserved.
ISBN: 0-08-043990-X

origin of human behavior) an inadequate explanation of social phenomena in learning. As Sorrentino and Higgins (1986) conclude, behavior is not a product of hot cognitions nor of cold cognitions, but rather motivation and cognition are inseparable.

Until the end of the 1980s, research on motivation had little contribution to research on learning. Even though detailed analyses of individual psychological processes of motivation in learning were evidenced, they very seldom were situated in classroom contexts or in processes of learning and instruction. Research was not focused on motivation during the learning process, since the conceptualization of learning was seen as an end product of certain task performance. Finally, an influential paper by Brown (1988) gave an impetus for researchers on learning and motivation to begin to design experiments in real contexts with increased interest in motivational issues (e.g. McGilly, 1994). Brown claimed that motivational aspects of learning had largely been ignored by many cognitive scientists and she called for researchers to take seriously motivational and emotional aspects of learning. Many researchers have since systematically examined the nature of the relations between different motivational constructs and students' cognitive engagement in academic tasks (e.g. Pintrich & Schrauben, 1992).

In the late 1990s educational psychologists' interest in contexts reflects trends in the study of cognitive development that emphasize the social nature of human learning (De Corte, 2000). During recent years there has been a lively discussion on whether we should follow individual or social perspectives on activity and on how we should conceptualize current understandings on situative or cognitive approaches (Anderson *et al.*, 2000). Through the influence of sociocultural and situated cognition theories, it has been recognized that motivation of individual learners is also influenced by social values and by the context in which the learning takes place. Motivation is no longer a separate variable or a distinct factor, which can be applied in explanations of an individual's readiness to act or learn — but it is reflective of the social and cultural environment. Finally, the gradual shift has occurred from learning and motivation research being almost different fields of research to a very integrated approach under the umbrella of the contextual perspective.

Issues Emerging when Considering Motivation in Context

This book considers the complex and still unclear issue of the dynamic relationships between context and motivation. While the role of contexts in shaping students' cognitions is becoming well integrated in the educational psychology literature (Anderman & Anderman, 2000), the construction of motivation in learning contexts still lacks a coherent theoretical foundation. Sociocultural, situative and socio-cognitive perspectives have questioned the ability of traditional motivation theory, focusing on general motivational beliefs and orientations, to adequately address the issue of situated motivation. These conceptual perspectives are dominant in this volume. They highlight the challenges created by trying to understand how learning activities provide support or constraints for learners' engagement in learning and at the same time how learners' subjective appraisals of situations play a mediating role in their commitment to engage in learning. Overall, there is widespread support for the view that understanding motivation in context is best achieved if conceptualized as a dual psychological and social phenomenon (Volet, this issue). By framing motivation in context from multiple conceptual perspectives and by examining its demonstration in real-life learning activities and contexts, this volume aims at making a conceptual advance to the field of motivation research and more broadly to research on learning and instruction.

Each chapter brings a unique research angle to the study of motivation in context. Conceptual and theoretical underpinnings have been given a special importance in order to strengthen the argument that the term contextual motivation should not be treated simply as a "concept in fashion". Together, the fourteen chapters propose original conceptual frameworks for researching and understanding motivation in context, examine epistemological issues underlying a contextualization of motivation, propose new distinctions for conceptualizing and operationalizing contexts, argue for the significance of multi-level, multi-dimensional and integrated theoretical models, and point to the significance of context sensitivity and situational dynamics alongside relatively stable motivational beliefs. The methodological implications of the conceptual shifts are addressed explicitly.

Reconceptualizing Motivation in Context

Because of historical roots in experimental and psychometric research, motivation researchers have been slow to develop or adapt contextual paradigms for their studies. The earlier motivational concepts were focused on the self while the context and social elements of the learning environment were left in the background. In recent years, researchers have focused less on stable personality characteristics and more on contextual factors, a trend consistent across all psychology and education research (Anderman & Anderman, 2000). Within a socio-cognitive perspective, contexts tend to be conceptualized as factors influencing the construction of motivation. Such factors can include schools, classrooms, family, peer groups, community, country, as well as culture, ethnicity and the historical context (Ames, 1992). In contrast, situative, socio-cultural perspectives conceptualize motivation in terms of active participation and engagement in learning activities and stress the importance of studying the learner-in-context (Turner & Mayer, 2000). The challenge for research on motivation is to integrate the notions of self and context. As some researchers have argued (Hickey, 1997; Järvelä & Niemivirta, 1999; Murphy & Alexander, 2000), the classical models of motivation may be inappropriate for studying newer forms of instruction, such as those grounded in a socio-constructivist tradition.

In her chapter "Context sensitivity: activated motivational beliefs, current concerns and emotional arousal" Monique Boekaerts provides arguments for reconceptualizing motivation in context and studying student motivation as a situated construct. Her position is that what students intend to do in the classroom and what they actually do to achieve these goals depends largely on how they appraise various learning situations and their contexts. In her chapter she reviews earlier studies on learning and motivation demonstrating that most motivation researchers have tended to study student motivation without taking adequate account of the immediate context that impacts on students' cognitions and effects and with little attention to the influence of appraisals, emotions and current concerns on the learning process. Her own studies during the past decade (Boekaerts, 1996; 1999) have shown how students' motivational beliefs interact with the cues present in diverse social, physical and instructional contexts in a student–situation transactional unit framework. Also reviewing other relevant research and providing examples, Boekaerts explains that, actually, it is not the learning situation itself that is crucial, but the meaning to a student of a learning or instructional situation. It is how he or she reacts to current concerns and to emotional arousals related to the context, on the basis of knowledge activated from his or her motivational knowledge base.

Daniel Hickey and Mary McCaslin's chapter "A comparative, sociocultural analysis of context and motivation" gives an impetus for further discussion on defining the conceptual and theoretical understanding of contextual motivation. Hickey and McCaslin explore context-oriented motivation from different epistemological perspectives, with a particular focus on sociocultural perspectives. Being "cautiously provocative" they argue that different assumptions about knowing and learning lead to very different assumptions about engagement in learning that, in turn, support different models of practice for motivating that engagement. They review how rationalist views of knowing and learning support a characterization of context as a source of information that can stimulate or inhibit the intrinsic sense making processes that are necessary for learning to occur. Empiricist assumptions about knowing and learning, instead, construe context as the source of both the associations that represent knowledge and the incentives for engaging in activity that causes those associations to be learned. Hickey and McCaslin also compare two very different ways of reconciling the differences between these perspectives, highlighting the shortcomings of the apparently popular "levels-of-aggregation" presented in recent discussion on cognitive and situative ideas of learning (Greeno *et al.*, 1996). In this approach, behavioral, cognitive, and situative perspectives are used to study thinking and learning at different levels of aggregation. What Hickey and McCaslin finally want to show is that any effort to define a contextual model of motivation must first set out assumptions about knowing and learning, and consider how those assumptions support additional assumptions about engagement in learning and principles of practice for motivating that engagement.

Simone Volet, in her chapter, "Understanding learning and motivation in context: a multi-dimensional and multi-level cognitive-situative perspective" discusses the conceptual and practical usefulness of adopting a multi-dimensional and multi-level cognitive-situative perspective for understanding learning and motivation in context. Her conceptual framework highlights the significance of mutual, reciprocal influences of individual effectivities and situational affordances. She makes a case for the criticality of understanding the person-context experiential interface from a combined cognitive and situative perspective. She presents research on transfer of learning across contexts to illustrate the usefulness of her conceptual framework for understanding international students' experiences in their familiar (home) learning environment and the less familiar (host) setting. Empirical evidence of subjective interpretations and ambivalence in what constitutes appropriate learning across cultural-educational contexts supports the usefulness of the multi-dimensional perspective and the significance of focusing on the person–context experiential interface. In the second part of her paper, she expands on her framework and locates the experiential interface within a multi-level perspective of person and context. She argues that conceptualizing contexts at different levels of specificity is critical for understanding the complex configuration of relatively stable motivational belief systems influencing behaviors, intra-individual variability across classroom activities, and individual tuning to the affordances of specific tasks and activities in that situation.

Motivational Concepts and Methodological Options for Studying Motivation in Natural Learning Settings

In recent years, a number of researchers have argued that applications of motivational theory have been limited by inadequate methodologies, research designs, and descriptions of what is actually happening in classrooms (Blumenfeld, 1992; Hickey, 1997; Järvelä *et al.*, 2001; Turner & Mayer, 2000). The dominance of deductive and quantitative methods of analyses, the use of research designs which involved only one or two points of data collection, and the scarce descriptions of classroom interactions are claimed to have led to little exploration of the how and why of motivation. The possibilities and limitations of combining different sets of methods in investigations of motivation in authentic contexts need to be examined.

Conceptualizing motivation in context challenges traditional research methodology and creates a need for the development of innovative approaches, which better capture the dynamic ways in which learners and context mutually interact in real-time in the classroom. The learner-in-context perspective has stressed the importance of revealing how subjective and dynamic processes generated within immediate tasks and situations mediate the impact of general and domain-specific belief systems, trait characteristics and tendencies. As a result, some researchers have drawn on multilevel approaches and methods for measuring motivation adequately. The research presented in this section examines various levels of motivation and motivated action and incorporates different planes of analysis.

Julianne Turner's chapter "Using context to enrich and challenge our understanding of motivational theory" illustrates how the notion of motivation in context and the use of mixed methods can challenge and enrich our theoretical understanding of motivation. The implications of context for the study of motivation are considered in relation to three perspectives on learning and motivation, and the assumptions underlying behavioral and cognitive approaches to learning and motivation are contrasted with the situative one. Turner claims that in an attempt to explore what motivation in context means, researchers need to move beyond and diversify traditional methods and foci of motivational research. She discusses methods appropriate for measuring motivation in context and introduces a mixed method approach. Use of mixed methods is a pragmatic perspective that incorporates both inductive and deductive, and both qualitative and quantitative methods simultaneously. An example from a program of research on motivation in context is presented to demonstrate the value of a situated approach to studying motivation, Turner also considers both the problems and opportunities emerging out of studying motivation in context.

Sanna Järvelä and Markku Niemivirta's chapter "Motivation in context: challenges and possibilities of studying the role of motivation in new pedagogical cultures" considers some theoretical and methodological issues in the research on motivation with a specific view to conceptualizing motivation from the situational and social cognitive perspectives. A special focus of their discussion is motivation and new pedagogical culture in terms of their characteristics for creating motivating learning environments. Järvelä and Niemivirta present a model that seeks to integrate the description of various aspects of a learning activity with a special emphasis on both students' motivational tendencies and situational interpretations, and their interaction with the contextual settings. Their theoretical underpinning for studying motivation in authentic learning situations derives from both action–theoretical and goal–theoretical perspectives on motivation. One of their arguments is that in order to gain some insight into the complexity of motivation in context, various sources of information need to be considered. That is, to draw valid inferences about how motivation comes about in natural learning settings, a variety of methods and analytical tools must be utilized. Finally, they introduce some methods used, such as questionnaires, video-tapings of students' learning activity, stimulated recall-interviews, and repeated process-oriented interviews for studying motivation in pedagogical contexts and present empirical examples (of data received).

In Marina Lemos' chapter "Context-bound research in the study of motivation in the classroom" an effort is made to show the importance of linking a relational goal-theory perspective with context-bound methodology and of describing variations in methodology associated with specific conceptions of motivation. The ideas presented are based on Lemos and her colleagues' studies aiming to describe students' motivation in the classroom with a special focus on students' goal orientations, and to identify conditions (person and environmental) that affect them. The emphasis on context-bound research derives from a general conceptualization of human motivation that argues for the centrality of meaningful behavior as opposed to behavior in itself. This conception has two major implications for research on motivated behavior: the examination of behavior-in-context and the concentration on motivational goals. In her chapter Lemos stresses a holistic dynamic interactionist model and context-bound methods where behavior is viewed as being determined by the reciprocal influences between the nature of the context and the individual's characteristics. In view of the reciprocal perspective, attention is also directed to subjective perspectives, as an example of the significance of the active role played by individuals in the determination of their own behavior.

In their chapter "What to learn from what we feel? The role of students' emotions in the mathematics classroom" Peter Op't Eynde, Eric De Corte and Lieven Verschaffel address a number of critical conceptual and methodological issues which have arisen from the most recent developments in the cognitive-situative debate (e.g. Anderson *et al.*, 2000). As part of their discussion of theoretical perspectives on emotions, they highlight a number of important points for mainstream research on the affective aspects of learning. In particular, they claim that in spite of the recognition of the interrelatedness of cognitive, conative and affective processes implied in socio-cognitive theory, most psychological and educational research favoring a social-historical perspective has focused mainly on cognitive and metacognitive processes. Affective and motivational factors are seldom intentionally studied within this theoretical framework. They take the discussion on the socio-historical perspective on learning further by stressing the conceptual and practical consequences of such a perspective for research on effect, next to but closely related to research on motivation. After exploring the conceptualization of motivation and effect within a socio-historical perspective, they elaborate on the socio-constructivist approach to the study of emotions and more specifically on how these relate to learning and motivation within that perspective. Their applied research in the mathematics classroom demonstrates the consequences of such a perspective for research on emotions and learning and the usefulness of combining quantitative and qualitative methods.

Students' Perceptions of the Learning Environment

Students' perceptions are thoughts, beliefs, and feelings about persons, situations and event. According to Schunk & Meece (1992), many types of student perceptions operate in classrooms, including self-perceptions, social perceptions and perceptions of tasks and environments. Self-perceptions, for example, involve perceptions of one's own abilities, self-concepts, goals, competence, effort, interest, attitudes, values, and emotions. Social perceptions refer to peers' abilities, self-concepts, goals, and so forth, as well as to perceptions of the various qualities of teachers and of the social processes of learning. Also important are students' perceptions of tasks and other classroom factors such as domain-related interest, task-type, classroom authority structure or pedagogical models used. Most motivation researchers have explicitly or implicitly defended the view that a student's actions in a classroom are affected jointly by personal characteristics and contextual factors. Yet the extent to which research acknowledges the influence of contextual variables on student behavior in the classroom varies. Students' current perceptions and interpretations of past experiences may play an essential role in contextual motivation. Recent studies examining the relationships between general motivational beliefs, situational appraisals, and performance have examined the importance of situation-specific self-appraisals in mediating the influence of general beliefs and prior achievements on later performance (Boekaerts, 1999; Niemivirta, 1999).

A contextual view of motivated learning, therefore, needs to describe how students' motivational beliefs interact with the cues present in diverse social, physical and instructional contexts. This means going beyond explanations of self-processes, and looking at the effects of collective experience where motivation is viewed as distributed among participants. The chapters in this section address a range of issues related to the conceptualization and operationalization of contexts. Psychosocial and future time perspectives, which are present in students' motivational interpretations in learning contexts, are discussed.

Marold Wosnitza and Peter Nenniger begin their chapter "Perceived learning environments and the individual learning process: The mediating role of motivation in learning" with a review of the traditions conceptualizing learning as an interaction between environment and personality coming from different historical roots of educational discussion. They claim that the issue of context has been subject to a traditional approach in the European history of instruction. The aim of their chapter is to discuss the possible interactions of external variables expected to be of significance within the individual learning process. For that purpose, Wosnitza and Nenniger conceptualize the learning environment at two different levels: the perspective of reality and the object of reality. They introduce the four combinations arising from the dimensions of the object and perspective of reality and from material and social objectives. They also examine the subjective perspective of social reality in more detail. The significance of aspects of a subjectively perceived learning environment on motivation within schools and universities is examined with descriptors such as student, class, and teacher. The influence of the subjective perception of a social learning environment on individual learning is taken as an illustrative example and supported by the results of an empirical study.

In a chapter entitled "Towards a multilayer model of context and its impact on motivation" Jean-Luc Gurtner, Isabelle Monnard and Philippe Genoud suggest a classification of contextual influences on students' motivation based on Bronfenbrenner's typology of environmental systems. According to the authors, an important contribution to the understanding of the interplay between an individual and its immediate environment is offered by Bronfenbrenner's ecological systems theory. They argue that the structure proposed by Bronfenbrenner to organize the various levels of influence of the environment on a person can prove useful to disentangle the various sorts of context discussed in motivation research even if one does not consider only contextual influences on a person's development, but use it more generally as a framework to understand the motives of a person's behavior or reaction. They see context as referring to the specific configuration of variables used by a given person or student to "recognize" and index a particular task or learning situation. Gurtner *et al.* report the results of a semi-longitudinal study, which observed the evolution of motivation and perceived classroom environment over two years among the 6th and 8th graders. These results highlight how different classroom environment variables contribute significantly to the students' motivation.

In their chapter "Development of interests and interest-based motivational orientations: a longitudinal study in vocational school and work settings" Andreas Krapp and Doris Lewalter discuss a theoretical framework which combines interest theory and person-object theory. The framework is found useful in making explicit statements about how an individual develops enduring preferences for specific subjects or contents of learning, and how the development of content specific motivational dispositions can be explained. They argue that research on motivation in longitudinal settings has been given little attention. Krapp and Lewalter provide an overview of their longitudinal research project in the field of vocational education. Their multi-level approach, combining quantitative and qualitative methods of analysis for studying the development of students' interest, illustrates how motivation can be studied with a variety of methods in authentic learning contexts. Besides questionnaires and tests, the use ESM-techniques (Experience Sampling Method) and interviews. These provide a broad variety of data on the conditions and effects of vocational education on the development of motivational variables such as motivational orientations and content-specific interests.

In their chapter "Student motivation and self-regulation as a function of future time perspective and perceived instrumentality", Willy Lens, Joke Simons and Siegfried Dewitte present a conceptual framework and empirical support for the role of future time perspective to commonly used motivational theories in educational psychology. Lens and his colleagues argue that contextual learning should not be limited to the present context. The anticipated individual future can create a meaningful context for learning and achieving. Student motivation is affected since people are aware that most of their behaviors, whether intrinsically or extrinsically motivated, have future consequences that may or may not be congruent with their present motivation. They also discuss the differential impact of several types of future goals on present motivation and goal orientation and illustrate this impact with empirical evidence.

Situational Dynamics of Motivation and Cognition

Sociocognitive perspectives on student motivation assume that both motivational and cognitive components are essential to describe students' actual learning in the classroom (Pintrich & Schrauben, 1992). Within this perspective, both motivation and cognition are influenced by the characteristics of the academic tasks that students confront in the classroom as well as by the nature of the instructional processes (Pintrich, 1989). More recent work adopting a dynamic approach regarding student adaptation and motivation to learning has revealed that different combinations of the learner's background, the social situation, the educational environment and the task characteristics result in different cognitive and emotional interpretations in different individuals (Lehtinen *et al.*, 1995; Lepola *et al.*, 2000). The last three chapters examine how various forms of context affect motivation, cognition and self-regulation in learning contexts.

The chapter entitled "Multiple goals, multiple contexts: the dynamic interplay between personal goals and contextual goal stresses" by Elizabeth Linnenbrick and Paul Pintrich provides a focused review of literature on the role and origin of multiple goals in learning contexts. In this chapter the authors extend goal theory to a consideration of multiple goals — rather than the traditional dichotomy of mastery and performance goal structure. The authors also discuss the dynamic interactions between multiple personal goals and multiple contextual goal stresses. When considering the impact of the environment, goal theory stresses the importance of examining both "objective" features of the classroom environment that can promote certain types of goals as well as more "subjective" and personal perceptions or construals of the context. Linnenbrink and Pintrich make a distinction between alpha (objective) and beta (subjective) presses as a framework for examining the relation of the classroom context to students' adoption of achievement goals. They argue that a multiple personal and contextual goal perspective leads to a more complex achievement goal theory, and that empirical support for this perspective would have to be sought in analyses of actual classroom interactions, including students' perceptions — the beta presses of the context.

Irini Dermitzaki and Anastasia Efklides' chapter "Age and gender effects on students' evaluations regarding the self and task-related experiences in mathematics" deals with metacognitive experiences, that is, feelings and judgments or estimates evoked during problem solving. Metacognitive experiences are the expression of the person's subjective evaluation of the task situation and the learning context and thus, they constitute the intrinsic context that accompanies learning. Their study on metacognitive experiences in mathematical problem solving highlights how the relationships between self-concept, metacognitive experience and performance change with increasing age in adolescence — which suggests that students interpret their intrinsic context in light of their already formed self-concept, of their growing expertise in the domain and of the learning context. These findings raise a number of questions as to the ways various forms of context affect motivation and self-regulation in specific learning contexts. In their discussion of contextual motivation perspectives, Dermizaki and Efklides warn of the risk of overlooking the more general or stable patterns of motivation across contexts if too much emphasis is placed on contexts and situational effects. They remind researchers not to lose track of the individual, in particular, how people interpret the various contexts in the light of their tendencies or abilities.

Finally, the chapter "Long-term development of motivation and cognition in family and school contexts" by Marja Vauras, Pekka Salonen, Erno Lehtinen and Janne Lepola discusses different motivational notions of achievement differences and presents an integrative, theoretical model of situational and developmental dynamics of cognitive–motivational interpretations and social interactions. They argue that their model can be used for analyzing the situational dynamics of student-task-teacher interaction as they relate to students' long-term development and to the institutional–cultural structures of the school. Their aim is to construct conceptual links between students' and teachers' situational adaptations, students' progressive and regressive learning careers, institutional–cultural frame factors and social regulation mechanisms. As their empirical work reveals, the origins of individual cognition and motivation can be traced to early social interactions within the home and family contexts. The authors review current research which helps understand how early family interactions contribute to later enhanced or retarded cognitive and motivational development. Cognitive and motivational development in conventional school contexts is related to research on reading and motivation. Finally, the motivational constraints which can be found in conventional and emerging learning contexts are compared and discussed.

The concluding chapter by Simone Volet, entitled "Emerging trends in recent research on motivation in learning contexts", discusses six major conceptual shift in the way research seems to be evolving and eight methodological implications of these conceptual shifts.

References

Ames, C. (1992), "Classrooms: goals, structures, and motivation". *Journal of Educational Psychology 84*, 261–271.

Ames, C., & Ames, R. (1989), *Research on motivation in education, Vol. 3: Goals and cognitions.* San Diego, CA: Academic Press.

Anderman, L. H. Y., & Anderman, E. M. (eds) (2000), "Considering contexts in educational psychology: Introduction to the Special Issue". *Educational Psychologist 35*(2), 67–68.

Anderson, J. R., Greeno, J. G., Reder, L. M., & Simon, H. A. (2000), Perspectives on learning, thinking, and activity. *Educational Researcher 29,* 11–13.

Bandura, A. (1986), *Social foundations of thought and action: a social cognitive theory.* Englewood Cliffs, NJ: Prentice-Hall.

Blumenfeld, P. C. (1992), "Classroom learning and motivation: clarifying and expanding goal theory". *Journal of Educational Psychology 84*, 272–281.

Boekaerts, M. (1996), "Personality and the psychology of learning". *European Journal of Personality 10,* 377–404.

Boekaerts, M. (1999), "Motivated learning: the study of student–situation transactional units". *European Journal of Psychology of Education 14*, 41–55.

Brown, A. L. (1988), "Motivation to learn and understand: on taking charge of one's own learning". *Cognition and Instruction 5*(4), 311–321.

De Corte, E. (2000), "Marrying theory building and the improvement of school practice: a permanent challenge for instructional psychology". *Learning and Instruction 10*(3), 249–266.

Greeno, J. G., Collins, A. M., & Resnick, L. B. (1996), "Cognition and learning". In: D. C. Berliner, & R. C. Calfee (eds), *Handbook of educational psychology* (pp. 15–46). New York: Simon & Schuster Macmillan.

Hickey, D. T. (1997), "Motivation and contemporary socio-constructivist instructional perspectives". *Educational Psychologist 32,* 175–193.

Hickey & McCaslin, this issue.

Järvelä, S., & Niemivirta, M. (1999), "The changes in learning theory and topicality of recent research on motivation". *Research Dialogue 2*, 57–65.

Järvelä, S., Salonen, P., & Lepola, J. (2001), "Dynamic assessment as a key to understanding student motivation in classroom context". Manuscript to be published in M. Maehr, & P. Pintrich (eds). *Advances in motivation and achievement: Vol. 12.*

Lehtinen, E., Vauras, M., Salonen, P., Olkinuora, E., & Kinnunen, R. (1995), "Long-term development of learning activity: motivational, cognitive, and social interaction". *Educational Psychologist 30*, 21–35.

Lepola, J., Salonen, P., & Vauras, M. (2000), "The development of motivational orientations as a function of divergent reading careers from pre-school to the second grade". *Learning and Instruction 10*, 153–177.

McGilly, K. (ed.) (1994), *Classroom lessons: integrating cognitive theory & classroom practice.* Cambridge, MA: MIT Press.

Murphy, P. K., & Alexander, P. A. (2000), "A motivated exploration of motivation terminology". *Contemporary Educational Psychology 25*, 3–53.

Niemivirta, M. (1999), "Cognitive and motivational predictors of goal setting and task performance". *International Journal of Educational Research 31*, 499–513.

Nisbett, R., & Ross, L. (1980), *Human inferences: strategies and shortcomings of social judgement.* Englewood Cliffs, NJ: Prentice-Hall.

Pintrich, P. R. (1989), "The dynamic interplay of student motivation and cognition in a college classroom". In C. Ames & M. Maehr (eds). *Advances in motivation and achievement: Vol. 6. Motivation enhancing environments* (pp. 117–160). Greenwich, CT: JAI.

Pintrich, P. R., & Schrauben, B. (1992), "Students' motivational beliefs and their cognitive engagement in classroom academic tasks". In D. Schunk, & J. Meece (eds). *Student perceptions in the classroom* (pp. 149–183). Hillsdale, New Jersey: Lawrence Erlbaum.

Schunk, D., & Meece, J. (eds) (1992), *Student perceptions in the classroom.* Hillsdale, New Jersey: Lawrence Erlbaum.

Sorrentino, R., & Higgins, T. (1986), "Motivation and cognition: warming up to synergism". In T. Higgins, & R. Sorrentino (eds). *Handbook of motivation and cognition: foundations of social behavior.* New York: Guildford Press.

Turner, J. C., & Mayer, D. K. (2000), "Studying and understanding the instructional contexts of classrooms: using our past to forge our future". *Educational Psychologist 35*, 69–85.

Volet, this issue.

Weiner, B. (1990), "History of motivation research in education". *Journal of Educational Psychology 82*, 616–622.

Part II

Reconceptualising Motivation in Context

Chapter 2

Context Sensitivity: Activated Motivational Beliefs, Current Concerns and Emotional Arousal

Monique Boekaerts

Motivational Beliefs: An Essential Knowledge Base

Mere observation of students' behavior in learning situations, reflection on our own actions, and questionnaire data reveal that behavior in a learning context is regulated by two main components, viz., (1) a domain-specific cognitive component and (2) a domain-specific motivation component. The domain-specific cognitive component pertains to factual and conceptual knowledge, skills, and abilities that one can bring to bear on the learning process itself. The domain-specific motivation component refers to students' motivational beliefs, including their attitudes, psychological needs, values and motives and how these beliefs affect their goal directed behavior. For a long time, researchers and teachers shared the view that students' actions in the classroom were a rational reaction to instruction and to teachers' requests to demonstrate learning. No distinction was made between learning that occurs spontaneously in natural learning situations (directed by the student's own goals) and learning that is the result of carefully planned teacher activities (teacher-directed learning). The rational view of learning is based on cognitive and metacognitive models of learning which have dominated the field for decades. It should come as no surprise that this view of learning has led to many misconceptions about classroom learning and to the design of sub-optimal learning environments.

Motivation researchers have argued that both the domain-specific motivation component and the domain-specific cognitive component are essential to understand students' behavior in the classroom. A large body of literature documents the claim that motivational beliefs have a strong effect on students' strategy use (for review, see Wigfield *et al.*, 1998). It should be noted, however, that motivation researchers have adopted various perspectives on classroom learning and on the impact that motivation has on it. It is not my intention to discuss these different perspectives here. Neither will I attempt to compare and contrast the constructs used in these different models. Instead, I will briefly point out, by way of illustration, that most motivation researchers tended to study student motivation without taking adequate account of the immediate context that impacts on students' cognitions and affects and with little attention to the influence of appraisals, emotions

Motivation in Learning Contexts: Theoretical Advances and Methodological Implications, pages 17–31.
Copyright © 2001 by Elsevier Science Ltd.
ISBN: 0-08-043990-X

and current concerns on the learning process. In the past, theories of motivation have dealt mainly with stable motivational traits. These traits can be split up into two main categories, namely general motivation traits and domain-specific motivation traits. The former refers to intra-individually invariant aspects of personality whereas the latter pertain to intra-individually invariant aspects across learning situations within a domain (e.g., Vicky is intrinsically motivated to solve math problems but extrinsically motivated to do history assignments).

It is a fact that most motivation researchers have explicitly or implicitly defended the view that a student's actions in the classroom are affected jointly by personal characteristics and contextual factors. Yet, the extent to which researchers believe that contextual variables influence student behavior in the classroom varies. Results obtained with self-report questionnaires, such as the Motivated Strategies for Learning Questionnaire (see, e.g., Pintrich, 1999), convinced researchers and educationalists that student motivation and cognitive strategy use differ by subject area. Since then, the study of motivation as a personality trait has been largely abandoned. Nevertheless, most of the current motivation research still deals with habitual or preferential behavior in the classroom, albeit in specific domains. Such an approach does not provide insight into students' goal setting and goal striving in actual learning situations. It is not my intention to discredit the work done by prominent researchers who focused on domain-specific motivation. Rather, I want to draw attention to aspects of motivation that have been under-explored in the literature so far.

Effect of Context on Classroom Behavior vs. Context Sensitivity

Firstly, I would like to point out that there is a difference between studies that investigated the effect of context on classroom behavior and studies that addressed contextual sensitivity. Many researchers have studied the effect that different instructional contexts have on students, as a group (e.g., Ames & Archer, 1988; Boggiano et al., 1989; Meece, 1991; Ryan & Deci, 1997). These authors showed that favorable domain-specific motivational beliefs, such as task orientation and intrinsic motivation, might be fostered by environmental conditions that the students themselves consider "favorable", such as autonomy and availability of peer support. Key variables that have been charted as "unfavorable conditions for learning" are teacher time pressure, emphasis on evaluation procedures, and instruction and support that is not adapted to the needs and values of the students. It is my contention that these studies have provided valuable insights with regard to the impact of the instructional procedures, teacher behavior, and the social environment on the activated motivational beliefs of students, *as a group*. However, the reflecting and feeling student who appraises the learning situation as it is unfolding, is absent from most of these studies. I argued elsewhere (Boekaerts, 1996) that researchers should go beyond the study of the antecedents of favorable motivational beliefs. They should register students' appraisals during actual learning episodes and study their effect on goal setting and goal striving.

For the past fifteen years, I have studied what motivates students to act in specific classroom situations. My research was guided by two main research questions: "How much of students' actual goal setting and goal striving is affected by (1) general, (2) domain-specific, and (3) situation-specific motivation?" and "In what way do emotions affect the students' actions in the classroom?" My main argument was that the context within which students must acquire new knowledge and skills appears to be quite stable because learning situations encountered at school are similar in many respects. Alleged stability in learning contexts suggests that students do not have to assess every learning situation in great detail before they can assign meaning to it. Yet, the content covered and the social context varies continuously in the classroom and this variability calls for context sensitive behavior on the part of the student. Are students able and willing to pay attention to cues in the learning environment that help them to assign meaning to the kaleidoscope of learning activities that are created in a school context? Such a question is generated from a theory of motivation that assumes variability in motivation across situations and time (situated motivation theory or context sensitive motivation theory).

The point I am making here is that adherents of situated motivation theories are not primarily interested in measuring students' desire to learn (stable trait), or their motivation to do math assignments (domain-specific trait). Rather, they want to document "stable" change in motivation. They consider stable change as an indicator of context sensitivity or intra-individual responsiveness to a learning situation and contrast it to unstable change, or in other words, to random behavior. For further discussion of these issues and of the distinction between structure-oriented and process-oriented models of motivation, see Boekaerts (1996, 2001) and Krohne (1996).

Empirical studies that focus on the dynamics of change in motivation are still relatively scarce (for exceptions, see Boekaerts, 1996, 1997, 1999; Krapp, 1999; Järvelä & Niemivirta, 2000; Schiefele, & Csikszentmihalyi, 1994; Volet, 1997). A dual focus is necessary to address this lacuna. Theories and models of motivation should reflect both the stable aspects of motivation (i.e., how general traits and domain-specific traits affect students' tendency to react favorably or unfavorably in relation to learning in a subject-matter domain) and a student's context sensitivity, given local conditions.

Context Sensitivity: Paying Attention to Environmental Cues

At this point in the discussion, I would like to raise the following question: "Why should motivation researchers address context sensitivity and incorporate it as a central construct in their current and future models of motivation?" What aspects of classroom learning make it necessary to incorporate context sensitivity, as a central construct, into current and future models of motivation? Before the 1990s, most educational psychologists accepted that there were individual differences in terms of ability and desire to learn. However, in the heydays of direct teaching and individual learning activities, educational psychologists neglected the learning context, even though they advocated that teachers who took account of individual differences in learning would achieve better results. For their part, motivation researchers described complex interactions between personal variables and subject-matter domains (state-trait interactions) and pointed to the importance of the instructional and social context for motivation and learning processes. Yet, their attempts to describe and measure components of the learning environment that facilitated or impeded learning were hindered by the typically teacher-directed learning environments that were in full swing at that time and by lack of adequate research methodology.

With the advent of teaching set up from a social constructivist perspective, major changes have swept the field of learning and instruction. Currently, there are strong pull and push phenomena at work. On the one hand, teachers are massively changing their teaching practice because research evidence as well as classroom observations show that students who are allowed to engage in social interaction in the classroom, learn in a fundamentally different way compared to students who are passively listening to the teacher's presentations (Slavin, 1996). On the other hand, examples of good practice in actual classroom settings invite researchers to adapt their research designs and methodology to be better equipped to describe and explain what is happening in actual learning situations. All over the world, collaborative innovation is being set up: teachers and teams of researchers work together, documenting that students are more willing to learn if they perceive the learning context as adapted to their needs (c.f. Randy & Corno, 2000).

Students' Goals may Change as a Function of Contextual Cues

My main argument has always been that motivation researchers should distinguish clearly between domain-specific motivational beliefs and appraisals of current learning situations (situation-specific motivational beliefs). Motivational beliefs refer to the opinions and judgments students hold about a specific aspect of reality, such as an object, event or domain (e.g., about a funfair or a subject-matter domain). The motivational knowledge base about a subject-matter domain, for example mathematics, includes the students' basic attitude, their psychological needs, motives and values in relation to the mathematics domain, but also the students' self-efficacy beliefs, outcome expectations, attributions, and perceived availability of social support. Information in the domain-specific motivational knowledge base is essential to appraise (perceive and interpret) cues in the actual learning situation. However, the environmental conditions are equally important to determine whether or not a learning opportunity is challenging, threatening or neutral for one's well-being. Students cannot appraise a present, past or future learning task unless they can take full account of the environmental conditions, including the local context and rivaling goals. The point being made is that learning intentions, which are generated in an actual learning situation, differ fundamentally from domain-specific commitments because they reflect "student by situation transactions." As such, learning intentions can be viewed as context specific commitment pathways (different from domain-specific commitment pathways), or students' decisions to engage in a specific activity, given local conditions.

In the last decade, researchers have used experience-sampling methods, which make it possible to record "student by situation transactions" while students are actually participating in unfolding learning episodes. These studies (e.g., Krapp, 1999; Vermeer, Boekaerts & Seegers, 2000; Volet, 1997) showed that students appraise learning tasks, and the social context within which they learn, differently. Several different types of appraisals can be discerned, such as task attraction, perceived relevance or utility, judgment of competence, perceived level of difficulty, success expectation, perception of control. These appraisals and concomitant emotions interact with the activated knowledge base.

It is important to realize that investigators who study context sensitivity do not claim that general or domain-specific motivational beliefs do not exist or are not important. On the contrary, this knowledge base is essential because the cues that students have to act on when assigning meaning to learning situations are usually not directly and unambiguously provided. This means that students have to infer the meaning of a learning activity from indirect cues, bringing their self-efficacy beliefs, expectations, and attributions into the picture (c.f., Boekaerts and Niemivirta, 2000). The following example illustrates that having insight into a student's domain-specific motivational beliefs is not sufficient to understand how he or she assigns meaning to a current learning situation.

Imagine that Vicky wants to become an engineer. She considers math competence as essential to achieve that goal and feels competent to solve mathematics problems. Under such conditions the chances are good that she will value math learning situations. One would expect that the activated motivational knowledge base that Vicky brings to bear on math learning situations is dominantly favorable. Does this statement imply that favorable motivational beliefs will always steer and direct Vicky's behavior in the math classroom? No it does not. Information that is present in the actual learning situation may modulate the domain-specific motivational beliefs, resulting in contextually sensitive behavior.

Indeed, context sensitivity draws students' attention to specific environmental cues, which have the potential to influence habitual or preferential behavior in the classroom. Imagine that Vicky's mother confronts the math teacher with the following concern: "I do not understand why my daughter got low marks for math this term and was expelled from class twice. She has always been highly motivated for math and, to my knowledge, she invests a lot of effort in her homework." The teacher may reply: "I agree with you that Vicky is generally a quiet, hard-working girl who invests a lot of effort in mathematics, except when she is with Kate." The qualifying statement "except when she is with Kate" points to contextually sensitive behavior. This example illustrates that context sensitivity gives rise to intra-individual differences in goal setting and goal striving. What the teacher's statement to Vicky's mother communicates is that in some learning environments (e.g., when Kate is not present) Vicky's achievement goals are activated and direct

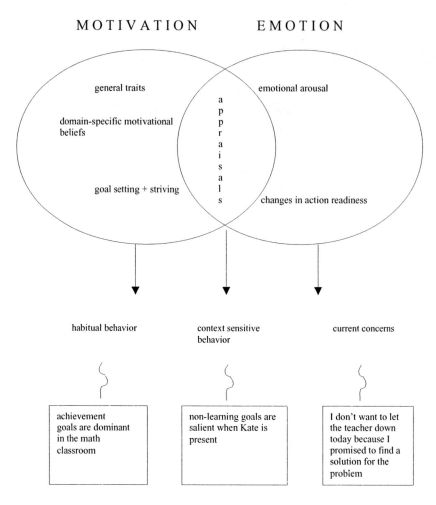

Figure 1: Relations between habitual behavior, context sensitive behavior and current concerns (top part) Illustrations of these three constructs with Vicky's example (see boxes).

her behavior. Apparently, other learning situations (e.g., having Kate as a neighbor) switch on non-learning goals, including social and well-being goals and this results in specific current concerns (see Figure 1, bottom part).

It is easy to imagine that students monitor the classroom environment and their own behavior as a function of the multiple goals they want to achieve. However, students are not always aware of the goals they are pursuing. They may become aware of their ever-changing goal structure when they experience imbalance in the goal system. Imbalance occurs when students perceive a misfit between what they believe should happen and what is, or when they perceive a conflict between the goals that different people hold for them (c.f. Boekaerts, 1998a,b, 1999; Boekaerts & Niemivirta, 2000). At such a point, students may experience emotional arousal due to feelings of disconnection, incoherence or conflict between goals. In our example, Vicky may orient differently to the learning process when Kate is present, because her friend expects her to give priority to private matters. Vicky may or may not be aware that her friend's goal is in disharmony with the teacher's goal, but her behavior suggests that her social goals have become salient in the math classroom.

Teachers and researchers should realize that different goals may become salient when the instructional or social context changes, or in other words, that the specific goals students set themselves (goal setting) may vary largely as a function of the perceived context. Granted, researchers and teachers are generally aware that students invest more effort when they are engaged in goal pursuits that reflect personal strivings. They also realize that negative affects experienced during the learning process, for example when bugs, obstacles or conflict arise, impede learning. Yet, direct discussions of the effect of emotional arousal and current concerns on the learning process have emerged infrequently in studies of motivation. Notable exceptions are discussions on the effect of anxiety on performance and learning (for review, see Zeidner, 1998), Pekrun's work on achievement-related emotions (Pekrun, 2000), Turner *et al.*'s (1998) work on the mediating effect of negative affect after failure, and my own work on coping with emotion in the classroom (Boekaerts, 1993, 1995, 1998a).

In the remainder of this chapter, I will argue that in the absence of salient contextual information, more habitual behavior (domain-specific behavior) will be noted. Detection of cues, which signal that learning tasks or interaction patterns are consequential in nature, may change students' motivation. They may then selectively attend to some cues (e.g., those that have consequences for their learner role) and ignore other cues (e.g., those that have consequences for their role as a "friend" or a "fun person"). I will refer to the results of some recent studies to illustrate these points.

Cues in the Environment may be Emotionally Arousing

In my double goal model of adaptable learning, two aspects of functioning in the real-life classroom are identified: mastering the content of the course and keeping positive emotional state (well-being) within reasonable bounds. It is assumed that students who have an emotionally sound personality strive to balance these two goals. How do they do that? And, what happens when they are not successful at striking that balance? I have argued elsewhere that optimistic appraisals are the key mechanism in goal setting and goal striving. Some students have the tendency to make optimistic appraisals whereas others rely heavily on loss or threat appraisals. I (Boekaerts, 1993, 1995, 1998a) explained that students who monitor for cues that signal uncertainty, difficulty and complexity experience negative affect and report pessimistic appraisals. These students are not primarily focused on the learning task. They are responding to environmental cues that are emotionally arousing and they are primarily concerned with restoring their well-being, rather than with learning (see also Salonen, Lethinen & Olkinuora, 1998).

Klinger's (1996) work is not so well-known in the field of motivation and learning. Yet, it can provide important insights into why students respond to some environmental cues and not to others. Klinger demonstrated that individuals always respond to cues that are emotionally arousing, mainly because some of these cues are innately linked to basic emotions (e.g., fear or anger) or are the result of conditioning (e.g., guilt or shame). Klinger also showed that individuals respond emotionally to current concerns. He described current concerns as internal states that are created by a commitment to the pursuit of a specific goal. He stated that an important property of a current concern is to make the individual emotionally alert to environmental cues associated with goal pursuit. Frijda (1986) defined emotions as changes in action readiness and current concerns as mental representations that turn an event into a satisfier (nonproblematic situation, associated with positive cognitions and emotions) or into an annoyer (situation that may cause damage, loss or harm). An extensive body of evidence (see Klinger for review) shows that current concerns govern people's perception, recall and thought processes. Also, these relations seem to be mediated by emotional arousal evoked by concern-related cues. As Klinger aptly puts it, the intensity of emotional arousal affects the probability that a person will continue to process given information in a certain way. In turn, continued cognitive processing modulates the intensity and nature of the emerging emotional state.

Pekrun (2000) provided a framework that clarifies how emotions may be evoked. He made a distinction between five different mechanisms. Two of these mechanisms concern us here, namely "cognitively mediated emotions" and "habitualized emotions". Pekrun explained that emotions may be induced by cognitive appraisals of current, past or future events. In our example, Vicky may feel worried, unhappy and tense when she realizes, for the first time, that she will not be successful in keeping both the teacher and her friend happy. I would like to speculate that the negative emotions that are evoked in that situation are cognitively mediated by pessimistic appraisals. In line with Pekrun's theorizing, it is hypothesized that this pattern of appraisal is stored as declarative knowledge in the motivational knowledge base. When Vicky encounters a similar situation, this knowledge may be activated, leading to similar emotions. Proceduralization of this knowledge may or may not occur. If it does, a direct link between environmental cues in the learning environment (perception) and emotion is established. Is there evidence that the distinction between cognitively mediated emotions and habitualized emotions is valid in a classroom context? Findings reported by Seegers & Boekaerts (1993), Boekaerts (1999) and by Turner et al., (1998a) suggest that motivational beliefs (opinions, judgments, and values attached to environmental cues in the learning environment) may trigger negative emotions directly (habitualized emotions).

Boekaerts and her colleagues (Boekaerts, 1999; Seegers & Boekaerts, 1993; Crombach et al., in press) explored the mediating role of appraisals. They

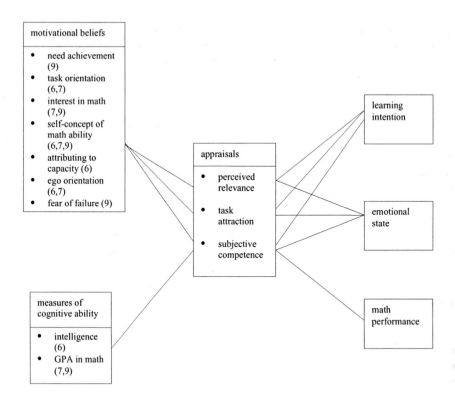

Figure 2: Summary of the structural models used to test the buffer hypothesis.

hypothesized that there is no direct link between domain-specific motivation beliefs, on the one hand, and emotional state, and willingness to invest effort in a concrete mathematics problem, on the other. Figure 2 summarizes the structural model that was tested on different data sets. As can be seen, a measure of cognitive ability was included in the model (intelligence in the 6th grade and Grade Point Average in mathematics in the 7th and 9th grade). At the beginning of each study the students completed several questionnaires that measured general or domain-specific motivation: ego/task motivation related to mathematics (6th and 7th grade), need achievement and fear of failure (9th grade), interest in mathematics (7th and 9th grade), self-concept of math ability (6th, 7th and 9th grade), attribution to math capacity (6th grade). The students' appraisals of math tasks were recorded with the on-line motivation questionnaire (perceived relevance, task attraction, and subjective competence) and used as mediators. No direct effects from general and domain-specific motivational beliefs on intended effort and emotional state were allowed. Rather, students' appraisals of the here-and-now-situation were considered to be the connecting link between stored motivational beliefs and their emotional states as well as willingness to invest effort.

A substantial percentage of the variance could be accounted for in emotional state (6th grade: 39 percent and 38 percent; 7th grade: 35 percent and 44 percent; 9th grade: 39 percent, 46 percent and 52 percent). In the 6th grade sample the percentage of the variance accounted for in emotional state and learning intention was roughly the same. In the 7th and 9th grade sample more variance could be explained in emotional state than in learning intention. There was no direct effect of domain-specific motivational beliefs on learning intention in any sample. All the variance was mediated by the appraisals, implying that whether or not students are prepared to invest effort in a math assignment depends largely on the way they appraise mathematics tasks in situ.

It is relevant to the present discussion that the effect of so-called "favorable" motivational beliefs on emotional state was also mediated by the appraisals (perceived relevance, task attraction, and subjective competence). This finding suggests that learning situations that have been positively valued in the past (reflected in domain-specific task orientation, interest, or a high self-concept) do not guarantee positive emotional state. Appraisals, recorded in situ, play a causal role in triggering emotional state. Interestingly, unfavorable motivational beliefs directly affected emotional state in the 7th grade sample (ego-orientation) and in the 9th grade sample (fear of failure) but not in the 6th grade sample. Hence, our hypothesis was violated in the 7th and the 9th grade sample. How can the observed direct link be explained? Fazio *et al.*, (1986)'s work on attitudes is informative here. These authors reported that strongly held positive and negative attitudes are activated automatically when individuals are exposed to objects that embody the attitude. In line with this finding, I suggest that a high score on fear of failure (personality trait) or ego orientation (domain-specific trait) may act as a strongly held negative attitude toward mathematics. This pessimistic "attitude" directly triggers negative affect in the older samples. In the 6th grade sample, the appraisals buffered the effect of both favorable and unfavorable motivational beliefs on emotional state. More specifically, students who had pessimistic motivational beliefs (high ego orientation, attribution of math results to capacity, or low self-concept of mathematics) judged their subjective competence as low when they were confronted with actual mathematics assignments. This, in turn, led to negative emotional state, low task attraction and low learning intention.

Taken together, these findings suggest that pessimistic motivational beliefs have a detrimental effect, not only because they have the power to trigger negative emotional state directly, but also because pessimistic motivational beliefs seem to counteract the positive effect that subjective competence may exert on emotional state and learning intention.

A recent study, Turner and her colleagues (Turner *et al.*, 1998b) also explored the relationship between goal orientation and affect. They found that students differ in their ability to ignore mistakes and tolerate errors during learning. Students who were task-oriented did not report negative affect after making mistakes. By contrast, students who were ego-oriented reported negative affect after failure (i.e., expressed negative emotions and the tendency to hide these feelings). In turn, negative affect impeded deep level processing, actions to promote learning, self-efficacy beliefs, and preference for difficulty. In line with

Klinger's work, I would like to speculate that students always react to environmental cues that emotionally arouse them, because these cues are the result of conditioning. Abundant research documents that students who believe that they cannot meet the learning goals in the math classroom may want to avoid these learning situations. Their current concern (or context-specific commitment pathway) is then to avoid the undesirable consequences of their actions in such problematic situations. In a similar way, students like Vicky, who experience a conflict of interest between learning goals and social goals, may want to avoid the undesirable consequences of their actions in social situations they have categorized as "annoyers". Very little is known about the way students deal with such conflict of interest in the classroom. Future research should address the ways students deal with conflicting goals in the classroom.

Conclusion and Guidelines for Further Research

At the beginning of the present chapter, an attempt was made to illustrate that there is a difference between studies that have explored the effect that different instructional contexts have on students' motivation, as a group, and studies that have addressed students' context sensitivity in actual learning situations. Researchers who draw their hypotheses from situated motivation theories are interested in how motivation changes as a function of environmental cues that students selectively attend to or ignore.

It was argued that Klinger's theoretical framework about emotions is a very powerful one for the study of context sensitivity in the classroom. He stated that an important property of current concerns is to make the individual emotionally alert to cues associated with goal pursuit. It is unfortunate that the construct of current concerns has not been used in the educational psychology literature so far. I would like to urge researchers to investigate the effect that distinct aspect of an emotional experience (see right ellipse in Figure 1) may have on students' perceptions of the learning content, their learning intention, well-being and learning processes. Attention was also drawn to the theoretical framework provided by Pekrun and the results of a few recent studies were used to explain the distinction that Pekrun made between habitualized emotions and cognitively mediated emotions. Both Boekaerts' and Turner's studies provided preliminary support for the validity of this distinction in the life classroom. Turner's findings revealed that not all students experience emotional arousal during learning experiences that involve mistakes and potential or actual failure. An interesting question raised by Boekaerts' study is why the habitualized emotion effect holds for negative emotions only. Most of what needs to be known about a student's cognitively mediated and habitualized emotions in class and the effect of various emotional states on learning still awaits empirical exploration. Questions that need to be answered are: To what extent can optimistic appraisals of a learning situation buffer negative attitudes/feelings about a subject-matter domain? Are strongly held positive and negative domain-specific motivational beliefs activated automatically when students are exposed to learning assignments in that domain? Which appraisals are most likely to buffer strong negative feelings about a subject-matter domain? Does perceived availability of social support buffer negative feelings about a subject-matter domain? To what extent do emotions, experienced during the learning process, affect effort investment? What does it take to turn a teacher-initiated learning goal into a student's current concern? Do all students become emotionally alert to cues associated with a current concern?

In this chapter a set of ideas that I think is important in conceptualizing student motivation was sketched. There is evidence that appraisal processes mediate the effect of information activated from the motivational knowledge base on emotional state and learning intention in actual learning tasks. It is essential to understand how students assign meaning to a learning activity and to the social and instructional context in which it is embedded. Questions such as these have been part of my research program for some time. I also recently began to explore the classroom as a social arena where students may cause stress but also provide social support. Indeed, classrooms are places where students have learning and social experiences. As Wentzel (1996) pointed out, the social world of youngsters and their social goals play a dominant role in their school life. This implies that social experiences and their mental representations, which are always impregnated with values, needs, expectations and norms, help students assign meaning to learning episodes. Put differently, learning situations in the life classroom are not static. They dynamically change as a function of the perception of cues in the social environment that are emotionally arousing or cues that have become salient because they are linked to current concerns.

Based on my work on social support and coping with stress, I believe that students who frequently report meeting with impediments in the classroom have learned to pay attention to cues in the learning environment that keep them into the "unsuccessful student" role. Teachers and fellow students who try to reassure these unsuccessful students can only help them if they have information about the cues in the learning environment that these students consider relevant. In one of our recent studies the effect of perceived social support on students' well-being at school was investigated (Boekaerts, Seegers & Vedder, in press). We found that specific cues in the social environment were associated with well-being in school. The perception of available teacher support is such a cue. Perception of peer support is not unambiguously linked to well-being in class and awaits further exploration.

The point that I am making is that students who are not motivated in the classroom identify many learning situations as "annoyers" and monitor for cues that signal uncertainty, disharmony, and complexity. In order to help these students, teachers need to have information about their context sensitivity. Motivation researchers are able to register the effect that motivational beliefs have on students' monitoring of the learning environment, provided that they are prepared to make use of new forms of measurement. In this respect, it is noteworthy, that at present most motivation researchers have shifted from quantitative-measures-only research designs to studies in which more qualitative methods, such as interviews, video observations, case studies, diaries, and stimulated recall are used alongside quantitative instruments.

I have already hinted at the present tendency to set up collaborative innovations. Researchers realize that good practice pushes theory ahead. For their part, teachers are increasingly aware that nothing is so practical than a theory that describes the strategies that are instrumental to motivated learning. Motivation researchers can profit from this interesting "Zeitgeist" phenomenon when they decide to address student context sensitivity and the effect it has on classroom learning. In doing so, they will further develop the theory of situated motivation and learn a lot about the cues in the learning environment that students consider "motivating" and "demotivating". I would like to invite all motivation researchers to put the prominent topic of context sensitive behavior on their research agendas.

References

Ames, C., & Archer, J. (1988), "Achievement goals in the classroom: Student learning strategies and motivation processes." *Journal of Educational Psychology 80*, 409–414.

Boekaerts, M. (1993), "Being concerned with well-being and with learning." *Educational Psychologist 28*, 149–167.

Boekaerts, M. (1995), "Self-regulated learning: Bridging the gap between metacognitive and metamotivation theories." *Educational Psychologist 30*, 195–200.

Boekaerts, M. (1996), "Personality and the psychology of learning." *European Journal of Personality 10*, 377–404.

Boekaerts, M. (1997), "Capacity, inclination, and sensitivity for mathematics." *Anxiety, Stress, and Coping 10*, 5–33.

Boekaerts, M. (1998a), "Coping in context: Goal frustration and goal ambivalence in relation to academic and interpersonal goals." In E. Frydenberg (ed.) *Learning to Cope: Developing as a Person in Complex Societies* (pp. 175–197). Oxford: Oxford University Press.

Boekaerts, M. (1998b), "Boosting student's capacity to promote their own learning: A goal theory perspective." *Research Dialogue 1* (1), 13–22

Boekaerts, M. (1999), "Motivated learning: studying student*situation transactional units." In M. Boekaerts & P. Nenniger (eds) Advances in motivation from the European viewpoint [Special Issue]. *European Journal of Psychology of Education 14* (1), 41–55.

Boekaerts, M. (2001), "Motivation, Learning, and Instruction." *International Encyclopedia of the Social & Behavioral Sciences*. Oxford: Elsevier.

Boekaerts, M. (in press), "The on-line motivation questionnaire: A self-report instrument to assess students' context sensitivity." In M. Maehr & P. Pintrich (eds) *Advances in Motivation and Achievement, Vol. 12, Methodology in Motivation Research.*

Boekaerts, M., & Niemivirta, M. (2000), "Self-regulated learning: Finding a balance between learning goals and ego-protective goals." In M. Boekaerts, P. R. Pintrich & M. Zeidner (eds) *Handbook of Self Regulation* (pp. 417–450). San Diego, C.A.: Academic Press.

Boekaerts, M., Seegers, G. & Vedder, P. The Tandem Social Support Questionnaire (TSSQ): Measuring the Distinction between Perceived Need and Availability of Social Support in the Classroom. Manuscript submitted for publication.

Boggiano, A. K., Main, D. S., Flink, C., Barrett, M., Silvern, L. & Katz, P. A. (1989), "A model of achievement in children: The role of controlling strategies in helplessness and affect." In R. Schwarzer, H. M. van der Ploeg & C. D. Spielberger (eds) *Advances in Test Anxiety Research* (pp. 13–26). Amsterdam: Swets & Zeitlinger.

Crombach, M. J., Voeten, M. J. M., Boekaerts, M., & Seegers, G. Development of a model to explain students' willingness to engage in actual curricular task situations. Manuscript submitted for publication.

Fazio, R. H., Sanbonmatsu, D. M., Powell, M.C., & Kardes, F. R. (1986), "On the automatic activation of attitudes." *Journal of Personality and Social Psychology 50*, 229–238.

Frijda, N. H. (1986), *The Emotions*. Cambridge (Great Britain): Cambridge University Press.

Klinger, E. (1996), "Emotional influences on cognitive processing, with implications for theories of both." In P. H. Gollwitzer & J. A. Bargh (eds) *The Psychology of Action* (pp. 168–192). New York: The Guilford Press.

Järvelä, S., & Niemivirta, M. (2000, May), *Motivation in Learning Context: The Interplay of Personal Beliefs and Situational Actions*. Paper presented at the 7th Workshop of Achievement and Task Motivation, Leuven, Belgium.

Krapp, A. (1999), "Interest, motivation and learning: An educational–psychological perspective." *European Journal of Psychology of Education 14*, 23–40.

Krohne, H. W. (1996), "Individual differences in coping." In M. Zeidner & N. S. Endler (eds) *Handbook of Coping. Theory, Research, Applications* (pp. 381–409). Wiley, New York.

Meece, J. (1991), "The classroom context and students' motivational goals." In M. Maehr & P. Pintrich (eds) *Advances in Motivation and Achievement 7* (pp. 261–285). Greenwich, CT: JAI Press.

Pekrun, R. (2000), "A social–cognitive, control–value theory of achievement emotions." In J. Heckhausen (ed.) *Motivational Psychology of Human Development* (pp. 143–163). Oxford: Elsevier.

Pintrich, P. R. (1999), "The role of motivation in promoting and sustaining self-regulated learning." *International Journal of Educational Research 31*, 459–470.

Randy, J., & Corno, L. (2000), "Teacher innovations in self-regulated learning." In M. Boekaerts, P. R. Pintrich & M. Zeidner (eds) *Handbook of Self Regulation* (pp. 651–685). San Diego, C.A.: Academic Press.

Ryan, R. M., & Deci, E. L. (1997), "Self-determination theory and the facilitation of intrinsic motivation, social development, and well-being." *American Psychologist 55*, 68–78.

Salonen, P., Lehtinen, E., & Olkinuora, E. (1998), "Expectations and beyond: The development of motivation and learning in a classroom context." In J. Brophy (ed.) *Advances on Research on Teaching 7* (pp. 111–150), London: JAI Press.

Schiefele, U., & Csikszentmihalyi, M. (1994), "Interest and the quality of experience in classroom." *European Journal of Psychology of Education*. Vol. IX, 3, 251–270.

Seegers, G., & Boekaerts, M. (1993), "Task motivation and mathematics achievement in actual task situations." *Learning and Instruction 3*, 133–150.

Slavin, R. E. (1996), "Research on cooperative learning and achievement: what we know, what we need to know." *Contemporary Educational Psychology 21*, 43–69.

Turner, J. C., & Meyer, D. K. (1998a), "Integrating classroom context into motivation theory and research: Rationales, methods, and implications." In T. Urdan, M. Maehr & P. Pintrich (eds) *Advances in Motivation and Achievement 11* (pp. 87–121).

Turner, J. C., Thorpe, P. K., & Meyer, D. K. (1998b), "Students' reports of motivation and negative affect: A theoretical and empirical analysis." *Journal of Educational Psychology 90*, 758–771.

Turner, J. C. (2000, May), *Enriching and Challenging Motivational Theory Through the Study of Situated Motivation*. Paper presented at the 7th Workshop of Achievement and Task Motivation, Leuven, Belgium.

Vermeer, H. J., Boekaerts, M., & Seegers, G. (2000), "Motivational and gender differences: sixth-grade students' mathematical problem-solving behavior." *Journal of Educational Psychology 92*, 308–315.

Volet, S. E. (1997), "Cognitive and affective variables in academic learning: The significance of direction and effort in students' goals." *Learning and Instruction 7*, 235–254.

Wentzel, K. R. (1996), "Social and academic motivation in middle school: Concurrent and long-term relations to academic effort." *Journal of Early Adolescence 16*, 390–406.

Wigfield, A, Eccles, J. S. & Rodriguez, D. (1998), "The development of children's motivation in school contexts." *Review of Research in Education 23*, 73–118.

Zeidner, M. (1998), *Test Anxiety: the State of the Art*. New York: Plenum Press.

Chapter 3

A Comparative, Sociocultural Analysis of Context and Motivation

Daniel T. Hickey & Mary McCaslin

The study of achievement motivation initially focused on the identification of enduring individual difference factors defined by maintenance over time and generalization over tasks and situations. Less attention has been paid to consideration of the broader and more particular social and physical aspects of the environment — the contexts — in which motivated activity occurs. Weiner (1990) concluded his history of achievement motivation research by stating that it has "overlooked the fact that achievement behavior influences and affects others, who have behavior expectations" and that motivation "must be considered within the context of social values and superordinate culture" (p. 620).

Mirroring a general trend in psychology, the last decade has seen increased concern for defining "context" among motivational researchers. The many thoughtful works in the present volume are but one example of the degree to which many educational researchers — particularly those concerned with motivation — are addressing non-individual factors such as task structure, social climate, culture, curricular context, authority, and rewards (c.f. Anderman & Anderman, 2000, Anderman & Maehr, 1994; Blumenfeld *et al.*, 1991; Boekaerts, 1998; Järvelä, 1998; Kaplan & Maehr, 1999; Paris & Turner, 1994; Volet, 1999).

Within the general trend away from enduring and stable personality traits and towards a better appreciation for situated contexts, the impetus for more contextual models of motivation and the initial conceptualization of "context" varies widely. Some researchers may be driven by the desire for a more comprehensive theory of motivation, while others may be driven by the desire to more directly inform educational practice. Some models may be limited to social factors, while others may consider physical factors as well. Some may be limited to classroom environments while others may include the broader community. As such, even relatively well-specified contextual variables (e.g., "classroom instructional context") can be operationalized in remarkably different fashions (Turner & Meyer, 2000). Most significantly from our perspective, the mere act of identifying a specific contextual motivation factor makes assumptions about knowing and learning that may not be apparent or be held by others. Practically, this means that one researcher's investigation of contextual motivation might be based on constructs that other researchers consider epiphenomena — and that some

Motivation in Learning Contexts: Theoretical Advances and Methodological Implications, pages 33–55.

educators, policy makers, and parents consider irrelevant. Indeed, it seems premature at this point in our discussion to craft even the most general definition of "contextual motivation."

This chapter considers how different views of knowing and learning support particular characterizations of context, principles of practice, and corresponding research. Specifically, we will consider "contextual motivation" from three different epistemological perspectives, generally corresponding with the theories associated with Skinner, Piaget, & Vygotsky. While acknowledging the potential peril of identifying and labeling such broad and potentially overlapping perspectives, we choose to label them *behavioral/empiricist*, *cognitive/rationalist*, and *situative/ sociocultural*, respectively. Several factors compel this consideration. One is the apparent resurgence of empiricist perspectives, particularly within the context of accountability-oriented educational reforms and renewed emphasis on standardized achievement tests. As we will argue, there are fundamental tensions between empiricist perspectives and the rationalist perspectives that underlie most modern motivation research. We believe that this tension can and will undermine educational reform efforts when researchers and educators assume that practices that follow from these two perspectives can readily coexist or complement each other.

A second factor compelling our effort is the ascendance of sociocultural perspectives. Perspectives generally associated with Vygotsky have become quite influential in education in the last decade, but their relationship with prior motivation research is complex and ill-defined (Hickey, 1997). Empiricism's re-emergence and socioculturalism's ascendance in the context of rationalism's continued, and dominant, influence has introduced unprecedented competition between educational practices that follow from the three perspectives. Greeno *et al.* (1996) and Case (1996) provide thoughtful descriptions of these three models of knowing and learning and associated principles of practice — but with limited consideration of motivation and engagement. Greeno *et al.* (1996, p. 40) argued that "in the next several years, one of the salient theoretical questions will be continuing clarification of the relations among these three perspectives." The present effort can be characterized as a response to Greeno, Collins, and Resnick's suggestion that "other issues can also be informed by the kind of discussion we have begun to develop in this chapter, perhaps organized by the same theoretical perspectives that we have used" (1996, p. 40). To this end, we will consider the notion of contextual motivation from the model of engagement that follows from each of the three views of knowing and learning. In doing so we try to show that one must first consider how "context" is conceptualized within a given theory of knowing and learning before considering the motivational implications of particular contexts. For the sake of clarity, we assign the term *motivation* to practices that are assumed to motivate engagement in learning, and focus our theory-building on the construct of *engagement*. This approach precludes discussion of motivation to learn without first specifying one's assumptions about the nature of learning.

Our contribution to this discussion is cautious. While our own perspective is most directly influenced by situative/sociocultural perspectives, our primary concern is the development of new and potentially more effective models of practice, rather than issues of sheer theory development. We acknowledge that our analysis is necessarily brief and emphasizes differences while ignoring similarities. More judicious and detailed analyses of competing perspectives (e.g., Tudge & Winteroff, 1993) have been criticized for overemphasizing initial conceptualizations of competing theories and ignoring their evolution (i.e., Zimmerman, 1993). However, we believe that a comparative consideration is useful in light of recent calls for research that emphasize the need for effective models of practice over traditional concerns with theoretical coherence and parsimony.

There has been a significant shift in the relationship between theoretical and practical work among many leading educational psychologists worldwide (see De Corte, 2000; Donovan *et al.*, 1999). This new approach simultaneously develops fundamental scientific understanding while designing learning environments, formulating curricula, and assessing learning. Coherence, parsimony, and predictive validity are no longer the sole questions or even the initial questions being asked of theories. This new approach presumes that research embedded in the activities of practical reform will yield theoretical principles with greater scientific validity than those developed within efforts focused on sheer theory development. In such an approach, the implicit and explicit assumptions of practitioners and practices become critical, if not paramount, because these assumptions influence whether and how new models of practice will be adopted. As such, we believe that scientifically valid consideration of something as far-reaching as "contextual motivation" must consider assumptions about knowing and learning behind existing or proposed practices and reforms.

Our ultimate goal is considering different ways to reconcile the competing assumptions and practices associated with the three different perspectives to better inform and improve practice. Reconciliation between rationalist and sociocultural perspectives is implied in recent efforts to consider motivational contexts (e.g., Anderman & Anderman, 2000, p. 67). It is our intent to make such reconciliation deliberate and explicit, and broaden it to include empiricist perspectives as well.

A Behavioral/Empiricist Focus on Lower-Level Associations

Empiricist views of the psychology of knowing and learning were initially refined in behaviorism, and later, within early human information processing models. They continue to provide the core assumptions of some models of human information processing theory (e.g., Anderson *et al.*, 1996), more recent connectionist information processing perspectives (e.g., Rumelhart, 1997), and prescriptive instructional systems design models (Visscher-Voerman *et al.*, 1999). Particularly relevant to our call for expanded epistemological reconciliation, empiricist views are also consistent with the naïve "folk psychology" worldview of most individuals who have not been schooled in a particular perspective (Olson & Bruner, 1996).

Empiricist perspectives construe the mind as a device for detecting and operating on patterns in the world. The "world" is construed as an objective knowable reality, offering some ultimate "truth" to be known. To "know" something means possessing associations that represent fragments of that external reality that include a repertoire of both patterns that the organism has learned to detect and operations that can be executed on those patterns. The mind is assumed to be initially a blank slate upon which associations are collected in an automatic and mechanistic fashion. Whether characterized as stimulus–response or cognitive associations, the fragments that represent one's knowledge of a domain are presumably arranged in a hierarchy, with "higher level" thought the function of "associations of associations" that occur prior in the hierarchy. Empiricist perspectives are inherently *reductionist* (assuming that complex behavior or concepts consist of smaller elements) and *additive* (assuming these smaller elements readily assemble into an accurate representation of the more complex entity).

When knowledge is viewed as an organized collection of associations, learning is by definition the process of forming, strengthening, and adjusting those associations. It occurs as organisms are exposed to patterns in the environment, enabling them to recognize and respond to them, and continues as smaller associations are assembled into larger ones. An obvious implication of this "bottom-up" view is that learning contexts can and should be characterized and structured as a network of associations and associations of those associations. In such a characterization, every level of context relative to the individual is construed as an aggregate of the same constructs used to characterize the activity of individuals. In other words, any aspect of the context where learning occurs, from individual interactions with the environment to the broader sociocultural community, is characterized using the same individually-oriented constructs — but at increasingly higher levels of aggregation. Another implication concerns the centrality of context. When learning is viewed solely as building or strengthening of internal representations of associations present in the environment, the nature of that environment — the context — is the sole determinant of learning.

Engagement as Extrinsically Motivated Activity. From an empiricist perspective, engagement is by definition the maintenance of the routines of activity that cause behavioral or cognitive representations of associations to be made and strengthened. The impetus for such engagement is always "extrinsic" in that it is derived from the environment, outside of the individual, in the form of incentives that the environment offers for engaging in those routines. The individual's goals, needs, and dispositions — things that are not context — are relevant only to the extent that they reveal prior learning history and define what is perceived as punishment and what is perceived as reward. Reflecting a mechanistic metatheoretical worldview, behavior is directly influenced by environmental contingencies, without conscious deliberation, in a manner that is qualitatively the same in all organisms and for all kinds of learning.

Behaviorists have traditionally defined activity that appears to be carried out for its own sake (what others call "intrinsically motivated") as behavior for which the controlling stimuli for the behavior have yet to be identified (Cameron & Pierce, 1994). Behaviorists acknowledge the value of intrinsic *rewards* — the natural consequences of the behavior — as distinct from intrinsic *motivation* that will be shown to follow from rationalist views. Reward is construed as reinforcement provided by the environment and the relationship between the reward and learning is seen as very direct and automatic: "We learn to cook from the pleasant sights and fragrances, and flavors that result from our culinary efforts; we learn to read from the understanding we get from the printed words" (Chance, 1992, p. 202).

An often-overlooked behaviorist presumption is that engagement in learning ideally occurs without artificially derived incentives. As long as the task or concept can be learned in sufficiently small units, the mastery of each is presumed to provide sufficient reward to maintain engagement. Nonetheless, proponents of empiricist approaches presume that there are many situations or instructional goals (particularly in formal educational contexts) where intrinsic rewards are problematic (Chance, 1992). For example, students may lack the necessary prerequisite skills, or the rewards may be too remote or too weak relative to the rewards for engaging in other less-desirable behaviors.

In order to "shape" the responses of the individual to ensure that needed associations are constructed and reinforced, one must first break down complex tasks and concepts into smaller components. These components are then sequenced from simple to complex. Because learners start at different levels and proceed at different speeds, self-pacing is a centerpiece of both behavioral and cognitive empiricist instructional approaches. While these approaches prescribe a great deal of control over the immediate learning environment, they pay little attention to the broader context in which that environment is situated:

> Teachers do not control the environments students come from, the knowledge they bring with them, whether they had breakfast before school or whether they will go home to an empty house. However, they do control the learning environment in the classroom (Fredrick *et al.*, 2000, p. 42).

Similarly, Anderson *et al.*'s (1985) Geometry Tutor provided a highly structured learning environment that represented a state-of-the-art instantiation of a theory of cognition in the form of organized pairs of tiny if-then associations. Tutors were deployed in classrooms with apparently very little consideration of the broader aspects of the classroom or school context in which they were being used.

Some empiricist models, however, have prescribed aspects of the broader contexts. However, because they used aggregated application of individual-level assumptions about learning and engagement, these models did not need to specify any particular assumptions or principles when prescribing broader school environments. Notable examples include Carroll's (1963) model of school learning and Engelmann's DISTAR (1988). Other school reformers, however, did attempt to transform society with their ideas, most notably Benjamin Bloom's (1976) model of "mastery learning." Because empiricist assumptions are so consistent with naïve folk-psychology views of motivation, many conventional educational practices are consistent with empiricist assumptions. While the use of more tangible rewards such as token economy practices remain controversial, typical grading practices, class competition, gold stars, breaking down complex tasks, and the like are all generally consistent with empiricist views. Perhaps most importantly, large-scale educational assessment practices (the apparent tool of choice for many contemporary reform efforts), like most classroom assessment practices, are generally consistent with empiricist assumptions (James & Gipps, 1998; Kelleghan *et al.*, 1996).

In summary, empiricist assumptions about knowing and learning construe "context" as the source of both the associations that represent knowledge and the incentives for engaging in activity that causes those associations to be learned. If one starts from an empiricist model of knowing and learning, a contextualist model of achievement motivation considers whether the context provides associations that need to be learned, along with sufficient incentives to keep the learner engaged in the routines of activity needed to build and strengthen behavioral or cognitive representations of those associations. Just as knowledge of the environment can be characterized as an aggregation of smaller associations, the incentives to maintain engagement in the environment can be characterized as an aggregate of the individual-level incentives. As such, no special constructs are needed to study the motivational aspects of the broader contexts. Therefore, prescriptions and constructs shown to be relevant to individual level activity are appropriate for designing learning contexts that motivate engagement and for studying the consequences of different contexts on engagement and learning.

A Cognitive/Rationalist Focus on Higher-Level Cognitive Structures

Rationalist perspectives emerged as a major orientation in research on learning and teaching in the 1970s. Although there was a shift away from the explicitly Piagetian "stage-theory" models (and the associated focus on very general reasoning abilities) in the 1980s, rationalist models continue to be very influential in educational, developmental, and cognitive psychology, and in the study of motivation (See Case, 1996). These perspectives view knowledge in terms of "structures of information" and processes that recognize and make sense of (i.e., "rationalize") symbols in order to understand concepts and exhibit general abilities. In contrast to the empiricist characterizations of human thought as higher-order instantiations of the same lower level processes in other organisms, rationalist perspectives view human thought as the result of intrinsic and uniquely human sense-making processes.

From this perspective, "knowledgeable" activity indicates the marshalling of knowledge structures needed to construct a solution for (i.e., make sense of) the demands of a particular task. This "top-down" approach is fundamentally antithetical to the "bottom-up" assumptions in empiricist models. Thus "context" is the source of new information and new associations that initiate the intrinsic sense-making processes that must occur for learning to take place, and is relevant to learning to the extent that it stimulates these internal processes.

Engagement as Intrinsic Sense-making Activity. When learning is viewed in terms of intrinsic sense-making processes, engagement in learning occurs quite naturally when experience is inconsistent with current understanding. Therefore, engagement in learning is a function of prior knowledge, experience, and understanding, relative to the environment in which learning is expected to take place. Generally, individuals must have an expectation that they will be able to make sense of the new information in the environment as well as some prior knowledge relevant to that learning environment if learning is to occur. In general, these two assumptions also underlie the expectancy X value model that underpins most modern motivation research. Well-known expectancy-related constructs include *self-efficacy* (e.g., Schunk, 1991), *goal orientation* (e.g., Schutz, 1991) and *self-determination* (e.g., Deci, 1980). Well-known value-related constructs include *task value* (e.g., Wigfield & Eccles, 1992), *individual interest* (e.g., Renninger, 1992), *personal interest* (e.g., Schiefele, 1991) and *situational interest* (e.g., Hidi & Anderson, 1992). Research in this tradition generally reflects a strongly organismic metatheoretical perspective, whereby theories about internal processes are tested in correlational or experimental studies of multiple subjects.

From a rationalist perspective, engagement in learning is enhanced when intrinsic sense-making is provoked and obstacles to intrinsic sense-making processes are removed. Expectancy-related obstacles include various negative self-perceptions that lead to ego-protective disengagement rather than sense-making. Perhaps the most salient value-related obstacles are explicit extrinsic rewards offered for learning, which are presumed to thwart intrinsic sense-making processes and form maladaptive attributions (as in the "overjustification effect" documented in Lepper & Greene, 1978, and emphasized by Kohn, 1993).

Rationalist views of engagement lead to a very different characterization of "contextual motivation" than the empiricist assumptions described earlier. Rather than serve as the source of the associations that represent knowledge, context is viewed as the source of uncertainty or disequilibria that cause the internal sense-making processes necessary for learning to occur. Rather than the source of incentives to maintain engagement in necessary routines of activity, context presents expectancy-related and value-related information that can encourage or discourage sense-making processes. Despite such differences, rationalist models of contextual motivation share an important characteristic with the empiricist models depicted earlier: In both cases, the same constructs are used to characterize multiple levels of context. As such, constructs developed in earlier personality-trait oriented models of individual motivation (e.g., performance orientation and learning orientation) are used in the aggregate to characterize broader social contexts. Thus, rationalist efforts to characterize contextual motivation primarily look at how aspects of classroom, school, and community contexts influence internal cognitive variables, such as goal orientation, that are presumed to impact engagement in intrinsic sense-making processes.

Epstien's TARGET framework (Task, Authority, Recognition, Grouping, Evaluation, and Time; 1989) is perhaps the most influential of the rationalist characterizations of context. An extensive body of research in this tradition has examined how these modifiable aspects of learning context foster appropriate goal states, expectations for success in learning, and value for mastery of tasks that afford that learning (e.g, Anderman & Young, 1994; Kaplan & Maehr, 1999). The majority of this research has relied on self-report measures to assess goals, expectations, and values within correlational or experimental designs; recent efforts have employed observational methods as well (e.g., Turner, 1995). In general, this research has documented how many common educational practices (i.e., normative grades, implicit or explicit competition, public displays of achievement, etc.) in classrooms and in the larger school environment serve to diminish students' intrinsic interest in academic domains and school in general. This research in turn has led to useful and influential sets of guidelines for creating motivated learning contexts — particularly regarding the needs of disadvantaged students (e.g., Bempechat, 1998; Corno & Randi; 1999; Covington & Teel, 1996; McCombs & Pope, 1994).

In summary, rationalist views of knowing and learning support a characterization of context as a source of information that can stimulate or inhibit the intrinsic sense-making processes that are necessary for learning to occur. This characterization fundamentally differs from the empiricist's. Consider, for example, that the decomposition of complex tasks and concepts that is central to empiricist views of engagement essentially removes the complexity that causes the disequilibrium necessary for rationalist learning processes to occur. Thus, it is not surprising that proponents of rationalist models of motivation have railed against educational practices that are consistent with empiricist models. As argued most vocally by Kohn (e.g., 1993) and perhaps most influentially by Anderman and Maehr (1994), rationalist views argue that many of the perceived problems in contemporary education are caused by maladaptive performance-oriented goals that are the result of empiricist practices that predominate school learning contexts — particularly starting in the middle grades when intrinsic motivation declines most sharply.

Given the general dominance of rationalist perspectives among motivational researchers, the preceding overview likely applies to many contemporary efforts to define "contextual motivation" and to prescribe motivating learning contexts (including those in the present volume). We acknowledge that this characterization is exceedingly brief and ignores the many continuing debates within the vast and diverse community of scholars to whom we refer. Indeed, many of these same researchers have questioned the dichotomizing of intrinsically-motivated and extrinsically-motivated activity (e.g., Pintrich & Garcia, 1991; Roeser, Midgely *et al.*, 1996) and some have begun to support the value of performance-oriented goals and some forms of competitive practices (e.g., Hidi & Harackiewicz, in press). Particularly problematic (as pointed out by Zimmerman, 1993, and, personal communication, 1999) is the application of a comparative analytic framework such as ours to approaches that are rooted in social learning, now, "social cognitive" theory (i.e., Bandura, 1989). Certainly we agree that there are aspects of social cognitive theory that are consistent with empiricist, rationalist, and, as we will see, sociocultural perspectives. However, we contend that both the intended and actual consequences of social cognitive models of motivation for educational practice are generally consistent with cognitive/rationalist perspectives.

More critically, we argue next that while social cognitive models have some overlap with situative/sociocultural perspectives, many of the key elements of these newer perspectives simply cannot be captured within social cognitive models.

A Situative/Sociocultural Focus on Participatory Rituals

Rooted in Vygotsky's seminal work following the Russian Revolution, sociocultural perspectives began to achieve prominence in the 1980s, and have continued to evolve within education, developmental psychology, and cognitive science. These perspectives view knowledge as a cultural entity that is distributed across the physical and social environment in which that knowledge is developed and used. Thus an individual's knowledge of a particular domain is presumed to be situated, or "stretched across" the people, books, computers, classrooms, worksheets, etc., present in the context in which the knowledge is being used. Reflecting an inherently contextualist metatheoretical perspective (and the associated metaphor of the historical event), every aspect of the context in which understanding is developed, is, at some level, part of that understanding. Because all knowledge is assumed to originate in the interaction of the social and material worlds, it is presumed that the social and material worlds are a fundamental part of all knowledge (Lave & Wenger, 1991).

In sharp contrast to the acquisition-oriented metaphors that epitomize both empiricist and rationalist models of knowing and learning, sociocultural views are epitomized via participation-oriented metaphors (see Sfard, 1998). Thus, "knowledge" is represented in the regularities of successful participation — rituals, rather than associations or concepts that individuals acquire. Regularity is presumed to be possible because the knowledgeable individual has become familiar with (i.e., "attuned to") the constraints and affordances that simultaneously bound and scaffold successful participation. Knowledgeable individuals use the physical and social tools that maximize successful participation and overcome the limitations of the mind. Given this view of knowledge and expertise, learning is construed as any meaningful participation in the construction of socially-defined knowledge and values, and occurs as communities of individuals co-construct understanding of a domain in whatever context it is encountered.

In the extreme, this perspective argues that both the empiricist's lower-level associations and the rationalist's higher-level conceptual structures are both epiphenomenal artifacts of an individual's participation in the particular test, task, or interview used to derive them. In other words, scores on a multiple choice content test as well as the responses to a clinical interview are both indicative of the degree to which the individual is attuned to the constraints and affordances on participation in those particular socio-physical contexts.

Engagement as Participation in a Community of Practice. As enumerated by Greeno *et al.* (1996), the core principles for designing effective learning environments from a sociocultural perspective are (1) fostering participation in social practices of inquiry and learning, (2) providing support for positive epistemic identity, (3) developing disciplinary practices of discourse and representation, and (4) providing practice in formulating and solving realistic problems. Learning environments that follow from these principles presume a characterization of engagement as meaningful participation in a context where to-be-learned knowledge is valued and used. This participation involves the maintenance of interpersonal relations and identities in that community, as well as satisfying interactions with the environments in which the individual has a significant personal investment. Because communities are defined by their participants, individuals do not independently choose to participate or not participate, or to participate actively or passively. Every member of a particular community of practice participates in the establishment and maintenance of the community that in turn impacts every other member as well as her own participation.

Viewing engagement as meaningful participation places more of the burden for motivating engagement on contexts and less on individuals, and presumes that individuals cannot and should not be solely responsible for compensating for inadequacies in learning environments. The perspective embodied in the principles enumerated above suggests that the "community" in many typical classrooms is not organized around or identified with the use of meaningful knowledge. If so, it will be difficult for a given individual to learn that knowledge. This is not to say that such students are not learning; by virtue of their presence in the classrooms, all students are arguably participating in, and therefore learning, the knowledge represented by whatever rituals in which they happen to participate. However, that knowledge may be unrelated to (or possibly antagonistic to) the knowledge ostensibly being taught. But contrary to common misperception, a sociocultural characterization does not presume that engagement occurs primarily, or even ideally, in collaborative, social, contexts. Because socially constructed knowledge is represented in books, lab materials, computers, and other physical artifacts, learners engaged in solitary activity around those artifacts can be meaningfully engaged in the practices of a larger knowledge community. Conversely, active participants in collaborative learning activities can be completely disengaged from the larger community to which they are ostensibly being acculturated (e.g., the practices of scientists), such as when ill-conceived activity structures more strongly reward participation in other less desirable practices.

The heightened emphasis on context in sociocultural approaches alters concerns with motivational contexts, relative to prior rationalist approaches. This difference is perhaps best epitomized by Dweck's rationalist argument that "effective interventions consist not simply of creating an environment in which children's maladaptive tendencies do not come into play, but in promoting more adaptive tendencies that will generalize to less utopian settings" (1989, p. 90).

A period of intensive development efforts carried out in Brown's (1992) "design experiment" tradition and exemplified by the work of Brown and Campione (e.g., 1996) and the Cognition and Technology Group at Vanderbilt (e.g., 1997) presumed that the lack of even remotely "utopian" learning environments was precisely the source of the enduring maladaptive tendencies of concern to trait-oriented theorists. This work also showed that creating such learning environments is anything *but* simple. However, these efforts have been carried out in relative isolation from modern motivation research (Hickey, 1997). As such, the implications of this work for motivation have been either ignored or misconstrued. Interestingly, though, a few studies (e.g., CTGV, 1992; Garrison *et al.*, 1994; Hickey *et al.*, forthcoming; Hickey *et al.*, 1993) have shown that even relatively isolated participation in socioculturally-inspired environments is a promising means of promoting the more "enduring adaptive tendencies" like personal interest and learning goal orientation that differential psychologists have focused on and tried to promote.

Using sociocultural perspectives to create motivational learning contexts raises many challenging new issues and sheds new light on old issues. Consider, for example, Bereiter and Scardamalia's (1989) notion of *intentional learning* as activity during which the "problem" that students are attempting to solve is the lack of knowledge itself. This is very different from the more rationalist "incidental" learning presumed to occur as a byproduct of students' efforts to solve problems in the environment. Even if those latter problems being solved are "authentic" and meaningful, it is a different and more challenging goal to orient learners towards genuinely intentional learning. Learning environments that follow from the four principles enumerated above should all support intentional learning by making it more salient and observable and, therefore, more acknowledgeable. As such, these environments provide heretofore unexplored avenues for rewarding intentional learning. In these contexts, the rationalist dichotomy between an extrinsic "performance orientation" and an intrinsic "learning orientation" should break down, because "demonstrating one's competence" and "engaging in learning-oriented activity" should become synonymous. If this is true, the presumed negative motivational consequences of common educational practices such as celebrating individual excellence and providing salient extrinsic rewards — and the resulting enhancement of performance-oriented goals — should have demonstrably less negative impact on outcomes in these learning contexts (see Hickey, 1997, and Collins *et al.*, 1989, p. 490).

Many theorists advancing sociocultural perspectives (e.g., Salomon, 1993) argue for a social cognitive model similar to Bandura's (1989), suggesting that we can and should maintain a clear distinction between the individual and the environment. While such perspectives presume that the individual is an active participant in learning and motivation, they nonetheless focus on constructs like self-regulation that are presumed to reside in the individual and interact with particular environmental contexts. However, when engagement is characterized as participation in knowledge communities, the social and physical aspects of that environment are ultimately responsible for scaffolding the learner's participation in inquiry and learning. From a sociocultural perspective, scaffolding is conceptualized within a master-apprentice relationship. The master's activity is deliberately selected to move the learner's activity further into the zone of proximal development. By coaching the student's activity towards proficiency and fading that assistance when no longer needed, the learner's participation (and the zone of proximal development) is continually advanced. Arguably, approaches that consider the individual in isolation from the environment place too much of the responsibility for engagement on the individual learner. From a sociocultural perspective, such approaches yield an impoverished model of scaffolding, precluding the development of the kinds of environments that afford participation in meaningful learning.

Within the present consideration of contextual motivation, this issue — the degree to which individuals are considered independently of contextual factors — is expected be a focus of vigorous, worthwhile, debate. Op't Eynde *et al.* (this volume) point out that researchers must prioritize their investigations and make critical decisions about factors such as the primary unit of analysis. Along with other leading researchers who are considering motivation from a sociocultural perspective (e.g., Järvelä & Niemivirta, 1999), Op't Eynde *et al.*, provide a spirited defense for the continued reliance on individually-oriented constructs like self-regulation as well as enhanced study of social and environmental preconditions and interactions. From our perspective, the question is not whether individuals should be considered in the study of contextual motivation — we believe that a multidimensional approach is both desirable and inevitable. (c.f., Volet, 1999). Rather, the question is how to prioritize individual, cognitive, and social issues, and how to reconcile the inevitably conflicting interpretations within multidimensional efforts (see McCaslin & Hickey, in press). As we will argue in the next section of this paper, multidimensional approaches raise a host of issues that must be addressed before real progress occurs.

Different Approaches to Reconciliation

The preceding discussion showed that the tension between different views of knowing and learning is most pronounced between empiricism and rationalism. Because of the fundamentally different assumptions about knowing and learning, it seems impossible to resolve these tensions. If so, the widely cited debate between Chance (e.g., 1992) and Kohn (e.g., 1993) over the consequences of extrinsic rewards for learning appears ill-focused. Similarly, we wonder about the ultimate value of the meta-analytic study which led Cameron and Pierce (1994) to dismiss concerns over the consequences of rewards, and the dismissal of that conclusion by Lepper *et al.*, (1996).[1] Without a broader consideration of assumptions of knowing and learning, arguments over empiricist and rationalist educational practices and associated research findings appear irreconcilable. While, to a lesser extent, we also wonder about the outcome of efforts to reconsider the negative consequences of extrinsic rewards from within largely rationalist perspectives (e.g.

---

[1] While the irreconcilable assumptions may limit the value of the debate, this was certainly a worthwhile example of scholarly advance. In particular, we found Lepper, Keavney, & Drake's (1996) discussion of the limitations of meta-analytic methods in general and the methods used by Cameron & Pierce (1994) invaluable.

Hidi & Harackiewicz, in press, Harackiewicz *et al.*, 1998). Most fundamentally to the present discussion, it seems problematic to use the constructs that follow from empiricist perspectives to characterize and study practices that follow from rationalist perspectives, and vice versa. While there are certainly tensions between sociocultural perspectives and the other two, these tensions do not appear as fundamental as the tension between empiricist and rationalist perspectives — a point we elaborate next.

We have alluded to two paths that might be followed to incorporate social factors into achievement motivation research. One uses individually-oriented constructs to characterize and study the broader contexts; the other starts from explicitly contextualist constructs and uses them to also characterize and study the activity of individuals. Following is a further consideration of these two paths, in light of prior efforts at reconciliation.

Epistemological Reconciliation via Levels-of-Aggregation

Greeno *et al.* (1996) acknowledged the *levels-of-aggregation* approach to reconcile competing perspectives. In this approach, behavioral, cognitive, and situative perspectives are used to study thinking and learning at different levels of aggregation. The behavioral analysis is used to study activities of individuals; the cognitive analysis also looks at individuals, but as a more detailed consideration of internal structures of information and their transformation; the situative analysis is an aggregated effort that "studies activity systems in which individual agents participate as members of social groups and as components of larger systems in which they interact with material resources" (p. 40). In such a reconciliation, the behavior of individuals is characterized within the mechanistic "individual-as-machine" metaphor associated with behaviorist perspectives. In contrast, the "individual-as-developing-organism" metaphor associated with cognitive/rationalist perspectives is used to derive the broader principles that best explain patterns of activity across individuals. At this intermediate level of aggregation, the units of analysis are the patterns of activities across individuals, as best explained by more general principles concerning the manner in which information about the environment is represented and transformed. Finally, a "historical event" metaphor and the contextualist worldview associated with the situative/sociocultural perspective is used to derive the principles that best explain the broadest patterns of activity across social groups.

The levels-of-aggregation approach to reconciliation seems implicit in most current efforts to address the relationship between individuals and contexts. Consider that one popular North American motivation text (Pintrich & Schunk, 1996) starts by characterizing behaviorist views of motivation as incomplete (p. 38), then focuses on largely individual-level rationalist constructs such as attributions and goals (Chapters 3–8), then concludes using these same constructs, primarily as embodied in the TARGET model, to consider classroom (Chapter 9) and school (Chapter 10) contexts. While other popular texts (e.g., Brophy, 1998) acknowledge the motivational appeal of practices associated with sociocultural perspectives, they do so primarily by arguing that such environments support intrinsically motivated information processing by the individuals.

In a similar vein, empiricist information processing theorists appear to reconcile the concerns that follow from sociocultural perspectives using the levels-of-aggregation approach. Anderson *et al.*'s (1996) influential counter to the claims of situative models of cognition assigns social aspects of learning to a higher level of aggregation than individual knowledge and skills. They argue both the social aspects of expert performance (such as an accountant working with the client), as well as the material aspects (using the calculator), have no relevance to more salient aspects of expert knowledge (e.g., tax laws). Accordingly, the value of complex social learning environments are construed in terms of their motivational utility or their introduction of skills that are unique to the situation. Initially, at least, this characterization seems consistent with a conceptualization of social activity as an aggregation of individual-level activity, (i.e., "composition of principles of individual behavior" in Greeno *et al.*, 1996, p. 40).

Despite its apparent popularity, we find a levels-of-aggregation reconciliation problematic for a number of reasons. For example, consider that Anderson *et al.*'s (1985) Geometry Tutor was carefully designed to reflect state-of-the-art information processing assumptions about learning, with little apparent consideration of the sociocultural context of classrooms. Yet Schofield's (1995) extended ethnographic analysis suggested that sociocultural factors were far more influential than information processing factors in determining whether the tutoring environment met its stated goals. Perhaps a more far-reaching problem with a levels-of-aggregation approach is that it does not address the tension between empiricist and rationalist perspectives. Consider for example, the issue of using extrinsic rewards to initiate engagement. At the behavioral analysis of individual activity, such a strategy makes sense, as it is seen as a useful way to engage learners at the level that is needed for meaningful successes in learning, which then provide a more appropriate form of reinforcement. At the cognitive analysis of the individual's information processing activity, however, the imposition of extrinsic rewards is likely to supplant the intrinsic interest that is needed to sustain the meaningful processing of that information. By not addressing these problems, the levels of aggregation approach leaves such obstacles in the path of both theoretical advances and more efforts to provide principles to transform educational practice.

Reconciliation of the former view of authenticity in learning environments with the latter view seems likely to foster the simplification and reduction of problem solving activities designed to foster a community of learners. Indeed, this is precisely what the first author observed in earlier research involving the *Jasper Woodbury* mathematical problem solving activities (CTGV, 1997). These video-based narratives were designed to facilitate the creation of a classroom culture of expert mathematical problem solvers. However, all of the teachers interviewed stated that their first goal for the activities was something like "showing how math is useful." In a few unfortunate classrooms, the activities were reduced to nothing more than a real-world example used to "motivate" participation in a direct instruction "game" around the relatively simple mathematical algorithms after they had been abstracted from the narrative adventures and placed on a worksheet (Hickey, 1996; Hickey *et al.*, forthcoming).[2] In a similar vein, Brown (1994) expressed concern that some of the practices associated with the Community of Learners model were being appropriated for use within very conventional direct instruction environments. Absurdities like the appropriately-labeled "Jasper Trivia Game," or highly scripted, choral reciprocal teaching exercises seem like inevitable consequences of the levels-of-aggregation approach to reconciliation.

The Dialectical Approach to Reconciliation

We have alluded to a very different approach to epistemological reconciliation that emerges when one starts from a sociocultural perspective. This dialectical approach to reconciliation is best understood in light of a Hegelian cycle of thesis–antithesis–synthesis, as suggested by Greeno and Moore (1993). This approach characterizes rationalism as the antithesis of behaviorism's initial thesis (emphasizing an inherent incompatibility) and characterizes socioculturalism as a higher-order synthetic perspective that unifies the strengths and minimizes the weaknesses of the other two. Such a view "supports an expectation of theoretical developments that will show how principles of individual behavior and information processing can be understood as special cases of more general principles of interactive function" (Greeno *et al.*, 1996, p. 40). In this approach to reconciliation, both the specific behaviors of individuals (in response to specific environmental stimuli) and the patterns of activity across individuals (in response to the way information in the environment is internally represented and transformed) are characterized as historical events, consistent with the contextualist sociocultural worldview. As such, both behavior and cognition are most fully explained in terms of the physical and social resources in the context in which those events occurred.

Whereas the levels-of-aggregation approach seems inevitable when reconciliation starts from a behaviorist or rationalist perspective, the dialectical approach seems inherent when reconciliation starts from a sociocultural perspective. Consider, for example, how a fundamentally sociocultural perspective led the second author's model of "adaptive learning" away from traditional views of development of self-regulatory skill:

> This concept of internalization embeds the individual within her culture; it blurs the distinction between self and other that is more readily accepted in mainstream American psychology. Within a Vygotskian framework, the interplay of the social/historical and the natural in the formation of consciousness informs questions about

[2] It should be noted that these events were observed during the first large-scale, independent implementation of these materials. Such concerns were effectively addressed in subsequent teacher training materials (see CTGV, 1997).

the relationship between social cognition and intrapersonal awareness and understanding. The individual is intricately a part of the
perceived social world; thus self-knowledge is not independent of
knowledge of others. One could argue then, that reports about self
are not interpretable without a context of "perception of others"
within which to analyze them; nor is a student's specific intrapersonal
approach and response apparent in a learning situation without
understanding the interpersonal influences of home and school
(McCaslin Rohrkemper, 1989, p. 148).

In short, this approach rejects the emphasis on the "self" in self-regulated activity.
The activity that has traditionally been characterized in terms of the way individuals process information is instead characterized as instances of events that are
fundamentally situated in the larger socio-physical context — as special cases of
more general principles of interactive functioning.

Indeed, more recent characterization of adaptive learning has supplanted the
entire notion of self-regulation with the notion of *co-regulated learning*. (McCaslin
& Good, 1996). Self-regulated learning has focused on the individual learners'
need to compensate for the inadequacies of the social/instructional environment in
order to make tasks and teaching more meaningful. In contrast, co-regulated
learning focuses on relationships, social supports, opportunity, and emergent interactions that empower the individual to seek new challenges within that scaffolded
environment, thereby internalizing those supports in a manner that is expected to
further enhance students' ability to participate in worthwhile school activity.
Reflecting the "competitive" aspects of a dialectical reconciliation, McCaslin and
Good argue that co-regulated learning "can take into consideration much of the
advances in research on the various component processes [of intrapersonal knowl-
edge] as it integrates the social/instructional environment with the learner in
mutual pursuit of a standard of excellence, within a setting of accountability"
(1996, p. 660).

Regarding practical conceptualizations, the preceding discussion also shows that
sociocultural practices are not necessarily antithetical to the practices of empiricism or rationalism, in the way that those two are antithetical to each other.
Consider, for example, the definition of engagement in learning as "participation
in a community where to-be-learned knowledge is used and valued." Such a
characterization is non-specific about how value is attached to that knowledge
or its use, so it provides a relatively objective perspective for considering
different ways of valuing the use of knowledge. From this perspective, attaching
extrinsic rewards to knowledgeable activity is not necessarily a good thing or a
bad thing. The negative consequences of competition and extrinsic rewards
documented previously may have occurred because students were not provided
useful tools for improving performance (Hickey, 1997). These issues are currently
being explored in classroom research now underway (Hickey, 2000). This research
considers the potentially divergent consequences of increasingly challenging
standards, and practices such as grading and public accountability associated with

those standards, within learning environments that follow from Frederiksen & Collins' (1989) "systemically valid" approach to assessment. The consequences of those manipulations on engagement and learning will then be examined by different teams of researchers from empiricist, rationalist, and sociocultural perspectives. Efforts to reconcile the expected conflicting research conclusions should shed light on the appropriateness of the two approaches to reconciliation described here.

In short, we believe that the dialectical approach to reconciliation should be considered as we broaden our models of motivation beyond the individual learner. We offer one very salient example of the value of this provocative, pragmatic approach by considering how such consideration has reshaped our understanding of (largely empiricist) educational measurement theory. While conventional measurement theorists acknowledged the importance of the broader context in which testing occurred, explicit consideration of context was limited to using psychometric methods to control the influence of test settings and cultural background. Renewed consideration of educational measurement from explicitly sociocultural perspectives and with an implicitly dialectical approach to reconciliation (e.g., Broadfoot, 1994; Frederiksen & Collins, 1989; Gipps, 1999; Moss, 1996; Shepard, 2000) supported wholesale reconsideration of longstanding measurement principles such as construct validity, and led to fundamentally new approaches to educational assessment (see Hickey *et al.*, 2000). The obvious implication is that a similar consideration of mainstream motivation research could lead to a similarly fundamental reconsideration of longstanding principles and practices regarding motivation.

Conclusion

In conclusion, we reiterate our belief that any effort to define a contextual model of motivation must first set out assumptions about knowing and learning, and consider how those assumptions support additional assumptions about engagement in learning and principles of practice for motivating that engagement. We have illustrated, however, that doing so suggests limitations in what appears to be the most likely approach. As such, we presume that our emphasis may not be welcomed by all. It is not our intention to help fan the flames that could ignite the sort of partisan battles that accompanied the emergence of the cognitive paradigm in the 1950s (see Melton, 1956). As we argue in more detail elsewhere (McCaslin & Hickey, in press, McCaslin & Hickey, 2001), we believe that a cautiously provocative approach can build on what is known without belittling the important work being carried out by others.

While our preceding initial analysis is certainly incomplete, we believe that our approach is theoretically sound, and warranted by recent developments in educational reform. As argued by Kelleghan *et al.* (1996), educational governing bodies in many countries have made far-reaching decisions regarding student and classroom accountability with no apparent consideration of how those changes might harm student motivation. Perhaps more significant is the way that mainstream motivation research has been ignored by educational research advisory boards (see Weston, 1991, in favor of more prosaic appeals such as the motivational affordances of increased expectations. We have illustrated how the dialectical reconciliation that follows from a sociocultural approach allows motivation research to address a broader range of assumptions about knowing and learning. As such, we believe that this approach will lead to models of practice and research findings that policy makers are less likely to ignore.

In closing, we refer to an additional conclusion that Weiner reached in his history of motivation research:

> school motivation cannot be divorced from the social fabric in which it is embedded, which is one reason that claims made upon motivational psychologists to produce achievement change must be modest. There will be no "person-in-space" for the field of classroom motivation unless there is corresponding social change (1990, p. 120).

Events during the intervening decade leave us doubtful that any development in education will be as consequential as John Glenn's flight. We offer our "cautiously provocative" approach as one possible route to new models of educational practice that yield achievement changes that may at least be more than "modest."

Acknowledgements

An earlier version of this paper was presented at the 8th European Conference for Research on Learning and Instruction, Göteborg, Sweden, in August, 1999. Work on this paper was carried out while the first author was supported by National Science Foundation Applications of Advanced Technology Program Grant RED-95-5348, and Research in Education and Communication Grants REC-9909732 and 0196225, Ann Kindfield, Peter Kindfield, Brandon Kyser, Peter Op't Eynde, Frank Pajares, Art Russell, Laura VandeWiele, Paul Pintrich, Nancy Schafer, Barry Zimmerman, and two anonymous reviewers provided invaluable feedback on earlier versions.

References

Anderman, L. H., & Anderman, E. M. (eds). (2000), "The role of social context in educational psychology: Substantive and methodological issues." Special issue of *Educational Psychologist 35* (2).

Anderman, E., & Maehr, M. L. (1994), "Motivation and schooling in the middle grades." *Review of Educational Research 64*, 287–309.

Anderman, E. M., & Young, A. J. (1994), "Motivation and strategy use in science: Individual differences and classroom effects." *Journal of Research in Science Teaching 31*, 811–831.

Anderson, J. A., Boyle, C. F., & Reiser, B. J. (1985), "Intelligent tutoring systems." *Science* 228, 456–462.

Anderson, J. R., Reder, L. M., & Simon, H. A. (1996), "Situated learning and education." *Educational Researcher 25* (4), 5–11.

Bandura, A. (1989), "Social cognitive theory." In R. Vasta (ed.) *Annals of Child Development* (Vol. 6, pp. 1–60). Greenwich, CT: JAI Press.

Bempechat, J. (1998), *Against the Odds: How "At Risk" Students Exceed Expectations.* San Fransico: Jossey-Bass.

Bereiter, C., & Scardamalia, M. (1989), "Intentional learning as a goal of instruction." In L. B. Resnick (ed.) *Knowing, Learning, and Instruction: Essays in Honor of Robert Glaser* (pp. 361–385). Hillsdale, NJ: Lawrence Erlbaum Associates.

Bloom, B. S. (1976), *Human Characteristics and School Learning.* New York: McGraw Hill.

Blumenfeld, P., Soloway, E., Marx, R. W., Krajcik, J. S., Guzdial, M. *et al.* (1991), "Motivating project-based learning: Sustaining the doing, supporting the learning." *Educational Psychologist 26*, 369–398.

Boekaerts, M. (1998), "Do culturally rooted self-construals affect students' conceptualization of control over learning?" *Educational Psychologist 33*, 87–108.

Broadfoot, P. (1994), *The Myth of Measurement.* Bristol, England: University of Bristol.

Brophy, J. E. (1998), *Motivating Students to Learn.* New York: McGraw-Hill.

Brown, A. L. (1992), "Design experiments: Theoretical and methodological challenges in creating complex interventions in classroom settings." *The Journal of the Learning Sciences 2*, 141–178.

Brown, A. L. (1994), "The advancement of learning." *Educational Researcher 23* (8), 4–12.

Brown, A. L., & Campione, J. A. (1996), "Psychological theory and the design of innovative learning environments." In L. Schauble & R. Glaser (eds) *Innovations in Learning: New Environments for Education* (pp. 289–235). Mahwah, NJ: Erlbaum.

Cameron, J., & Pierce, W. D. (1994). "Reinforcement, reward, and intrinsic motivation. A meta-analysis." *Review of Educational Research 64*, 363–423.

Carroll, J, (1963), "A model of school learning." *Teacher's College Record 64*, 723–733.

Case, R. (1996), "Changing views of knowledge and the impact on educational research and practice." In D. R. Olson & N. Torrance (eds) *The Handbook of Education and Human Development*, (pp. 75–99). Blackwell: Cambridge.

Chance, P. (1992), "The rewards of learning." *Phi Delta Kappan 73*, 200–207.

Cognition and Technology Group at Vanderbilt. (1992), "The Jasper series as an example of anchored instruction: Theory, program description, and assessment data." *Educational Psychologist 27*, 231–315.

Cognition & Technology Group at Vanderbilt. (1997), *The Jasper Project: Lessons in Curriculum, Instruction, Assessment, and Professional Development.* Erlbaum: Mahwah, NJ.

Collins, A., Brown, J. S., & Newman, S. E. (1989), "Cognitive apprenticeship: Teaching the craft of reading, writing, and mathematics." In L. B. Resnick (ed.) *Knowing, Learning, and Instruction: Essays in Honor of Robert Glaser* (pp. 453–494). Hillsdale, NJ: Lawrence Erlbaum Associates.

Corno, L., & Randi, J. (1999), "A design theory for classroom instruction in self-regulated learning?" In C. M. Reigeluth (ed.) *Instructional-design Theories and Models: A New Paradigm of Instructional Theory, Vol. II* (pp. 293–318). Mahwah, NJ: Earlbaum.

Covington, M. V., & Teel, K. M. (1996), *Overcoming Student Failure: Changing Motives and Incentives for Learning.* Washington, DC: American Psychological Association.

Deci, E. L. (1980), *The Psychology of Self-determination.* Lexington, MA: D. C Heath.

De Corte, E. (2000), "Marrying theory building and improvement of school practice: A permanent challenge for instructional psychology." *Learning & Instruction 10*, 249–266.

Donovan, M. S., Pellegrino, J. W., & Bransford, J. D. (eds). (1999), *How People Learn: Bridging Research to Practice*. Washington, DC: National Academy Press.

Dweck, C. S. (1989), "Motivation." In R. Glaser & A. Lesgold (eds) *Foundations for a Psychology of Education* (pp. 87–136). Hillsdale, NJ: Erlbaum.

Engelmann, S. (1988), "The direct instruction/follow through model: Design and outcomes." *Education and Treatment of Children 11*, 303–317.

Epstein, J. (1989), "Family structures and student motivation. A developmental perspective." In C. Ames & R. Ames (eds) *Research on Motivation in Education* (Vol. 3, pp. 259–295. San Diego: Academic Press.

Frederiksen, J. R., & Collins, A. (1989), "A systems approach to educational testing." *Educational Researcher 18* (9), 27–32.

Fredrick, L. D., Deitz, S. M., Bryceland, J. A., & Hummel, J. H. (2000), *Behavior Analysis, Education, and Effective Schooling*. Reno, NV: Context Press.

Garrison, S. J., Barron, B. J., Hickey, D. T., & Morris, J. (1994, April), *Building a Learning Community for Mathematical Problem Solving: Changes in Student Attitudes*. Presentation at the meeting of the American Educational Research Association, New Orleans.

Gipps, C. (1999), "Sociocultural aspects of assessment." *Review of Research in Education 24*, 355–392.

Greeno, J. G., Collins, A. M., & Resnick, L. (1996), "Cognition and learning." In D. Berliner & R. Calfee (eds) *Handbook of Educational Psychology* (pp. 15–46). New York: MacMillan.

Greeno, J. G., & Moore, J. L. (1993), "Situativity and symbols: A response to Vera and Simon." *Cognitive Science 17*, 49–60.

Harackiewicz, J. M., Barron, K. E., & Elliot, A. J. (1998), "Rethinking achievement goals: When are they adaptive for college students and why?" *Educational Psychologist 33*, 1–21.

Hickey, D. T. (1996), Constructivism, Motivation, and Achievement: The Impact of Classroom Mathematics Environments & Instructional Programs. Unpublished doctoral dissertation: Vanderbilt University.

Hickey, D. T. (1997), "Motivation and contemporary socio-constructivist instructional perspectives." *Educational Psychologist 32*, 175–193.

Hickey, D. T. (2000), *Assessment, Motivation, and Epistemological Reconciliation in a Technology-supported Learning Environment*. Grant REC-9909732 from the National Science Foundation, Division on Research, Evaluation, & Communication to Georgia State University.

Hickey, D. T., Moore, A. L., & Pellegrino, J. W. (forthcoming), "The motivational and academic consequences of two innovative mathematics environments. Do innovation and reform make a difference?" *38*, (3) *American Educational Research Journal*.

Hickey, D. T., Pellegrino, J. W., Goldman, S. R., Vye, N. J., & Moore, A. L. (1993, April), *Interests, Attitudes, and Anchored Instruction: The Impact of One Interactive Learning Environment*. Paper presented at the meeting of the American Educational Research Association, Atlanta.

Hickey, D. T., Wolfe, E. W., & Kindfield, A. C. H. (2000), Assessing learning in a technology-supported genetics environment: Evidential and consequential validity issues." *Educational Assessment 6*, 155–196.

Hidi, S., & Anderson, V. (1992), "Situational interest and its impact on reading and exposi-
tory writing." In K. A. Renninger, S. Hidi & A. Krapp (eds) *The Role of Interest in
Learning and Development* (pp. 215–238). Hillsdale, NJ: Erlbaum.
Hidi, S., & Harackiewicz, J. (in press), "Motivating the academically unmotivated: A critical
issue for the 21st century." *Review of Educational Research.*
Järvelä, S. (1998), "Socioemotional aspects of students' learning in cognitive–apprenticeship
environments." *Instructional Science 26*, 439–472.
Järvelä, S., & Niemivirta, M. (1999), "The changes in learning theory and the topicality of
the recent research on motivation." *Research Dialogue 2*, 57–65.
James, M., & Gipps, C. (1998), "Broadening the basis of assessment to prevent the narrow-
ing of learning." *The Curriculum Journal 9*, 285–297.
Kaplan A., & Maehr, M. L. (1999), "Achievement goals and student well-being." *Contem-
porary Educational Psychology 24*, 330–358.
Kellaghan, T., Madaus, G. F., & Raczak, A. (1996), *The Use of External Examinations to
Improve Student Motivation.* Washington, DC: American Education Research Association.
Kohn, A. (1993), "Rewards versus learning. A response to Paul Chance." *Phi Delta Kappan*
74, 783–787.
Lave, J., & Wenger, E. (1991), *Situated Learning. Legitimate Peripheral Participation.* New
York: Cambridge University Press.
Lepper, M. R., & Greene, D. (eds). (1978), *The Hidden Cost of Reward.* New Perspectives on
the Psychology of Human Motivation. Hillsdale, NJ: Erlbaum.
Lepper, M. R., Keavney, M., & Drake, M. (1996), "Intrinsic motivation and extrinsic
rewards: A commentary on Cameron & Pierces' meta-analysis." *Review of Educational
Research 66*, 5–32.
McCaslin, M., & Good, T. (1996), "The informal curriculum." In D. Berliner & R. Calfee
(eds) *The Handbook of Educational Psychology* (pp. 622–670). New York: American
Psychological Association/Macmillan.
McCaslin, M., & Hickey, D. T. (in press), "Self-regulated learning and academic achieve-
ment: A Vygotskian view." In B. Zimmerman & D. Schunk (eds) *Self-regulated Learning
and Academic Achievement: Theory, Research, and Practice, Second Edition.* (Forthcoming
volume to be published by Erlbaum).
McCaslin, M., & Hickey, D. T. (2001), Educational psychology, social constructionism,
and educational practice: A case of emergent identity. *Educational Psychologist 36*, 133–
140.
McCaslin Rohrkemper, M. (1989), "Self-regulated learning and academic achievement: A
Vygotskian view." In B. Zimmerman & D. Schunk (eds) *Self-regulated Learning and
Academic Achievement: Theory, Research, and Practice* (pp. 143–167). New York:
Springer Verlag.
McCombs, B. L., & Pope, J. E. (1994), *Motivating Hard to Reach Students.* Washington,
DC: American Psychological Association.
Melton, A. W. (1956), "Present accomplishments and future trends in problem solving and
learning theory." *American Psychologist 11*, 278–281.
Moss, P. A. (1996), "Enlarging the dialogue in educational measurement: Voices from inter-
pretive research traditions." *Educational Researcher 25* (1), 20–28.
Olson, D. R., & Bruner, J. S. (1996), "Folk psychology and folk pedagogy." In D. R. Olson
& N. Torrance (eds) *The Handbook of Education and Human Development* (pp. 9–27).
Blackwell: Cambridge.
Op't Eynde, P., De Corte, E., & Verschaffel, L. (this volume), "What we learn from what we
feel: The role of students' emotions in the mathematics classroom." In S. Volet & S.

Järvelä (eds) *Motivation in Learning Contexts: Theoretical and Methodological Implications.*

Paris, S. G., & Turner, J. C. (1994), "Situated motivation." In P. Pintrich, D. Brown & C. Weinstein (eds). *Student Motivation, Cognition, and Learning: Essays in Honor of Wilbert J. McKeachie* (pp. 213–237). Hillsdale, NJ: Erlbaum.

Pintrich, P. R., & Garcia, T. (1991), "Student goal orientation and self-regulation in college classrooms." In M. L. Maehr & P. R. Pintrich (eds) *Advances in Motivation and Achievement* (Vol. 7, pp. 371–402). Greenwich, CT: JAI Press.

Pintrich, P. R., & Schunk, D. H. (1996), *Motivation in Education: Theory, Research, and Applications.* Englewood Cliffs, NJ: Prentice Hall.

Renninger, K. A. (1992), "Individual interest and development: Implications for theory and practice." In K. A. Renninger, S. Hidi & A. Krapp (eds) *The Role of Interest in Learning and Development* (pp. 361–395). Hillsdale, NJ: Erlbaum.

Roeser, R. W., Midgley, C. & Urdan, T. (1996), "Perceptions of school psychological environment and early adolescents' self-appraisals and academic engagement: The mediating role of goals and belonging." *Journal of Educational Psychology 51*, 519–529.

Rumelhart, D. E. (1997), "The architecture of mind: A connectionist approach." In J. Haugeland (ed.) *Mind Design: Philosophy, psychology, and Artificial Intelligence* (pp. 205–232). Cambridge: The MIT Press.

Salomon, G. (1993), "No distribution without individual's cognition: A dynamic interactional view." In G. Salomon (ed.) *Distributed Cognition* (pp. 111–138). New York: Cambridge University Press.

Schiefele, U. (1991), "Interest, learning, and motivation." *Educational Psychologist 26*, 299–323.

Schofield, J. W. (1995), *Computers and Classroom Culture.* New York: Cambridge University Press.

Schunk, D. (1991), "Self efficacy and academic motivation." *Educational Psychology Review 1*, 173–208.

Schutz. P. (1991), "Goals in self-directed behavior." *Educational Psychologist 26*, 55–67.

Sfard, A. (1998), "On the two metaphors for learning and the danger of choosing just one." *Educational Researcher 27* (2), 4–13.

Shepard, L. A. (2000, April), *The Role of Assessment in a Learning Culture.* Presidential Address at the Annual Meeting of the American Educational Research Association, New Orleans. (Forthcoming in *Educational Researcher*).

Tudge, J. R. H., & Winterhoff, P. A. (1993), "Vygotsky, Piaget, and Bandura: Perspectives on the relations between the social world and cognitive development." *Human Development 36*, 61–81.

Turner, J. C. (1995), "The influence of classroom contexts on young children's motivation for literacy." *Reading Research Quarterly 30*, 410–441.

Turner, J. C., & Myer, D. K. (2000), "Studying and understanding the instructional contexts of classrooms: Using our past to forge our future." *Educational Psychologist 35*, 69–85.

Visscher-Voerman, I., Gustafson, K., & Plomp, T. (1999), "Instructional design and development: An overview of the paradigms." In J. van den Akker, N. Nieveen, R. M. Branch, K. L. Gustafson & T. Plomp (eds) *Design Methodology and Developmental Research in Education and Training* (pp. 15–28). The Netherlands: Kluwer Academic Publishers.

Volet, S. (1999), "Motivation within and across cultural-educational contexts: A multidimensional perspective." In T. C. Urdan (ed.) *Advances in Motivation and Achievement, Vol. 11, The Role of Context* (pp. 185–231). Stamford, CT: JAI Press.

Weston, P. (ed.). (1991), *Assessment of Pupil Achievement: Motivation and School Success.*

Report of the Education Research Workshop Held in Liège 12 –15 September. Amsterdam/Lisse:Swets & Zeitlinger.

Weiner, B. (1990), "History of motivation research in education." *Journal of Educational Psychology 82*, 616–622.

Wigfield, A., & Eccles, J. (1992), "The development of achievement task values: A theoretical analysis." *Developmental Review 12*, 265–310.

Zimmerman, B. J. (1993), Commentary. *Human Development 36*, 82–86.

Zimmerman, B. J. (personal communication, September 14, 1999).

Chapter 4

Understanding Learning and Motivation in Context: A Multi-dimensional and Multi-level Cognitive–Situative Perspective

Simone Volet

Studying psychological phenomena in social contexts, rather than with a sole focus on the individual agent represents one of the major shifts in educational psychology research in the last decade. This shift, accompanied by tensions between mainstream theorists, prepared to take into account contextual influences on individual endeavours, and those promoting the view that the situative perspective subsumes the individual, is noticeable across several fields of research. This chapter discusses the conceptual and practical usefulness of adopting a multi-dimensional and multi-level cognitive–situative perspective for understanding learning and motivation in context. After a brief review of the emergence of the person-in-context position, recent research on transfer of learning across contexts is presented to illustrate the usefulness of the framework for understanding international students' experiences in their familiar (home) learning environment and the less familiar (host) setting. Empirical evidence of subjective interpretations and ambivalence in what constitutes appropriate learning across cultural–educational contexts supports the usefulness of the multi-dimensional perspective and the significance of understanding the experiential interface of learning and motivation in context.

In the second part of the paper, the framework is expanded into a multi-level perspective of person in context. It is argued that conceptualising contexts at different levels of specificity is critical for understanding the complex configuration of relatively stable motivational belief systems influencing behaviours, intra-individual variability across classroom activities, and individual continuous attuning to the affordances of specific tasks and activities in situation. Empirical evidence of differentiated patterns of stability and change in goals and self-efficacy, when students move across contexts and communities of learning, provide support for a multi-level framework. The findings are interpreted in light of dynamic interactions between relatively broad and enduring socio-cultural influences at the societal and general educational levels, the affordances created by the cultural educational practices of specific communities of learning at home and abroad, and the meaning given by students to their experiences in the two contexts.

Motivation in Learning Contexts: Theoretical Advances and Methodological Implications, pages 57–82.
ISBN: 0-08-043990-X

Emergence of the "Person in Context" Position

The conceptual shift towards a person-in-context perspective can be observed in at least three fields of research related to learning and motivation The first is *cognitive psychology*, which has found itself under attack from situativity theory and socio-cultural perspectives in the last decade. These latter perspectives have stressed the significance of socio-cultural influences in the development of cognition, motivation and learning and reciprocally how students' beliefs and behaviours affect the community of learning that they belong to. The mutual influence of socio-cultural, situative perspectives and individual cognitions can be found in recent models of self-regulation of learning, which have become more systemic in nature (e.g. Biggs, 1996; Boekaerts, 1992; 1999). Although there is a general consensus on the view that multi-dimensional and dynamic models are required for further conceptual advances in understanding and designing instruction (Salomon, 1991; Cobb & Bowers, 1999), there is less agreement on which dimension should become the central part of such models. Cognitive theorists such as Vosniadou (1996) have claimed that, cognitive psychology can provide a unified perspective if it "take[s] into consideration the biological, environmental and sociocultural constraints in which mental activity takes place" (p. 106). In contrast, others such as Greeno (1998), have argued that the situative perspective can provide, "a synthesis that subsumes the cognitive and behaviourist perspectives" (p. 5).

Recent attempts to reconcile the cognitive and situative epistemological positions have highlighted some of the fundamental tensions (Anderson *et al.*, 1996; 1997; Billett, 1996; Greeno *et al.*, 1996; Greeno, 1997; 1998; Hickey, this volume) but also some important points of agreement (Anderson *et al.*, 2000). Many researchers seem to agree on the complementary rather than contradictory nature of the cognitive and situative approaches for understanding the learner in context. According to Billett (1996, p. 277), the two perspectives can enrich each other "by providing a basis for understanding thinking and acting which they could not achieve on their own". For Anderson *et al.* (2000, p. 12) in order to progress towards more "useful design principles for resources and activities of productive learning", "both are needed" and "both should be pursued vigorously".

Similar trends towards a person-in-context perspective can be observed in *motivation research*. Already ten years ago, Weiner (1990) had argued that "school motivation cannot be divorced from the social fabric in which it is embedded" (p. 120). Ten years later, sociocultural dimensions in the construction of motivation feature in most theory developments worldwide. As stated by Maehr *et al.* (1999), the latest shift in motivation research is from, "thinking about motivation as an internal disposition that differentiates individuals, towards a consideration of the construction of motivation in context" (p. 17). This shift, therefore, does not only focus on the influence of school policies and classroom practices on motivation, which had long been acknowledged in the literature, but recognises and systematically investigates the ways in which organisational settings, school cultures and practices interact dynamically with students' motivational beliefs during experiences of learning. In other words the shift calls for a closer examination of the dynamics of motivation in situation.

Boekaerts' (1999) theory of motivated learning, for example, has stressed how "students and instructional contexts influence one another", and more specifically how "students' motivational beliefs interact with the cues present in diverse social, physical and instructional contexts" (p. 43). As part of her argument for researching the dynamics of change in motivation, she claims that although the instructional context within which students acquire new knowledge and skills can be quite stable and trigger "habitualised" behaviours, the content covered and the social context vary continuously, which calls for investigations of "context-sensitive" behaviours (Boekaerts, this volume). A similar position combining context sensitive appraisals with relatively stable motivational beliefs is adopted by Op't Eynde *et al.* (this volume). Both claim that emotions in the classroom are contextualised and unstable since they are based on students' unique continuous appraisals and interpretations of events as they unfold. They also recognise that event-specific appraisals are influenced by students' identity, prior experiences, belief systems and knowledge developed over participation in numerous other practices — and which can reflect age, personal history and home culture variables. There is growing empirical evidence of cognitive, motivational, volitional and emotional sensitivity to tasks and activities in relation to relatively stable factors and macro-level contextual influences (Boekaerts, 1997; 1999; Schiefele & Csikszentmilhalyi, 1995; Turner *et al.*, 1998; and Volet, 1997) and of knowledge structures activated in response to situational cues and circumstances (Boekaerts & Niemivirta, 2000; Pintrich, 2000). Overall, this research highlights the mediating role of subjective interpretations and appraisals of situations on learning goals and engagement.

The growing importance of the person-in-context position is also noticeable within mainstream cross-cultural psychology. A body of so called *cultural or contextualist cultural* research has emerged as an alternative to the mainstream cross-cultural universalist research orientation. Like situated cognitive theorists, cultural/contextualists psychologists, many of them from non-western countries (Bond, 1986; Bergen *et al.*, 1996; Kagitcibasi, 1996; Sinha, 1986) have claimed that cognition, motivation and behaviours have little meaning outside the specific cultural environments in which they are embedded and therefore cannot be compared in abstraction across contexts — a typical approach adopted by cross-cultural psychologists. Studies which simply compare the cognitive or motivational characteristics of groups of students from different countries or ethnic groups and do not identify or measure the aspects of culture assumed to be responsible for observed variations (Betancourt & Lopez, 1993) have been criticised. Yet, according to Bergen *et al.* (1996), Kagitcibasi (1992), Kim & Berry (1993) and Sinha (1996), the cross-cultural and cultural positions do not need to be in competition. They should rather be seen as complementary, each enriching the other. Misra, in Bergen *et al.* (1996), argues that the aim of an indigenous Indian psychology, for example, is "not to generate a set of mutually exclusive, culturally-based orientations that fail to regard or appreciate the alternatives" but rather to "generate orientations that intersect and interpenetrate" (p. 498). Similarly, Valsiner &

Lawrence (1997) argue that cultural psychologies distinguish themselves from cross-cultural traditions by their effort "to provide a systemic account of how culture participates in the psychological functioning of human beings" (p. 82).

Overall, the rationale for the emergence of a cultural perspective alongside mainstream cross-cultural psychology (Berry, 1997) bears some functional resemblance to the emergence of a situative perspective alongside mainstream cognitive psychology (Vosniadou, 1996) and motivation theory (Hickey, 1997). Attempts at reconciliation also have been proposed (Katcibasi, 1996), but the respective benefits and possible integration of the cultural and cross-cultural approaches are still being debated. In neither field of research does theory development seem to be mature enough to provide a coherent framework which reconciles the different epistemological perspectives. Yet, consistent across all three fields is the growing importance given to contexts as providing the socio-cultural conditions which support or alternatively constrain the development of cognitions, motivations, emotions, attitudes and behaviours. Whereas most educational psychologists would agree with the importance of contexts in their work, the major challenge is how to conceptualise the learner in context and how to analyse their mutual interactions (Anderman & Anderman, 2000). For Hickey (this volume), an additional challenge is how to reconcile "the inevitably conflicting interpretations within multidimensional efforts".

A Multi-dimensional Cognitive–Situative Perspective for Understanding the Person–Context Experiential Interface

The basic framework presented in Figure 1 illustrates the person-in-context from a combined cognitive and situative perspective, loosely conceptualised at the level of the classroom. The top part represents a student's cognitions, motivations and emotions related to learning or "effectivities" to use a term coined by Snow (1994). The bottom part represents the affordances (Gibson 1979/1986; Greeno, 1998; Gruber et al., 1995) of the social and physical learning context. It refers to the instruction and support provided by the teacher, the behaviour of other students, and the cultural norms, value systems, and social expectations prevailing in that setting, and which are assumed to be understood and shared by all individuals participating in those activities. In the middle part of the framework are the mutual interactions between the two components during a learning experience. Finally, the overall enclosure stresses the view that while from a psychological viewpoint, the two components can be conceptualised and examined as distinct entities, from a situative perspective all participants and physical and social dimensions form an integral part of the so called socio-cultural context, or community of practice. The notion of "experiential interface", which is at the core of a (socio)-cognitive perspective, may be substituted by the notion of "experiential engagement" within a situative perspective.

The layout of Figure 1 highlights the tensions which arise when trying to conceptualise and visually represent context from a combined cognitive and situative

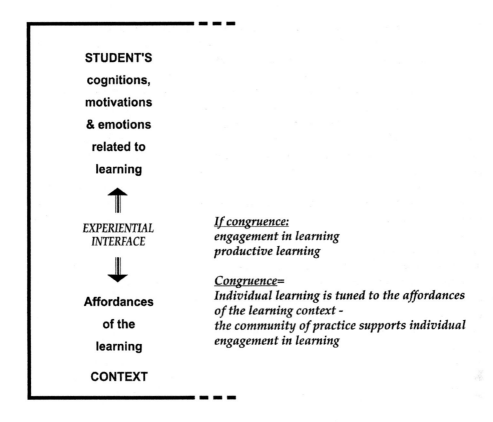

STUDENT'S
cognitions,
motivations
& emotions
related to
learning

EXPERIENTIAL
INTERFACE

Affordances
of the
learning
CONTEXT

If congruence:
engagement in learning
productive learning

Congruence=
Individual learning is tuned to the affordances
of the learning context -
the community of practice supports individual
engagement in learning

EXPERIENTIAL ENGAGEMENT
IN COMMUNITY OF PRACTICE

Figure 1: A multi-dimensional cognitive-situative framework for understanding learning and motivation experiences in context.

perspective. From a cognitive perspective, the most critical aspect is the interface between an individual's effectivities and the (affordances of the) context — whether perceived, observed or inferred. The activation of prior knowledge and beliefs, situational interpretations, immediate emotions and the construction of meaning take place at this experiential interface. In contrast, from a situative perspective, the most critical aspect is the *experience* and engagement in the community of practice. Although a combined cognitive–situative framework may be cumbersome to conceptualise and represent, it is argued that the complementary nature of concepts, perspectives and analyses is critical for enriching our understanding of learning and motivation in context. In our research on international students' experience of learning across contexts, a pragmatic approach (Cobb &

Bowers, 1999; Hickey, 1997; McCaslin & Good, 1996) bringing together concepts from both perspectives was considered desirable to reveal the significance of subjective, culturally and experientially based interpretations of educational practices.

Figure 1 shows congruence at the interface, when the learning context supports students' engagement and learning, and reciprocally when students are attuned to the affordances of the learning environment. Depending on the learner's characteristics, prior experience, motives and preferences, and their cognitive, motivational and emotional online appraisals of the immediate task, congruence may be achieved by teacher-regulation, shared regulation or self-regulated learning practices (Vermunt & Verloop, 1999). In other words, what produces congruence is expected to vary across groups and individuals, task purposes and subject matter. It is also expected to change for the same person over time and across situations, although some consistency is expected overall.

The two-way arrow, at the interface, highlights the mutual, reciprocal influences of effectivities and affordances. It is important at that point, to specify that shared standards and subsequent expectations by students and teachers are subjective, and thus may not necessarily reflect context-independent principles of effective learning and motivation. While there is an assumption that productive learning could not be achieved without minimal shared standards and expectations, there is no assumption that congruence in academic and social expectations will necessarily lead to productive learning in real-life situations — due to possible competing local circumstances. In most cases, however, the effectivities–affordances interface in the classroom does reflect congruence. Teachers are attuned to the characteristics of their students, and design educational activities which produce "constructive frictions" for effective learning (Vermunt & Verloop, 1999). Reciprocally, students are attuned to the expectations of their familiar educational environment and keen to participate productively in learning activities. The notion of congruence at the experiential interface highlights the subjective nature of what students and teachers perceive as appropriate learning. Occasional mismatch is observed when some students are unwilling or unable to benefit from the opportunities provided by the learning environment, or reciprocally when the instructional approach does not support their special needs or circumstances, and ends up inhibiting their motivation, engagement and learning.

Criticality of the Experiential Interface

More substantial mismatch in intersubjective perceptions, and consequent lack of congruence, is noticeable when students move across different educational settings. The educational literature has highlighted the multi-dimensional, mutual adjustments experienced by students and teachers or supervisors in the first year of high school, the first year at university, the first year of postgraduate study, or the first weeks in a new job. The norms and expectations that are prevailing in a particular context are often tacit rather than explicit. Their significance becomes more salient when newcomers join a community of practice and attempt to apply the knowledge and skills — which were valued in their previous learning environment — within the new setting. Re-establishing congruence can be difficult because of the subjectively perceived nature of what are appropriate cognitions, motivations and behaviours. According to Rogoff & Chavajay (1995), students have to learn to "discern the relations ('transfer') between genres of activity across contexts as they, together with others, participate in and contribute to bringing about those activities" (p. 871). When communities of practice do not assign the same meaning or value to given behaviours, the transition process required to re-establish congruence in expectations among participants can be difficult, making the promotion of "adaptive dispositions" (Hess & Azuma, 1991) in both students and teachers critical.

This psycho-social phenomenon will be illustrated by two examples from research related to international students from Singapore and Hong Kong studying at high school in their home country, and then at university in Australia (Volet, 1999a; 1999b). This research, which has taken a dual cognitive–situative perspective, has compared the nature and significance of perceived (students, teachers) socio-cultural appropriateness of transfer of learning at the experiential interface in the two learning contexts. Using the original framework as a basis, the left-hand part of Figure 2 assumes that after multiple mutual interactions and years of participation in the same cultural educational context, congruence has been achieved in students' familiar home community of practice.

The challenge starts when these students move to the Australian university context. The right-hand part of Figure 2 shows four types of subjective experiences in the transfer of learning across contexts: congruence, ambivalence, difficulty, and incongruence (see Volet, 1999b). Congruence is re-established in the host environment, if the learning practices which students bring with them travel well, and like at home, are perceived by all parties as congruent with what is valued in the new setting. One example of re-establishment of congruence across the two cultural–educational contexts, is the development of informal study groups or peer support groups (See Figure 3a). As illustrated in this figure, there is converging evidence from multiple studies and data sources such as observations, questionnaires, personal accounts and reflection in interviews, that the majority of Singaporean and Hong Kong students spontaneously form study groups at high school in their home country, and that once at university in Australia, they tend to re-create similar groups. Tang's (1996) studies in the Hong Kong context converge with Singaporean students' own accounts (Volet & Kee, 1993; Tan *et al.*, 1999) to show that spontaneous collaborative learning and interdependent practices are common in both Asian countries. The collaborative activities carried out in these groups appear to have functional similarity across contexts and are widely perceived in each setting as adaptive to the characteristics of that environment.

With regard to the host university setting, our own studies (Volet, 1999b; Renshaw & Volet, in progress) have shown significant differences in the amount of spontaneously formed study groups among international students from Confucian Heritage Countries backgrounds in comparison to local Australian students. They also revealed that the typical informal peer support groups of

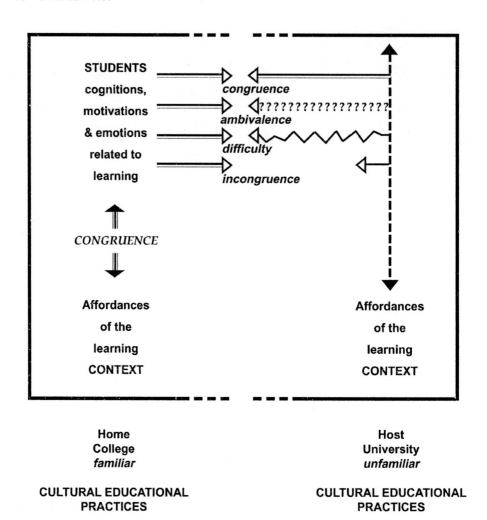

Figure 2: Different experiences of learning and motivation in familiar vs. unfamiliar contexts/cultural educational practices.

students from Asian backgrounds almost exclusively consist of co-nationals or other international students from Asian backgrounds (Volet & Ang, 1998; Smart *et al.*, 2000). Questionnaire as well as interview data have highlighted the positive impact of these groups on students' emotional and academic adjustment in the new cultural–educational context. From a cognitive, motivational or emotional perspective, these practices represent evidence of effective self-regulation of learning to adjust to an unfamiliar learning setting. It may be argued, however, that these regulatory behaviours were necessary (for cognitive, motivational as well as emotional purposes) to "compensate for inadequacies" (McCaslin & Good, 1996) in the induction process (or lack of) in the host environment.

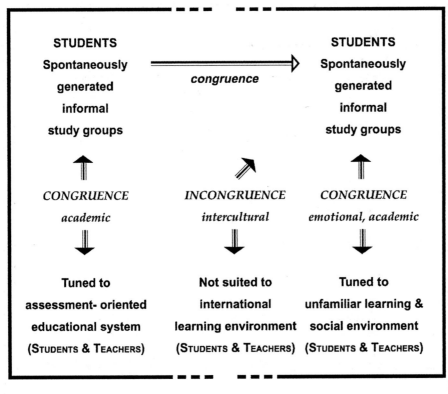

Figure 3a: Experiencing *congruence/incongruence* in learning across contexts/cultural educational practices.

Regardless of the cultural–educational setting, there is evidence that informal support groups are perceived by both students and teachers as being well attuned to the learning environment and to the special circumstances of international students. With one exception, however. From the perspective of educators (and many students) who consider international campuses as creating unique opportunities for intercultural learning, informal peer support groups which include only international students are maladaptive since they prevent students from engaging in cross-cultural encounters and ultimately achieving intercultural learning (Volet, 1999c; Volet & Ang, 1998). This phenomenon highlights the subjective and multidimensional nature of the notion of appropriateness of learning. Appropriate for what and under what conditions? With regard to international students at university in Australia, informal study groups of peers experiencing similar socio-cultural adjustments appear ideal to meet their members' emotional and academic needs. But at the same time, mono-cultural groups are perceived by the same individuals as maladaptive and incongruent from a perspective of international education and intercultural learning. Our preliminary work on the issue of social cohesion at university in Australia (Smart *et al.*, 2000) revealed that teachers, as well as students, are well aware of the difficulty of simultaneously addressing emotional needs and intercultural development. This is reflected in the following comments, *"we will stick to our own culture and friends ... you are more comfortable with them"* or *"only when you are working with friends of your own culture can you really tell them how you feel"* (Volet & Ang, 1998, p. 10), but also *"we prefer mixed group, cross-culture group, we want to know what each other's culture offers"* or *"I prefer mixed group because of the new experience and new ideas"* (p. 11).

A second example of the significance of mutual dynamic interactions between effectivities and affordances in an international education context is reflected in the practice of cue-seeking in order to conform to task requirements (see Figure 3b). Cue-seeking refers to students' deliberate, systematic search for information related to forthcoming assignments and tests. It can involve, for example, quizzing teachers, searching for model answers or checking on past examination questions. Extensive use of such strategies was revealed in research with Hong Kong (Tang & Biggs, 1996; Biggs, 1996) and Singaporean students (Volet & Kee, 1993) studying in their home country. That research has shown how assessment-oriented systems in both countries have created students who are street-wise when it comes to test-taking. They have learnt to deliberately look for cues for each specific academic task and to adjust their learning strategies accordingly. Within the highly assessment-oriented educational systems in Hong Kong and Singapore, cue-seeking has traditionally been assigned a positive connotation, and is perceived by both students and teachers as adaptive and appropriate to the characteristics of the learning context. Reciprocally, the learning context supports active use of these strategies, as revealed in Singaporean students' accounts of some teachers assisting them analyse past examination papers for hints about possible questions in future papers (Volet & Kee, 1993).

Once transferred to the host university context, however, that same strategy acquires an ambivalent status. Interview data with staff and students revealed feelings of frustration and anger by both students and teachers created by a division of opinion as to whether cue-seeking behaviours represent appropriate learning strategies. From the point of view of students, this strategy was seen to be highly adaptive to find out about learning requirements in the new unfamiliar learning environment, even though they realised that the system was not as highly assessment-oriented as in their home country. But some teachers did not agree. They viewed students' cue-seeking behaviours as inappropriate at university. They expressed the belief that students who behaved in that way were only interested in getting the right answers to get good marks, at the expense of understanding the materials, *"... they feel that teachers are meant to teach and students are meant to*

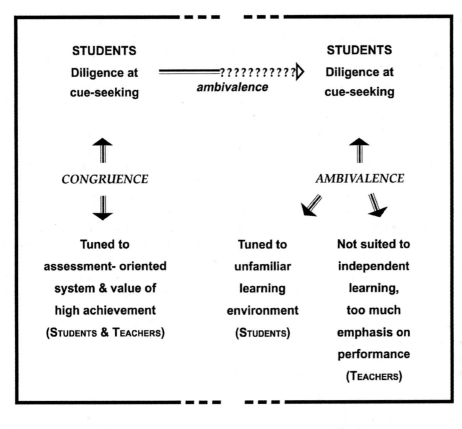

Figure 3b: Experiencing *ambivalence* in learning across contexts/cultural educational practices.

work hard and give the right answer", so they ask *"What am I supposed to do?"*, *"You are responsible for teaching me. You must tell me what to do"*. Many teachers thought that such beliefs were nurtured by educational practices in students' home country, *"... [they] are used to be directed"*. On the one hand, these teachers praised the diligence and engagement of students, but at the same time, they thought that cue-seeking was a bad coping strategy since it demonstrated a dependency in learning and a lack of disposition to exercise self-direction. Teachers' reactions revealed frustration and resistance, *"I have to resist [telling them] and keep throwing the responsibility to them"*. Yet, whether these same teachers' instructional and assessment practices do support and scaffold students' development of more autonomous forms of learning was unclear.

Furthermore, one could argue that the value of, respectively, teacher-regulated and student-regulated learning practices vary across cultural–educational contexts, and this would contribute to the experience of ambivalence in international education settings. Theories of the self in different cultural contexts (Markus & Kitayama, 1991; Triandis, 1989) have highlighted how independent vs. interdependent construals of the self affect cognition, motivation, emotions and behaviours. Singaporean students' accounts of their learning at college back home revealed that reliance on the teacher for close guidance was valued and encouraged. (Note: The recent promotion of "being able to think independently and creatively" across the whole educational system in Singapore (Chang & Hung, 1999) may produce changes in expectations and practices). Nevertheless, while it seems reasonable to expect that all students would have developed some skills for self-regulated learning by the time they start university study, this may only be achieved once they have "internalised the social structural supports" of that environment (MacCaslin & Good, 1996, p. 660). In the context of international education, which requires studying in a relatively unfamiliar cultural educational environment, co-regulated learning (MacCaslin & Good, 1996) or shared regulation of learning (Vermunt & Verloop, 1999) practices seem best suited for scaffolding and socially situating students in the host learning context.

In conclusion, these examples illustrate the significance of multidimensional and dynamic aspects of learning and motivation in context. Studying practices in different contexts (Anderson *et al.*, 2000) and at the experiential interface of learner and context (multiple perspectives) have revealed that what constitutes adaptive or appropriate learning is not only subjectively perceived but is also situated in particular communities of practice. Exploring the extent of congruence in expectations and interpretations — or alternatively ambivalence, difficulty or incongruence — was found critical to address some of the misconceptions related to international students' learning at the individual level (cognitive angle, the level misunderstood by teachers) and to interpret their origin at the systemic level (situative angle) which gives meaning and authenticity to cognitions and behaviours (Salomon, 1991). Findings of continuous adjustments by both students and teachers at the experiential interface highlight how groups and individuals provide the social context for each other's practices. Contexts, therefore, should not be conceived as static entities but as dynamic communities in need of individual reciprocal understanding (Volet & Tan-Quigley, 1998) in order to ensure that the dynamic interactions between participants support productive learning.

Locating the Experiential Interface within a Multi-level Perspective of Person and Context

The second part of this chapter proposes to locate the dynamic experiential interface within a broader, multi-level perspective of person and context. Starting from

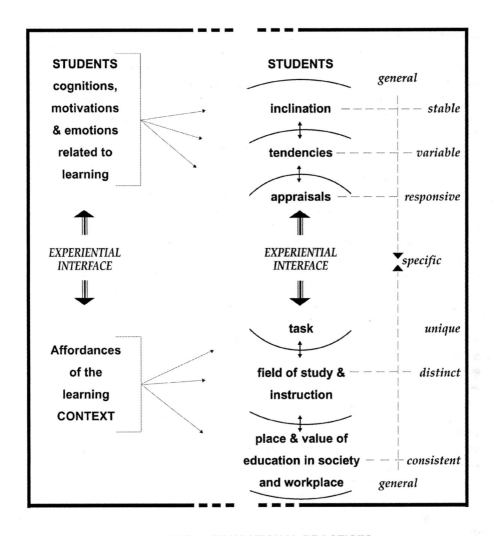

CULTURAL EDUCATIONAL PRACTICES

Figure 4: A multi-dimensional and multi-level cognitive-situative framework for understand learning and motivation in context.

the basic cognitive–situative framework presented earlier, Figure 4 shows how person and context can be conceptualised at different levels of specificity. As illustrated by the vertical arrow, the most specific and critical level is the experiential domain, i.e. the level of an individual's appraisals of the current activity in its real life social setting. More general levels of both "students" and "context" are conceptualised at the periphery, away from the immediate experience but with an overarching influence on the interactive and dynamic processes that are activated during a learning experience.

Rationale for a Multi-level Perspective

Although the influence of macro- and micro-level aspects of individuals and contexts are acknowledged in the literature (c.f. Anderman & Anderman, 2000), there have been few attempts to integrate all aspects into a single conceptual framework. The epistemological tensions discussed earlier may have contributed to this situation. Consequently, research exploring the complex configuration and interactions of multi-level dimensions on student learning, motivation and achievement is still limited and fragmented.

The most elaborated model available comes from a cognitive–motivational constructivist perspective (Boekaerts, 1992; 1999). Boekaerts' model of adaptive learning, which incorporates multi-level dimensions of individual (e.g. motivational beliefs, appraisals) and context/situation (subject matter domain, concrete task), provides a theoretically sound basis for examining how domain-specific motivational and appraisals of current learning situations affect learning intentions, goal setting and goal striving in actual learning situations. Boekaerts' empirical research as well as the work of a few others has provided support for the significance of a multi-level conceptualisation in understanding the dynamic experience of learning and motivation in real learning episodes and over a period of time (Boekaerts, 1997; 1999; Krapp, 1999; Volet, 1997).

Given the applied interest in this chapter on learning and motivation across cultures, another multi-level model, this time coming from an anthropological and cross-cultural psychology perspective is also briefly mentioned. Schneider, Lee & colleagues (Schneider & Lee, 1990; Schneider et al., 1994) developed and validated a dynamic and interactive model to explain East Asian academic success. Their work, inspired by Spindler & Spindler's (1987) multi-level conceptualisation of culture uses a "holistic research methodology", including questionnaires and interviews with students, parents, teachers and school administrators, and focuses on a range of macro- and micro-level educational, instructional and learning issues. Their findings suggest that the academic success and high educational aspirations of East Asian Americans are related to a combination of macro-level cultural and socio-economic characteristics, and micro-level interactive relationships among children, parents, teachers and peer groups. The usefulness of combining macro-sociocultural and micro-interpersonal analyses to explain complex patterns of academic achievement across ethnic groups was also highlighted in Ogbu's research (1992).

Describing the Multi-level Framework

The top part of Figure 5, is inspired by Boekaerts' (1992; 1997; 1999) theory of motivated learning. It shows how students' cognitions, motivations and emotions related to learning can be conceptualised and empirically examined at three or more levels of specificity. At the most general, and assumed relatively stable level is a student's inclination to engage in learning in particular ways. Inclination

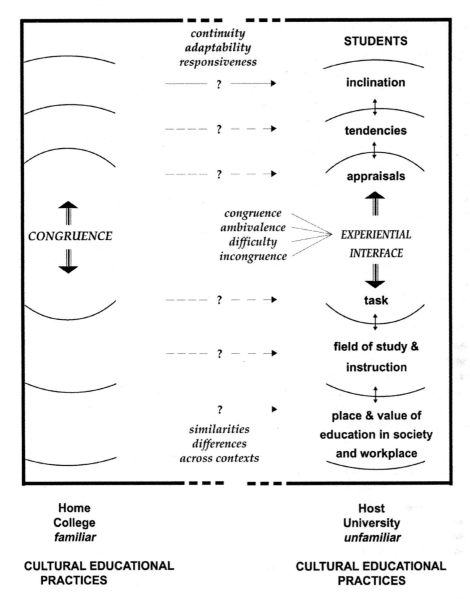

Figure 5: A multi-dimensional and multi-level cognitive-situative framework for understanding experiences of learning and motivation across contexts/cultural educational practices.

reflects overall beliefs and traits characteristics. At university (the applied focus for this chapter), these can include, for example, overall achievement motivation, intrinsic and extrinsic goal orientation, self-efficacy, preferred learning styles and personal views of the value of academic study. At the next level down in the figure are students' tendencies to engage in learning in particular ways. In Boekaerts' model, tendencies refer to cognitions and motivational beliefs similar to those at the general level, but as they relate to a particular field of study. Our conceptualisation is similar to Boekaerts' but in an addition to field of study, we added a range of other, distinct types of learning environment (described below). At that level, some variability is expected. Studies with school children, for example, have revealed evidence of intra-individual variability in goal orientation and self-efficacy across school subjects (MacCallum, in press) and between cooperative vs. competitive learning environments (e.g., Ames & Archer, 1988). At the most specific level are students' cognitive, motivational and emotional appraisals of their current, immediate task or learning activity. Appraisals are part of the experiential domain which incorporates the most specific level of context. An example of appraisals would be a student's perception of self-competence to complete a particular task and their emotional feelings toward that task. At this level, context sensitivity and responsiveness are expected to dominate, and to mediate the impact of the more general influences, although, as cogently argued by Boekaerts (this volume), habitualised or preferential behaviour may prevail "in the absence of salient contextual information" which are of high personal importance.

The bottom part of Figure 5 expands on the notion of context and situation. At the most general level — represented at the bottom — are macrosocio-cultural societal dimensions. These refer to the values and belief systems which tend to dominate in a community, in particular the dominant views of the *place and value of university education in society and the workplace*. Societal dimensions are assumed to provide a relatively consistent and coherent framework for the development of overall educational policies and priorities, and the design of new courses, curricula, accreditation and assessment practices at university. At the next level up are the characteristics of a range of distinct and diverse learning environments, for example, overall field of study (environmental sciences or psychology) or form of instruction (teacher-regulated or student-centered; technologically-mediated or face-to-face) but also type of knowledge (scientific or philosophical; theoretical or practical), assessment practices (examinations or assignments carried out in students' own time; multiple choice tests, essays or research projects) and the nature of social learning setting (competitive or collaborative; fostering dependent, independent or interdependent learning). Combining dimensions produces a multiplicity of distinct learning environments which support or inhibit the activation of favourable or unfavourable motivational beliefs and trigger "cognitively mediated" or "habitualised" emotions (Pekrun, 2000). Finally, one level up in the figure is the experiential domain, the most specific level represented by the current task or activity that a student is currently engaged in — the "here and now" of learning. It includes the immediate socio-cultural surroundings, such as current classroom climate, role of peers and degree of social support provided by the teacher for the completion of that particular activity. The experiential interface thus presents a unique configuration of person-in-context dimensions.

Although the framework represents different levels of individual (and context) as nested within one another, there is no assumption that a nested component will necessarily reflect its encompassing structure. For example, a student's perception of low self-competence for a particular activity may not reflect that student's general tendency to perceive him/herself as competent for similar types of activities. Local circumstances encountered during the activity may trigger different appraisals on that occasion. Salient personal and situational cues can re-arrange the configuration of elements by highlighting powerful physical or social dimensions (such as mood of the day, perception of competing priorities, temporary interference of peer support, anticipation of immediate returns or long-term benefits).

While the significance of examining students' motivational beliefs at different levels of specificity has been highlighted (Boekaerts, 1999), the theoretical and practical importance for educational practice of examining the complex patterns of effectivities–affordances interactions within and across different levels of context has received less attention. One can assume, for example, that university students' general motivational beliefs about learning reflect the macro-level value of university education in their future profession, community and society at large. But alternatively, these beliefs may be mediated by academic priorities, forms of instruction or assessment practices, which themselves could be at odds with the macro-level aspects. Tensions between economic and academic agendas, for example, can create confusion and conflicting influences on educational practices and in turn on students' motives and engagement in academic study at the specific level of units of study and even learning tasks.

Similarly, students' appraisals of a current activity are expected to reflect sensitivity to specific self-task conditions and to the immediate social and physical environment. Yet, there is evidence that students' appraisals also reflect consistency across tasks and situations, which stresses the enduring influence of prior educational experience, typical assessment practices, and the value placed on education in a person's family. Examining the nature and significance of dynamic interactions within and across levels of specificity is therefore important for understanding stability and change in student learning and motivation over a period of time, or when students move across cultural–educational contexts, as in the case of international education and migration.

Criticality of a Multi-level Perspective to Understand Macro- and Micro-level Interactions in Learning and Motivation

Our own research on learning and motivation within and across cultural–educational contexts provides preliminary support for the usefulness of a multi-level perspective. Figure 5 illustrates the multi-level dynamic interactions within an international education setting, and some questions which can be generated. The left hand side of the figure represents the situation in the students' home country with evidence of congruence at the person-in-context experiential interface. The right hand side represents the host university context with multiple levels of specificity for both "students" and "context". As indicated by the question marks in the top and bottom parts of the figure, the socio-cultural conditions which foster continuity, adaptability or responsiveness in students' motivational beliefs over time and across contexts are not well known. For example, it seems reasonable to assume that the socio-cultural conditions leading to immediate re-establishment of congruence in the host setting have some degree of similarity with the home context. But what type of similarity, to what degree, and at what level of specificity? In the example of spontaneously formed informal study groups, discussed earlier, the similarity was in the function played by such groups at the person-in-context interface, and not between some characteristics of either individuals or contexts.

Acknowledging the situated, multi-dimensional and multi-level nature of the person-in-context perspective raises new questions for learning and motivation research, some related to tensions and possible conflicts between different layers of context. For example, while cross-cultural research has provided evidence that the cultural–educational practices which are valued in particular educational systems tend to foster the development of distinct motivational beliefs, it is unclear whether such beliefs are activated across all situations and tasks. Under what conditions do students' domain-specific, instruction-specific or assessment-specific experiences mediate their general motivational beliefs? What types of motivational beliefs are relatively stable and which ones vary across contexts, situations and tasks? After how much and what kind of participation? What is the magnitude of inter- and intra-individual differences in motivational orientations within and across different levels of context? The research questions which can be generated within a multi-dimensional contextual perspective are endless.

Our research has started to explore the interplay of broad socio-cultural and specific contextual aspects on the construction of different forms of motivation. The presence of large numbers of Singaporean students studying alongside local Australian students in the same classes at two Australian universities created a unique opportunity to explore the issue of stability and change in university students' motivational patterns over time, within and across cultural–educational contexts. On the one hand, evidence of stability over time would support the view that international students' motivational beliefs are not significantly affected by their specific experience in the Australian university setting. On the other hand, evidence of change over time would indicate that students' motivational profiles are malleable and readjusted within a different academic environment. In other words, maintenance of cross-group differences over time would highlight the enduring influence of substantial cultural–educational experiences, while a decrease in cross-group differences would stress the impact of the current specific academic situation in which all students study. Only a few selected findings are presented in this chapter (see Volet [1999a] for an overview).

In a short-term longitudinal study (Volet et al., 1994) with two matched groups of Singaporean and Australian students, we examined the interplay of prior cultural–educational background and current specific learning environment on the development of study motives (using Bigg's Study Process Questionnaire, Biggs, 1987). We found that all significant changes over one semester were in the same direction for the two groups. Both groups' motivation scores had decreased over time regardless of whether motives were deep, achieving or surface oriented. The decrease in achieving motivation, however, was of a lesser magnitude for the Singaporean group, yielding a significant group difference at the end of the semester. These results suggest that different layers of contextual influences may interact in dynamic ways in students' minds, and can even conflict with one another. Interview data revealed tensions experienced by some students between their overall academic achievement goals and their specific learning intentions for a unit of study, when the latter was not perceived as interesting or directly relevant to their programme of study.

In another small-scale longitudinal study (Volet & Renshaw, 1995), Singaporean and Australian students' learning goals for their first unit of study at university, and their perceptions of study settings for achieving these goals were collected at the beginning and the end of that semester-long unit. The issue of cultural specificity of the instrument for measuring goals was first addressed by analysing whether there were any qualitative differences in the two groups' conceptualisation of goals at the beginning and the end of the unit. The Rasch analyses, conducted separately for each group and for each occasion, revealed that the two groups' perceptions of the stimulus items and their relationships were different at the beginning but that these differences had disappeared by the end of the semester. By then, the ordering and location of the goals were almost identical for both groups. Since the Singaporean students were new to the Australian cultural–educational system, this finding suggests that students' prior cultural–educational experience supported the generation of different conceptualisations of goals (thus the group differences at the onset) but then, the specific study context of the unit and students' experiences within it had influenced both groups' conceptualisation of the relationships of the five goals in a similar way. Furthermore, comparisons of the two groups' learning goals at the beginning and end of semester showed that, after participating in the same learning activities over a semester, Singaporean students' levels of goals (measured with an instrument based on a hierarchy of goals customised to the specific unit of study) had become more like those of the group of local students. The significant relationships between the shift downwards in Singaporean students' levels of goals and their appraisals of the relevance of the unit content to their programme of study (measured with an adaptation of Boekaerts (1999) Online Motivation Questionnaire), provided support for the mediating role of subjective appraisals on the generation of learning goals.

The similar pattern of change for both groups, in their perceptions of the usefulness of different study settings was consistent with the data on learning goals, providing further support for the influence of specific learning experiences (via subjective appraisals) on students' beliefs about learning. The quantitative analyses of change over time in Singaporean students' appraisals of "Consulting with their tutor outside tutorial classes" provided results which were consistent with the interview data on home and host experience. On arrival, students were thinking that asking clarification questions was expected after class rather than during class. This reflected their experience at college in Singapore, where students were expected to *"ask the friends first"*, and once they had formulated a common question, they would *"go as a group to ask her. Because the teacher feels that you will be a distraction to the others ... if you are the only one who doesn't understand"* (Volet & Kee, 1993, p. 15). After one semester at university in Australia, students' appraisals reflected local practices. They were aware of their lack of confidence in speaking up, *"... lack the confidence ... so we dare not speak up"* and *"... tutors could encourage ... quite intimidating in the big group"* p. 41).

Other investigations of the impact on student motivation of respectively broad socio-cultural and specific cultural–educational aspects of context were carried out by sub-dividing the Australian student group on the basis of students' ethnic background (country of birth). Three groups of students studying in the same programme of study at the same university in Australia could therefore be compared: Australian students born, and fully educated in Australia and of dominant anglo-saxon backgrounds; Australian students born in Singapore but fully or partly educated in Australia due to migration; international students just arrived from Singapore for the duration of their university degree. Each group was expected to have encountered a unique configuration of socio-cultural and educational experiences, characterised by some similar and some different characteristics to the other groups. The results of this study (which used an adaptation of Pintrich's MSLQ 1991; Volet, 2001) revealed that socio-cultural experiences had a significant and lasting impact on students' levels of extrinsic goal orientation (regardless of whether goal orientation was conceptualised with a self or a social focus). As expected, and in line with other research evidence of the higher achievement motivation of students from Confucian Heritage Cultures (Salili, 1995), the group of Australian students born and fully educated in Australia scored significantly lower on both measures of extrinsic goal orientation than either the group of Australian students from Singaporean background or the group of international students from Singapore.

The lack of significant differences in extrinsic goal orientation between the two groups of students from Singaporean backgrounds suggests that schooling in an Australian vs. a Singaporean setting had a minimal impact on their motivational orientation for their business studies. Similar results were obtained with matched sub-groups of students (age, gender and program major taken into account). Evidence of the enduring impact of broad socio-cultural influences on the value of education among Asian groups has also been reported in American research (Schneider *et al.*, 1994). Consistent with our findings, Schneider & colleagues found that Japanese American parents of 4th generation children placed a higher intrinsic value on education for self-improvement in comparison to parents of European American descent. On other aspects of education, however, they found that the Japanese American parents' responses reflected the impact of American cultural–educational practices.

Differentiated findings also emerged with our cross-group comparisons of self-efficacy which showed an opposite pattern of results. Unlike for extrinsic goal orientation, the significant differences for self-efficacy were between the two groups of students from Singaporean backgrounds and not between the two sub-groups of Australian students. These results do not agree with repeated findings in cross-cultural studies, of Chinese-ethnic students' tendency to display lower levels of self-efficacy in comparison to their Western counterparts (Triandis, 1995; Salili, 1995). Our research, using a multi-level operationalisation of context, suggests that such differences may in fact disappear after a period of time in a different learning setting. The group differences in the cross-national studies, thus, may have to be interpreted as evidence of adaptation to specific educational practices rather than as the product of cultural values grounded in essentialist, static conceptions of culture (as context). In Singapore (Chew, 1997; Gopinathan, 1997) as in Hong Kong (Salili, 1995; Stevenson & Stigler, 1992) students are typically faced by highly competitive school systems, which put pressure on them to continuously strive for high levels of excellence — whether for maintaining the public ranking of their school or for the purpose of securing a place in the best possible college or university. Under such circumstances, it seems reasonable to assume that once in the less harsh study environment of an Australian university and given their relatively high academic achievement in comparison to their Australian counterparts, it is not surprising to find that the group of Singaporean students' level of self-efficacy is boosted. These interpretations are consistent with Zimmerman's (2000) claim that students' self-perceptions of efficacy are distinctive from related motivational constructs because of "their specificity and close correspondence to performance tasks" and "their sensitivity to variations in experience and task and situational context" (p. 89).

Conclusion

In this chapter, it has been argued that a multi-dimensional and multi-level cognitive–situative perspective is essential for understanding learning and motivation in context. A framework incorporating these elements was discussed and data from research on international students' experience of learning and motivation in different cultural–educational contexts was provided as preliminary support of the usefulness of the framework.

Within a combined cognitive–situative perspective, the experiential interface of the learner in context and the learner's experiential engagement in learning are emphasised. It is assumed that when learners participate in a learning experience (whether a learning task, classroom activity or unit of study), their motivational beliefs, orientations and habitualised forms of engagement for this type of learning are activated. These cognitions — which have developed over years of participation in various cultural–educational activities and contexts — interact with subjective appraisals of the affordances and constraints perceived in the immediate learning situation. These subjective appraisals mediate the direct impact of activated beliefs and orientations, and lead to goals, engagement and forms of participation which reflect context-sensitivity — rather than simply habitualised approach. Our research at the micro-level of learning showed that when individual learning is attuned to the affordances of the learning context and reciprocally when the community of practice supports individual engagement in productive learning, congruence is achieved and productive learning can occur. Alternatively, when there is a mismatch between learners and teachers' subjective perceptions of what constitutes appropriate learning and motivation, ambivalence and difficulties are experienced.

Our proposal to locate the experiential interface within a multi-level perspective of person and context aims at capturing the holistic nature of the acting person in context (Ford, 1992) and the complexity of real-life learning situations. Within a multi-level cognitive–situative perspective, experiential engagement is conceived as socially situated, multi-dimensional, reflecting the past and at the same time oriented towards the present and the future. The learning situation in which a person participates is conceptualised as social and physical, complex and dynamic, and providing proximal and distal levels of affordances and constraints. Moving from naturalistic classroom studies to global and multi-level research settings is conceptually and methodologically challenging. Within a multi-level, cognitive–situative perspective, it becomes possible to explore, for example, how and why short-term goals for an immediate activity may interfere with future aspirations, how some behaviours may be at the same time congruent and adaptive to satisfy immediate motivational needs and incongruent and maladaptive for long-term well-being, or how local educational practices may enhance or alternatively inhibit the development of positive appraisals of students who belong to communities with different self-systems (Markus & Kitayama, 1991; Volet 2000).

One major issue related to multi-level research is the nested nature of some contexts. To date, little attention has been given to the dynamic interactions of cultural–educational practices in contexts which are nested within one another — as is the case with learning contexts. Classroom activities (micro-level) take place within educational institutions which prioritise certain policies, instructional approaches and assessment practices (meso level). Yet, these activities and practices may not always be congruent, which creates confusion in learners. At another level, schools and universities operate within broader communities with close links to the world of work. The value placed within educational institutions on critical thinking, and intellectual rigour may clash with vocational and instrumental views of schooling and higher education in society (macro-level). Gurtner *et al*'s research (this volume) revealed how a lack of congruence between messages conveyed at macro- and micro-levels can inhibit efforts to foster engagement in learning. Investigating the dynamics of motivation across levels of specificity ideally requires the use of mixed research methodologies, where traditional surveys, involving multi-level designs and person-centered analyses are combined with repeated experience sampling, classroom observations, discourse analysis, online and video-recall interviews and other evidence of typical and specific cultural–educational practices.

To conclude, it is argued that motivation in learning contexts is best understood if conceptualised as a dynamic construct, and as a dual psychological and social phenomenon. The interplay of relatively consistent, distinct and unique aspects of contexts with relatively stable, variable and responsive motivational beliefs and appraisals highlights the systemic and situated nature of learning, where both individual and situational dimensions affect students' motivation and engagement in learning.

References

Ames C., & Archer, J. (1988), "Achievement goals in the classroom: Students' learning strategies and motivational processes." *Journal of Educational Psychology 80*, 260–267.

Anderman, L. H. Y., & Anderman, E. M. (eds), (2000), "Considering contexts in educational psychology: Introduction to the Special Issue." *Educational Psychologist 35* (2), 67–68.

Anderson, J. R., Greeno, J. G., Reder, L. M., & Simon, H. A. (2000), "Perspectives on learning, thinking and activity." *Educational Researcher 29* (4), 11–13.

Anderson, J. R., Reder, L. M., & Simon, H. A. (1996), "Situated learning and education." *Educational Researcher 25* (4), 5–11.

Anderson, J. R., Reder, L. M., & Simon, H. A. (1997), "Situative versus cognitive perspectives: Form versus substance." *Educational Researcher 26* (1), 18–21.

Bergen, K. J., Gulerce, A., Lock, A., & Misra, G. (1996), "Psychological science in cultural context." *American Psychologist 51* (5), 496–503.

Berry, J. W. (1997), Preface. In J. W. Berry, P. R. Dasen & T. S. Saraswathi (eds), *Handbook of Cross-cultural Psychology (Vol. 2) Basic Processes and Human Development* (pp. xi–xvi) Boston: Allyn & Bacon.

Betancourt, H., & López, S. R. (1993), "The study of culture, ethnicity and race in American psychology." *American Psychologist 48* (6), 629–637.

Biggs, J. B. (1996), "Approaches to learning of Asian students: A multiple paradox." In J. Pandey, D. Sinha & D. P. S. Bhawuk (eds) *Asian Contributions to Cross-cultural Psychology* (pp. 180–199). Sage Publications: New Delhi.

Biggs, J. B. (1987), *Student Approaches to Learning and Studying*. Hawthorn, Vic.: Australian Council for Educational Research.

Billett, S. (1996), "Bridging sociocultural and cognitive theorising." *Learning and Instruction 6* (3), 263–280.

Boekaerts, M. (1992), "The adaptable learning process: Initiating and maintaining behavioral change." *Journal of Applied Psychology: An International Review 41* (3), 377–397.

Boekaerts, M. (1997), "Self-regulated learning: A new concept embraced by researchers, policy makers, educators, teachers and students." *Learning and Instruction 7* (2), 161–186.

Boekaerts, M. (1999), "Motivated learning: studying student*situation transactional units." In M. Boekaerts & P. Nenniger (eds), Advances in Motivation from the European Viewpoint [Special Issue]. *European Journal of Psychology of Education 14*, 41–55.

Boekaerts, M., & Niemivirta, M. (2000), "Self-regulated learning: Finding a balance between learning goals and ego-protective goals." In M. Boekaerts, P. R. Pintrich & M. Zeidner (eds) *Handbook of Self-regulation* (pp. 417–450). San Diego, C.A.: Academic Press.

Bond, M. H. (1986), *The Psychology of the Chinese People*. Hong Kong: Oxford University Press.

Chang, S. C. A., & Hung, W. L. D. (1999), "Development of a thinking culture within the Singaporean university context." *Asia Pacific Journal of Education 19* (2), 72–85.

Chew, O. A. J. (1997), "Schooling for Singaporeans: The interaction of Singapore culture and values in the school." In J. Tan, S. Gopinathan & H. W. Kam (eds) *Education in Singapore* (pp. 75–91). Singapore: Prentice Hall.

Cobb, P. & Bowers, J. (1999), "Cognitive and situated learning: Perspectives in theory and practice." *Educational Researcher 28* (2), 4–15.

Ford, M. (1992), *Motivating Humans: Goals, Emotions and Personal Agency*. Sage: Newbury Park, CA.

Gibson, J. J. (1979/1986), "The theory of affordances." In J. J. Gibson. (ed.) *The Ecological Approach to Visual Perception* (pp. 127–143). Hillsdale, NJ: Erlbaum. (Original work published in 1979).

Gopinathan, S. (1997), "Education and development in Singapore." In J. Tan, S. Gopinathan & H. W. Kam (eds) *Education in Singapore* (pp. 33–53). Singapore: Prentice Hall.

Greeno, J. G. (1997), "On claims that answer the wrong questions." *Educational Researcher 26*, 5–17.

Greeno, J. G. (1998), "The situativity of knowing, learning and research." *American Psychologist 53* (1), 5–26.

Greeno, J. G., Collins, A. M., & Resnick, L. (1996), "Cognition and learning." In D. Berliner & R. L. Calfee (eds) *Handbook of Educational Psychology* (pp. 15–46). New York: Macmillan.

Gruber, H., Law, L. C., Mandl, H. & Renkl, A. (1995), "Situated learning and transfer." In P. Reimann & H. Spada (eds), *Learning in Humans and Machines: Towards an Interdisciplinary Learning Science* (pp. 168–188). Oxford: Pergamon.

Hess, R. D., & Azuma, H. (1991), "Cultural support for schooling: contrasts between Japan and the United States." *Educational Researcher 20* (9), 2–8, 12.

Hickey, D. (1997), "Motivation and contemporary socio-constructivist instructional perspectives." *Educational Psychologist 32*, 175–193.

Kagitcibasi, C. (1992), "Linking the indigenous and universalist orientation." In S. Iwawaki, Y. Kashima & K. Leung (eds) *Innovations in Cross-cultural Psychology* (pp. 29–37). Lisse: Swets & Zeitlinger.

Kagitcibasi, C. (1996), *Family and Human Development Across Cultures: A View from the Other Side*. Mahwah N.J.: Erlbaum.

Kim, U., & Berry, J. B. W. (eds). (1993), *Indigenous Psychologies: Research and Experience in Cultural Context*. Newbury Park, CA: Sage.

Krapp, A. (1999), "Interest, motivation and learning: An educational–psychological perspective." *European Journal of Psychology of Education 14*, 23–40.

MacCallum, J. (2001), "Motivational change in transition contexts." In A. Efklides, J. Kuhl & R. M. Sorrentino (eds) *Trends and Prospects in Motivation Research* (pp. 121–143). Dordrecht, The Netherlands: Kluwer.

Maehr, M. L., Shi, K., Kaplan, A., & Wang, P. (1999), "Culture, motivation and achievement: Toward meeting the new challenge." *Asia Pacific Journal of Education 19* (2), 15–29.

Markus, H. R., & Kitayama, S. (1991), "Culture and the self: Implications for cognition, emotion and motivation." *Psychological Review 98*, 224–253.

McCaslin, M., & Good. T. (1996), "The informal curriculum." In D. Berliner & R. Calfee (eds) *Handbook of Educational Psychology* (pp. 622–670). New York: MacMillan.

Ogbu, J. G. (1992), "Understanding cultural diversity and learning." *Educational Researcher 21* (8), 5–14.

Pekrun, R. (2000), "A social–cognitive, control–value theory of achievement emotions." In J. Heckhausen (ed.) *Motivational Psychology of Human Development* (pp. 143–163). Oxford: Elsevier.

Pintrich, P. (1991), *A Manual for the Use of the Motivated Strategies for Learning Questionnaire (MSLQ)*. Ann Arbor, Michigan: National Centre for Research to Improve Postsecondary Teaching and Learning and the School of Education, University of Michigan.

Pintrich, P. R. (2000), "An achievement goal theory perspective on issues in motivation terminology, theory and research." *Contemporary Educational Psychology 25*, 92–104.

Rogoff, B., & Chavajay, P. (1995), "What's become of research on the cultural basis of cognitive development?" *American Psychologist 50* (10), 859–877.

Salili, F. (1995), "Explaining Chinese students' motivation and achievement: A sociocultural analysis." In M. L. Maehr & P. R. Pintrich (eds) *Advances in Motivation and Achievement: Culture, Motivation and Achievement (Vol. 9)* (pp. 73–118). Greenwich, Connecticut: JAI Press.

Salomon, G. (1991), "Transcending the qualitative–quantitative debate: The analytic and systemic approaches to educational research." *Educational Researcher 20* (6), 10–18.

Schiefele, U., & Csikszentmihalyi, M. (1995), "Interest and the quality of experience in classroom." *European Journal of Psychology of Education 9*, 251–269.

Schneider, B., & Lee, S. (1990), "A model for academic success: The school and home environment of East Asian students." *Anthropology and Education, 21* (4), 358–377.

Schneider, B., Hieshima, J. A., Lee, S., & Plank, S. (1994), "East-Asian academic success in the United States: Family, school and community explanations." In P. Greenfield & R. Cocking (eds), *Cross-cultural Roots of Minority Child Development.* (pp. 323–350). Hillsdale, NJ: Erlbaum.

Sinha, D. (1986), *Psychology in a Third World Country: The Indian Experience.* New Delhi: Sage.

Sinha, D. (1996), "Cross-cultural psychology: The Asian scenario." In J. Pandey, D. Sinha & D. P. S. Bhawuk (eds), *Asian Contributions to Cross-cultural Psychology.* (pp. 20–41). New Delhi/Thousand Oaks/London: Sage Publications.

Smart, D., Volet, S. E., & Ang, G. (2000), *Fostering Social Cohesion in Universities: Bridging the Cultural Divide.* Murdoch/Canberra: Murdoch University/Australian Education International.

Snow, R. (1994), "Abilities in academic tasks." In R. Sternberg & R. Wagner (eds) *Mind in Context: Interactionist Perspectives on Human Intelligence* (pp. 3–37). Cambridge: Cambridge University Press.

Spindler, G., & Spindler, L. (1987), *The Interpretive Ethnography of Education: At Home and Abroad.* Hillsdale, NJ: Erlbaum.

Stevenson, H. W., & Stigler, J. W. (1992), *The Learning Gap: Why our Schools are Failing and What We Can Learn from Japanese and Chinese Education.* New York: Summit Books/Simon & Schuster.

Tan, J., Goh, J., & Volet, S. E. (1999, January), *The significance of cultural values on the study approaches of students across Australia, Malaysia and Singapore.* Paper presented at the International Conference on New Professionalism in Teaching:Teacher Education and Teacher Development in a Changing World. Hong Kong.

Tang, C. (1996), "Collaborative learning: The latent dimension in Chinese students' learning." In D. Watkins & J. Biggs (eds) *The Chinese Learner: Cultural, Psychological and Contextual Influences* (pp. 183–204). CERC The University of Hong Kong/ACER.

Tang, C., & Biggs, J. B. (1996), "How Hong Kong students cope with assessment." In D. Watkins & J. Biggs (eds) *The Chinese Learner: Cultural, Psychological and Contextual Influences* (pp. 159–182). CERC The University of Hong Kong/ACER.

Triandis, H. C. (1989), "The self and social behavior in differing cultural contexts." *Psychological Review 96* (3), 506–520.

Triandis, H. C. (1995), "Motivation and achievement in collectivist and individualist cultures." In M. L. Maehr & P. R. Pintrich (eds) *Advances in Motivation and Achievement: Culture, Motivation and Achievement (Vol. 9)* (pp. 1–30). Greenwich: JAI.

Turner, J. C., Meyer, D. K., Cox, K. E., Logan, C., DiCintio, M. *et al.* (1998), "Creating contexts for involvement in mathematics." *Journal of Educational Psychology 90*, 730–745.

Valsiner, J., & Lawrence, J. A. (1997), "Human development culture across the life span." In J. W. Berry, P. R. Dasen & T. S. Saraswathi (eds) *Handbook of Cross-cultural Psychology (Vol. 2)* (pp. 69–106). *Basic Processes and Developmental Psychology*. Boston: Allyn & Bacon.

Vermunt, J. D., & Verloop, N. (1999), "Congruence and friction between learning and teaching." *Learning and Instruction 9* (3), 257–280.

Volet, S. E. (2001), "Significance of cultural and motivational variables on students' appraisals of group work." In F. Salili, C. Y. Chiu, & Y. Y. Hong (eds) *Student Motivation: The Culture and Context of Learning* (Ch. 15) (pp. 309–334). New York: Kluwer/Plenum.

Volet, S. E. (1999a), "Motivation within and across cultural–educational contexts: A multidimensional perspective." In T. Urdan (ed.) *Advances in Motivation and Achievement: The Role of Context (Vol. 11)* (pp. 185–231). Stanford, CT: JAI Press.

Volet, S. E. (1999b), "Learning across cultures: Appropriateness of knowledge transfer." *International Journal of Educational Research 31*, 625–643.

Volet, S. E. (1999c), "Internationalisation of higher education: Oportunities for intercultural development of Chinese and Australian students." In LuJie (Ed.) *Education of the Chinese: The Global Looking on Traditions of the Chinese Nation* (pp. 240–256) Nanjing: Nanjing University Press.

Volet, S. E. (1997), "Cognitive and affective variables in academic learning: The significance of direction and effort in students' goals." *Learning and Instruction 7* (3), 235–254.

Volet, S. E., & Ang, G. (1998), "Culturally mixed groups on international campuses: An opportunity for intercultural learning." *Higher Education Research & Development 17* (1), 5–23.

Volet, S. E., & Kee, J. P. P. (1993), *Studying in Singapore — Studying in Australia: A Student Perspective*. Occasional Paper No. 1, Murdoch University Teaching Excellence Committee, Murdoch.

Volet, S. E., & Renshaw, P. D. (1995), "Cross-cultural differences in university students' goals and perceptions of study settings for achieving goals." *Higher Education 30* (4), 407–433.

Volet, S. E., & Tan-Quigley, A. (1998), "Interactions of South-east Asian students and administrative staff at university in Australia: The significance of reciprocal understanding." *Journal of Higher Education Policy and Management 20* (2), 295–315.

Volet, S. E., Renshaw, P. D., & Tietzel, K. (1994), "A short-term longitudinal investigation of cross-cultural differences in study approaches using Biggs' SPQ questionnaire." *British Journal of Educational Psychology 64*, 301–318.

Vosniadou, S. (1996), "Towards a revised cognitive psychology for new advances in learning and instruction." *Learning and Instruction 6* (2), 95–109.

Weiner, B. (1990), "History of motivation research in education." *Journal of Educational Psychology 82*, 616–622.

Zimmerman, B. J. (2000), "Self-efficacy: an essential motive to learn." *Contemporary Educational Psychology 25*, 82–91.

Part III

Studying Motivation in Natural Learning Settings

Chapter 5

Using Context to Enrich and Challenge our Understanding of Motivational Theory

Julianne C. Turner

Until recently, it was assumed that motivation could be studied and its influences and outcomes understood without knowing the situation or context in which it occurred. This now seems like an absurd notion. Motivation is influenced by multiple and overlapping contexts. Nothing is "decontextualized" despite efforts to make it so. Investigations of the influence of educational contexts range from macro views of "culture as context" (e.g., Volet, 1999) to micro studies of two people interacting (e.g., Rogoff, 1990; Wertsch, 1985). Educational contexts include social elements such as teachers and peers, cultural elements such as norms and expectations, and instructional and material elements such as content area, curricula and tasks. However, more recent motivational constructs have been focused on the self while regarding context as "background." The present challenge to motivational research is to integrate the notions of self and context. The situative approach attempts to understand persons-in-situations and provides an alternative to both traditional behavioral and cognitive approaches to motivation.

This chapter will focus on four related issues. First, assumptions underlying behavioral and cognitive approaches to learning and motivation will be contrasted with the situative one. Second, methodologies more appropriate to measuring motivation from a contextual or situative perspective are proposed. Third, a research example is offered to illustrate how a more situated notion of motivation can illuminate traditional interpretations and enrich motivational theory. Finally, the problems and opportunities associated with such an approach are considered.

What is Motivation in Context?

The conceptual and theoretical bases of motivation to learn have been closely tied to parallel notions of cognition and learning. The roles of environmental, individual, and social factors have been central to our understandings of cognition and motivation. These foci represent the three major perspectives that have developed in psychological research: behaviorist, cognitive, and situative (Greeno *et al.*, 1996).

Motivation in Learning Contexts: Theoretical Advances and Methodological Implications, pages 85–104.

Behavioral and Cognitive Views of Learning and Motivation

In the behavioral perspective on learning and motivation, the environment plays a crucial role. Learning is viewed as the accumulation of associations and components of skills while motivation supplies incentives so that the learner will attend to specific aspects of the situation and will respond appropriately (Skinner, 1953). Motivation is extrinsic to the learner, although dependent on the relative effectiveness of the reward for the student. Learning and motivation are individual to the extent that certain incentives may be attractive to individuals, but the assumption is that the process itself is not situational.

Conversely, in the cognitive perspective, learning is viewed as the construction of concepts and the growth in general problem-solving abilities and metacognitive processes (Anderson *et al.*, 1996). The cognitive approach treats processes of individual cognition as the basic unit and explains social interactions in terms of individuals' perceptions, goals, inferences, and so on.

The cognitive perspective on motivation is the most dominant currently. Theories of achievement motivation tend to focus on the self and the person's perception of the environment. The context is a source of information that can provoke sense-making processes that are expected to influence engagement (e.g., expectancy). For example, flow theory (Csikszentmihalyi & Csikszentmihalyi, 1988) describes an optimal situation in which the perceived challenges of a situation are closely in tune with the person's perceived skills. This theoretical perspective has mostly been used to investigate the frequency of certain psychological states (such as flow, boredom, etc.) and the affective correlates of these states (e.g., involvement) for individuals across time and contexts. The development of meta-skills can help the individual tailor environments to be more personally satisfying (Csikszentmihalyi & Nakamura, 1989). Self-determination theory has defined intrinsic motivation as the satisfaction of human needs such as competence, control, and relatedness, but suggests that motivation will still vary with the individual depending on initial interests (Ryan & Deci, 2000). In undermining situations where individuals must perform extrinsically motivated actions, they can often transform such actions so that they internalize the value or utility of the task and regain control. Goal theory proposes that motivation is related to the purposes for pursuing academic activities, and that differing purposes will be related to specific programs of beliefs and affects (Pintrich, 2000). Much of this program of motivational research has focused on personal goal orientations and the more or less adaptive patterns that students adopt in academic situations (e.g., Ames & Archer, 1988; Dweck & Leggett, 1988; Midgley *et al.*, 1996). In these cognitive theories of motivation the emphasis is often on understanding what motivates students (e.g., developing competence) or on devising ways to foster students' natural tendencies to learn such as by increasing competence and autonomy, or responding to interests. Because the focus is on perceptions, cognitive theories of motivation also emphasize individual differences in learners, sometimes rendering the environment a "source of information" rather than an integral part of the experience of motivation to learn.

In sum, the behavioral and the cognitive perspectives of motivation emphasize either the role of the environment or the individual, placing one in the foreground while relegating the other to the background; an outside vs. inside dichotomy.

The Situative Perspective on Learning

The situative, or interactional, perspective on learning attempts to avoid the outside vs. inside dichotomy by giving priority to activity or doing rather than knowing (Bredo, 2000; Greeno, 1997). For example Lave contends that the

> ... cognitive view of learning as cognitive acquisition — whether of facts, knowledge, problem-solving strategies, or metacognitive skills — seems to dissolve when learning is conceived of as the construction of present versions of past experience for several persons acting together (Lave, 1993, p. 8).

Learning becomes the appropriation of socially derived forms of knowledge through transformation and a reciprocal constructive process (Billet, 1996). Whereas the cognitive perspective emphasizes that all knowledge is, to a great extent, personal, there are two arguments for regarding knowledge not as purely personal but as interactive (Eraut, 2000). First, in some situations, students are not able to perform alone, as when students are learning something new. For example, cooperative learning and jigsaw procedures are designed specifically so that not all participants have the same knowledge or skill base (Aronson *et al.*, 1978; Cohen, 1994). Second, knowledge or understanding is inevitably shaped by the situations in which it is learned and used. The surrounding social interactional context structures individual thinking such that participants share understandings. As Newman *et al.* (1984) point out, the very definition of a task changes when it becomes a shared, versus an individual, endeavor. Thus knowledge and learning will be found distributed throughout the complex structure of persons-acting-in-settings (Lave, 1993, p. 9).

Critics such as Anderson *et al.* (1997) question the meanings of situative terminology like "identity as a learner" and whether the individual is subsumed as a group identity. They also suggest that the situative perspective has not demonstrated

> ... that it provides the right theoretical or experimental tools for understanding social cognition (p. 20).

Indeed, exactly how to conceive of the role of person in situation is complex. Cognitive activities are not completely specific to the context in which they were learned. Personal knowledge is interdependent with social context and this interdependence raises the question of whether any knowledge (or motivation) is either individually or socially constructed. For example, Eraut (2000) argues that the knowledge gained in a classroom (e.g., curricular knowledge, knowledge of the "informal curriculum," and norms, beliefs, and attitudes generated from peer interaction) is constructed in a social context whose influence cannot be denied. Nevertheless, because individuals do not enter settings with the same cognitive resources such as prior knowledge, and because they are rarely treated in identical ways, their experiences are different. Thus, Eraut (2000) believes one must adopt two complementary perspectives:

> One should focus on the situation itself — its antecedents, wider context and ongoing interaction with its environment — and the transactions of its participants throughout the period of enquiry. The other should focus on the contributions of the situation to the learning careers of individual participants, the learning acquired during their "visit" (p. 132).

Motivation from a Situative Perspective

The situative view of motivation is much less theoretically developed than its counterpart in learning. It attempts to explain not only the self-processes, but also the effects of collective experience. The situative view of motivation focuses on the ways that social practices provide for the engaged or disengaged participation by members of communities. Engagement depends on interpersonal, or social, relations (not just individual perceptions) in learning communities and the continuing development of personal identities. Motivation is viewed as distributed among participants. Thus context is no longer a background variable but a major constituent of motivation. Similarly, motivation, while incorporating individual experience, is integrally intertwined with group experience.

According to this view, students can become engaged in learning by participating in classroom communities that value learning. Lave and Wenger (1991) described how people could establish their identities by functioning in the communities they join. In a mathematics classroom, for example, students can become legitimate members of the mathematics community, sharing expertise and ownership. As they become more important to their community, their identity becomes enhanced by virtue of their participation.

Motivation researchers have begun to acknowledge the importance of context (e.g., Anderman & Anderman, 2000; Turner & Meyer, 2000), but tend to approach a context as the sum of its parts rather than as integral and holistic. For example, goal theorists have demonstrated that students may report similar perceptions of the goal structure in their classrooms, thus suggesting that there is a shared cultural understanding (e.g., Meece, 1991, Ryan *et al.*, 1998). Similarly, Turner and her colleagues (Turner *et al.*, 1998) have described how teacher-initiated instructional environments are related to students' perceptions of motivation. However, construction of the environment is usually portrayed as unidirectional, flowing from teacher to student, rather than as multidirectional, constituted by group members in their activities.

Situative theorists interpret motivation as a social phenomenon, yet have not yet clearly described the psychological dimensions of such experience. For example, we have yet to explore what norms and values mean from a motivational and affective stance. Goldstein (1999) examines the affective importance of "the other" in the social organization of learning. She contends that the interpersonal character of the teaching–learning relationship (or perhaps of learners to each other) resembles Noddings's (1984) notion of caring. Vygotskian perspectives, as applied to motivation, imply that members of a learning community internalize, and then exercise, the actions, beliefs and affects of their co-participants. Similarly, Brophy's (1999) notion of an "optimal match" suggests that affordances of contexts may create a "motivational zone of proximal development". That is,

> ... features of a learning domain or activity must line up with the learner's prior knowledge and experiences in such a way as to stimulate interest in pursuing the learning (Brophy, 1999, p. 77).

Such a situation has the potential to increase value for learning among the participants.

Cognitive theories of motivation may also be useful in explaining how participation enhances identity. The notion of modeling, as explained by Self-Efficacy theory (e.g., Schunk & Hanson, 1985), suggest that seeing how similar others participate can increase self-efficacy to master new competencies, be they individual or group processes. It seems reasonable that when students share expertise and ownership they may increase collective self-efficacy (Zimmerman, 2000), expectancy for success and task value (Wigfield & Eccles, 2000), become more focused on learning meaningful content (Pintrich, 2000), and develop a greater interest in the task itself (Ryan & Deci, 2000). These outcomes could occur at the level of the collective group as well at the individual level. Such motivational outcomes increase the group's identity with the situation because they help satisfy needs and goals.

However, current cognitive theories, because of their reliance on individual perceptions, do not appear to adequately address how participants develop a shared view of what counts as learning, how one participates, and what is valued. Greeno and his colleagues (1998) describe this process as dependent on a unique set of constraints and affordances. Constraints involve the ability to anticipate outcomes while affordances are qualities of systems that support interactions. Students become attuned to the regularized conventions and develop well-coordinated patterns of participating in social practices. Of course, group activity could also foster disengagement in learning through classroom communities that devalue learning. Regardless of the positive or negative character of the motivations that students develop in their classrooms, all classrooms appear to construct such constraints and affordances as part of their culture.

It is a challenging and exciting opportunity to try to advance our theoretical and empirical understandings of motivation as situated or contextualized. The concept of "motivation in context" means that we assume that motivation is an interactive experience, depending on the influences of students and their environments on each other, although different students will make different contributions and may also have different interpretations of the context. Environments, broadly defined, will include teachers, peers, activities, the content area, and the instructional discourse, as well as the norms and beliefs promoted or accepted by the participants. From a theoretical perspective, the situative view, closely related to the socio-cultural perspective of Vygotsky (1978), holds that the practices of the classroom community can either facilitate or inhibit motivational patterns. These patterns, in turn, influence the group's activities and the participation of students who are attuned to them. For example, discourse practices, such as scaffolding (Brophy, 1999; Gallimore & Tharp, 1990; Hogan & Pressley, 1997), can help students develop ways to participate and gain membership as disciplinary thinkers in the classroom community. Such practices help students identify with the community and seek to participate fully.

Approaches to Studying Motivation in Context

As views of the nature of motivation change, so too must the methods devoted to their study. The typical methods used to study motivation, such as experimental and laboratory manipulations and self-reports, have often been more suited to investigating motivation from either the behavioral or the cognitive perspectives. Hickey (1997) has proposed a new "principled, pragmatic motivation research model" (p. 184). He argues that older models of motivation may be inappropriate for studying some newer forms of instruction, such as those in the socio-constructivist tradition. Newer instructional models, as discussed above, assume that learning (and motivation) are not confined to individual representations, but are, to some degree, distributed, and thus necessitate reconsideration of traditional assumptions and methods. Indeed, even traditional instruction can be studied from a situative perspective if one believes that instructional practices have historical roots, that they are constructed in joint activity with students, and that they inculcate beliefs, values, and motivations (Lave, 1993; Minick, 1993).

In an attempt to explore just what "motivation in context" means, researchers will need to move beyond and diversify the traditional methods and the traditional focus of motivational research. In terms of method, Hickey (1997) and Blumenfeld (1992) assert that applications of motivational theory have been limited by methodologies, research designs, and the lack of description of what is actually happening in classrooms. Methodologies have been mostly deductive and quantitative, research designs have involved one or two snapshots of phenomena, and there has been little exploration of the *how* and *why* of motivation because there have been few descriptions of classroom interactions. Blumenfeld suggested that researchers should: (a) use better sampling techniques, such as descriptions of classroom structures, discourse, and tasks in addition to (or instead of) questionnaires; (b) pay specific attention to the influence of the content area, such as what counts as learning in mathematics; and (c) follow students and teachers over time so that they may discover the ebb and flow of motivation and emotion in relation to classroom learning and also the long-term motivational effects of learning in specific contexts.

One response to those critiques, is to adopt a *mixed method approach* to studying motivation in context (e.g., Turner & Meyer, 1999, 2000). Use of mixed methods is a pragmatic perspective that incorporates both inductive and deductive, and both qualitative and quantitative methods simultaneously and as complementary modes of inquiry (Tashakkori & Teddlie, 1998). For example, Turner and her colleagues have used deductive measures such as surveys and experience sampling forms in combination with inductive approaches such as interviews, observations of students and teachers, and analyses of teacher discourse during instruction. They combine both quantitative and qualitative measures in an attempt to capture not only the *what*, but also the *why* and the *how* of students interacting in contexts. Observations, interviews, and discourse analysis are tools to help us begin to understand how classroom communities are formed, how they function, and what they value. Student self-reports such as experience sampling and surveys enable us to see how students interpret classroom goals and sanctioned practices.

Similarly, the focus of research should move beyond students alone. If we believe that motivation is situated in contexts, then we must consider the major features of an instructional context and their reciprocal effects. Although this is clearly very complex, one might begin with a consideration of the interaction of students, teachers, and several features of the instructional context such as classroom tasks, teachers' instructional practices as revealed in their classroom discourse, and the academic content area. One advantage of this approach is that it does not force an artificial dichotomy between cognition and motivation (c.f. Hickey, 1997). Motivation and cognition are interrelated. For example, by studying instruction as revealed in teacher discourse, the motivational messages are embedded in the very acts of teaching and learning, thus unifying the constructs that co-exist in classrooms, but have been separated in research.

A mixed method approach to studying motivation has several advantages:

- *Triangulation*, or seeking convergence of results. Four types of triangulation include: data triangulation (use of a variety of data sources), investigator triangulation (use of several researchers), theory triangulation (use of multiple perspectives, like goal theory and discourse theory), and methodological triangulation (use of multiple methods).
- *Complementarity*, or examining overlapping and different facets of a phenomenon such as motivation from different perspectives.
- *Initiation*, or discovering paradoxes, contradictions, or fresh perspectives: "Pushing theory" (Tashakkori and Teddlie, 1998).

The most valuable outcome of mixed methodology may be Initiation, or uncovering paradoxes and contradictions. In mono-method research, the risk is that the construct being measured is difficult to differentiate from its particular (mono-method) operational definition (Cook & Campbell, 1979). When focus is enlarged and student, teacher, and other contextual influences are measured simultaneously, the result might be that we find certain formerly acceptable theoretical explanations to be wanting or at odds with the data. The fruitful tension between and among deductive and inductive approaches makes it impossible to gloss over inconsistencies and potentially rival or "messy" interpretations (Blumenfeld, 1992). Findings from multiple methods must be reconciled, providing a more stringent test of motivation theories in classrooms. The benefit is that we can, by integrating and explaining these interactions, enrich and contextualize our theories of motivation. The following section provides an illustration of the use of mixed methods from one research program and discusses the theoretical and practical implications of such methods.

Some Research Examples

The examples chosen are based on research in one classroom and these data were part of a larger study (see Turner *et al.*, 1998, for details). This classroom posed several contradictions and became a fruitful example of how using contextual data, or knowing what was happening in classrooms, can help us expand our notions of what our theoretical constructs mean.

Theoretical Background

The original research question was, Which instructional practices are related to students' involvement in mathematics instruction? One perspective that informed the work was that of Csikszentmihalyi's flow theory. Csikszentmihalyi's (Csikszentmihalyi & Csikszentmihalyi, 1988; Csikszentmihalyi & Nakamura, 1989) work in intrinsic motivation predicts that students will experience involvement when there is an optimal balance between the challenges of a learning situation and the skills that students bring to the situation. When students experience a moderately challenging situation and when they possess adequate skills to meet that challenge, the resulting experience, called flow, is very positive because it allows students to operate at their fullest capacity. Conversely, when challenges and skills are not balanced, situations may be perceived as boring (e.g., challenges low and skills high), or promoting either anxiety or apathy. Csikszentmihalyi has argued that when students are involved they will indicate positive feelings such as "happy" vs. "sad" and "proud" vs. "ashamed." Students should have different responses to situations when they are bored, anxious, or apathetic because the quality of experience should be diminished.

In order to involve students in learning, teachers would have to be skillful at calibrating instruction so that it offered moderate challenges, *yet also* enabled students to meet challenges by helping them to continuously increase their skills (e.g., Vermunt & Verloop, 1999). Scaffolding, or "assisting instruction" (Brophy, 1999; Gallimore & Tharp, 1990) is an instructional approach that may foster involvement because it supports students cognitively, motivationally, and emotionally in learning while helping students take control of their learning. During scaffolding, teachers perform two crucial functions, negotiation and transfer. In *negotiation of meaningful learning*, the teacher supports students' understanding in order to help them build skills. In *transfer of responsibility*, the teacher offers opportunities for students to demonstrate and apply what they have learned by asking them to think on their own, without teacher support. Thus scaffolding is an instructional vehicle for building skills students will need for learning and then offering them challenges to which they can apply their skills. In addition to academic support, teachers also provide emotional and motivational support such as encouraging persistence, teaching the constructive value of errors, encouraging intrinsic interest in, and modeling value for the subject, and even making content-related jokes. It was hypothesized that scaffolded instruction would be related to students' reports of involvement because it helped students build skills and meet academic challenges.

However, other forms of discourse may work against such goals. Initiation–Response–Evaluation (IRE) (Mehan, 1985) consists of the teacher asking a question, eliciting a student answer, and then evaluating the answer. Often the emphasis is on asking a "known answer" question. Such discourse does not appear to help students build skills, as no new knowledge is introduced, explained or modeled. Another form of discourse is "teacher telling" in which the teacher gives answers (pre-empting student responses) or insists on a "correct" set of procedures to be followed, discouraging student initiative. Such discourse, if overused, subverts challenges because it does not offer students the chance to apply skills in new situations. Some emotional and motivational strategies also appear to work against involvement. Extrinsic motivation strategies, such as threats or praise for superficial accomplishments, are designed to focus students on compliance, but not necessarily on learning. It was hypothesized that these forms of non-scaffolded discourse would be associated with boredom, anxiety, or apathy because they did not contribute to building skills and meeting new challenges.

Data Collected

Students' involvement was measured by asking them to fill out an experience sampling form (ESF) (Csikszentmihalyi & Larson, 1987) during each of the five days of instruction in their classroom. Students responded to "How challenging was math class today?" and "How were your skills in math today?" by circling a number from zero (low) to nine (high) with four and five labeled "average." In addition, students circled a set of semantic differential items designed to provide an index of their quality of experience during mathematics (e.g., happy" vs. "sad" and "proud" vs. "ashamed"). Students' responses were directly tied to the individual math lessons and were representative of their personal experiences in those lessons. Observers also visited each math lesson and tape-recorded all teacher discourse. Discourse was transcribed and coded using the scaffolding and non-scaffolding categories described above.

Paradox 1: Boredom as a "Positive" Quality of Experience

One of the seven classrooms in the study challenged traditional cognitive assumptions about the theoretical relationships between motivation and instruction. In Ms. Grant's class, students reported that they found mathematics lessons in general to be of low challenge while they rated their skills as quite high in relation to the instructional requirements. Such ratings of "boredom," however, were associated with very positive qualities of experience in the classroom. There were no significant differences in the semantic differential responses of students in "flow" classrooms and students in the "boredom" classroom. Students reported feeling as cooperative, alert, strong, proud, relaxed, clear, open, and involved as students who reported moderately high challenges and skills in their classes.

Because existing theory did not explain this situation well, a more situated view of the patterns in classroom participation seemed to offer an opportunity for meaningful interpretation. The focus became how teachers and students co-constructed a view of "mathematics class" and how they became attuned to the constraints and affordances of their situation. The discourse data was a useful source of evidence to help understand the relationship between the instruction and the student responses to it. The following is an excerpt from a mathematics lesson. The teacher had designed an application lesson to follow several weeks of the study of decimals, fractions, and percents. The students were to participate in a survey by walking around the room and recording their responses to survey questions posted on the walls. Then each student was to represent the data from one survey question graphically, such as in a pie chart. In order to do this, students had to change the raw frequencies into percentages by categories, such as the percentages of students who preferred certain kinds of fast food.

The teacher began the lesson by trying to appeal to the students affectively, using an extrinsic approach. Through her overuse of the word "little" she may have focused attention on establishing a cooperative relationship with the students and (perhaps unwittingly) trivializing the mathematics. Then she began one of several long "telling" sequences in which she explained things that students appeared to know already, such as how to make tally marks and what a nickname was.

T: Eyes on me ... OK, I have made *little* things here with *little* questionnaires and you have to take your *little* pencil now and follow the directions and we are going to go single file and we are going to mark our *little* categories. There's lots to fill out here and then we are going to turn these into our *little* graphs that we have been making. Now this is what you are going to do ... if you come up here and answer this question. "Do you prefer to be called by a nickname? It says use a tally mark." What they mean is when you are doing a survey and they say to use a tally mark is that they want you to put a little line (draws on the board). When you are the fifth one, what do you mark ... Larry (says a slash through) ... OK so if you are the fifth one up here then you are going to make a diagonal. Do you prefer to be called by a nickname? So that means if your name is Jonathan and you like to be called by the name Jon, then you have a nickname ...

After the students completed marking the surveys, the teacher introduced the idea of converting the frequencies into percentages. Even though the students had studied this topic for weeks, the teacher began to "tell" them how to do it. Unlike a scaffolding teacher, who would ask the students to do the thinking, Ms. Grant did it for them. This decision served to keep challenge very low, and the students' skills very high, the definition of boredom in the theory. It is interesting to see how "telling" contributes to this low challenge situation.

T: We need to figure out how many people we have here to make the total 100 per cent. Let's count how many people will make the 100 percent total. Twenty-nine people is the total amount for the survey ...

T: Now we should have 29 surveys to tally up here ... so I will pass out these surveys (T passes out sheets for students to count the number of tally marks on each question).

T: If you have a chart that not all students answered the questions ... the total number of tally marks on the sheet is the total 100 percent. I will come around here ... Annie, out of 29 what were your results? 100 percent is 29.

S: Only 28 (people) answered my question (as opposed to the class total of 29).

T: Only 28 answered that question ... OK now if you have a chart that only 28 answered, your total amount will change ... you better count your total and be like Anna and change your 100 percent ...

In contrast to students' comments in scaffolding classrooms — where students were explaining and solving the problems — these students focused on superficial aspects such as how many respondents they had and whether they could make a different kind of graph. There was no indication that students were focusing on the meaning of the numbers and how that could be accurately and clearly presented. This student response was consistent with the teacher expectations that appeared to be set at the beginning of the class. Thus teacher and students seemed to be cooperating in keeping the lesson at a procedural level.

The next class, students had completed the graphs for homework and the teacher was commenting on them. Some students may have missed the point of the lesson, because they made circle graphs but did not compute percentages for their frequencies. In the excerpt below, the teacher again "tells" the student how to do that, missing another opportunity for the students to demonstrate knowledge and gain ownership.

T: OK let's figure out the percents since you did a circle graph, OK twelve out of 28 we are going to turn this into a decimal, would it be helpful to reduce it maybe first?
Reduce it first ... it would be helpful ... what would go both into twelve and 28?

S: It would be 3/7ths
    The teacher continued to demonstrate the algorithm for computing a percent.

In the second set of comments, the teacher complimented the students on the graphs. These comments were notable for their focus on the superficial (not mathematical) aspects of the work and also the overly effusive praise for work that appeared to be very easy for these students. Following are two examples of how the teacher used extrinsic supports.

T: You guys have to see this one. This one is excellent here. She's got pretty bubble letters here colored in. Excellent. Outstanding.
T: ... that was a tough one. Look at the way he did that! Oh that was awesome — look at those solid colors!

When students[1] completed their ESF's at the end of this class, the observer asked them to explain why they selected their levels of challenge and skills. Two students circled zero for challenge and nine for skills (on a nine-point scale). These students commented: "It's so easy. I've done it before" and "It's too easy." Three other students indicated a three to a six-point discrepancy between higher skills and lower challenges. One typical comment was: "We've done it before. I knew how." However, two students responded differently. One student circled nine for both challenges and skills. He said, "It was hard work trying to make the graph, but I could do it." One student matched challenges and skills at four and five respectively, and commented "I already knew it. I would like to be doing it all the time."

This transcript is from the end of the school year and represents a pattern that became the standard in this classroom. In fact, the lesson went very smoothly — there were no disruptions or reprimands — with both teacher and students playing their roles. It appears that the participants cooperated in maintaining a climate that stressed relaxation, friendliness, warmth, and low expectations. Compared to other classrooms observed in this school and in this district, this classroom privileged social, rather than content, goals and demanded minimal responsibility from students to demonstrate their understanding of mathematics. This situation was especially puzzling because the students in this class scored well above the national average for mathematics achievement. In addition, students appeared to accept the praise that the teacher gave for the graphs even though many of them had not completed the assignment correctly (i.e., they had not converted frequencies to percentages). The teacher ignored this fact and proceeded smoothly to do it for them again, thus maintaining the pleasant and supportive environment. Only by understanding the roles that students and teacher played and their joint responsibility for maintaining the climate can one begin to understand the seeming contradiction between students' assessment of the classroom as offering low challenge and their expressed satisfaction with that

---

[1] There were six student informants in each classroom.

environment. As seen from the situative perspective, communities share standards of what defines worthwhile modes of engagement and solutions to problems. They develop expectations of participating authoritatively or in subservient relations to others on matters of knowing. In this classroom, it appears that the teacher used certain discourse patterns to maintain her role of expertise, but in doing so, she gained participation by acting benevolently. For the students, there were constraints to demonstrating expertise, but there were affordances to compliant behavior and they had become attuned to this pattern.

Paradox 2: A "Mastery" Orientation in a Classroom Little Focused on Mastery

Students also completed surveys asking them to indicate their perceptions of the goal orientation in the classroom, or the reasons that were communicated for trying to achieve. Two types of goal structures, mastery and performance, were measured. Mastery goals are focused on developing competence and gaining content mastery. Performance goals are focused on demonstrating superior ability relative to others. Theory predicts that mastery goals will be associated with teacher support of learning. In this study, teacher support for learning was expected to operate through scaffolding moves such as negotiation and transfer of responsibility and by providing encouragement and intrinsic support for learning mathematics. Non-scaffolding discourse was expected to be associated with a perception of performance goals (overuse of IRE statements, which are evaluative) or with a perception of mastery goals as low ("teacher telling"). Because there was such a low percentage of scaffolding discourse (15 percent) and such a high percentage of non-scaffolding discourse (58 percent) across Ms. Grant's lessons, it was expected that the students would view the classroom as significantly less mastery oriented than the classrooms with high percentages of scaffolded discourse.

Surprisingly, there were no significant differences among students' perceptions of the mastery goal structure across the seven classrooms. That is, the students in Ms. Grant's classroom perceived their classroom as mastery oriented just as the students in classrooms with scaffolded instruction did. This was puzzling because the instructional practices in Ms. Grant's classroom differed from those related to mastery goals (e.g., Ames, 1992) that focused on the importance of learning, the value of challenge, the importance of effort and persistence, and intrinsic reasons for engaging in tasks. Rather, the discourse in this classroom seemed to convey quite different messages. It suggested a more trivial view of learning, exemplified by the way the teacher introduced the task. It appeared to avoid challenge, as shown in the way that the teacher answered questions *for* the students. Because students were not asked to find solutions, such as how many participants would comprise 100 percent, the discourse seemed to avoid effort and persistence. Finally, the use of extrinsic reasons for doing tasks dominated. For example, students received praise for superficial aspects of their work and the teacher seemed to try to cajole students into working on the task rather than representing it as having interest or learning value.

Resolving the Paradoxes and Enriching Theory

The puzzle of Ms. Grant's classroom can only be addressed if one has knowledge of the social practices of the classroom. Through the discourse it becomes more clear how

> People's everyday practices ... exhibit — indeed generate — the social structures of the relevant domain (Mehan, 1993, p. 243).

Over the school year, Ms. Grant and her students had co-constructed the discourse, norms, and practices of their classroom mathematics community. These norms and practices privileged low expectations for students, teacher control of responsibility for learning, praise for insignificant accomplishments, and student self-satisfaction. From a motivational perspective, they had created a comfortable, non-threatening climate in the classroom.[2]

In contrast to Csikszentmihalyi's more organismic contention that all people will enjoy an optimal experience when meeting moderate challenges with increasing skill, these students expressed satisfaction with a surfeit of skills and low challenges. A more situated perspective helps us see that meeting challenges is only an "optimal" experience in a context in which such goals are valued. In the context of this classroom, easy success and "feeling good" were the values jointly and cooperatively constructed by the participants. As one student said, "I would like to do it (i.e., easy work) all the time."

The students' interpretation of the classroom goal structure as mastery oriented also challenged theoretical understandings. Mastery goals have been defined as a general orientation to developing skills and valuing learning for its own sake. Such norms have implied that specific instructional practices would contribute to that interpretation. Because those kind of instructional practices were rare in this classroom, one conclusion is that students interpreted survey items differently than intended. For example, they agreed that "In math class, the teacher thinks mistakes are OK" and "In math class the teacher tells us if our work is getting better." We found little evidence that students ever made mistakes in this class because the teacher anticipated student errors and often supplied the answer for them. The teacher did, indeed, compliment students on their work, but it was not focused on improvement, but on fairly mundane accomplishments. Students were well aware of this as their self-reports indicated.

Although the researchers who developed the survey items clearly meant them to reflect the teacher's messages about reasons for achievement, it appears that the students in this class did not interpret them that narrowly. Rather, the students may have interpreted them as indicators of the social environment of the classroom. Because they regarded their teacher as nice, as supportive, and as caring about them, they would agree that a "nice" teacher "thinks mistakes are OK." It

---

[2] Such environments do not need to be created *at the expense of* fostering involvement and mastery goals as our research has demonstrated (Turner *et al.*, 1998).

appears that the meaning of constructs, despite indications of good reliability, may change depending on the context. Such findings raise questions about our accepted notion of construct validity and suggest the need for more contextualized and mixed method investigations of theories of motivation. The more situative view provided a vehicle to advance an explanation for the seeming contradiction between students' perceptions of a mastery goal orientation in a classroom with little emphasis on learning, effort, and improvement.

A Contextual Perspective: Problem or Opportunity?

Taking a contextual perspective on motivation highlights issues that are just beginning to be raised in the theoretical and methodological discussions in our research community. While some would frame them as problems, they can also be seen as opportunities. These issues raise several important questions.

First, what kinds of problems or opportunities are there in triangulating different theories, such as goal theory and discourse analysis? These theories come from distinct intellectual traditions, one explicating individual construction, and the other social construction, of reality. They represent different levels of analysis. As discussed earlier, cognitive theories such as goal theories place emphasis on how one constructs individual reality in the classroom and how one meets goals in that setting. Discourse theory assumes that the social context is the reality and that it represents a joint understanding constructed by participants. Although these theories can be interpreted as conflicting views of truth or reality, and incompatible, their triangulation offers an opportunity to explore the phenomenon of person-in-situation. As Eraut (2000) indicated, the situative perspective must be able to explain how individuals enter, engage in, and leave shared experiences with shared constructions of reality while retaining individuality. Until our theoretical understandings of motivation and persons in contexts develops further, it may be fruitful to try to integrate two powerful theories and use one to complement the other. Advantages would include the acknowledgement that both individual perceptions and the cultural context influence motivation, that they work reciprocally rather than uni-directionally, and that descriptions of the context can be useful in speculating on the causes of the participants' actions, beliefs, and affects.

Second, what kinds of problems or opportunities are there in using methods that hail from different epistemological and disciplinary traditions? Positivist traditions underlie quantitative methods while Constructivist or Naturalist traditions underlie qualitative methods. These two perspectives have differed on several major tenets of research such as: (1) the nature of reality (e.g., is there a single or are there multiple realities?); (2) epistemology (e.g., are the knower and known independent or inseparable?); (3) the role of values (e.g., is research value free or value laden?); (4) generalizations (are context-free generalizations possible or not?); (5) causal linkages (e.g., can one distinguish cause from effect?); and (6) logic (does one reason deductively or inductively?) (Tashakkori & Teddlie, 1998). Although both traditions have argued that there can be no rapprochement, more recently social scientists have taken a "pragmatic" perspective based on "what works." Theorists (Reichardt & Rallis, 1994) have argued that these perspectives share some fundamental agreements that make them compatible. These include belief in the value-ladenness of inquiry, the belief that reality is multiple and constructed, and that any given set of data can be explained by many theories, among others.

Quantitative and qualitative, as well as deductive and inductive, methods are complementary in the sense that the strengths of one offset the weaknesses of the other. On the one hand, deductive methods offer the strength of using a theoretical orientation to interpret findings and quantitative data are more easily generalizable than qualitative data. They represent well the "what" of motivation, such as "intrinsic motivation". On the other hand, only qualitative data can adequately describe "how" motivation is constructed in settings. As a result, qualitative data are more idiosyncratic and less generalizable, yet crucial to the meaning of the participants. Inductive methods offer the benefit of moving from empirical facts to initiation of new theoretical inferences. Such complementarity offers an exciting opportunity for motivational research; one does not have to sacrifice the benefits of either tradition and the research is enriched as one method informs the other.

Third, what kinds of problems or opportunities are inherent in trying to present qualitative data in a compact way? Qualitative reports tend to be longer than quantitative ones because they are verbal rather than symbolic. For some, this may suggest issues of efficiency and parsimony. Indeed, journal editors, more accustomed to the goals of succinctness, do urge authors to shorten, shorten, shorten. Qualitative data must be adequate to present the case intended. Just as one must report N, degrees of freedom, and effect size for quantitative data, the amount of qualitative data must be sufficient to allow others to test the authors' interpretations of the data. Therefore, standard notions of efficiency, succinctness, and parsimony need to be reconsidered in light of the author's purpose. As use of qualitative data increases in the study of motivation, journal editors have an opportunity to support more contextual studies of motivation by adjusting page length guidelines to the purpose of the study.

Fourth, what are the risks of reporting or not reporting qualitative data? Because psychologists have followed a mostly quantitative and deductive tradition, these methods have become privileged in academic presentations and journals. Therefore, it has been considered risky by some to use qualitative methods. However, with discussions of how one can adequately understand and represent the role of context in motivation, it may become risky to ignore such a potent contribution to our research methodologies. Mixed method and mixed model studies (Tashakkori & Teddlie, 1998) make it possible to use both approaches so that research questions about the "what" and "how and why" can inform each other.

A major goal of studying motivation in context is to understand how participants construct motivational meanings. Traditional approaches to studying motivation, while useful in building theory, have not contributed enough to our understanding of how and why motivation develops in contexts. Theoretical constructs are necessarily abstract and are rarely able to convey how participants construct motivations. Constructs reflect the products of motivation from an individualistic perspective and their interrelationships, but do not describe well the process of understanding how motivation emerges, changes, and endures in a variety of contexts. Thus the thinking about how motivation actually develops is confined to logical speculation. Studying motivation in context allows us to test our theoretical assumptions, leading to more nuanced understandings or even to reformulation. The examination of classroom context using multiple methods, as described in the examples above, has presented some paradoxes and fresh perspectives. These approaches have helped to enrich our understanding of motivation in the classroom.

If researchers believe that motivation is jointly constructed by teachers and students in situations, then we must develop approaches and interpretations consistent with this view. As Chaiklin (1993) concludes,

> ... there is a dialectic between the actions of individual and the more collective units of analysis such as members of a ... society. An important problem for future development is to develop our theoretical and practical understanding of how to work with these relationships in the context of analyzing particular practices (p. 390).

Acknowledgements

Preparation of this chapter was supported by a grant from the Spencer Foundation to Julianne Turner and Carol Midgley. I am grateful for the perceptive comments of my colleague, Debra Meyer, and to the editors on drafts of this chapter.

References

Ames, C. (1992), Classroom: Goals, Structures, and student motivation. *Journal of Educational Psychology 84*, 261–271.

Ames, C., & Archer, J. (1988), "Achievement goals in the classroom: Goals, structures, and student motivation." *Journal of Educational Psychology 80*, 260–267.

Anderman, L. H., & Anderman, E. M. (2000), "Considering contexts in educational psychology: Introduction to the special issue." *Educational Psychologist 35*, 67–68.

Anderson, J. R., Reder, L. M., & Simon, H. A. (1996), "Situated learning and education." *Educational Researcher 25*, 5–11.

Anderson, J. R., Reder, L. M., & Simon, H. A. (1997), "Situative versus cognitive perspectives: Form versus substance." *Educational Researcher 26*, 18–21.

Aronson, E. *et al.* (1978), *The Jigsaw Classroom.* Beverly Hills, CA: Sage.

Blumenfeld, P. C. (1992), "Classroom learning and motivation: Clarifying and expanding goal theory." *Journal of Educational Psychology 84*, 272–281.

Billet, S. (1996). "Situated learning: Bridging sociocultural and cognitive theorizing." *Learning and Instruction 6*, 263–280.

Bredo, E. (2000), "Reconsidering social constructivism: The relevance of George Herbert Mead's interactionism." In D. C. Phillips (ed.) *Constructivism in Education* (Ninety-ninth Yearbook of the National Society for the Study of Education, pp. 127–157). Chicago: University of Chicago Press.

Brophy, J. (1999), "Toward a model of the value aspects of motivation in education: Developing appreciation for particular learning domains and activities." *Educational Psychologist 34*, 75–85.

Chaiklin, S. (1993), "Understanding the social scientific practice of Understanding Practice." In S. Chaiklin & J. Lave (eds) *Understanding Practice: Perspectives on Activity and Context* (pp. 377–401). Cambridge, UK: Cambridge University Press.

Cook, T. D., & Campbell, D. T. (1979), *Quasi-experimentation: Design and Analysis Issues for Field Settings.* Boston: Houghton Mifflin.

Cohen, E. (1994), *Designing Groupwork: Strategies for the Heterogeneous Classroom* (2nd ed.). New York: Teachers College Press.

Csikszentmihalyi, M., & Csikszentmihalyi, I. S. (1988), *Optimal Experience: Psychological Studies of Flow in Consciousness.* Cambridge, England: Cambridge University Press.

Csikszentmihalyi, M., & Larson, R. (1987), "Validity and reliability of the experience-sampling method." *The Journal of Nervous and Mental Disease 175*, 526–536.

Csikszentmihalyi, M., & Nakamura, J. (1989), "The dynamics of intrinsic motivation." In R. Ames & C. Ames (eds) *Handbook of Motivation Theory and Research* (Vol. 3, pp. 45–71). New York: Academic Press.

Dweck, C. S., & Leggett, E. L. (1988), "A social–cognitive approach to motivation and personality." *Psychological Review 95*, 256–273.

Eraut, M. (2000), "Non-formal learning and tacit knowledge in professional work." *British Journal of Educational Psychology 70*, 113–136.

Gallimore, R., & Tharp, R. (1990), "Teaching mind in society: Teaching, schooling, and literate discourse." In L. Moll (ed.) *Vygotsky and Education: Instructional Implications and Applications of Sociohistorical Psychology* (pp. 175–205). Cambridge, UK: Cambridge University Press.

Goldstein, L. S. (1999), "The relational zone: The role of caring relationships in the co-construction of mind." *American Educational Research Journal 36*, 647–673.

Greeno, J. G. (1997), "On claims that answer the wrong question." *Educational Researcher 26*, 5–17.

Greeno, J. G., Collins, A. M., & Resnick, L. B. (1996), "Cognition and learning." In D. C. Berliner & R. C. Calfee (eds) *Handbook of Educational Psychology* (pp. 15–46). New York: Simon & Schuster/Macmillan.

Greeno, J. G., & the Middle School Mathematics Through Applications Project Group. (1998), "The situativity of knowing, learning, and research." *American Psychologist 53*, 5–26.

Hickey, D. T. (1997), "Motivation and contemporary socio-constructivist instructional perspectives." *Educational Psychologist 32*, 175–193.

Hogan, K., & Pressley, M. (eds). (1997), *Scaffolding Student Learning: Instructional Approaches and Issues.* Cambridge, MA: Brookline Books.

Lave, J. (1993), "The practice of learning." In S. Chaiklin & J. Lave (eds) *Understanding Practice: Perspectives on Activity and Context* (pp. 3–32). Cambridge, UK: Cambridge University Press.

Lave, J., & Wenger, E. (1991), *Situated Learning: Legitimate Peripheral Participation.* Cambridge, UK: Cambridge University Press.

Meece, J. L. (1991), "The classroom context and students' motivational goals." In M. L.

Maehr & P. R. Pintrich (eds) *Advances in Motivation and Achievement* (Vol. 7, pp. 261–286). Greenwich, CT: JAI Press.

Mehan, H. (1985), "The structure of classroom discourse." In T. van Dijk (ed.) *Handbook of discourse analysis* (Vol. 3, pp. 119–131). London: Academic Press.

Mehan, H. (1993), "Beneath the skin and between the ears: A case study in the politics of representation." In S. Chaiklin & J. Lave (eds) *Understanding Practice: Perspectives on Activity and Context* (pp. 241–268). Cambridge, UK: Cambridge University Press.

Midgley, C., Arunkumar, R., & Urdan, T. (1996). " 'If I don't do well tomorrow, there's a reason': Predictors of adolescents' use of academic self-handicapping strategies." *Journal of Educational Psychology 88*, 423–434.

Minick, N. (1993), "Teachers' directives: The social construction of 'literal meaning' and 'real worlds' in classroom discourse." In S. Chaiklin & J. Lave (eds) *Understanding Practice: Perspectives on Activity and Context* (pp. 343–374). Cambridge, UK: Cambridge University Press.

Newman, D., Griffin, P., & Cole, M. (1984), "Social constraints in laboratory and classroom tasks." In B. Rogoff & J. Lave (eds) *Everyday Cognition: Its Development in a Social Context* (pp. 172–193). Cambridge, MA: Harvard University Press.

Noddings, N. (1984), *Caring*. Berkeley: University of California Press.

Pintrich, P. R. (2000), "An achievement goal theory perspective on issues in motivation terminology, theory, and research." *Contemporary Educational Psychology 25*, 92–104.

Reichardt, C. S., & Rallis, S. F. (1994), "Qualitative and quantitative inquiries are not incompatible: A call for a new partnership." In C. S. Reichardt & S. F. Rallis (eds) *The Qualitative–Quantitative Debate: New Perspectives* (pp. 85–92). San Francisco: Jossey-Bass.

Rogoff, B. (1990), *Apprenticeship in Thinking: Cognitive Development in Social Context*. New York: Oxford University Press.

Ryan, R. M., & Deci, E. L. (2000), "Intrinsic and extrinsic motivations: Classic definitions and new directions." *Contemporary Educational Psychology 25*, 54–67.

Ryan, A. M., Gheen, M. H., & Midgley, C. (1998), "Why do some students avoid asking for help? An examination of the interplay among students' academic efficacy, teachers' social–emotional role, and the classroom goal structure." *Journal of Educational Psychology 90*, 528–535.

Schunk, D. H., & Hanson, A. R. (1985), "Peer models: Influence on children's self-efficacy and achievement." *Journal of Educational Psychology 77*, 313–322.

Skinner, B. F. (1953), *Science and Human Behavior*. New York: Free Press.

Tashakkori, A., & Teddlie, C. (1998), *Mixed Methodology: Combining Qualitative and Quantitative Approaches*. Thousand Oaks, CA: Sage.

Turner, J. C., & Meyer, D. K. (1999), "Integrating classroom context into motivation theory and research: Rationales, methods, and implications." In T. Urdan (ed.) *Advances in Motivation and Achievement: The Role of Context* (Vol. 11, pp. 87–121). Stamford, CT: JAI Press.

Turner, J. C., & Meyer, D.K. (2000), "Studying and understanding the instructional contexts of classrooms: Using our past to forge our future." *Educational Psychologist 35*, pp. 69–85.

Turner, J. C., Meyer, D. K., Cox, K. E., Logan, C., DiCintio, M. *et al.* (1998), "Creating Contexts for Involvement in Mathematics." *Journal of Educational Psychology 90*, 730–745.

Vermunt, J. D., & Verloop, N. (1999), "Congruence and friction between learning and teaching." *Learning and Instruction 9*, 257–280.

Volet, S. (1999), "Motivation within and across cultural–educational contexts: A multi-dimensional perspective." In T. Urdan (ed.) *Advances in Motivation and Achievement: The Role of Context* (Vol. 11, pp. 185–231). Stamford, CT: JAI Press.

Vygotsky, L. S. (1978), *Mind in Society: The Development of Higher Psychological Processes* (M. Cole, V. John-Steiner, E. & Souberman, eds). Cambridge, MA: Harvard University Press.

Wertsch, J. V. (1985), *Vygotsky and the Social Formation of Mind*. Cambridge, MA: Harvard University Press.

Wigfield, A., & Eccles, J. S. (2000), "Expectancy–value theory of achievement motivation." *Contemporary Educational Psychology 25*, 68–81.

Zimmerman, B. J. (2000), "Self-efficacy: an essential motive to learn." *Contemporary Educational Psychology 25*, 82–91.

Chapter 6

Motivation in Context: Challenges and Possibilities in Studying the Role of Motivation in New Pedagogical Cultures

Sanna Järvelä & Markku Niemivirta

Introduction

During the past years we have witnessed a lively discussion on whether we should follow individual or social perspectives in studying learning activity (Anderson *et al.*, 1996; Cobb & Bowers, 1999; Greeno, 1997). Recently, Anderson *et al.* (2000) proposed that, there is no reason for contradictory approaches. Rather, we should progress towards an integrative theory, which included more specific explanations of differences between learning environments and individual students' participation in social and contextual interactions. However, since the debate concerning the relative merits of the situative and cognitive approaches to studying learning has merely focused on knowledge and knowing, some other fundamentally important issues such as affect and motivation have been neglected. The growing interest in studying the processes of learning and instruction in actual classrooms rather than in laboratory settings has resulted in an understanding that students' perceptions, cognitions, and actions are often contextually bound, and that knowledge is situated being in part a product of activity, context, and culture in which it is developed and used (Alexander, 2000; De Corte, 2000). This implies that students' conceptual structures and the cognitive strategies available to them are influenced by the environment in which they have been acquired (Mischell & Schoda, 1995). At the same time, it means that the social and cultural environment in which learning processes take place is reciprocally affected by students' actions. It is, therefore, timely to consider motivation in learning context.

The aim of this paper is to discuss some theoretical and methodological issues in the research on motivation with a specific view on conceptualizing motivation from the situational and social cognitive perspectives. In the beginning of the chapter, motivation and new pedagogical culture are discussed in terms of their characteristics for creating motivating learning environments. Then, a working model is presented that seeks to integrate the description of various aspects of learning activity with a special emphasis on both students' motivational tendencies and situational interpretations, and their interaction with the contextual settings.

Motivation in Learning Contexts: Theoretical Advances and Methodological Implications, pages 105–127.
Copyright © 2001 by Elsevier Science Ltd.
ISBN: 0-08-043990-X

The theoretical underpinnings for studying motivation in authentic learning situations derive from both action–theoretical and goal–theoretical perspectives on motivation. However, since these views strongly emphasize individual aspects of motivation we will elaborate their core ideas with a view on situative and socio-cognitive perspectives on learning. Also in line with the above, we will further argue that in order to gain some insight into the complexity of motivation in context, various sources of information need to be considered. That is, to draw valid inferences about how motivation comes about in natural learning settings, a variety of methods and analytical tools must be utilized. Finally, empirical data from series of intensive case studies in computer supported inquiry are presented.

Motivation and New Pedagogical Cultures

Research on motivation has elicited some common principles about how certain aspects of the classroom, such as task, authority, evaluation, recognition, and grouping, can be structured to enhance and support task-focused motivation. (Ames, 1992). The task dimension concerns the design of learning activities that make learning interesting and include variety and personal challenges (Meece, 1991). It also includes helping students to establish realistic goals (Schunk, 1991). The authority dimension stresses students' opportunities to take leadership roles, develop a sense of personal control and ownership in the learning process (DeCharms, 1976; Grolnick & Ryan, 1987). Evaluation and recognition concern the formal and informal use of rewards, incentives, and praise in the classroom. This issue includes guidelines, such as recognizing individual student effort, accomplishment, and improvement and giving all students opportunities to get rewards and recognition (Ames & Archer, 1988). The grouping dimension focuses on students' ability to work effectively with others on school tasks. This includes providing opportunities for social interaction, collaboration and varied group arrangements (Ames, 1992).

Related empirical studies have demonstrated how common practices such as normative evaluation or an emphasis on isolated individual performance can lead to maladaptive motivational tendencies in students (e.g., Anderman & Maehr, 1994; Meece, 1991; Slavin, 1989). On the other hand, other studies have shown how classroom arrangements such as using meaningful and differentiated tasks, building on students' interests, or using collaborative learning activities (e.g., Ames, 1992; Corno & Rohrkemper, 1985) can enhance and maintain motivation. Nevertheless, despite their undisputed merits, such studies have often been carried out in rather traditional instructional contexts. Therefore, the pedagogical implications derived from the findings may not be fully appropriate in some other, say technology-intensive, learning environments.

Several reasons have led educational researchers to develop new pedagogical practices and models of modern learning environments. Educational institutions are forced to find better pedagogical methods for future learners to cope with the continuous challenges of information flow and life-long learning (De Corte, 2000).

Simultaneously, the rapid development in information and communication technology has given new possibilities for restructuring teaching–learning processes to help the students to be better prepared for such challenges (Koschmann, 1996). As a consequence of the above, providing students with support to participate and engage in meaningful and in-depth learning has become a necessity (Brandsford *et al.*, 1991; Brown & Campione, 1996).

New powerful learning environments (Brown & Campione, 1996; Cognition and Technology Group at Vanderbilt, 1997; Salomon, 1996) aim at turning classrooms of students into communities of learners and learning situations into challenging and interesting projects with authentic problems. Although it is the students themselves who construct and test their own conceptual understanding, the community of learners and the interactions with different cultures of expertise have a notable bearing on the quality of learning (Brown & Campione, 1996). In contrast to traditional school settings, which usually are well prepared, organized, and controlled by the teachers, the goals of self-organized learning and true student responsibility characterize these new pedagogical cultures. The motivational implications are quite clear: The process of knowledge-seeking inquiry starts from cognitive or epistemic goals that arise from the learner's cognitive needs that cannot be achieved by relying on available knowledge. The learner has a close and meaningful cognitive relationship with the learning task, which contributes to the intrinsic quality of motivation (Ames, 1992). An essential aspect of knowledge-seeking inquiry is also the generation of one's own explanations, hypotheses or conjectures (Brown & Campione 1996; Scardamalia & Bereiter, 1994). Participation in a process of generating one's own explanations fosters a dynamic change of conceptions, produces knowledge that is likely to be connected with the learner's other knowledge, and, thereby, facilitate purposeful problem solving. The learner and the task create a new kind of cognitive relationship. This — to some extent, at least — contradicts the configuration common in traditional classroom settings where information is frequently produced without any guiding questions or personal ambitions.

The facilitation of higher-level practices of inquiry at school also requires a change in the cognitive division of labor between the teacher and the students. Traditionally, the teacher takes care of a major part of all higher cognitive functions at school, such as planning, questioning, explaining and evaluating, while the students are required to understand, restore and reproduce the transmitted information. Based on studies of expertise, Bereiter and Scardamalia (1993) argued that an important prerequisite for the development of higher-level cognitive competencies is that students themselves take the responsibility for all cognitive (e.g., questioning, explaining) and metacognitive (e.g., goal-setting, monitoring and evaluating) aspects of inquiry. A further assumption is that the transfer of responsibility between the teacher and student increases student autonomy and sense of personal control, which, in turn, facilitates intrinsic motivation and task commitment (Grolnick & Ryan, 1987; Turner, 1995).

Another important characteristic of computer-supported collaborative learning (CSCL) is the potential it offers for effective social interaction. Although there are contradictory findings concerning the success of collaboration in learning (Salomon & Globerson, 1989), some aspects of social interaction bear motivational implications. For example, peers provide models of expertise; observing the progress of other students may increase confidence in one's own ability to succeed (Bandura, 1997; Schunk, 1991). Furthermore, peer models provide a benchmark for students' own self-evaluations, thereby helping them to set proximal or more accurate goals.

Despite the intuitively appealing motivational implications, the empirical research focusing on such issues within the framework of computer-supported collaboration and learning is rather rare. The evaluation of projects introducing technology-based support for learning and collaboration often focuses on interactivity and quality of learning outcomes. Therefore, if we are to move towards a more situative account of motivation, we must also address issues such as the inability of theories to describe how individual motivation manifests itself in different contexts, how this adaptability develops, and what influences its characteristics. Accordingly, research should intensify its emphasis on the learner's intrinsic processes such as cognitive activities, emotional states, and motivational interpretations of situations, *as well as* their social preconditions and interactivity. Methodologically, achieving this challenging goal requires an intrinsic and reciprocal consistency of the theoretical methods, of the basic axioms and phenomena connected with them, and of the means of data collection and analysis (c.f. Valsiner, 1996). The integrated study of the intentional and developmental nature of motivated action in learning context should, therefore, include both the comprehensive description of the student's motivational tendencies, situational interpretations, and their interactive processes, and the methods to make the processes of thinking and interpretation during learning processes transparent.

Studying Motivation in Context: Theoretical Rationale and Methodological Considerations

Within personality research, the shift from a static trait-based conceptualization of individual differences to a dynamic conceptualization of person–situation transactions was grounded on repeated observations that an individual's behaviors can significantly fluctuate from the "average level" for that person, depending on the situation he or she is in (Higgins, 1990; Mischel & Schoda, 1995). However, it also become clear that such situation-to-situation variations are not random, but rather reflect stable characteristics of the individual (e.g., Schoda *et al.*, 1993). Accordingly, the acknowledgement of such complex patterning of person–situation transactions not only necessitated a more process-oriented conception of personality but also means to address the issue of stable variability across situations.

In an attempt to respond to this challenge, Mischel and Schoda (1995) introduced a cognitive–affective process system model of personality, which sought to incorporate the role of situations, events and contexts into the conception of personality. According to the theory, individuals differ in "how they selectively focus on different features of situations, how they categorize and encode them cognitively and emotionally, and how those encodings activate and interact with other cognitions and affects in the personality system" (Mischel & Schoda, 1995, p. 252). Furthermore, people are not seen as blind recipients passively reacting to situations, but as active and goal-directed agents, who construct plans and generate changes, and as such, partly create the situations themselves. These very same assumptions also lie at the bottom of our model of motivation in context.

Figure 1 illustrates our conceptual framework and the accompanying methods for studying the different aspects motivation in context — i.e., the situated nature of students' motivation and classroom engagement. In our description of motivation in learning context we focus on the situational construals students create/ form in different contexts. Our basic assumption is that students' subjective interpretations of classroom situations largely determine the goals they choose. This situational construal is, however, dependent on students' motivational beliefs and perceptions of themselves, and, even though students' situational construal may well define the goals they choose to strive for, the actual engagement is also dependent on their volitional control — their ability to support and maintain the chosen paths of engagement — and the supportive (or inhibiting) configuration made available by the instructional and social setting. The theoretical framework for conceptualizing our view on motivational beliefs, situational interpretations and

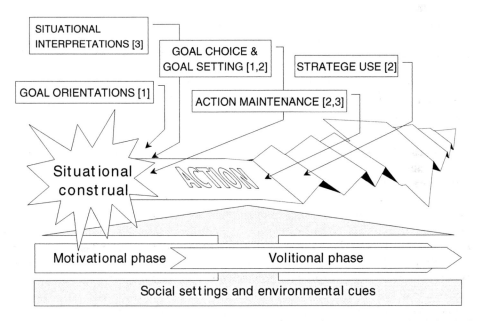

Figure. 1. The conceptual framework and the accompanying methodological means for studying motivation and learning activity in context. [1] = self-reports, [2] = observations, [3] = stimulated-recall interviews.

motivated action will be presented in the following. These descriptions are further associated with empirical methods we consider appropriate and relevant for studying each phenomena.

Goal Orientations and Motivational Beliefs

Achievement goal (or goal orientation) theory represents one prominent perspective on the study of motivation. A notable feature of this approach is that individual and environmental factors are both believed to be necessary components of motivation (Pintrich & Schunk, 1996). Typically goal orientations refer to the purposes individuals are striving for in academic settings; they provide an organizing framework through which a variety of cognitive and affective responses to achievement situations can be interpreted (Ames, 1992; Dweck & Leggett, 1988). The concept goal orientation is used here to reflect a student's general orientation towards classroom situations and tasks, which, as such, is tightly associated with other related beliefs about purpose, competence, success, ability, effort, errors and standards (Pintrich, 2000). It is the integrated and organized nature of these different beliefs that provides the theoretical utility and predictive power of the achievement goal construct.

As suggested by Niemivirta (1998) and Pintrich (2000), goal orientations can be viewed as knowledge structures that become activated depending on the contextual setting and environmental cues. In other words, various achievement-related elements such as purposes, definition of success, role of effort and errors, and standards are nodes in a network that display different patterns of activation as a function of contextual and internal personal factors. This type of representational model thus suggests that goals are dynamic states, which fluctuate in response to contextual information as well as to internal feedback between the different nodes or units in the network. This view also implies that goal orientations, defined as individuals' general preferences for certain classes of desired end-states — whether specific goals, outcomes or consequences — influence the very way individuals perceive their present social and contextual arena.

Since goal orientations are assumed to reflect individuals' preferences — although they functionally appear to operate in an implicit and even automatic way (c.f. Bargh, 1990) — they are assumed to manifest themselves in a form of explicit self-representations. Accordingly, goal orientations are commonly assessed by means of self-reports and questionnaires. Students are, for example, asked to rate the extent to which claims such as "I always try to outperform my classmates" or "I prefer challenging tasks that I can learn something new from" describe themselves. In some studies, the items are designed to tap very general orientations, whereas in some others, the content is delimited to a given context (e.g., "In this class, I try ..."). Two of the most studied goal orientations are learning orientation and performance orientation. The former reflects an emphasis on task- and learning-related goals or outcomes, whereas the latter stresses students' focus on either relative ability or general success, depending on the quality and function — e.g., approach vs. avoidance, self-enhancement vs. self-protection — attached to the construct. Another rather common type of goal orientation is avoidance orientation, which generally refers to students' tendency to avoid work and effort expenditure in performance situations and school contexts in general. In short, goals orientations have been found to be differentially related to self-regulative efforts, classroom perceptions, academic performance, and informational preferences (e.g., for a review, see Pintrich, 2000).

Situational Interpretations and Appraisals

Following Higgins (1990), we argue that the psychological significance of an event is a critical determinant of how a person responds to the event, and that the psychological significance of an event is a product of both the person and the situation. As elaborated by Boekaerts and Niemivirta (2000), the way students give meaning to situations proceeds through the processes of identification, interpretation and appraisal. That is, students' situational construals are not based on their mere perceptions of the situation as such (data-driven processing). Much of the significance of events, situations, and other social objects derives from how individuals categorize them (theory-driven processing). To put it simply: subjective meaning is a joint construction of previous experiences and current informational input from the given situation (Higgins, 1990; Higgins & Bargh, 1987).

Identification is the first stage in a student's situational construal. It refers to the recognition of the input and the resulting activation of related knowledge. For example, when facing the quiz, students recognize the stimulus (given that it is not a totally novel situation) to be an instance of previously established class of events — i.e., a specific type of classroom episodes with specific implications. Thus, in addition to identifying the situation as a "test situation", also certain characteristics are attached to it. The second phase can be conceptually partitioned into two tightly interwoven processes, namely to interpretation — an inference of the implications of the stimulus, and to appraisal — an estimation of the personal significance of that implication. These processes are distinguishable from identification in that they are often, if not always, related to some kind of a standard or reference point (Higgins *et al.*, 1986). The latter process, an individual appraisal of the personal significance of a situation, is of specific interest here, because it is — by definition — a motivationally charged process.

At this point, is must be noted that although the theoretical descriptions provided above clearly rely on a cognitively and individually oriented jargon, we do not deny — on the contrary — the fact that all "previously established classes of events" become as such only as parts and products of the socioculturally shaped common practices embedded in the context. That is, what really constitutes "a classroom episode" and what becomes "a characteristic attached to it" is solely dependent on the socially shared meanings developed within the classroom, school, or even a larger cultural community.

The empirical documentation of a student's situational construal and its personal significance is methodologically very challenging. One major difficulty concerns the limits of conscious awareness and availability for verbal expressions in general, and the accuracy of individual reports, in particular (Murphy & Alexander, 2000). Some of the cognitive processes and psychological meanings always remain unconscious and include tacit knowledge that cannot be explicitly expressed (Ericsson & Simon, 1980). Another problem deals with the fact that monitoring one's own mental processes (metacognitive awareness) is not very well developed in younger students. There are also rather extensive individual differences in students' way of expressing their thoughts and opinions verbally. We have tried to overcome some of these difficulties by examining students' interpretations of contextual features and their motivational significance through interviews. The aim of process-oriented interviews is to reveal the subjective essence of students' motivational and emotional interpretations during a learning situation (Järvelä, 1995). In what we call "on-line interviewing" students are interviewed *during* the classroom activity. They are asked questions about their goals ("Please, try to describe and justify, why you are working on this particular task?"), self-related beliefs ("Would you tell us what expectations you had when you came to the class today?"), learning strategies ("Could you describe one complicated phase during your work?" "How did you overcome it?"), and the type and quality of social interaction ("What role did the teachers play in your working?").

On-line interviewing can be further supported by stimulated recall interview methods (STRI), which are based on Bloom's (1953) studies on teachers' thinking processes. During the interview, students are encouraged to describe their current task in details, and express their feelings, goals and reasons for their actions. In STRI, students' thought processes are investigated by interviewing them while they watch a videotape of themselves working in a lesson. Validity problems caused by forgetting and misinterpreting the events can partially be eluded, if the learning situation is recalled in the interview. By interviewing students during different kind of tasks, different phases of learning projects and varying activities, it is possible to consider a variety of situational settings and unmask their psychological meaning for the students. In general, process-oriented interview methods make it possible to investigate thought processes that cannot be put under investigation by conventional observational research.

From Situational Construals to Action

Students' situational construals are assumed to set the scene for further engagement. However, in order to transform an appraisal of a situation into desired action, the student must first set (or activate) appropriate goals and create a corresponding action plan (for discussions on habitual behavioral responses and automatic goal processes, see Bargh & Chartrand, 1999, and Boekaerts & Niemivirta, 2000). Here, a qualitative distinction can be made between the issue of goal setting and the issue of goal striving (Lewin *et al.*, 1944; c.f. Nie-mivirta, 1999a). For example, Kuhl (1984) refers to the former as a motivational phase concerning the decision on what goals to adopt, whereas the latter refers to the determined pursuit of goal completion. As it has been described in previous sections, the factors and processes leading to a goal choice are largely based on subjective interpretations and appraisals of prevailing situations. However, once the choice has been made, the initiation and execution of corresponding actions themselves must take place.

Going beyond the conceptual distinction of goal setting and goal striving, the action phase model suggested by Heckhausen and Gollwitzer (1987; Gollwitzer, 1990) provides a coherent framework for bridging different aspects of motivation and volition. The model incorporates the issues of initiating and maintaining action into a process-like continuum. The temporal phases of goal-directed engagement are partitioned into four phases, which in turn are separated by particular transition points (the decision, action initiation, and action outcomes, respectively) that give rise to subsequent engagement. Following this framework both appraisals and the process of forming a goal intention can be described as characteristic of a predecisional phase — a phase in which people translate their wishes into intentions. In other words, during the predecisional phase individuals weigh the desirability and feasibility — or outcome-expectancy and subjective value — of different alternative goals and their potential outcomes or consequences on the basis of various subjective criteria. This "relative preference expressed in a context of conflicts, alternatives and trade-offs" (Mischel *et al.*, 1996; p. 333) manifests itself in a commitment to the chosen goal. The formation of a goal intention thus represents a leap from a state of uncertainty to a goal state where the desired outcome becomes an end state that the individual feels committed to attain (Gollwitzer, 1990).

The subjective criteria that define the desirability and feasibility of goal choices are in part determined by individuals' situation-specific judgements. In contrast to goal orientations, which are considered as general or relatively context-free sets of motivational beliefs, some other types of motivational beliefs can be viewed as more situational in nature. Three important classes of personal judgements that are likely to influence individuals' goal choice and their subsequent action are self-efficacy beliefs, task value, and anticipated interest. Self-efficacy refers to individuals' judgements about their ability to carry out specific actions in specific situations (Bandura, 1997). Such beliefs have found to be highly influential in predicting individuals' actual behavior and task performance (c.f. Pajares, 1996). Task value refers to the degree value and worthiness individuals attach to the future task and/or its outcomes, whereas anticipated interest reflects individuals' expectations about the extent to which the upcoming activity will be experienced as interesting. Recent studies examining the relationships between general motivational beliefs, situational appraisals, and performance have supported the assumption of the importance of situation-specific self-appraisals in mediating the influence of general beliefs and prior achievements on later performance (Boekaerts, 1999; Niemivirta, 1999; see also Pajares, 1997).

The outcomes of students' situational construals define the course of further engagement, but they are not sufficient determinants of actual engagement (Boekaerts & Niemivirta, 2000; Kuhl, 2000). Sometimes students fail to realize their intentions or attain desired goals, and sometimes they carry out even the most boring or unpleasant tasks with great effort and commitment. One explanation of how students can become active in tasks that may initially seem frustrating is through effective volitional control. It comprises of the strategies and plans invoked after decisions to pursue certain goals have been made. According to Kuhl (1984; see also Corno, 1993), volition can be characterized as a dynamic system of psychological control processes that protect concentration and directed effort in the face of personal and environmental distractions.

We believe that the potential for making valid inferences about the unique and subjective nature of students' goal-oriented action and motivational interpretations in a learning context — i.e., what students actually do and experience in the classroom — lies in observational data. By observing the student's behavior his or her motivational orientations can be tied to contexts, tasks and instructional situations (Salonen et al., 1998; Turner, 1995). However, the challenge is to make the process transparent: how do students construct and set goals; what kind of processes are related to that; how do students' emotional and motivational interpretations relate to different phases of goal achievement? Students' motivational tendencies and emotional expressions are very difficult to observe on-site, and as such, the observers' descriptions and interpretations tend to be too global. Therefore, video-recordings instead of participant observation appear to be a more appropriate means for such data collection. Video-data can be recalled and thus the detailed nuances of interaction and student expression can be interpreted (e.g., Järvelä, 1995).

In a study by Järvelä, Niemivirta & Hakkarainen (2001), the conceptual basis of both goal– and action–theoretical perspectives on motivation was applied to create a system of categories for analyzing on-line video-data on students' learning processes. Three modes of classroom engagement were derived from the theoretical framework: task-focused, outcome-focused, and avoidance-focused engagement, respectively. Each of these three modes were further specified along different domains of content, such as goals, self-appraisals, quality of learning processes and the use of learning strategies, and the type and quality of social interaction.

Our experiences support the claim that observations as data source have important strengths for evaluating behavioral indications of motivated action (See also Winne & Perry, 2000 for measures of self-regulation). First, they reflect what learners actually do versus what they say they do, and second, they illuminate links between features of the teaching–learning context and the features of the learning environment and student engagement in general. The limitations, instead, concern with the issues of subjective and inappropriate interpretations made by the observer. Further, some aspects of goal striving and other motivational processes are very difficult to observe due to their intraindividual nature. It is also important for researchers to recognize that what is actually observed often reflects what is considered worth observing.

Studying Motivation in New Pedagogical Contexts — Empirical Examples

We have recently carried out a series of case studies that focus on students' motivation and activity within the context of computer-supported collaborative learning (Järvelä *et al.*, 2001; Rahikainen *et al.*, 2000). In the following excerpts we illustrate few empirical findings along with the accompanying methods used from our initial efforts to examine the interaction of students' motivational orientations and situational motivation during a classroom study project. The data were collected using questionnaires, videotapings of students' learning activity, stimulated recall-interviews, and repeated process-oriented interviews. The learning environment provided was Computer Supported Intentional Learning Environment (CSILE) and its more recent version, Knowledge Forum. These applications are based on the assumption of learning as a communal knowledge-building process that progresses through inquiry-based activities (Scardamalia *et al.*, 1994.). Eighteen secondary school students worked in inquiry-based projects to study the topics "Racism", "Time" and "Science fiction". The topics were part of literature curriculum and in each project the students conducted a small-scale inquiry about a more specific question they had formulated of the overall topic. Each project lasted for six weeks and the students had project lessons (each lasting for 75 minutes) three to four times a week.

To What Extent are Students' Self-reported Goal Orientations and Strategy Use Related to Their Observed Behavior?

Students' goal orientations were assessed by means of self-reports. Before participating in the project, students responded to a questionnaire tapping three types of goal orientations, learning ("The most important goal for me in school is to learn new things"), performance ("It is important for me get better grades than other students in my class"), and avoidance orientation ("I always to try to get off without putting much effort to my school work"), respectively, and four types of -strategy use, organizing ("When I'm studying, I try to analyze and organize the material into meaningful wholes"), superficial engagement ("When I study for a test I try to learn the material just by saying to myself over and over"), metacognitive regulation ("When studying for a test I often stop reading and ask myself questions to see if I have understood anything"), and elaboration ("When I study for a test I try to translate the material into my own words"), respectively. To examine how students' self-reported goal orientations and the corresponding classroom behavior were related, we first grouped students based on their responses to the goal orientation scales and then compared the extent of different types of engagement observed during the actual classes among the groups. Cluster analysis was used as a tool for classification. A three-group solution, which seemed to describe the data best, was used for subsequent comparison. According to each group's score profile, the groups were labeled as learning-oriented, performance-oriented, and avoidance-oriented, respectively.

Students' classroom engagement was observed during four different classes. The coding-scheme for the observations was built on the theoretical principles described above. Accordingly, observers rated each student's behavior in terms of the quality and type of goals they appeared to strive for and the form of strategies they employed in the pursuit of those goals. For the present purposes, the scores (i.e., the time students exhibited specific types of engagement) over all four classes were aggregated. This is due to the fact that despite some clear situational fluctuations students' behavioral profile was found to be surprisingly stable over time (stability coefficients across the classes ranged from 0.63 to 0.90).

As illustrated in Figure 2, students with a different type of goal orientation profile differed from each other in rather parallel ways. That is, learning-oriented students exhibited more task-focused classroom behavior than the others did, whereas the behavior of performance- and avoidance-focused students was inclined towards outcome- and avoidance-focused concerns. Due to the small number of participants, both conventional (ANOVA) and non-parametric procedures (Kruskal-Wallis ANOVA) were used to analyze group-level mean differences. Conventional analysis of variance resulted in significant overall effects for both task- and outcome-focused engagement ($p < 0.05$), and a moderate effect for avoidance-focused engagement ($p < 0.07$) was found. With a non-parametric procedure only the effect for task-focused engagement was found statistically significant ($p < 0.05$).

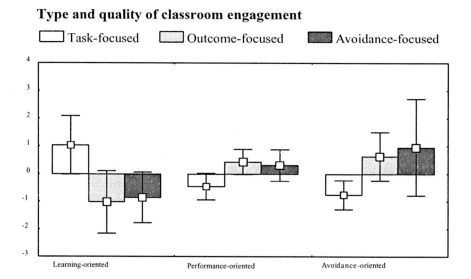

Figure 2. The relationship between self-reported motivation and observed classroom engagement.

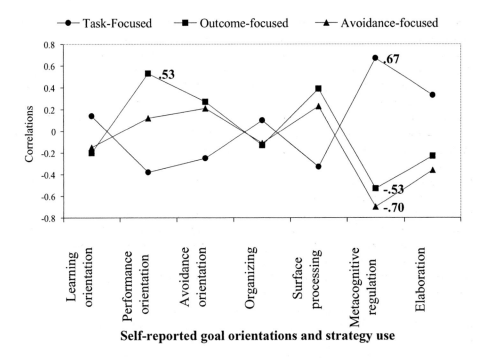

Figure 3. The profiles of correlational relationships between self-reported goal orientations and strategy use and observed learning activity (inserted coefficients denote significant correlations at p < .05).

To further illustrate the relationships between various self-reported factors and observed behavior, simple zero-order correlations were calculated across the domains. As can be seen in Figure 3, not many statistically significant associations were detected.

However, the patterning of correlations demonstrates some level of correspondence between self-reported and actual engagement. For example, task-focused engagement was clearly associated with higher scores in metacognitive regulation and elaboration and with lower scores in performance orientation and superficial engagement. However, is must be noted that the correspondence was clearly higher between observed behavior and variables reflecting behavioral tendencies (i.e., strategy use) than between observed behavior and variables reflecting goals and motivational beliefs. This observation could be interpreted as reflecting the important differentiation between individuals' preferences and intentions and their actualized behavior. Further, the accentuated relationships between the self-reported use of metacognitive regulation and classroom behavior suggests that students' assessment of their own metacognitive activity is a rather solid global indicator of the quality of their true strategic engagement in the classroom.

How Do Students with Different Goal Orientation Profiles Interpret Actual Learning Situations?

One of the core assumptions in our model of motivation in context is that students with different motivational tendencies view classroom events and situations in somewhat different ways. We believe that such contextual interpretations together with students' situational appraisals provide a structure according to which individuals form their decisions about the goals they will pursue, the personal meaning they attach to the situations, and the emotional significance associated with those meanings.

In one of our studies, the personal meaning students attached to different classroom events were probed from students within the context of computer-supported collaborative inquiry in literacy. Repeated process-oriented interviews were conducted in order to investigate how students with different goal orientation profiles (See Niemivirta, 1998b) interpreted actual learning situations. The students were interviewed four times during a learning project that lasted for six weeks (involving three 75 minute lessons per week). Students' actual goals, strategies for achieving their goals, self-related beliefs and their interpretations of the learning environment were inquired during the lessons. The interview data was transcripted, coded according to the principles of content analysis (Chi, 1997), and analyzed with the help of Nudist qualitative data analysis program. Responses to questions concerning students' actual goals are displayed in Table 1. Responses

Table 1. Percentages of student responses to process-oriented interviews concerning their actual goals in learning context

Goals students reported during process interviews	Goal orientation groups based on self-reports				
	Performance N = 6	Learning N = 4	Avoidance N = 3	Opportunist N = 5	Total N = 18
Learning	13*	5	2	5	25
	39%	26%	13%	19%	27%
Performance	15	12	5	19*	51
	45%	63%	34%	70%	54%
Ego/Avoidance	5	2	8*	3	18
	16%	11%	53%	11%	19%
Total	33	19	15	27	94
	100%	100%	100%	100%	100%

Note. Significance tests are based on hypergeometric probability estimations (see Bergman & El-Khouri, 1987); * = Observed frequency larger than expected by chance alone ($p < 0.05$).

were divided into three categories indicating learning goals (e.g., *"I want to know more about Racism which is the topic of my inquiry"*), performance goals (e.g., *"To complete the task in time"*) or ego/avoidance goals (e.g., *"I don't know if I have any goals"*) and then compared to students' self-reported goal orientation.

Most students reported striving for goals similar to their self-reported motivational tendency, as evidenced by the frequency patterns for especially performance-oriented and avoidance-oriented students (overall χ^2 (6) = 18.02, $p < 0.05$). However, it must be noted that contrary to our predictions, also learning-oriented students expressed more outcome-related goals than learning goals. Since the emphasis on performance-focused engagement appeared to be a somewhat general trend among the students, we may assume that the classroom events and situational features, in general, were likely to elicit such responses. A plausible explanation in line with our prior findings (Hakkarainen et al., 2001) would be that the students had not yet adapted to the "adequate culture of CSCL", but were more inspired by the production-oriented and surface level activities associated with the technological features of the environment.

We also recorded students' responses to questions concerning their self-related beliefs during the lessons (see Table 2). Responses were divided into four categories indicating positive situational interpretations (e.g., *"I was waiting for the*

Table 2. Percentages of student responses to process-oriented interviews concerning their self-related beliefs in learning context

Self-related beliefs reported during process interviews	Goal orientation groups based on self-reports				
	Performance N = 6	Learning N = 4	Avoidance N = 3	Opportunist N = 5	Total N = 18
Posit. situational interpretation	28 52%	32 60%	17 61%	22[†] 41%	99 52%
Negat. situational interpretation	7 13%	7 13%	10* 36%	15 28%	39 21%
Motivational control strategies	18* 33%	11 21%	1[†] 4%	13 24%	43 22%
Emotional control strategies	1 2%	3 6%	0 0%	4 7%	8 4%
Total	54 100%	53 100%	28 100%	54 100%	189 100%

Note. Significance tests are based on hypergeometric probability estimations (see Bergman & El-Khouri, 1987); * = Observed frequency larger than expected by chance alone ($p < 0.05$); = Observed frequency smaller than expected by chance alone ($p < 0.05$).

lesson because I'm working for such an interesting project"), negative situational interpretations (e.g., *"I am frustrated because I should know so much"*), motivational control strategies (e.g., *"Reading a novel was boring and I nearly gave up, but then I decided to try and concentrate and afterwards I felt very good"*), or emotional control strategies (e.g., *"I was irritated because I couldn't progress, but then I decided to try something else and refresh my mind that way"*), respectively.

In general, students mentioned more positive than negative interpretations in different situations (overall χ^2 (9) = 20.56, $p < 0.05$). Students having self-reported performance orientation were more likely to report on motivation control during the lessons while the avoidance students reported hardly none. The qualitative process-oriented analysis revealed differences in students' contextual interpretations and displayed different patterns of actions and interpretations than expected. For example, a positive finding has been that working with a novel learning environment (computer-supported collaborative inquiry) seem to facilitate non-learning oriented students' active task-related participation and positive self-beliefs even though they first had difficulties to cope with new demands of the learning environment. They had problems such as regulating their learning goals, and committing themselves to sustained processes of inquiry (Järvelä *et al.* 2000; Rahikainen *et al.* 2000).

What is the Importance of Students' Contextualised Interpretations of Classroom Action? The Emergence of Contradictory Cases

Having students' self-reported motivation as a "baseline" for evaluating their interpretations in different situations we were not only able to follow how the different patterns of motivation were interacting with the context, but also look for unexpected patterns of motivational interpretations. A detailed description of a student's learning process, motivational interpretations and actions sheds light on the possible emergence of individual–contextual patterns which may restructure students' earlier patterns of motivation. Our series of case-studies has elucidated that there indeed are students who benefit from the change into a new pedagogical context, and whose situational interpretations are therefore not in line with their prior self-reported motivational tendencies (see Järvelä *et al.*, 2000).

The video-tapings of students' learning processes were used to analyze an individual student's motivational involvement and action during a computer-supported inquiry in literacy. A theory-based category was created in order to code his or her involvement. The main categories were: task-orientation, performance orientation, social orientation and volitional processes. The videodata were analyzed with the help of Noldus Observer computer program having units of analysis ranging from 30 seconds to two minutes unity behavior. Utilizing the process-oriented interview- and video-data individual case descriptions were constructed on students' working and motivational processes in a classroom learning context (See Case Hanna for an example).

Case Hanna

Hanna is a 14-year-old girl whose self-reported motivational patterns indicated avoidance type of orientation. Her responses revealed that she did not really believe that her own efforts would make any difference in relation to school performance, she possessed a rather negative view of her abilities, and she placed hardly any value on schooling in general. Further, her motivational profile also suggested a tendency to give up (i.e., lack of action control) when dealing with demanding study tasks.

In the beginning of the computer-supported collaborative inquiry in literacy (science fiction) Hanna was slightly avoidant and expressed a tendency towards performance goals. She did not have clear goals in her work, which is illustrated in her responses to on-line interview:

> INTERVIEWER: First of all, tell me what were your feelings in the beginning of the lesson?
> HANNA: Nothing, I did not expect anything.
> INTERVIEWER: Can you tell me what is your goal in this "science fiction" project?
> HANNA: Well, to make a good inquiry.
> INTERVIEWER: Could you be more specific, please?
> HANNA: To read as many books as possible.
> INTERVIEWER: Why do you have set such a goal??
> HANNA: I don't know. I don't have any reasons.

The summary of Hanna's coded motivational involvement and action during the three lessons suggested an increase in task-focused activity (see Figure 4). The coded video-data (three hours and 50 minutes altogether) involved 29 percent of task-focused and 29 percent of performance-focused activity (as well as 42 percent of zero-orientation, which refers to data not been able to code) during the first lesson. The analysis of the second lesson's video-data showed that 50 percent of her learning activity was task-focused and 38 percent performance-focused (twelve percent of zero-orientation), respectively, while the third lesson indicated her high task-involvement with 91 percent of activity coded as task-focused and 4 percent as performance-focused (5 percent of zero-orientation), respectively.

Hanna's task-involvement during the three lessons

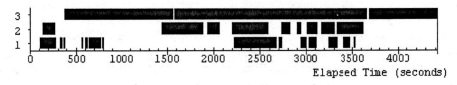

Figure 4. The summary of Hanna's coded task-involvement and action during the three lessons.

The most typical observation of her working process referred to classroom situations where task involvement paralleled with her individual work, reading a book, thinking alone or working with a computer by herself. Other students' company made her socially oriented and distracted her task-involvement. It is plausible that the new learning environment with its accompanying pedagogical features and computer support bolstered her task-focused activities, self-regulation and interest in reading, which can be seen in an excerpt of an interview conducted during the third lesson. In this interview Hanna reports on being able to utilize the features of the learning environment.

> INTERVIEWER: Can you tell me what has been your best situation in your inquiry this far? I mean when you have felt good.
> HANNA: Reading, I think.
> INTERVIEWER: Why?
> HANNA: I like reading. Then I don't need to focus on thinking so much, or to consider the school-tasks.
> INTERVIEWER: What about working with the Knowledge Forum (the computer program for collaborative knowledge building), what is your opinion about it?
> HANNA: It helps me to structure my thoughts. While I try to report on my ideas in a compact way I get to know them better. And also the other students can read and comment them.

Conclusions

The aim of this chapter has been to discuss some theoretical and methodological issues emerging when studying motivation in context. The model introduced here places an emphasis on students' situational construals and the accompanying processes in his or her involvement. Our aim has been to integrate not only the trait- and state-like constructs of motivation, but also the individual and contextual determinants of how motivation manifests itself in natural learning settings without the cost of conceptual clarity. Due to the fact that the contemporary study of motivation has its historical roots in both experimental research and individual difference approaches to motivation, we have followed a bottom-up strategy in our quest of conceptualising motivation in context. In other words, we have utilized the theoretical frameworks and core concepts identified in prior research, but elaborated and extended the use of them in order to capture some aspects of the contextual nature of motivational phenomena. That is, we have tried to give some theoretical and empirical body to the definition of motivation as a function of the person and the context.

The focus on students' situational interpretations and construals, however, does not imply that the social and cultural aspects of the environment are of less importance. Rather, we do stress the necessity of acknowledging the social and contextual planes of activity in order to understand the origins and especially the development of motivational processes and their individual antecedents. On the other hand, since the impetus has been to understand how an individual student interprets and constructs his or her environment, the model presented here may not provide accurate nor adequate explanations of how some motivational phenomena — e.g., student motivation as a socially shared experience — come about within their sociocultural frame of reference. It is nevertheless argued that an insight into individual psychological experiences is a necessary prerequisite in order to follow their dynamics within the social field, since the context not only stimulates these internal processes, but also provides a framework for further actions, such as goal achieving or motivation control. One may argue that motivation is always contextually bound and based on individuals' situational interpretations. However, no interpretations are made without any reference to prior experiences — no matter how novel the given situations are. Further, what really constitutes "a situation" is not independent of the culturally shared meanings embedded in the given context. From this point of view, the perspective presented here should not be considered as an alternative, but rather as a "situationally sensitive extension", and as such, complementary to the other contemporary approaches to motivation.

As there are different dynamic levels of classroom social context, there are also different channels for examining students' motivation. First, motivation in learning context can be considered as an individual student's psychological construction process that takes the form of situational interpretations and an appraisals, but still has its origin in students' motivational tendencies and prior experiences (c.f. Higgins, 1990). Second, the social dynamics of classroom context — such as pedagogical acts, conventions of interaction processes, or classroom community — provide another framework for understanding how motivation manifests itself through the way students engage in classroom activities (Cobb & Bowers, 1999). Third, the cultural conventions at home and societal levels situate changes in students' motivational beliefs or values in a broader framework (e.g., Murdock, 2000). A dialog is presumed to take place between the interpretations and actions of individuals and the more collective units of analysis such as classroom interactions (student–student or teacher–student) or the systemic structure of the pedagogical environment (teaching practices, tasks, values, norms, artifacts).

The increased agreement with the importance of considering context in research on motivation (e.g., Anderman & Anderman, 2000) challenges not only the conceptual issues, but also methodological issues in terms of how to measure and analyze the way persons and situations interact. As a result, some researchers have drawn on multilevel approaches and methods for measuring motivation adequately. In line with this, also the empirical experiments presented in this chapter have incorporated different planes of analysis that focus on various levels of motivation and motivated action. At this stage, the emphasis has been on personal and interpersonal structures and processes, but in the near future the analyses will be extended to include the complex practices of classroom community as well.

The conscious aim has been to develop a set of methods that correspond to the conceptual and theoretical framework in order to avoid some of the problems associated with multilevel and multifaceted data collection and analysis. Because such approaches generate rich and labour-intensive data to deal with, there is a clear danger of drawing either overly general and theoretically loose or too specific and empirically trivial inferences. We do acknowledge that fact that some of these problematic stages in data analyses simplify the nature of the phenomena at hand (e.g., the nature of interaction between individuals and the social context), and as such, easily lead to vague instead of conceptually coherent descriptive interpretations.

The future goals for our work are thus threefold: First, we need to continue our theoretical exploration in order to build a network of concepts that adequately and extensively describe the complexity of motivation in natural learning contexts. Second, we must also further develop methodological means and analytical tools in order to validly and reliably capture the empirical nature of the phenomena we seek to conceptualise and operationalise. Third, without a thorough analysis of what changes new learning environments are to bring about and what sort of pedagogical implications they embody, much of the intended efforts described in relation to the first two goals become far less meaningful. In other words, in order to truly advance the study of motivation in context, the development of both theoretical and empirical means must walk hand in hand with the study of the nature and significance of new pedagogical cultures.

References

Alexander, P. A. (2000), "Toward a model of academic development: Schooling and the acquisition of knowledge." *Educational Researcher 29*, 28–33.

Ames, C. (1992), "Classrooms: goals, structures, and motivation." *Journal of Educational Psychology 84*, 261–271.

Ames, C., & Archer, J. (1988), "Achievement goals in the classroom: Goals, structures, and student motivation." *Journal of Educational Psychology 80*, 260–267.

Anderman, L. H., & Anderman, E. M. (2000), "Considering contexts in educational psychology: Introduction to the special issue." *Educational Psychologist 35*, 67–68.

Anderman, E. M. & Maehr, M. L. (1994), "Motivation and schooling in the middle grades." *Review of Educational Research 64*, 287–309.

Anderson, J. R., Reder, L. M., & Simon, H. A. (1996), "Situated learning and education." *Educational Researcher 25*, 5–11.

Anderson, J. R., Greeno, J. G., Reder, L. M., & Simon, H. A. (2000), "Perspectives on learning, thinking, and activity." *Educational Researcher 29*, 11–13.

Bandura, A. (1997), *Self-efficacy: The Exercise of Control*. New York: Freeman.

Bargh, J. A. (1990), "Auto-motives. Preconscious determinants of social interaction." In E. T. Higgins & R. M. Sorrentino (eds) *Handbook of Motivation and Cognition. Foundations of Social Behavior* (pp. 93–103). New York: Guilford.

Bargh, J. A., & Chartrand, T. L. (1999), "The unbearable automaticity of being." *American Psychologist 54*, 462–479.

Bereiter, C., & Scardamalia, M. (1993), *Surpassing Ourselves. An Inquiry into the Nature and Implications of Expertise*. Chicago, IL: Open Court.

Bloom, B. (1953), "Thought processes in lectures and discussions." *Journal of General Education 7*, 160–169.

Boekaerts, M. (1999), "Motivated learning: The study of student–situation transactional units." *European Journal of Psychology of Education 14*, 41–55.

Boekaerts, M., & Niemivirta, M. (2000), "Self-Regulation in learning: Finding a balance between learning and ego-protective goals." In M. Boekaerts, P. R Pintrich & M. Zeidner (eds) *Handbook of Self-Regulation* (pp. 417–450). San Diego, CA: Academic Press.

Brandsford, B. J., Goldman, S. R., & Vye, N. J. (1991), "Making a difference in people's abilities to think: Reflections on a decade work and some hopes for the future." In L. Okasagi & R. J. Sternberg (eds) *Directors of Development: Influences on Children* (pp. 147–180). Hillsdale, NJ: Erlbaum.

Brophy, J. (1999), "Toward a model of the value aspects of motivation in education: Developing appreciation for particular learning domains and activities." *Educational Psychologist 34* (2), 75–85.

Brown, A. L., & Campione, J. A. (1996), "Psychological theory and the design of innovative learning environments." In L. Schauble & R. Glaser (eds) *Innovations in Learning: New Environments for Education* (pp. 289–235). Mahwah, NJ: Erlbaum.

Chi, M. T. H. (1997), "Quantifying qualitative analyses of verbal data: A practical guide." *Journal of the Learning Sciences 6*, 271–315.

Cobb, P., & Bowers, J. (1999), "Cognitive and situated learning: Perspectives in theory and practice." *Educational Researcher 28*, 4–15.

Cognition and Technology Group at Vanderbilt. (1997), *The Jasper Project: Lessons in Curriculum, Instruction, Assessment and Professional Development*. Mahwah, NJ: Erlbaum.

Corno, L. (1993), "The best-laid plans: Modern conceptions of volition and educational research." *Educational Researcher 22*, 14–22.

Corno, L., & Rohrkemper, M. (1985), "The intrinsic motivation to learn in the classroom." In C. Ames & R. Ames (eds) *Research on Motivation in Education* (Vol. 2, pp. 53–90). New York: Academic Press.

DeCharms, R. (1976), *Enhancing Motivation: Change in the Classroom*. New York: Irvington.

De Corte, E. (2000), "Marrying theory building and the improvement of school practice: a permanent challenge for instructional psychology." *Learning and Instruction 10* (3), 249–266.

Dweck, C. S. (1986), "Motivational processes affecting learning." *American Psychologist 41*, 1040–1048.

Dweck, C. S, & Leggett, E. L. (1988), "A social–cognitive approach to motivation and personality." *Psychological Review 95*, 256–273.

Ericsson, K. A., & Simon, H. A. (1980), "Verbal reports as data." *Psychological Review 87*, 215–251.

Gollwitzer, P. M. (1990), "Action phases and mind-sets." In E. T. Higgins & R. M. Sorrentino (eds) *Handbook of Motivation and Cognition: Foundations of Social Behavior* (pp. 52–92). New York: Guilford Press.

Greeno, J. G. (1997), "On claims that answer the wrong questions." *Educational Researcher 26*, 5–17.

Grolnik, W. S., & Ryan, R. M. (1987), "Autonomy support in education: Creating the facilitating environment." In N. Hastings & J. Schwiesco (eds) *New Dimensions in Educational Psychology: Behaviour and Motivation*. London: Falmer Press.

Hakkarainen, K., Lipponen, L., & Järvelä, S. (2001), "Epistemology of inquiry and computer-supported collaborative learning." An article to appear in T. Koschmann, N. Miyake, & R. Hall (eds) *CSCL2: Carrying Forward the Conversation*. Mahwah, NJ: Erlbaum, in press.

Heckhausen, H., & Gollwitzer, P. M. (1987), "Thoughts contents and cognitive functioning in motivational versus volitional stages of mind." *Motivation and Emotion 11*, 101–120.

Higgins, E. T. (1990), "Personality, social psychology, and person-situation relations: Standards, and knowledge activation as a common language." In L. A. Pervin (ed.) *Handbook of Personality: Theory and Research.* New York: Guilford.

Higgins, E. T., & Bargh, J. A. (1987), "Social cognition and and social perceptions." *Annual Review of Psychology 38*, 369–425.

Higgins, E. T., Strauman, T., & Klein, R. (1986), "Standards and the process of self-evaluation: Multiple affects from multiple stages." In E. T. Higgins & R. M. Sorrentino (eds) *Handbook of Motivation and Cognition: Foundations of Social Behavior* (pp. 229–264). New York: Guilford.

Järvelä, S. (1995), "The cognitive apprenticeship model in a technologically rich learning environment: Interpreting the learning interaction." *Learning and Instruction 5*, 237–259.

Järvelä, S., Hakkarainen, K., Lehtinen, E. & Lipponen, L. (2001), "Creating Computer Supported Collaborative Learning (CSCL) Culture in Finnish Schools: Research Perspectives on Sociocognitive Effects." *International Journal of Continuing Engineering Education and Life-Long Learning*, in press.

Järvelä, S., Lehtinen, E., & Salonen, P. (2000), "Socioemotional orientation as a mediating variable in teaching learning interaction: Implications for instructional design." *Scandinavian Journal of Educational Research 44*, 293–307.

Järvelä, S., Niemivirta, M., & Hakkarainen, K. (2001), *The interaction of students' Self-reported Motivation and Strategies and Situational Motivation and Action During a Computer Supported Collaborative Learning Project.* Submitted.

Koschmann, T. (1996), *CSCL: Theory and Practice of an Emerging Paradigm.* Mahwah, NJ: Lawrence Erlbaum.

Kuhl, J. (1984), "Volitional aspects of achievement motivation and learned helplessness: Toward a comprehensive theory of action control." In B. A. Maher & W. B. Maher (eds) *Progress in Experimental Personality Research* (pp. 99–171). New York: Academic Press.

Kuhl, J. (2000), "A functional–design approach to motivation and self-regulation." In M. Boekaerts, P. R. Pintrich & M. Zeidner (eds) *Handbook of Self-regulation* (pp. 111–169). San Diego, CA: Academic Press.

Lewin, K., Dembo, T., Festinger, L. A., & Sears, P. S. (1944), "Level of aspiration." In M. J. Hunt (ed.) *Personality and the Behavior Disorders* (pp. 333–379). New York, NY: Ronald Press.

Meece, J. (1991), "The classroom context and students' motivational goals." In M. Maehr & P. Pintrich (Eds.) *Advances in Motivation and Achievement 7* (pp. 261–285). Greenwich, CT: JAI Press.

Mischel, W., Cantor, N., & Feldman, S. (1996), "Principles of self-regulation: The nature of will-power and self-control." In E. T. Higgins & A. W. Kruglanski (eds) *Social Psychology: Handbook of Basic Principles.* New York, NY: The Guilford Press.

Mischel, W., & Schoda, Y. (1995), "A cognitive–affective system theory of personality: Reconceptualizing situations, dispositions, dynamics, and invariance in personality structure." *Psychological Review 102*, 246–268.

Murdock, T. B. (2000), "Incorporating economic context into educational psychology: Methodological and conceptual challenges." *Educational Psychologist 35*, 113–124.

Murphy, P. K., & Alexander, P. A. (2000), "A motivated exploration of motivation terminology." *Contemporary Educational Psychology 25*, 3–53.

Niemivirta, M. (1998a, August), *Stability and Change in Goal Orientations and Motivational*

Beliefs — A Pattern-Oriented Approach. A paper presented at the 24th International Congress of Applied Psychology, San Francisco.

Niemivirta, M. (1998b), Individual differences in motivation and cognitive factors affecting self-regulated learning — A pattern-oriented approach. In P. Nenniger, R. S. Jäger, A. Frey & M. Wosnitza (eds) Advances in motivation (pp. 23–42) Landau: Verlag Empirische Pädagogik.

Niemivirta, M. (1999), "Cognitive and motivational predictors of goal setting and task performance." *International Journal of Educational Research 31*, 499–513.

Pajares, F. (1996), "Self-efficacy beliefs in academic settings." *Review of Educational Research 66*, 543–578.

Pajares, F., & Valiante, G. (1997), "Predictive and mediational roles of the writing self-efficacy beliefs of upper elementary school students." *Journal of Educational Research 90*, 353–360.

Pintrich, P. (2000), "An achievement goal theory perspective on issues in motivation terminology, theory and research." *Contemporary Educational Psychology 25*, 92–104.

Pintrich, P. R., & Schunk, D. H. (1996), *Motivation in Education: Theory, Research, and Applications.* Englewood Cliffs, NJ: Prentice Hall.

Rahikainen, M, Järvelä, S., & Salovaara, H. (2000), "Motivational Processes in CSILE-based Learning." In *Proceedings of the International Conference for Learning Sciences,* June 14–17, Michigan, USA. Mahwah: Lawrence Erlbaum Associates.

Salomon, G. (1996), "Studying novel learning environments as patterns of change." In S. Vosniadou, E. De Corte, R. Glaser & H. Mandl (eds) *International Perspectives on the Psychological Foundations of Technology-based Learning Environments.* Hillsdale, NJ: Erlbaum.

Salomon, G., & Globerson, T. (1989), "When teams do not function as they ought to." *International Journal of Educational Research 13*, 89–100.

Salonen, P., Lehtinen, E., & Olkinuora, E. (1998), Expectations and Beyond: The development of motivation and learning in a classroom context." In J. Brophy (ed.) *Advances on Research on Teaching 7* (pp. 111–150), London: JAI Press.

Scardamalia, M., & Bereiter, C. (1994), "Computer support for knowledge building communities." *The Journal of the Learning Sciences 1*, 37–68.

Scardamalia, M., Bereiter, C., & Lamon, M. (1994), "The CSILE project: Trying to bring the classroom into world 3." In K. McGilly (ed.) *Classroom Lessons; Integrating Cognitive Theory & Classroom Practice* (pp. 201–228). Cambridge, MA: MIT.

Schoda, Y., Mischel, W., & Wright, J. C. (1993), "Links between personality judgments and contextualized behavior patterns: Situation–behavior profiles of personality prototypes." *Social Cognition 4*, 399–429.

Schunk, D. H. (1991), "Self-efficacy and academic motivation." *Educational Psychologist 26*, 207–232.

Slavin, R. (1989), "Cooperative learning and students achievement: Six theoretical perspectives." In Teoksessa Maehr, M. L. & Ames, C. (eds) *Advances in Motivation and Achievement. Vol. 6. Motivation Enhancing Environments.* JAI Press, 161–178.

Turner, J. C. (1995), "The influence of classroom contexts on young children's motivation for literacy." *Reading Research Quarterly 30*, 410–441.

Valsiner, J. (1996), "Development, methodology, and recurrence of unsolved problems: On the modernity of 'old' ideas." *Swiss Journal of Psychology 55*, 119–125.

Winne, P. H., & Perry, N. E. (2000), Measuring self-regulated learning. In P. Pintrich, M. Boekaerts & M. Zeidner (eds) Handbook of Self-regulation (pp. 531–566). Orlando, FL: Academic Press

Chapter 7

Context-Bound Research in the Study of Motivation in the Classroom

Marina S. Lemos

Introduction and Conceptual Framework

This article shows the importance of linking theory with methodology and of describing variations in methodology associated with specific conceptions of motivation. Our discussion draws heavily from our previous research (e.g., Lemos, 1993, 1996, 1999a, 1999b; Lemos & Almeida, 1997; Lemos & Estrela, 1990; Lemos *et al.*, 2000), which has been informed by a relational goal perspective of motivation and has been based on a context-bound methodological approach. The aims of these studies have been to describe students' motivation in the classroom, with special reference to their goal orientations, and to identify personal and environmental conditions that affect them. Many of the propositions that underlie our research program have already been supported. The aim of this chapter is to provide empirical evidence of the links between goal orientations, personal and environmental conditions.

Context-bound research is defined not only by its methods but also in relation to the objectives of a given study. Therefore it is probably correct to say that the only common denominator of context-bound studies is the observation of an entity in its "natural" context (e.g., Creswell, 1998; Denzin & Lincoln, 1998a, 1998b). Our emphasis on context-bound research stems from a general conceptualization of human motivation that argues for the centrality of meaningful behavior as opposed to behavior itself. This conceptualization has two major implications for research on motivated behavior: (a) the examination of behavior-in-context, and (b) the emphasis on motivational goals. The elucidation of the meaning of a behavior is enhanced by placing that behavior in its context, for contexts are physical and relational systems that set limits and affordances to behavior. The importance attached to meaning in motivational research also makes goals stand out as privileged research targets. Motivational goals are viewed as representing finalities or purposes. Thus, goals confer direction, meaning, and functional unity to the diversity of observable behavior; they transform a set of behaviors into one purposeful action (Lemos, 1996). Moreover, goals themselves are intimately linked to the contexts where individuals reside, because, basically, concrete goals are projects to change an actual state of relations between the individual and his

Motivation in Learning Contexts: Theoretical Advances and Methodological Implications, pages 129–147.
Copyright © 2001 by Elsevier Science Ltd.
ISBN: 0-08-043990-X

environment (Nuttin, 1980/84). Therefore, the focus on goals further justifies the importance of a contextual approach to motivation. The context-bound approach to motivation is founded also in current holistic and dynamic interactionist models of behavior, which conceive of behavior as determined by the reciprocal influences between the nature of the context and the individual's characteristics (e.g., Magnusson, 2000).

Recently, the term "situated motivation" has been used precisely to underscore the importance of examining the contextual embededdness of motivated behavior and motivation development (Paris & Turner, 1994). The term underlines the idea that motivation theory and research should conceive of the situational conditions as the stage for the emergence and functioning of motivation. In our view, situated motivation will be more thoroughly understood once motivation is included in a general theory of behavior, a theory that avoids an excessive environmentalism to the detriment of the role of the person, and that argues for an integrated rather than a dualistic view of person–environment relations (in line with dynamic interactionism). In the field of motivation, Nuttin's (1953, 1965, 1980/84) relational theory is fundamentally in accordance with the priority assigned to meaningful behavior, and with the tenets of modern interactionism.

Overview of Conceptualization of Motivation and Research Implications

Our conception of situated motivation is thus inspired by Nuttin's theory and it includes three main interrelated propositions, each with important implications for the definition of relevant issues for, and corresponding methodology in, motivational research. The first proposition refers to the *relational and goal oriented nature* of human motivation. As noted by Nuttin (1980/84), "behavior involves a subject's entering into *relation* with his world ... (and) ... motivation, as the dynamic element of behavior, must be studied within the framework of this relationship, ... linking the individual to his physical and social environment" (p. 57). Within this view, individuals and environments constitute a functional unit — an I-E unit — that cannot be understood separately. Moreover, goals are essential to motivation, in that the behavior process begins with the construction of a goal, which further directs the course of action. In other words, motivated behavior is goal-directed, and goals are intimately linked to contextual characteristics (e.g., Brandtstadter, 1984; Freese & Sabini, 1985; Nuttin, 1980/84). The theoretical importance given to the contextual embededdness of motivational processes calls for the empirical identification of the particular forms that motivation assumes in actual contexts. The assessment of motivational variables in their environmental context requires adequate methodological techniques, as will be detailed later in this chapter.

As we argued, the term situated motivation should not be equated with unidirectional environmental determinism. The second proposition underscores precisely that *motivation is a reciprocal process*. Motivational processes in general, and goals in particular, develop within a reciprocal relation between the individual and the environment. Individuals are not passive partners in this relation; rather, they play an active role in the dynamic individual–environment system. The intrinsic complementarity of individuals' behavior and their environment is well captured in Nuttins' (1980/84) contention that "The individual continually acts upon its world (of objects) and thereby transforms them (into tools). In turn, persons themselves are continually shaped by the very objects they produce and use" (p. 64). Within the I-E unit, "the *individual is a subject-in-situation*, and the *environment is the situation-of-a-subject*, i.e., constructed by his behavioral operations" (p. 77). These assumptions underline the importance of enriching our thinking and of rephrasing our research questions concerning the determinants of motivation, namely (a) by framing the study of motivational determinants in terms of both constancy and change (or malleability), and focusing on the complex whole of influencing conditions, instead of just analyzing changes produced by isolated factors, and (b) by including subjective perspectives.

The core assumption of "situated motivation" research is that motivated behavior changes with changing situational conditions. However, the acknowledgement that the conditions of constancy and change necessarily involve both individual and contextual features, as well as contemporary and past influences, asks for increased efforts to more accurately evaluate those conditions. Later in this chapter we propose ways to examine the circumstances of students' motivational malleability.

In view of the reciprocal perspective, attention is also directed to subjective perspectives, as an example of the significance of the *active role played by individuals* in the determination of their own behavior. Individuals' interpretation of events partly accounts for the impact of the environment in motivational functioning. Empirical methods will be illustrated that stimulate and identify individuals' subjective perspectives.

The third proposition defining our conception of motivation emphasizes that *individuals function as holistic, total* systems, that are best characterized by the patterning of relevant aspects of structures and processes (e.g., Bergman, 2000), rather than by isolated variables. Within this view, the components of motivated behavior constitute functional units of the total motivational functioning. Therefore, challenging assumptions of additivity, one important task of empirical research is to identify the ways in which these components are arranged, particularly in real life functioning.

In sum, a context-bound approach is particularly pertinent to this conceptual framework of motivation. Within this approach four guidelines orient classroom motivation research: (a) the description of the contextual manifestations of motivation, (b) the examination of constancy and change in motivation (c) the identification and assessment of subjective perspectives, and (d) the identification and analysis of patterns of motivational functioning. These guidelines correspond to the conceptual features outlined above: (a) the relational and goal-directed nature of motivation, (b) the reciprocal nature of motivation, with special mention of (c) the role of an individual's interpretations and the (d) the holistic character of the multidimensional motivational functioning.

Before expanding on these issues, we will present a brief overview of selected methods to classroom context-bound inquiry.

Methodological Issues in the Assessment of Motivation in the Classroom

If the purpose of the research is to examine the relative impact of specific contextual and individual influences, it is important that methods afford an in-depth description of students' motivation in particular classroom situations, and also account for unique variations, which can offer a sophisticated understanding of the range of diversity in students' motivation. One efficient strategy to capture context-bound manifestations of classrooms is to select one only (allowing for in-depth analysis) entire school class (allowing for holistic analysis and within-classroom diversity), and assess these students in a variety of contextual conditions (allowing for between-classrooms diversity). At this point a remark must be made: the description of what is singular might move motivational research away from the goal of most scientific inquiries, namely, the search for regularity. However, the emphasis on specificity should not lessen the importance of finding regularities. In an in-depth context-bound approach, regularities can be searched through the comparison of particular cases in contrast to random sampling, which excludes particular cases because it is aimed at generalization. Furthermore, several methodological techniques are useful to derive and analyze context-bound manifestations of classroom motivation, for example, purposeful sampling, repeated sampling, semi-structured interviewing, confronting interviews, and inductive content analysis.

Purposeful Sampling is critical for conceptual–methodological coherence. It consists of deliberately selecting cases that best elucidate the research questions. In classroom research the choice of the classroom group as the sampling unit is especially important. Classrooms form the natural school group, and consist of complex wholes of variables that configure particular environments. Thus, any other group of students, belonging to different school classes, would reduce the context in the interpretation of data (Ford, 1975; Lincoln & Guba, 1985; Patton, 1980).

Repeated Sampling consists of the use of direct repeated measurement of the same entity, with the aim of identifying intra-individual change. It is also a valuable tool for the study of motivational determinants because through this procedure the more enduring processes remain quite stable, thus enabling a more direct estimation of the context effects. The repeated sampling procedure allows a more precise answer to such questions as: Do individual students react similarly to a variety of situations? Are there individual or contextual characteristics that affect students' classroom motivation, regardless of other circumstances?

In contrast with questionnaire measures that tend to isolate variables and their relations (Blumenfeld, 1992), **Semi-Structured Interviewing** provides descriptions of patterns of students' motivation through a direct, intensive, and open questioning about motivational cognitions and emotions. This technique is especially suited to capture subjective perspectives, including the psychological meaning of the environment, perceptions about the self, and the subjective definitions of the individual's purposes.

Confronting Interviewing is intended to detail motivation specific to concrete situations. This technique uses video-recordings to present individuals with their own actions in context, and it tries to elicit motivational accounts related to specific activities.

Categorizing a given sequence of statements as an exemplar of a specific type of goal-directed behavior involves an interpretative process that goes beyond the immediate observable data. The value of semi-structured interviewing would be severely wasted if only theoretically driven rating systems were used in this process. A more "open" approach to content analysis is needed to capture previously unidentified aspects of motivational phenomena. One such approach is **Inductive Content Analysis**, whereby the meaning of the interviewee's statements is progressively inferred during several stages of protocol analysis (for a detailed description of its application to classroom motivation, see for example Lemos, 1996).

Description of Contextual Manifestations of Motivation

As we have emphasized, motivation is a relational and goal-directed process. Each of these features is intimately linked to context, which means that one needs to study motivation partly as a function of that context. This idea will be discussed and illustrated at greater length in the present section.

Research has identified several variables and processes that are relevant for motivation in educational settings, such as intrinsic *versus* extrinsic orientations, perceived competence, control beliefs, level of achievement motivation, and mastery *versus* performance goals (e.g., Ames, 1992, Ames & Archer, 1988; Skinner *et al.*, 1990). However, very little is known about the contextual manifestations of these variables within the classroom. There are several arguments that underscore the need to describe motivation variables as they arise in the classroom setting. One is that it is plausible that once activated in a specific context, individual motivation gains specific contours related to the particular contextual opportunities, values, and contingencies. Novel manifestations of motivational constructs might also come into play. This might complete the potentially limited range of empirical referents of these motivational variables, and contribute to adjusting potentially inaccurate definitions. Moreover, extended knowledge of situated indicators contributes to a better understanding of their impacts. Finally, after recognizing the contextual manifestations of motivation, it becomes possible to explore the fundamental issue of individual–environment determinants by comparing typical (dispositional-like) motivation with situational specific motivation.

Illustration: The Case of Students' Classroom Goals

Traditional goal theories have concentrated on two achievement goals — task or mastery goals, and ego or performance goals (Ames & Archer, 1988; Dweck & Leggett, 1988; Nicholls, 1990). We believe that mastery and performance goals do not fully reflect the complexity of motivation orientation in the classroom. A number of researchers (e.g., Blumenfeld, 1992; Wentzel, 1991, 1993, 1994) have already underlined the need to consider also affiliative and social goals in relation to achievement and engagement in the classroom. Despite the promise of a thorough analysis of the full range of students' goals, relatively little research has been conducted in real classroom contexts. Moreover, typically, goals are inferred only indirectly, on the basis of classroom structure. In our conceptualization, the term "goal" is about the content of individual goals, not classroom goal orientations. However, goals cannot be understood isolated from the context in which they are pursued. This is why we have directly assessed students' specific purposes accompanying particular classroom activities. In order to contribute to advances in classroom applications of goal theory, methodological approaches must be tailored to identify students' individual goals, to describe the contextual manifestations of goals, and to document the variety of classroom goals, namely allowing for the emergence of potential new goals. The techniques of semi-structured confronting interviewing, and of inductive content analysis proved useful to such an exploration.

Using such techniques, our research produced empirical evidence of several types of goals which could be classified and operationally defined using classroom-bound formulations (Lemos, 1993, 1996). This research provided a detailed picture of the manifestations that the goal orientation phenomena assume in the classroom. For example, using students' reports of what they are trying to achieve while performing several classroom activities, seven different types of goals were found (Lemos, 1993). The five main types of goals included three types of academic goals — learning, evaluation, and working goals — all directly related to needs for competence; two other types of goals were detected — relational and complying goals — which seem to reflect the social–relational dimension of students' classroom activities. These findings add to the growing interest in the content and diversity of goals in achievement settings (Ford, 1992; Urdan & Maehr, 1995; Volet & Chalmers, 1992; Wentzel, 1993, 1994). They also offer empirical support for these extensions of goal theory. It is worth noting that "complying goals" and "working goals" had not been articulated in theories about student motivation. Yet, they are of the utmost relevance in daily classroom activities. Moreover, the methodological approach allowed the detection of different levels[1] of intentionality in students' activities — intentional (referring to activities supported by goal-setting and planning) or unintentional (referring to automatic behavior) — which in a later study (Lemos, 1999a) were

---

[1] Goal type and goal level are two separate dimensions of goal classification. However, they are not mutually exclusive — certain types of goals are mostly classified in certain goal levels.

found to be related to self-determination and autonomy in the classroom context.

In summary, the use of semi-structured confronting interviewing about individual purposes for classroom behavior, combined with an inductive content analysis, allowed the empirical identification of students' individual goals, some of them not previously identified. Moreover the study supported the notion that goals are context-specific and revealed the relevant dimensions of the classroom setting implied in students' behavior orientations. Although it is important to organize the variability of human behavior into a more limited set of workable forms of behavior, we must caution against reductionism. The identification of a variety of goals, and the development of classroom-bound definitions of these goals appear well suited to an educational application of goal theory. Also, a new dimension of students' classroom orientation — intentionality — emerged. This finding indicates that goal-setting and planning are active processes in the classroom setting, and our research provided a description of their contextual manifestations.

Constancy and Change in Motivation

We approach the study of motivational determinants by focusing on the conditions of both constancy and change (or malleability). That is, we trace observed (in)variations in motivation and search the circumstances under which they occur. Moreover, we rely on motivational variations of the same individuals, rather than just drawing from different individuals in different circumstances. Traditional research on motivational determinants has focused the study of individual differences. Expanding on this research we emphasize that a distinction must be made between inter-, and intra-individual differences. Inter-individual differences refer to variability between individuals within contexts, whereas intra-individual differences refer to variability of the same individual across contexts (Nesselroad & Baltes, 1979; Valsiner, 1998). The methodological procedures used to disentangle these two types of individual differences, and some of the more interesting results will be highlighted. Finally, subscribing to a reciprocal perspective, the search for the conditions of constancy and change will involve both individual and contextual influences. To illustrate our approach to constancy and change (both inter- and intra-individual) in motivation we will address two issues: (a) malleability in relation to motivational dispositions, and (b) malleability in relation to motivational functioning in specific contexts. Our focus is on the study of individuals' motivational functioning from a contemporaneous perspective. However, we are also concerned with how developmental results interact with current context to determine how individuals function. Through early interactions with their environments individuals develop rather stable motivational characteristics (e.g., expectations, motivational orientations, pathways to valued goals, beliefs, or attributional styles), which define the individual's typical or habitual motivational functioning. Nevertheless, to the extent that these dispositions have been shaped by the environment, they may still be challenged by current contextual factors. Therefore, research on situated motivation must examine the influence of these dispositions on context-specific motivation. To the same effect, we (Lemos, 1993, 1996; Lemos & Estrela, 1990) have tried to determine if an individual's dispositional-like motivations (i.e., individual's typical motivation) are directly reflected in motivational functioning in specific contexts, or if they undergo changes, as well as the direction of those changes. This research is illustrated in the section "Constancy, change, and motivational dispositions". Because the plasticity of behavior is not unlimited, behavior is expected to change only partially across situations. Some of our research addresses how ongoing situations determine constancy and change in individuals' motivation. Also, we try to identify the quantitative and/or qualitative variations in situational conditions associated with change in motivated behavior. This research is illustrated in the section "Constancy, change, and contexts".

Constancy, Change, and Motivational Dispositions

The understanding of situated motivation cannot rely solely on descriptions of context-specific, motivation-related variables and ignore the individuals' motivational history and its resulting, more or less enduring, dispositions (Boekaerts, 1994). To proceed otherwise is to suggest, misleadingly, that motivation is a fluctuating state that changes continually according to the particular situation.

Research is needed that examines whether trait-like motivational variables show qualitative and/or quantitative specifications, as we approach the real and concrete activities of an individual. For example, do students enact their intended motivational orientations when enrolled in the real classroom setting? Which orientations are activated and deactivated in the classroom? Design, measurement, and analysis issues especially relevant for these purposes are discussed. Following from the same argument, we also want to draw attention to the role of theory and concepts in guiding context-bound research. For example, the comparison of typical motivation with context-specific motivation brings to the foreground the theoretical question of the relevance of the same constructs to describe motivational functioning at different levels of specificity. Thus, empirical work is needed that operationalizes motivational constructs at the different levels of specification. Based on the conceptual definitions of the constructs under examination, we selected from interview protocols ecologically valid empirical referents of these constructs. In our studies the referents tapped the constructs in progressively closer levels of proximity to the concrete classroom setting, allowing conceptually coherent comparisons.

To estimate students' motivation in situations progressively closer to the classroom, we (Lemos, 1993, 1996) defined three levels of approach to the classroom situation, and used the same students in these levels. At the first and most distant level, questionnaires were used to assess students' trait-like motivational dispositions; these data were considered as reflecting students' typical patterns of classroom motivation. At the second level, the same students were interviewed individually to elicit their motivation for spcific classroom activities. At the third level, and in order to access students' ongoing motivation within real-life class-room settings, lessons from each of six subject-matters were video-taped. Students were again interviewed individually while they were presented with these videos, exploring their motivation for particular classroom activities.

This research (Lemos, 1993, 1996; Lemos & Estrela, 1990) documented differ-ences in the quality (variety of dimensions) and degree (low-high) of motivation-related variables, when assessed at a general and distant level, or at a more context-specific level. For example, students demonstrated significantly lower self-perceptions of competence in the real-life classroom (third level) than they had reported. They also showed a significantly more extrinsic orientation in the class-room (third level) than they had reported in the interview about their classroom activities (second level), and in a questionnaire measure (first level). These results suggest a powerful classroom effect over students' motivational dispositions.

Inter-Individual Differences in Intra-Individual Change

From an interactionist perspective, the determinants of a motivational outcome are located in the dynamic interaction between a particular individual and contex-tual factors. Therefore, the suggestion made above that the real classroom context enhances extrinsic motivation can be fully asserted only by comparing the results of each individual student at the three levels of approach. Such comparison evi-denced, for example, that every individual student changed in the same direction — to a more extrinsic orientation. The figures reveal no inter-individual differ-ences in the direction of intra-individual change. This type of finding is specially relevant to understanding the malleability and direction of motivational changes. Despite students' intrinsic dispositions, extrinsic reasons take precedence over intrinsic interest as they approach the performance of concrete activities. This might help teachers balance more accurately the activation of intrinsic and extrin-sic motivational systems in learning contexts. In sum, the proposed research strategy enables the determination of inter- and intra-individual differences, as well as of inter-individual differences in intra-individual change.

Constancy, Change, and Contexts

An outgrowth of the contextual perspective of motivation in education is the appreciation for the diversity of patterns of motivation across settings (Pintrich & Schunk, 1996). Motivation may exhibit either constancy or change within various settings, or it may exhibit some features of both constancy and change depending on the particular interaction between the context and the individual.

A large body of work identified a variety of instructional and social contextual characteristics that influence students' motivation (see for example, Eccles *et al.*, 1998). In this line, researchers have focused mainly on the effects of particular structures, and sought to isolate those effects from confounding contextual and individual variables. Typical research usually compares classroom structures that represent contrasting examples concerning the selected factors. This procedure does not reflect the natural ongoing classroom setting, and reduces the complexity of the setting to elementary constituents. Moreover it is possible that the conditions that matter for a particular student's outcomes lie in differences in the intensity, frequency or temporal duration of some structures or events, rather than in their presence or absence. They may also relate to the relative proportion of enhancing and debilitating dimensions rather than in the absolute amount of each of these, or alternatively in the occurrence of significant single events that may exert a profound impact on a student's motivation.

Research is needed that examines the impact of learning contexts from a more global and integrated view, conceptualizing the classroom context as a set of conditions that describe a particular case, in line with a holistic view. The need for such an approach is partly supported by research that suggests that environmental features are interdependent (Ames, 1992; Epstein, 1989). Within this conception of classroom effects, researchers describe and then try to explain differences between students' motivation in particular kinds of classroom contexts. Likewise, Talbert & McLaughlin (1999) proposed a "bottom-up research strategy", which begins with the dependent variable (students' motivation), and works upward to find which classroom contexts "shape a phenomenon of interest" (p. 198). In a similar vein, in our own research, the relevance of the contextual features is an empirical question, rather than an independent variable. We ask, for example, how much students' perceived competence or goal orientation varies in a diversity of classroom contexts. Next, we try to identify the conditions that eventuate in those differences (usually a combination of conditions; see below). We (Lemos, 1993, 1996) used the same students in six different courses in order to understand what happens to their motivation when they move from class to class, facing in each a different teacher and a different subject-matter. In sum, our methods apply a holistic view to assess contexts, examine integral classrooms, and compare the results of person–context interactions.

Results showed a remarkable consistency in students' goal orientations across the six classroom environments. Whereas these findings may suggest that neither different subject-matters, nor different teachers, significantly affected these students' classroom goal orientation, there was one exception. In one of the courses, students diverged significantly from their characteristic goal orientations. Specifically, and in contrast with all other courses, complying goals systematically led students' goal priorities in this course. This unique finding appeared to be related to a combination of specific, subtle, but insidious quantitative and qualitative environmental conditions. This particular teacher held different expectations for the students, when compared with the other teachers. However, teacher expectations alone were not a sufficient condition to alter students' goal orientations. In addition to different expectations, this teacher also placed a strong emphasis on one specific requirement — students' compliance — largely overseeing other aspects of classroom learning and management. Therefore, and in contrast with what was found in the other classroom contexts, it is suggested that one particular combination of environmental factors (in the present case, a very intense and exclusive teacher requirement) may be capable of influencing students' goal orientations in the direction intended by the teacher.

The utilization of the preceding methods revealed that in the natural classroom setting students seem to share rather generalized schemas of motivational functioning, which change only under exceptional conditions. It also contributed to identifying the specific characteristics of the situation that students encounter, characteristics that presumably explain the stability of their motivated behavior across situations.

The Assessment of Subjective Perspectives

This section deals with a specific aspect of the active role of the individual in the I-E functional unit. More precisely, it concentrates on the role of subjective perspectives in motivated behavior: (a) subjective perspectives about the external world, and (b) subjective perspectives about the inner world (in this respect, we will specifically discuss individuals' subjective definitions of their goals).

One fundamental environmental component of motivated behavior is the meaningful situation constructed by the individual. The importance of the personal meaning of the situation was first underscored by Lewin (1935) who argued that organisms act in a perceived rather than in a real world. In the domain of motivation in education it has also been emphasized that the main function of the environment in the processes of motivation operates through the perceived environment. For example, the term psychological situation (first presented by Rotter, 1955) refers to the situation as it is interpreted and assigned meaning by the individual (Ames, 1992). Similarly, the individual's mental organization of the social environment of the classroom was stressed by Magnusson and Stattin (1998) as a prerequisite for the "individual's experience of the networks as meaningful, (and) for the individual's purposeful current functioning..." (p. 704). Students' subjective perspectives have also been referred to as personal meaning (Maehr, 1984) or functional significance (Ryan & Grolnick, 1986) of classroom events.

On the grounds that there are behavioral determinants that delimit the variety of behavioral options, and which lie partly or even completely outside of one's effective range of control, it is critical to examine how individuals construe their actions, and personal development, namely by selecting and interpreting stimulus and events. Subjective measures are therefore recommended to capture an individual's experiences and constructions of the self and the contexts, which in turn affect motivation.

One important consequence of the previous discussion for classroom motivation research is the necessity to assess individuals' subjective definition of their goals. Although the contextual and the individual foundations of motivational goals are inseparable, in this chapter they are treated in different sections because distinct methodological implications derive from each. We have already dealt with the contextual aspects of goals (in the first section); now we will emphasize the individual counterpart, clearly expressed in our conceptualization of goals, which directly refers to the individuals' active stand in the process of goal-setting, and to the uniqueness of individuals' purposes. In this respect, it should be reminded that general motives or needs and goals are related but conceptually distinct constructs. As Nuttin (1980/84) contended, needs are behaviorally undetermined, thus allowing for a multitude of different specific goals to realize them. These goals are personally constructed, based on the individuals' perceptions about the self and the world. As stated earlier, research on motivation in education has focused on the effects of different goals. However, little consideration has been given to the prior question of what students are trying to achieve when performing classroom activities. Unlike other motivational variables (e.g., self-perceptions, beliefs, self-judgments) the subjective dimension of goals has been largely overlooked in empirical work. In our studies, goals are assessed in terms of the individuals' subjective definition of their purposes for particular activities.

Illustration: The Actual Situation, Students' Perceptions, and Students' Goals

To illustrate the role of subjective realities we will elucidate the influence of the classroom environment on students' orientations. A large body of research has concluded that classroom structures influence the salience of a particular goal, and consequently its adoption (see for example Ames, 1992; Blumenfeld, 1992; Meece, 1991). These studies focus on whether a mastery or performance orientation is elicited by specific task designs and deliveries, evaluation practices, availability of social comparison information, and locus of authority. Overall, conclusions about the effects of classroom structures on students' goals cannot yet be made. However, one problem is that students' perceptions of classroom orientations are often used as indicators of students' goals. A second limitation is that the actual and perceived salience of classroom goal orientations are frequently used interchangeably. To clarify these imprecisions, in our studies (Lemos, 1993, 1996) a strategy was developed that included three main types of data: (a) The direct assessment of the subjective definition of the goals pursued by students, cautioning against undue assumptions that students adopt the goal orientations that characterize the classroom structures; (b) direct questioning of students' perceptions of classroom goals was used to disentangle pursued and perceived goals; and, (c) the assessment of teachers' goals for the students was also a key target because teachers are important agents in structuring the classroom goal orientations. Students and teachers were individually interviewed facing the same classroom episodes. On the one hand, students were asked about their own goals for their particular activities as well as about the goals that the teacher held for them in those activities. On the other hand, teachers were asked about their goals for the students.

Considering that students are active agents in the construction of their motivational orientations, we presumed that they would not necessarily adopt the goal orientations promoted by their teachers. Students' orientations may resemble more their own perceptions of teachers' expectations, than the teachers' expectations themselves. In the same line of thinking, we would not expect a perfect match between students' goals and their perceptions of teachers' goals. The comparison of the teachers' goals for the students, the students' perceptions about the teachers' goals, and the students' behavioral goals, for the same classroom activities, yielded some interesting results. Whereas teachers emphasized mainly learning and complying goals, the goals that were salient to students in the classroom were mainly evaluation goals. Moreover, under these perceived circumstances, students pursued mainly working ("get by") goals. These results suggest nonlinear processes of influence between classroom orientations and students' goals in the classroom. First, there was evidence that students did not accurately perceive teachers' intentions. The analysis of the confronting interviews revealed that, frequently, teachers' activities intended to stimulate students' curiosity and exploration were interpreted by students' as having evaluative purposes. As students' perceptions were similar in different courses, it is suggested that through early classroom experiences students' developed stable expectations about teachers' values and goals. Second, students' reactions were more closely related to their perceptions than to teachers' goals. However, students reacted to a perceived evaluative environment by concentrating just on working goals. In other words, in the face of perceived challenges or threats (represented by evaluation goals), students tended to adopt easy and immediate goals (working goals), apparently enhancing the probability of goal achievement. Moreover, by restricting themselves to this type of goal and showing "on task" behavior, students may also try to avoid negative judgments of their overall classroom behavior. These results reveal that students' perceptions of classroom goals are not directly transformed into goal orientations, suggesting that these perceptions only partly influence a more complex process of goal-setting.

In sum, by considering students' perceptions and personal goal definitions, we were able not only to map the diversity of students' goals (mentioned above), and their partly unique set of goals in objectively similar situations (Lemos, 1993, 1996), but also to reveal some of the processes favoring students' adoption of certain goal orientations in the classroom. As argued, subjective perspectives, namely those that operate in the real contextual environments, add interesting contributions to the understanding of students' classroom action orientations.

Patterns of Classroom Motivational Functioning

The patterning of motivational functioning is specially relevant to an interactionist perspective in the understanding of the lawfulness of behavior. As we have stressed, an interactionist view does not contradict research and theorizing on behavior consistency or regularity. The argument is about what remains consistent and what changes. Constancy in motivation is conceived as the continuous organization of motivation. Constancy may be ensured despite changes in specific behaviors, inasmuch as the same pattern or profile of motivation is maintained. The variable approach must then be complemented with a pattern approach, with the aim of representing the phenomena under study in terms of the several relevant attributes. As Magnusson and Stattin (1998) observed, "In pattern analysis, the specific individual datum for a certain variable gets its psychological significance because of the role it plays in the configuration of scores on the relevant dimensions for the same individual" (p. 737). In sum, patterns best reflect the multidimensionality and wholeness of motivational functioning.

Some methodological strategies were used in our own research (e.g., Lemos, 1996, 1999b) in an effort to capture whole totalities in every phase of data collection, analysis and interpretation. These include (a) the elicitation of a wide range of motivational responses (e.g., cognitions, behaviors and emotions) concerning natural and semi-natural specific events, (b) the identification of the configurations assumed by these components, namely relying on vertical content analysis (Krippendorf, 1980), which utilizes global units of analysis, thereby maintaining the component parts nested in their signifying sites, and (c) the comparison of whole patterns derived in this manner.

The utilization of those methods shed some light upon the working patterns of students. For example, in our recent work on students' classroom coping strategies (Lemos, 1999a, b; Lemos & Almeida, 1997; Lemos *et al.*, 2000), we observed that students' active behavior in stressful circumstances was associated with constructive coping strategies. A closer analysis revealed that this association was mainly found among students who showed a combination of behavioral and cognitive involvement, intentional goal-setting and planning, and emotional responsiveness. There were other students who, in spite of reporting active behavior, did not exhibit goal-planning, and subsequently showed qualitatively different (poorer) coping strategies. In a similar vein, goal-valuing was associated with good coping strategies only if other aspects of their goals were present, notably goal personalization. On the other hand, some students, in spite of showing no behavioral activity, revealed an overall pattern of action that is representative of competent coping. One first suggestion is that judgments about the quality of motivational functioning should be derived from the comparison of whole patterns, not of single variables. Moreover, the finding of diverse variants of the same good (or maladaptive) patterns, supports the hypothesis that similar functions might be served by multiform structures (or configurations), and similar structures might serve multiple functions.

It was also found (Lemos 1999a, 1999b) that students could be classified into four patterns with reference to five dimensions of motivation, thus evidencing ways in which the motivational factors are arranged. Moreover, these results support Gangestad and Snyder's (1985) argument that there is a limited number of patterns of behavior organization. In fact, it was interesting to note that some dimensions were clearly incompatible, while others were indissolubly linked, and still others could be part of different combinations.

Finally it is suggested that patterning procedures that rely on a dimensional perspective have important advantages over categorical perspectives of motivated behavior. We would argue that the assessment of students' motivation should incorporate various motivational dimensions, rather than be reduced to discrete, mutually exclusive, categories of dimensions. Based on this perspective, we (Lemos, 1993; Lemos & Estrela, 1990) have highlighted that students' reasons for performing classroom activities were seldom purely intrinsic or extrinsic but were often motivated by both reasons; moreover, it was also revealed that students typically pursue multiple goals simultaneously.

These examples illustrate the wealth of theoretically and empirically accounting for the complex nature of motivational functioning, and concentrating on the organizing principles underlying the variability of ongoing motivated behavior. In this respect, the analysis of profiles and patterns is of unquestionable value.

Conclusion

In this chapter we have outlined a dynamic interactionist view of motivation. The major point made is that motivation is an individual process that cannot be understood separately from the environment in which it emerges and develops. Context-bound research was underscored as a methodological approach that is consistent with this motivational conceptualization, rather than just as a mere methodological perspective. A judicious use of context-bound methods is a critical component in the study of relevant classroom motivational phenomena. This entails an approach that accounts for contextual factors, as well as for the individuality of one's experiences in the environments, for the individual history, and for subjective perspectives. We have described and illustrated several methodological strategies and techniques that meet these requirements, and suggested how they might contribute to extend and integrate the field. To conclude, we will single out the more innovative and generative strategies and techniques in the domain of motivation in learning contexts.

Each of the major facets of the conceptual framework of motivation presented is associated with specific procedures of data collection and analysis. First, a relational and goal oriented perspective of motivation leads to the need to describe its contextual manifestations, utilizing methods that preserve the diversity and uniqueness of the phenomena under study. With respect to goal orientations in particular, our conceptualization of goals as individual constructions in a given situation, emphasizes the importance of both goal-content and of goal-setting in motivated behavior. Corresponding with this view, in empirical work, methods of direct assessment of individual student's specific purposes were utilized, which elicited a variety of goals pursued in the classroom context and also informed about the quality of the goal-setting process. These two aspects of goals were found to be interrelated and both are reflected in the quality of students' motivational functioning. The application of in-depth, open, and context-specific methods in our research revealed that a wide range of classroom dimensions are relevant to students' motivation and indicated the most influential ones. For example, it was suggested that students' main preoccupation in the classroom is to strive for academic and psychological survival, leaving less than satisfactory room for learning. Overall, the classroom setting does not seem to be prepared to stage the development of students' motivation in general, and hence, motivation to learn. The search for contextual manifestations of motivation also revealed novelty in motivational constructs, as the evidencing of a new type of goal, and of the scarcity of pure intrinsic and extrinsic orientations in the classroom.

Second, the conception of motivation as a dynamic reciprocal process leads to a re-conceptualization of the conventional ways of studying the determinants of motivation. The acknowledgement of reciprocal influences focuses the investigation of determinants on the analysis of constancy and change in motivation. Research on this issue requires methods that illuminate the conditions that shaped an observed variation in motivation, and that identify those patterns and components of motivation that are vulnerable, resistant or resilient to real-life activity and to changing conditions. To this effect, the use of the same individuals in different conditions becomes central to motivational research. Moreover, the active role played by the individuals stresses the need to assess subjective perspectives. In our studies, the aforementioned methods, combined with semi-structured interviewing and inductive content analysis, yielded some results that complement and even challenge some views of motivation in education. Notably, it was found that the hierarchy of students' goals, namely the position of learning goals in students' goal priorities, did not vary as a function of the subject-matter or the teacher's instructional strategies, as would be expected. Those methods were also essential to examine entity-specific (rather than just the average) intra-individual change, and inter-individual differences in intra-individual change, in a variety of situations. In addition, the development of a three-level design was essential to detect the motivational dimensions that undergo transformations as individuals approach the real-life situation, and the direction of these transformations. An interesting line of inquiry would be to explore the extent to which context specific motivation represents the outcome of the individual's typical patterns interacting with a particular environment, and the extent to which typical patterns subsume specific patterns, i.e., whether or not they are continuously (re)constructed by the specific patterns of functioning in various situations.

Finally, the holistic character of motivational functioning requires the use of entire profiles as the units of analysis. In our empirical work, the patterning of multiple specific measures enabled the detection of indissoluble links as well as incompatibilities among component variables, thus clarifying the reciprocal influences between them, and the role they play in determining the overall quality of students' motivation.

References

Ames, C. (1992), "Classrooms: Goals, structures, and student motivation." *Journal of Educational Psychology 84*, 261–271.

Ames, C., & Archer, J. (1988), "Achievement goals in the classroom: Students' learning strategies and motivation processes." *Journal of Educational Psychology 80*, 260–267.

Bergman, L. R. (2000), "The application of a person-oriented approach: Types and clusters." In L. R. Bergman, R. B. Cairns & L-G. N. L. Nystedt (eds) *Developmental Science and the Holistic Approach*. Mahwah, NJ: Erlbaum.

Blumenfeld, P. C. (1992), "Classroom learning and motivation: Clarifying and expanding goal theory." *Journal of Educational Psychology 84*, 272–281.

Boekaerts, M. (1994), "The interface between intelligence and personality as determinants of classroom learning." In D. H. Saklofsky & M. Zeidner (eds) *Handbook of Personality and Intelligence*. New York: Plenum.

Brandtstadter, J. (1984), "Personal and social control over development: Some implications of an action perspective in life-span developmental psychology." In P. B. Baltes & O. G. Brim (eds) *Life-Span Development and Behaviour* (Vol. 6, pp. 1–32). New York: Academic Press.

Creswell, J. W. (1998), *Qualitative Inquiry and Research Design. Choosing Among Five Traditions*. London: Sage.

Denzin, N. K., & Lincoln, Y. S (1998a), *Strategies of Qualitative Inquiry*. London: Sage.

Denzin, N. K., & Lincoln, Y. S. (1998b), *Collecting and Interpreting Qualitative Materials*. London: Sage.

Dweck, C. S., & Leggett, E. (1988), "A social–cognitive approach to motivation and personality." *Psychology Review 95*, 256–273.

Eccles, J. S., Wigfield, A., & Schiefele, U. (1998), "Motivation to succeed." In W. Damon & N. Eisenberg (eds) *Handbook of Child Psychology: Vol. 3. Social, Emotional, and Personality Development* (pp. 1017–1095). New York: John Wiley.

Epstein, J. L. (1989), "Family structures and student motivation: A developmental perspective." In Ames, C. & Ames, R. (eds) *Research on Motivation in Education: Vol. 3 Goals and Cognitions* (pp. 25–295). San Diego: Academic Press.

Ford, J. (1975), *Paradigms and Fairy Tales*. London: Routledge & Kegan Paul.

Ford, M. E. (1992), *Human Motivation: Goals, Emotions, and Personal Agency Beliefs*. Newbury Park, CA: Sage.

Freese, M., & Sabini, J. (eds). (1985), *Goal-Directed Behaviour: The Concept of Action in Psychology*. Hillsdale, NJ: Erlbaum.

Gangestad, S., & Snyder, M. (1985), "To carve nature at its joints: On the existence of discrete classes of personality." *Psychological Review 92*, 317–349.

Krippendorf, K. (1980), *Content Analysis: An Introduction to its Methodology*. London: Sage.

Lemos, M. S. (1993), *A Motivação no Processo de Ensino/Aprendizagem, em Situação de Aula* [Motivation in the instructional process, in the classroom setting]. Doctoral dissertation. University of Porto, Faculty of Psychology and Education.

Lemos, M. S. (1996), "Students' and teachers' goals in the classroom." *Learning and Instruction 6* (2), 151–171.

Lemos, M. S. (1999a), "Students' goals and self-regulation in the classroom." *International Journal of Educational Research 31* (6), 471–485.

Lemos, M. S. (1999b, August), *Coping Strategies in the Classroom — The Functions of Students' Goals*. Paper presented at the 8th European Conference of the European Association for Research on Learning and Instruction (EARLI), Goteborg (Sweden).

Lemos, M. S., & Almeida, C. (1997, August), *Students' Motivational Strategies in Stressful Classroom Situations*. Paper presented at the 7th European Conference of the European Association for Research on Learning and Instruction (EARLI), Atenas.

Lemos, M. S., & Estrela, A. (1990, September), *Students' Motivation in the Classroom Setting*. Paper presented at the International Symposium "Research on Effective and Responsible Teaching" Friburg (Switzerland).

Lemos, M. S., Soares, I. C., & Almeida, C. (2000), "Estratégias de motivação em adolescentes" [Pre-adolescents' motivational strategies]. *Psicologia: Teoria, Investigação e Prática 1*, 41–55.

Lewin, K. (1935), *A Dynamic Theory of Personality*. New York: McGraw-Hill.

Lincoln, Y. S., & Guba, E. G. (1985), *Naturalistic Inquiry*. Beverly Hills, CA: Sage.

Maehr, M. (1984), "Meaning and motivation: Toward a theory of personal investment." In R. Ames & C. Ames (eds) *Research on Motivation in Education: Vol. 1. Student Motivation* (pp. 115–143). New York: Academic Press.

Magnusson, D. (2000), "The individual as the organizing principle in psychological inquiry: A holistic approach." In L. R. Bergman, R. B. Cairns & L-G. N. L. Nystedt (eds) *Developmental Science and the Holistic Approach*. Mahwah, NJ: Erlbaum.

Magnusson, D., & Stattin, H. (1998), "Person–context theories." In W. Damon & R. M. Lerner (eds) *Handbook of Child Psychology: Vol. 1. Theoretical Models of Human Development* (pp. 685–759). New York: John Wiley.

Meece, J. (1991), "The classroom context and students' motivational goals." In M. L. Maehr & P. R. (eds) *Advances in Motivation and Achievement* (Vol. 7, pp. 261–286). Greenwich, CT: JAI Press.

Nesselroad J. R., & Baltes, P. B. (eds). (1979), *Longitudinal Research in the Study of Behaviour and Development*. New York: Academic Press.

Nicholls, J. G. (1990), "What is ability and why are we mindful of it? A developmental perspective." In R. J. Sternberg & J. Kollogian (eds) *Competence Considered*. New Haven, CT: Yale University Press.

Nuttin, J. (1953), *Tâche, Réussite et Échec. Théorie de la Conduite Humaine* (Studia Psychologica). Louvain: Publications Universitaires.

Nuttin, J. (1965), "La structure Moi-Monde." In J. Nuttin (ed.) *La Structure de la Personnalité*. Paris: PUF.

Nuttin, J. (1980/84), *Motivation, Planning, and Action: A Relational Theory of Behaviour Dynamics*. Leuven & Hillsdale, NJ: Leuven University Press & Erlbaum.

Paris, S. G., & Turner, J. C. (1994), "Situated motivation." In P. R. Pintrich, D. R. Brown & C. E. Weinstein (eds) *Student Motivation, Cognition, and Learning: Essays in Honor of Wilbert J. McKeachie* (pp. 213–237). Hillsdale, NJ: Erlbaum.

Patton, M. Q. (1980), *Qualitative Evaluation Methods*. Beverly Hills, CA: Sage.

Pintrich, P. R., & Schunk, D. H. (1996), *Motivation in Education. Theory, Research, and Applications*. New Jersey: Prentice Hall.

Rotter, J. B. (1955), "The role of the psychological situation in determining the direction of human behaviour." In M. R. Jones (ed.) *Nebraska Symposium on Motivation* (pp. 245–268). Lincoln: University of Nebraska Press.

Ryan, R. M., & Grolnick, W. S. (1986), "Origins and pawns in the classroom: Self-report and projective assessments of individual differences in children's perceptions." *Journal of Personality and Social Psychology 50* (3), 550–558.

Skinner, E. A., Wellborn, J. G., & Connell, J. P. (1990), "What it takes to do well in school and whether I've got it: The role of perceived control in children's engagement and school achievement." *Journal of Educational Psychology 82*, 22–32.

Talbert, J. E., & McLaughlin, M. W. (1999), "Assessing the school environment: Embedded contexts and bottom-up research strategies." In S. L. Friedman & T. D. Wachs (eds) *Measuring Environment Across the Life Span. Emerging Methods and Concepts*. Washington, DC: American Psychological Association.

Urdan, T. C., & Maehr, M. L. (1995), "Beyond a two-goal theory of motivation and achievement: A case for social goals." *Review of Educational Research 65* (3), 213–243.

Valsiner, J. (1998), "The development of the concept of development: Historical and episte-mological perspectives." In W. Damon & R. M. Lerner (eds) *Handbook of Child Psychology: Vol. 1. Theoretical Models of Human Development* (pp. 189–232). New York: John Wiley.

Volet, S. E., & Chalmers, D. (1992), "Investigation of qualitative differences in university students' learning goals, based on an unfolding model of stage development." *British Journal of Educational Psychology 62* (1), 17–34.

Wentzel, K. R. (1991), "Social competence at school: Relationship of social responsibility and academic achievement." *Review of Educational Research 61*, 1–24.

Wentzel, K. R. (1993), "Motivation and achievement in early adolescence: The role of multiple classroom goals." *Journal of Early Adolescence 13* (1), 4–20.

Wentzel, K. R. (1994), "Relations of social goal pursuit to social acceptance and perceived social support." *Journal of Educational Psychology 86*, 1273–182.

Chapter 8

"What to Learn from What We Feel?": The Role of Students' Emotions in the Mathematics Classroom

Peter Op't Eynde, Erik De Corte & Lieven Verschaffel

Introduction

Recent theories on cognition and learning (e.g., Greeno *et al.*, 1996; Salomon & Perkins, 1998; Wenger, 1998), inspired by the works of Vygotsky and his fellow researchers (Luria, Leont'ev, and others), point to the social–historical embeddedness and the constructive nature of thinking and problem solving. In spite of the recognition of the interrelatedness of cognitive, conative and affective processes implied in this perspective, most psychological and educational research favoring a social–historical perspective has focused only on cognitive and metacognitive processes (situated knowledge, the zone of proximal development, etc.). Affective and motivational factors are seldom intentionally studied within this theoretical framework. Most researchers investigating affect and motivation still favor more traditional perspectives (e.g., appraisal theories of emotions, goal theories, attributional theories) that, in general, do not treat the social–historical context as a major factor influencing students' behavior.

After all, research on affective issues has traditionally been individual and trait oriented, looking for factors such as attitudes that are stable and can be measured by questionnaires. More dynamic affective variables as, for example, feelings and emotions have always been less extensively studied (see Boekaerts, 1994; Pekrun, 1990). Moreover, researchers in the affective domain generally take a rather narrow perspective on studying affective variables. Not only do they focus on investigating affective variables in isolation, but they tend to work also in relative separation from each other, and from other, neighboring domains in psychology, sociology, and education (Pekrun, 1990).

In general, a focus on trait-like concepts and the individual also characterizes the post-behavioristic research approaches in motivational research (Hickey, 1997; Volet, 1999). The role of the context is perceived as facilitating or inhibiting change, but does not fundamentally change the course of the learning process.

Recently, several researchers have called for a rethinking of research on motivation and affect in line with socio-historical approaches of cognition and learning. Turner and Meyer (1999) argue for a theory of motivation in context that can account for the results of empirical studies illustrating the impact of contextual

Motivation in Learning Contexts: Theoretical Advances and Methodological Implications, pages 149–167.
Copyright © 2001 by Elsevier Science Ltd.
All rights of reproduction in any form reserved.
ISBN: 0-08-043990-X

factors on motivation. In a similar way, Hart and Allexsaht-Snider (1996) suggest that research on affect should closely analyze the social organization of schools as well as the specific characteristics of the mathematics learning in the classroom. On a more theoretical level, Hickey (1997) points to the different worldviews that ground a socio-historical approach compared to the more traditional motivational approaches, respectively a contextualized versus an organismic worldview. Implying different epistemological stands, these worldviews might be very hard to reconcile (see the competitive approach, Hickey & McCaslin, this volume). Consequently, studying motivational and affective issues in relation to learning and problem solving from a social–historical perspective asks for a fundamental reconceptualizing of motivational and affective research.

Nowadays, there is a growing interest in affect and motivation-in-context supported by an increasing body of empirical data (e.g., Järvelä & Niemivirta, this volume; Locke Davidson & Phelan, 1999). The theoretical and practical consequences of this shift in perspective are, however, less clear. Many authors refer in some way to socio-historical or socio-constructivist perspectives to justify their research approach, but these theoretical frameworks are far from solid research paradigms. As Cole (1995, p. 187) points out, we cannot:

> refer to them as a mature scientific paradigm with generally accepted theoretical foundations, a methodology, and a well-delineated set of prescriptions for relating theory to practice.

It comes as no surprise then that these research perspectives are not yet widely accepted and that lively discussions on their characterization and relevance are coloring the research journals (e.g., Anderson *et al.*, 1996; 1997; Cobb & Bowers, 1999; Greeno, 1997; O'Connor, 1998). Motivational and affective issues are, however, hardly touched on in this literature. Only in their chapter for the *Handbook of Educational Psychology* (1996) Greeno *et al.* have tried to trace the consequences of, what they called, the situative/pragmatist–sociohistoric perspective for the conceptualization of motivation and engagement. They point to the issues of identity and interpersonal relations as critical in defining engagement from a socio-historic perspective.

In this chapter, we want to take the discussion of a socio-historical perspective on learning a bit further along that line, focusing on the theoretical and practical consequences of such a perspective for research on affect, next to but closely related with, research on motivation. In the first part, we will investigate the conceptualization of motivation and affect within a socio-historical perspective, developing more specifically a socio-constructivist perspective on emotions. Taken into account that the focus of this book is on motivation in learning contexts, we will discuss at some length how emotions relate to learning and motivation within a socio-constructivist perspective. In the second part, we will study the consequences of such a perspective for research on emotions and learning in the mathematics classroom. A discussion of some critical issues will conclude the chapter.

To avoid confusion, a little side-step on the use of terms to describe the perspective seems in place here. Different terms are actually used as illustrated already above: the situative/pragmatic–sociohistoric perspective (Greeno *et al.*, 1996), socio-constructivism (Hickey, 1997), the socio-cultural perspective (Wertsch, 1991). It is not always clear to what extent they are identical or expressing different theoretical views. O'Connor (1998), for example, clearly illustrated the complexity of the matter pointing to the heterogeneous collection of research that describes itself as socio-constructivist. He interprets the term in a very broad sense, including perspectives from sociology of knowledge, ethnomethodology, Piagetian and Vygotskian perspectives. Used in this way, socio-constructivism refers to such a broad area of viewpoints that it stays far from a coherent theoretical perspective that can function as a framework for educational research.

Therefore, in this chapter, we will limit the use of the term socio-constructivist to describe a theoretical position that is grounded in a Vygotskian theory on cognition and learning, but accentuates more explicitly the mutual interaction between the individual and the context, that sometimes seems to be lost in other interpretations of Vygotsky's work.[1] To refer to the Vygotskian perspective in a more general sense, i.e., talking about an approach that is concerned with the social construction of cognition, learning, etc., inspired by the work of Vygotsky, we will use the term social–historical.

1. Affect and Learning from a Socio-Constructivist Perspective

Learning as Engagement

Wertsch (1991, p. 86) defines the basic assumption of the socio-historical paradigm as follows:

> Human mental functioning is inherently situated in social interactional, cultural, institutional, and historical context.

People are always situated in and constituted by the social and historical context(s) in which they find themselves. They give meaning to themselves and the surrounding world by interacting with it. Meaning becomes jointly constructed in the sense that it is neither handed down ready-made nor constructed by individuals on their own (Salomon & Perkins, 1998). Well-established meanings might be implied in practices characterizing a specific community for many years, but it is through engaging in such a practice anew that the individual experiences meaning. In doing so:

---

[1] Basically, we refer to the theoretical position developed by Vygotsky as a social–historical theory. We assume that most of the different terms that are actually used to describe a similar perspective refer to different interpretations of his work or want to stress a particular aspect of it (e.g., a socio-cultural perspective).

> we produce again a new situation, an impression, an experience: we
> produce meanings that extend, redirect, dismiss, reinterpret, modify
> or confirm — in a word, negotiate anew — the histories of meaning
> of which they are part. (Wenger, 1998, pp. 52–53)

By engaging in the practices of a community, people can discover meaning, come to know, but in doing so they at the same time renegotiate the meaning. "Negotiated meaning is at once both historical and dynamic, contextual and unique" (Wenger, 1998, p. 54). It is always a function of the interplay between the individual and the social–historical context.

To discover the meaning, to know, to understand, for instance, a word, a theory, a phenomenon, etc. ..., are all processes fundamentally constituted by their social–historical situatedness. Consequently, knowledge and knowing go beyond the individual. They reside in the various practices that characterize a specific community. Knowledge is intimately related to the context and the activity in which and by means of which it is constructed (Salomon & Perkins, 1998). It is distributed in the world among individuals, the language, the tools and the books that are used (Greeno *et al.*, 1996). The truth of a proposition no longer primarily depends on its correspondence with an "objective", "external" reality, because one cannot think a reality outside of the social–historical context. The truth of a proposition is determined by the criteria of truthfulness governing the practices of a specific community. Following Wittgenstein's epistemology (1953), knowledge and meaning reside in various "language games", embedded in organized social "forms of life" (Ernest, 1998). This implies that meaningful learning has to be conceived as a fundamentally social activity.

Learning is getting acquainted with the language, rules and practices that govern the activities in a certain community. It is becoming attuned to the constraints and affordances of a specific activity system through participation (Greeno *et al.*, 1996). Participation in the activities in a specific context becomes the process and the goal of learning. Greeno *et al.* (1996, p. 26) clarify that:

> The view of learning as becoming more adept at participating in distributed cognitive systems focuses on engagement that maintains the person's interpersonal relations and identity in communities in which the person participates.

The narrow intellectual view on learning is replaced here by a broader view that recognizes the conative aspects, i.e., motivation and volition, as central in learning. The learning process is characterized as a form of engagement that enables one to actualize his identity. Our engagement in specific communities is determined by, and constitutive for, our identities. Who we are and what we value, is derived from, and expressed in, our participatory relationships in specific contexts.

Students' Identity and Engagement

As an individual we participate in different ways in different communities, all of which are constitutive for our identity. To avoid fragmentation and to keep a sense of self, of being one person, requires some work to reconcile our membership in these respective communities. This reconciliation is to a large extent a private enterprise that entails, however, a potential for social change. As argued by Wenger (1998, p. 161):

> ... the work of reconciliation is an active, creative process. As we engage our whole person in practice, our identities dynamically encompass multiple perspectives in the negotiation of new meanings. In these new meanings we negotiate our own activities and identities, and at the same time the histories of relations among our communities of practice. The creative negotiation of an identity always has the potential to rearrange these relations.

From this perspective, the on-going creation of a person, of one's identity, is a social activity that potentially creates bridges between different practices, actualized in the particular engagement of the person in the respective communities.

In this way, students' learning in the mathematics classroom is characterized by an actualization of their identity through the interactions with the teacher, the books, and the peers, they engage in. On the one hand, these interactions are determined by the class and school context in which they are situated, and as such the *social context* is constitutive for students' identities. But, on the other hand, students bring with them to the classroom the experiences of numerous other practices in other communities they have participated and/or are participating in. Continuously challenged to integrate these in one self, this wide spectrum of past experiences determines the specific way students find themselves in the class context and its practices, discover meaning, and renegotiate or construct new meanings through their way of engaging in the class activities.

> Cast in this way, the relation between individual students' reasoning and communal practices is viewed as reflexive in that students contribute to the evolution of the classroom practices that constitute the immediate social situation of their mathematical development as they learn. (Cobb & Bowers, 1999, p. 9)

To accentuate this reflexive character between the social–historical context and the constructing individual, we will use from now on the term socio-constructivist perspective instead of social–historical perspective.

The way students engage in classroom activities is a function of the interplay between their identity and the specific classroom context. Their motivation to participate in a specific way in certain classroom activities is grounded in the way they find their "selves" in that context. However, their self, their identity, is only partially transparent to them. Who they are, what they value in this context, what they find worthwhile acting upon is seldom known a priori, it emerges in the situation. It is through their experienced motivations and emotions that subjects recognize the value a situation bears for them (Taylor, 1985). After all, what is sensed as important is grounded in our being a subject *as* a subject. As a subject we are constituted by the socio-historical context, the "form of life", we find ourselves in, the practices in which we participate. Through language, acting and interacting, meaning and values are constructed. Our feelings and emotions incorporate articulations of these specific meaning and values. Taylor (1985, p. 65) clarifies that:

> ... our feelings always incorporate certain articulations; while just they do so they open us on to a domain of imports which call for further articulation. At each stage what we feel is a function of what we have already articulated and evokes the puzzlement and perplexities which further understanding may unravel.

A Socio-Constructivist Perspective on Emotions

Although certain cognitive theories of emotion (e.g., Frijda, 1986; Lazarus, 1991; Mandler, 1989, Ortony *et al.*, 1988) clearly recognize the nature of emotions as articulations of our (self)understanding and revealing the importance a situation bears for the subject, they never integrate the fundamental social nature of emotions into their theories. They consider emotions to arise from an individual's construction and appraisal of his ongoing interactions with the world.

> Emotions arise in response to meaning structures; different emotions arise in response to different meaning structures. (Frijda, 1986, p. 349)

Consequently, emotions are a function of appraisal processes in which the situation is evaluated in the light of a current concern. Klinger (1996, p. 184) clarifies that:

> When people become committed to pursuing a goal, that event initiates an internal state termed a "current concern", one of whose properties is to potentiate emotional reactivity to cues associated with the goal pursuit.

Frijda (1986) further explains that emotional experiences also imply a state of action readiness, an impulse to act in a certain way. People feel urged to run, when they have fear or feel a need to act when they are interested. Next to this, the appraisal processes that constitute emotions might be accompanied by physiological change and some conscious awareness of being in an emotional state. From a cognitive perspective then, an emotion is fundamentally perceived as a

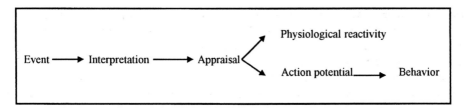

Figure 1: A cognitive perspective on emotions.

process consisting of the defining components depicted in Figure 1 (Power & Dalgleish, 1997, p. 149).

Although a cognitive perspective allows us to understand some of the characteristics of emotions, it does not succeed in clarifying the whole spectrum of emotional experiences that color people's daily lives. A cognitive approach is most successful in explaining the nature of a person's fear when he meets an elephant in the jungle. Confronted with the elephant he will perceive an elephant approaching him, making a lot of noise and flapping his ears. He will interpret this behavior as aggressive (interpretation) and finds himself in a dangerous situation (appraisal). His heartbeat will raise, he starts to sweat (physiological reactivity) and he feels the urge to run (action potential). Finally, he runs in the bush as fast as he can. This emotional episode can be nicely explained by a cognitive theory of emotions. However, what can be done with more casual and less intense emotions. What about jealousy, proud, shame, frustration, boredom, etc?

These emotions are rarely accompanied by a clear physiological reaction and for some of them there might not even be a specific action potential. More importantly, the experience of these emotions presupposes implicit or explicit knowledge of the rules and norms of the social context that are constitutive for them. Someone can only be proud of someone else if there is a relation of responsibility or personal relevance present. For example, a father can only be proud of his son's achievements if he regards himself as in some way responsible and able to take credit for it (Armon-Jones, 1986a). Consequently, his feeling proud presupposes an understanding of proud as used in a specific cultural setting. Harré (1986) points out that emotions can differ depending on the social context in which they are embedded and this as well in terms of the different kinds of emotions that are experienced, as in the specific characteristics of what on first sight appear to be the same emotions. Research in the mathematics classroom (e.g., Cobb *et al.*, 1989; Goodlad, 1983) shows that depending on the social norms that govern the activities in the classroom, students in one classroom can frequently experience joy and do not evidence any embarrassment or jealousy whatsoever, while in another class, negative affect might be highly present, or more likely, affect as such could be virtually absent. Similarly, being proud in a performance-oriented, competitive classroom will refer to being better than others, while in a mastery-oriented classroom it will originate from the successful completion of a difficult task. Students' knowledge and beliefs about the rules that govern classroom behavior, in interaction with other personal beliefs, are claimed to be an important part of the context within which emotional responses develop (Cobb & Yackel, 1998; McLeod, 1992; Op't Eynde *et al.*, 1999). More generally, according to a socio-constructivist perspective:

> emotions are characterized by attitudes such as beliefs, judgments and desires, the contents of which are not natural, but are determined by the systems of cultural belief, value and moral value of particular communities. (Armon-Jones, 1986b, p. 33)

The point we want to make here is not that the cognitive approach to emotions is of rather limited use or completely wrong. We only want to stress that the interpretation and appraisal processes that characterize emotions in cognitive theories are not grounded in nature, but in culture. The emotions we experience and the interpretation and appraisal processes that ground them are not primarily determined by us being an individual subject, a human being, irrespective of the social–historical context in which we live. On the contrary, the structure of an emotion is fundamentally constituted by the social–historical context in which it is situated. This does not imply that there are no emotions that are natural responses to natural situations. Some might be less socially colored (more natural) than others, like the fear of a wild animal, but to some extent primary and non-primary emotion types are all culturally constituted. An emotion(al process) can therefore better be schematized as shown in Figure 2.

A socio-constructivist perspective on emotions stresses their situatedness. An emotion is no longer the most individual expression of the most individual feeling. It is always grounded in, and bounded by, the broader social–historical context that constitutes the individual as well as by the immediate social-context where the act is situated. For students this context is in the first place the instructional context. In line with Paris and Turner's (1994) characterization of situated motivation, one can claim then that every emotion is situated in its instructional context by virtue of four characteristics. First, emotions are based on students' cognitive interpretations and appraisals of specific situations. Second, students construct interpretations and appraisals based on the knowledge they have and the beliefs they hold, and thus they vary by factors such as age, personal history and home

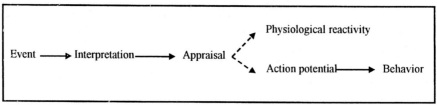

Figure 2: A socio-constructivist perspective on emotions.

culture. Third, emotions are contextualized because individuals create unique appraisals of events in different situations. Fourth, emotions are unstable because situations and also the person-in-the-situation continuously develop.

One can conclude that emotions clearly have a rationale with respect to the local social order (Cobb *et al.*, 1989). As Vygotsky (cited in van der Veer & Valsiner, 1994, p. 342) already pointed out:

> in an emotional experience we are always dealing with an indivisible unity of personal characteristics and situational characteristics, which are represented in the emotional experience.

In summary, characterizing students' learning as a form of engagement that enables one to actualize his identity, does not only acknowledge the central role of motivation and volition, but also of emotions and other affective factors as, for example, attitudes and desires. Students' behavior in the classroom is a function of the interplay between who they are (their identity), and the specific classroom context (c.f. supra). What they value, what matters to them, in what way, in this situation, is revealed to them through their emotions. They might even be perceived as elements of an affective representational system that in close interaction with several cognitive systems determines students' behavior (Goldin, 2000). Therefore, a socio-constructivist perspective on learning is clearly not only characterized by its focus on the interplay between the social context and the individual, but also by the recognition of the close interaction between cognitive, conative and affective factors in students' learning.

2. Investigating Learning Taking a "Holistic" and "Multilevel" Approach

The Study of Emotional Experiences: a "Holistic" Approach

Reflecting on the methodological consequences of the presented view on emotional experiences for research, Vygotsky (cited in van der Veer & Valsiner, 1994, p. 342) claims:

> from the methodological point of view it seems convenient to carry out an analysis when we study the role the environment plays in the development of a child, an analysis from the point of view of the child's emotional experiences.

Although surely not the only possible focus of attention when studying students' development and learning, students' emotional experiences are worthwhile to analyze. Grounded in socially colored interpretation and appraisal processes, these experiences represent not only students' individual characteristics and the context features in their interdependence, but also embody an integration of cognitive, conative and affective processes.

It has to be clear, however, that emotions are not perceived here as primarily subjective and internal phenomena, as in the more traditional cognitive approach. It is not the ambition of research from a socio-constructivist perspective to search for a clear-cut universal definition and/or theory of certain (basic) emotions, i.e., the identification of characteristic *internal* appraisal processes with their typical physiological complements and action potentials (see e.g., Power & Dalgleish, 1997). Emotions are not treated as objects that can be studied as independent and detachable from the specific individual and context (Cobb *et al.*, 1989). On the contrary, emotions are perceived as an act of participating in certain practices and contexts. To study, for example, joy, then implies an analysis of joyful acts as they occur in the concrete world of contexts and activities, in our case, in the context of learning in the mathematics classroom.

Analyzing the emotional or affective dimension of students' activities in the mathematics classroom, however, cannot take place in isolation from the study of cognitive and conative processes. Although different in nature, we have shown above that there are close interactions between these processes. Studying the affective dimension separated from the cognitive and conative dimension, would never fully grasp the complexity of a student's activity. He is never only feeling, but always also thinking and wanting. A unidimensional analysis of the learning activity would neglect the complexity of a student's personality and life. Thus it is only when a more holistic approach is taken that the study of emotional experiences can provide us with valuable insights in a student's learning and development.

Studying the Person-in-Context: a "Multilevel" Approach

The situatedness of emotions or emotional experiences, and of classroom learning in general, forces research from a socio-constructivist perspective to take place in the classroom. This does, however, not imply that the classroom level composed of interacting individuals, situations, activities, and contents would be the only relevant unit of analysis (Salomon & Perkins, 1998). This is a widely held misunderstanding by opponents of the socio-constructivist perspective. Anderson *et al.* (1997), for example, describe the difference between the situated and cognitive perspective on learning as the choice for the social collective or the individual as the primary unit of analysis. In a recent article (Anderson *et al.*, 2000), however, rephrased and moderated this opposition, describing it as a different focus of attention on learning activity that does not have to be framed as social versus individual. Indeed, pointing to the reflexive relation between the individual and the context and claiming that the study of emotional experiences of students can teach us a lot about their learning and development; we already argued that also from a socio-constructivist perspective, the study of an individual's emotions and learning is crucial. The individual student is still an important unit of analysis. Research that focuses on the individual has to document how students engage and reorganize their ways of participating in classroom practices. This approach stresses intentionality and emotionality, next to intellectuality, and takes activity and meaning as its basic currency. It implies a shift for researchers from an observer's perspective to an actor's perspective (Cobb & Bowers, 1999). What matters is not the classroom environment and practices as observed by the researcher, but the meaning students (and teachers) give to it and upon which they act. In their actions they re-negotiate the meanings that are prevailing, continuously creating new situations to which they relate in different ways. To grasp this dynamic interplay between the student and the class context that fundamentally determines his behavior, new research methods have to be used. Interviews, observations and discourse analysis seem to be more appropriate methods for revealing the meanings that students give to situations and how they are constituted through interactions in class, than, for example, questionnaires (see e.g., Cobb *et al.*, 1989; Turner & Meyer, 1999). However, to really grasp the dynamics of the interplay between student and context, methods have to be developed and applied that allow the on-line tracing of the different processes that are taking place. On-line questionnaires, experience sampling methods, and video-based stimulated recall interviews, are examples of appropriate techniques in view of reaching the intended goals (see e.g., Boekaerts 1987; Leder, 1999; Prawatt & Anderson, 1994).

We agree with Cobb and Bowers (1999, p. 6) when they state that a socio-constructivist perspective on learning:

> admits a range of units of analysis, the choice in any particular case being a pragmatic one that depends on the purposes at hand.

This position can be expanded to the study of emotions or emotional experiences in students' learning. The analysis of the emotional experiences of an individual student in the classroom can reveal how he continuously interprets the situation and acts upon it, and can teach us about his beliefs and knowledge underlying these actions. However, to fully understand the nature of these beliefs and the consequences of the actions, it is also necessary to analyze the norms and practices that characterize the class of which he is a member. One might even take it one step further and study the rules and values that are dominant in the school community and the society as a whole. A "multilevel" approach that incorporates these three planes of analysis, corresponding to personal, interpersonal, and community processes (see Rogoff, 1995), will probably result in the most complete understanding of the emotional experiences studied. This is a rather idealistic position. In most cases studies are confined to one level of analysis, due to limited resources and practical reasons. For one, research in the classroom is always constrained by the fact that, as a researcher, one is responsible for the learning of 20 or more students. Combining (video)taping of classroom interactions, on-line measurements of student processes, interviews with different participants, and sometimes intentionally creating new instructional contexts, is not always possible on a large scale. Consequently most studies of emotional experiences in the classroom done within this perspective will take the form of an in-depth investigation of a limited number of cases, i.e., classes or individuals, and will focus either on the individual or on the interactions in the classroom context.

An Illustration: Investigating the Role of Emotions in Mathematical Problem Solving

In the last decade several researchers in the field of mathematics education advocating a situated perspective have investigated students' learning and problem solving including analyses of motivational and affective processes, next to cognitive processes (e.g., Isoda & Nakagoshi, 2000; Lester *et al.*, 1989; McLeod, 1992; Prawatt & Anderson, 1994; Seegers & Boekaerts, 1993). They all focused mainly on the individual, using research methods (e.g., interviews, on-line questionnaires, video-stimulated recall interviews, on-line heart rate measures) that should enable them to represent the student's (actor) perspective on problem solving, rather than the researcher's (observer) perspective. Their results point to several important relations between the classroom context, students' beliefs, their emotions and their problem-solving behavior.

To further investigate these relationships and to advance the search for appropriate research instruments, we developed in our center a research project to study the role of emotions in students' mathematical problem solving, taking individual students as the unit of analysis (Op't Eynde *et al.*, 2000). The focus of this project is an analysis of the relations between students' mathematics-related beliefs, their emotions, and their problem-solving behavior in the classroom. The aim is to document how students engage in solving a mathematical problem in class, stressing especially the emotional dimension of their behavior, next to the motivational and intellectual aspects. Consequently, students' activities and the meaning they give to them, will be our basic research objects.

In the next section we will present some data from the pilot study which mainly aimed at testing the research methodology and instruments. Basically, we wanted to know if the chosen approach and the instruments we used would enable us to learn something more about the relationship between students' beliefs, their emotions and their problem-solving behavior. We opted for a very individualistic approach that to a lesser extent pays attention to the social context. The main study stays much closer to the assumptions that characterize a socio-constructivist perspective.[2] Consequently, the results presented here are tentative and in need of further validation.

Our study took place in the second year of junior high school (age 14) in three classes in different schools. The classes had basically the same curriculum for math but differed in the general level of secondary education they followed. Students of these classes were presented a self-developed questionnaire on mathematics-related beliefs (De Corte *et al.*, in press). Two months later (after presenting the questionnaire to the classes) we made a selection of six students, one high- and one low-achiever out of each class as evaluated by the teacher. They

---

[2] In the pilot study one student was isolated in the class to solve a mathematical problem while the other students were making other exercises. In the main study, one student of the class is followed when solving a mathematical problem that is given to the whole class by the teacher. The student and teacher activities were much more like their regular classroom practices, than was the case in the pilot study.

were asked to solve a complex realistic mathematical problem in class during a regular lesson and had to fill in the first part of the "On-line Motivation Question-naire (OMQ)" (Boekaerts, 1987) after they had skimmed the task and before they actually started to work on it.

Every student was asked to think aloud during the whole problem-solving process, which was also videotaped. Immediately after finishing, the student accompanied the researcher to a room adjacent to the classroom where a "Video-based stimulated recall interview" took place (Prawatt & Anderson, 1994). The interview procedure consisted of three phases. In the first phase the student and the researcher watched the videotape and the student was asked to recall what he did, thought and felt while he was solving the problem, especially during those episodes that he was not thinking aloud. In the second phase the interviewer asked questions for clarification, more specifically "what and how questions" relating to what he saw on the screen, what the student told him, what the student wrote down on the OMQ, and what he wrote on the answer form. Finally, in the third phase, the researcher tried to unravel the subjective rationale for the student's problem-solving behavior. He looked for the interpretations the student gave to certain situations. The "why questions" that were asked made underlying beliefs more visible and as such clarified the relation between beliefs, emotions and problem-solving behavior.

The results indicate that, in general, there is an individually changing flow of emotional experiences that follows from students' interpretations and appraisals of the different events that occur during problem solving in class. We found, on the one hand, that solving a problem in class, even the same problem, usually consists of an individually different chain of events for each student. For instance, some students' were confronted with a lot of obstacles when solving the problem, others encountered less difficulties they had to deal with. On the other hand, our analyses showed that comparable events are in some cases interpreted and appraised differently according to the person and the class context.

For example, our results show that negative emotions were usually experienced at moments that students were not able to solve the problem as fluently as they expected. Experiencing the inadequacy of the cognitive strategies used, is appar-ently as much an emotional as a (meta)cognitive process (see also Mandler, 1989). However, the nature and the intensity of the emotion experienced, when con-fronted with a comparable cognitive block, can significantly differ between students. Confronted with a difficulty in an early stage of the problem-solving process, one of the students became hopeless, stating that "If I'm already not able to solve this, then I surely will not be able to solve the rest of the problem". Another student also got stuck at the same point, became a bit annoyed, but experienced this as a challenge, and tried to find a way around it.

This also reveals another aspect of the role of emotions in mathematical problem solving. In most of our cases, the emotional experience always triggered students to redirect their behavior looking for alternative cognitive strategies or heuristics to find a way out of the problem. However, big differences were observed in the effectiveness and/or efficiency of the cognitive strategies used.

None of the students in the pilot study really used coping strategies or emotional regulation strategies to control their behavior. Some thought of it, but did not use it, explaining their behavior in the video-based stimulated recall interview as follows:

Int.:   "You notice that it is not working and still you persist in going on, although you are very angry. Why?"

Ellen.: "It is important ..."

Int.:   "Would you act the same if I wasn't here, or if you were home?"

Ellen: "No, then I would take a break and relax for a moment, so that I can try it again afterwards."

Int: "You don't do it here, why not?"

Ellen: "Because I have to keep on working. You are not allowed. You don't do that in class. You are not just going to stop and leave, telling just leave me alone for a while guys, I will continue in a few minutes."

Int: "But that's what you would do at home and does it work better afterwards?"

Ellen: "Sometimes."

This example illustrates how students' behavior is determined by the beliefs they have about the practices that are or are not allowed in the class context. More generally, students' descriptions and explanations of their emotional experiences in the video-based stimulated recall interviews usually refer to underlying belief-systems. When we combined these data with the results on the mathematics-related beliefs questionnaire and the on-line motivation questionnaire, we found that specifically students' general and task-specific competence and value beliefs appeared to determine the interpretation and appraisal processes underlying the emotional experiences. For example, the experience of a cognitive block as challenging rather than frightening in many cases seemed to depend a lot on students' beliefs about their competence. Although, one might assume that also their specific beliefs about the nature of solving these kinds of problems and the class teacher's acceptance of getting stuck in the process color their interpretations and appraisals. However, neither these very specific beliefs nor their social correlates, i.e., the classroom norms and practices, were the focus of attention in this study.

Affordances and Constraints

The presented data (for a more detailed description, see Op't Eynde *et al.*, 2000) illustrate the relevance of analyzing students' emotional experiences when solving a mathematical problem in class as a means of advancing our understanding of students' learning and problem solving. It shows how the use of a variety of research methods and instruments (e.g., thinking aloud, observation, question-naires, interviews, etc.) in a complementary way can enable researchers to trace students' ongoing interpretations and appraisals of events constituting their problem-solving processes. As such the analysis of students' emotional experiences inevitably also includes an analysis of cognitive and conative processes, on the one hand, and of characteristics of the task context (the events), on the other hand. It allows us to grasp the student's, actor's, perspective and the meanings underlying his/her activities when solving a problem, clarifying the dynamics that constitute his problem solving in class. In this way, this kind of research is a good example of how one can study the individual from a socio-constructivist perspective and what can be learned from it. Although there is a lot to gain from these kinds of in-depth studies of students' behavior, one has to stay aware of the restrictions implied in the methods and instruments used. For one, bringing a researcher, video and audio equipment into the classroom always interferes in some way with normal classroom life. There is sometimes a very clear influence on students' experiences in class, as can be illustrated by the following clarification given by a student during the video-based stimulated recall interview "I was nervous in the beginning, because there was a camera". However, we have learned from this study that after a few minutes students' behavior in presence of the camera becomes more and more normal, i.e., similar to their behavior when the camera is not present. Teacher's observations in the classroom confirm this. Nevertheless, researchers have to be aware that the "research setting", even when it is situated in the classroom and stays as close as possible to authentic classroom activities, does influence students' behavior. By explicitly allowing students to deal with these aspects in the interviews (see supra) researchers are able to trace some of these unintended influences and take them into account when interpreting the results.

Another way around this problem is of course the development of more sophisticated and less interfering on-line instruments. The more frequent use of on-line questionnaires or other on-line registration systems, for example measuring physiological parameters like heart rate (see Isoda & Nakagoshi, 2000) look like alternatives worthwhile considering. Both of them, on-line questionnaires as well as sophisticated heart rate registration equipment, do not necessitate the immediate presence of the researcher in the classroom and seem to enable more authentic classroom activities to take place. However, even these methods have their limitations. On the one hand, it seems very difficult to trace the dynamic dimension of problem solving using on-line questionnaires. They usually only give an indication of students' experience(s) at one or several discrete moments in time. For example, the motivation on-line questionnaire enabled us to understand the task-specific perceptions of students when they just had read the problem, but the interviews revealed that some of these perceptions had already changed two minutes later, determining the subsequent problem-solving behavior. Using the questionnaire at several points during the process might give a more complete picture, but would imply interfering quite strongly. On the other hand, the use of physiological parameters can currently indicate the presence of some (emotional) arousal, but the present state of the art of research on the typical physiological processes accompanying different emotions does not allow us to unambiguously define the emotional nature of the arousal, let alone the consequences.

In general, we are convinced that a deeper understanding of students' mathematical problem solving can only be reached if researchers study students' activities in a setting that is as close as possible to the natural class environment and interferes as little as possible with their usual activities. Next, as already pointed out, the focus on the individual ideally should be complemented with an analysis of classroom interactions (see e.g., Cobb *et al.*, 1989) to fully grasp the background and the consequences of students' behavior. The use of qualitative methods and instruments like observations and interviews, and also discourse analyses, currently, seem to be most appropriate to understand the dynamics of students' problem-solving behavior.

3. Conclusion

We have been developing in this chapter a socio-constructivist perspective on emotions in learning contexts, stressing the close interactions between affective, cognitive, and conative (motivational and volitional) processes that characterize learning constituted by a continuous interplay between individual and context. This situated perspective on emotions does not imply, however, that the situation, the context, is the only relevant unit of analysis. We have argued that a socio-constructivist perspective admits a range of units of analysis and has to study (1) processes at the level of the broader society, (2) processes and interactions characterizing life in the classroom, (3) and processes characterizing an individual student's learning.

Although the focus on the individual is shared with cognitive approaches of emotions in learning context, the theoretical perspective taken clearly differs, resulting in different views on the goals of research and the relation between theory and practice.

Research on emotions from a socio-constructivist perspective focuses on the activity of students in specific contexts, in our case the learning context. It wants to understand the emotional processes present in these situated activities that are inevitably linked with the other dimensions of the activity and framed by the meaning structure students give to it. In this way, emotions in learning contexts are fundamentally determined by the specific individual and the specific learning context. A theory on "the (basic) emotions" or about the role of emotions in learning in general, neglects these fundamental insights. Theories necessarily need to evolve from, and stay close to, activities in the classroom. As a consequence, theoretical constructs, as emotions, developed in this way cannot stand apart from classroom practices, but must stay grounded in it (Cobb & Bowers, 1999). A theory of emotions in the classroom that grows out of an analysis of students' situated activities in class, will more accurately define the relevant emotional processes and their role in the classroom context. The lack of such a theory until now might explain why affect is so often claimed to be virtually absent in the classroom (e.g., Goodlad, 1983).

The further development of appropriate research methods and instruments that allow researchers to analyze on-line in the classroom the different processes that characterize students' learning activities, is crucial. Only then we will be able to document in a reliable and valid way the emotional experiences of students in the classroom and advance the development of a theory of emotion in (the classroom) context.

References

Anderson, J. R., Reder, L. M., & Simon, H. A. (1996), "Situated learning and education." *Educational Researcher 25* (4), 5–11.

Anderson, J. R., Reder, L. M., & Simon, H. A. (1997), "Situative versus cognitive perspectives: Form versus substance." *Educational Researcher 26* (1), 18–21.

Anderson, J. R., Greeno, J. G., Reder, L. M., & Simon, H. A. (2000), "Perspectives on learning, thinking, and activity." *Educational Researcher 29* (4), 11–13.

Armon-Jones, C. (1986a), "The social functions of emotions." In R. Harré (ed.) *The Social Construction of Emotions* (pp. 57–82). Oxford, UK: Basil Blackwell Ltd.

Armon-Jones, C. (1986b), "The thesis of constructionism." In R. Harré (ed.) *The Social Construction of Emotions* (pp. 32–56). Oxford, UK: Basil Blackwell Ltd.

Boekaerts, M. (1987), "Situation specific judgements of a learning task versus overall measures of motivational orientation." In E. De Corte, R. Lodewijks, R. Parmentier & P. Span (eds) *Learning and Instruction*. Oxford, UK: Pergamon Press.

Boekaerts, M. (1994), "Action control: How relevant is it for classroom learning?" In J. Kuhl & J. Beckmann (eds) *Volition and Personality: Action Versus State Orientation* (pp. 427–435). Seattle: Hogrefe & Huber Publishers.

Cobb, P., & Bowers, J. (1999), "Cognitive and situated learning: Perspectives in theory and practice." *Educational Researcher 28* (2), 4–15.

Cobb, P., & Yackel, E. (1998), "A constructivist perspective on the culture of the mathematics classroom." In F. Seeger, J. Voigt & U. Waschescio (eds) *The Culture of the Mathematics Classroom* (pp. 158–190).

Cobb, P., Yackel, E., & Wood, T. (1989), "Young children's emotional acts while engaged in mathematical problem solving." In D. B. McLeod & V. M. Adams (eds) *Affect and Mathematical Problem Solving: A New Perspective* (pp. 117–148). New York: Springer-Verlag.

Cole, M. (1995), "Socio-cultural-historical psychology: Some general remarks and a proposal for a new kind of cultural–genetic methodology." In J. V. Wertsch, P. del Rio & A. Alvarez (eds) *Socio-Cultural Studies of Mind* (pp. 187–214). Cambridge, UK: Cambridge University Press.

De Corte, E., Op't Eynde, P., & Verschaffel, L. (in press), "Knowing what to believe: The relevance of students' mathematical beliefs for mathematics education." In B. K. Hofer & P. R. Pintrich (eds) *Personal Epistemology: The Psychology of Beliefs About Knowledge and Knowing*. Mahwah, NJ: Lawrence Erlbaum Associates.

Ernest, P. (1998), "The culture of the mathematics classroom and the relations between personal and public knowledge: An epistemological perspective." In F. Seeger, J. Voigt & U. Waschescio (eds) *The Culture of the Mathematics Classroom* (pp. 245–268). Cambridge, UK: Cambridge University Press.

Frijda, N. (1986), *The Emotions*. Cambridge, UK: Cambridge University Press.

Goldin, G. A. (2000), "Affective pathways and representation in mathematical problem solving." *Mathematical Thinking and Learning 2* (3), 209–219.

Goodlad, J. I. (1983), *A Place Called School: Prospects for the Future*. New York: McGraw-hill.

Greeno, J. G. (1997), "On claims that answer the wrong questions." *Educational Researcher 26* (1), 5–17.

Greeno, J. G., Collins, A. M., & Resnick, L. B. (1996), "Cognition and learning." In D. C. Berliner & R. C. Calfee (eds) *Handbook of Educational Psychology* (pp. 15–46). New York: Simon & Schuster Macmillan.

Harré, R. (1986), "An outline of the social constructionist viewpoint." In R. Harré (ed.) *The Social Construction of Emotions* (pp. 2–14). Oxford, UK: Basil Blackwell Ltd.

Hart, L. E., & Allexsaht-Snider, M. (1996), "Sociocultural and motivational contexts of mathematics learning for diverse students." In M. Carr (ed.) *Motivation in Mathematics* (pp. 1–23). Cresskill, NJ: Hampton Press.

Hickey, D. T. (1997), "Motivation and contemporary socio-constructivist instructional perspectives." *Educational Psychologist 32* (3), 175–193.

Hickey, D. T., & McCaslin, M. (this volume).

Isoda, M., & Nakagoshi, A. (2000), "A case study of student emotional change using changing heart rate in problem posing and solving Japanese classroom in mathematics." In T. Nakahara & M. Koyama (eds) *Proceedings of the 24th Conference of the International Group for the Psychology of Mathematics Education* (pp. 387–394). Hiroshima: Hiroshima University.

Järvelä, S., & Niemivirta, M. (this volume).

Klinger, E. (1996), "Emotional influences on cognitive processing, with implications for the theories of both." In P. M. Gollwitzer & J. A. Bargh (eds) *The Psychology of Action: Linking Cognition and Motivation to Behavior*. New York: The Guilford Press.

Lazarus, R. S. (1991), *Emotion and Adaption*. New York: Oxford University Press.

Leder, G. C. (1999), "Measuring mathematical beliefs and their impact on the learning of mathematics: A new approach." In E. Pehkonen & G. Törner (eds) *Mathematical Beliefs and Their Impact on Teaching and Learning of Mathematics; Proceedings of the Workshop in Oberwolfach* (pp. 57–65). Duisburg, Germany: Gerhard Mercator Universität Duisburg.

Lester, F. K., Garofalo, J., & Kroll, D. L. (1989), "Self-confidence, interest, beliefs, and metacognition: Key influences on problem-solving behavior." In D. B. McLeod & V. M. Adams (eds) *Affect and Mathematical Problem Solving: A New Perspective* (pp. 75–88). New York: Springer-Verlag.

Locke Davidson, A., & Phelan, P. (1999), "Students' multiple worlds: An anthropological approach to understanding students' engagement with school." In T. C. Urdan (ed.) *Advances in Motivation and Achievement, Vol. 11. The Role of Context* (pp. 233–273). Stamford, Connecticut: JAI Press Inc.

Mandler, G. (1989), "Affect and learning: Causes and consequences of emotional interactions." In D. B. McLeod & V. M. Adams (eds) *Affect and Mathematical Problem Solving: A New Perspective* (pp. 3–19). New York: Springer-Verlag.

McLeod, D. B. (1992), "Research on affect in mathematics education: a reconceptualization." In D. A. Grouws (ed.) *Handbook of Research on Mathematics Teaching and Learning: a Project of the National Council of Teachers of Mathematics* (pp. 575–596). New York: Macmillan.

O'Connor, M. C. (1998), "Can we trace the 'efficacy of social constructivism'?" In P. D. Pearson & A. Iran-Nejad (eds) *Review of Research on Education, Vol. 22* (pp. 1–25). Washington, DC: American Education Research Association

Op't Eynde, P., De Corte, E., & Verschaffel, L. (1999), "Balancing between cognition and affect: Students' mathematics-related beliefs and their emotions during problem solving."

In E. Pehkonen & G. Törner (eds) *Mathematical Beliefs and Their Impact on Teaching and Learning of Mathematics. Proceedings of the Workshop in Oberwolfach, November 21–27, 1999* (pp. 97–105). Duisburg, Germany: Gerhard Mercator University.

Op't Eynde, P., De Corte, E., & Verschaffel, L. (2000), *From Trait to State: Analyzing Students' Beliefs and Emotions During Mathematical Problem Solving.* Paper presented at the 7th Workschop on Achievement and Task Motivation, May 2000 in Leuven, Belgium.

Ortony, A., Clore, G. L., & Collins, A. (1988), *The Cognitive Structure of Emotions.* New York: Cambridge University Press.

Paris, S. G., & Turner, J. C. (1994), "Situated motivation." In P. R. Pintrich, D. R. Brown & C. E. Weinstein (eds) *Student Motivation, Cognition, and Learning: Essays in Honor of Wilbert J. McKeachie* (pp. 213–238). Hillsdale, NJ: Lawrence Erlbaum Associates.

Pekrun, R. (1990), "Emotion and motivation in educational psychology." In P. J. D. Drenth, J. A. Sergeant & R. J. Takens (eds) *European Perspectives in Psychology: Theoretical, Psychometrics, Personality, Development, Educational, Cognitive, Gerontological Vol. 1* (pp. 265–295). Chichester, UK: John Whiley & Sons.

Power, M., & Dalgleish, T. (1997), *Cognition and Emotion: Form Order to Disorder.* Sussex, UK: Erlbaum Taylor & Francis Ltd.

Prawat, R. S., & Anderson, A. L. H. (1994), "The affective experiences of children during mathematics." *Journal of Mathematical Behavior 13*, 201–222.

Rogoff, B. (1995), "Observing sociocultural activity on three planes: participatory appropriation, guided participation, and apprenticeship." In J. V. Wertsch, P. del Rio & A. Alvarez (eds) *Sociocultural Studies of Mind* (pp. 139–164). New York: Cambridge University Press.

Salomon, G., & Perkins, D. N. (1998), "Individual and social aspects of learning." In P. D. Pearson & A. Iran-Nejad (eds) *Review of Research on Education, Vol. 23* (pp. 1–25). Washington, DC: American Educational Research Association.

Seegers, G., & Boekaerts, M. (1993), "Task motivation and mathematics in actual task situations." *Learning and Instruction 3*, 133–150.

Taylor, C. (1985), *Human Agency and Language: Philophical Papers I.* New York: Cambridge University Press.

Turner, J. C., & Meyer, D. K. (1999), "Integrating classroom context into motivation theory and research: Rationales, methods, and implications." In T. C. Urdan (ed.) *Advances in Motivation and Achievement, Vol. 11. The Role of Context* (pp. 87–121). Stamford, Connecticut: JAI Press Inc.

van der Veer, R., & Valsiner, J. (eds). (1994), *The Vygotsky Reader.* Oxford, UK: Blackwell Publishers Ltd.

Volet, S. (1999), "Motivation within and across cultural-educational contexts: A multidimensional perspective." In T. C. Urdan (ed.) *Advances in Motivation and Achievement, Vol. 11. The Role of Context* (pp. 185–231). Stamford, Connecticut: JAI Press Inc.

Wenger, E. (1998), *Communities of Practice: Learning, Meaning, and Identity.* Cambridge, UK: Cambridge University Press.

Wertsch, J. V. (1991), "A sociocultural approach to socially shared cognition." In L. B. Resnick, J. M. Levine *et al.* (eds) *Perspectives on Socially Shared Cognition* (pp. 85–100). Washington, DC: American Psychological Association.

Wittgenstein, L. (1953), *Philosophical Investigations/Philosophische Untersuchungen.* Oxford, UK: Basil Blackwell.

Part IV

Perceived Learning Environments and Motivation

Chapter 9

Perceived Learning Environments and the Individual Learning Process: The Mediating Role of Motivation in Learning

Marold Wosnitza & Peter Nenniger

Questions about the mode and impact of conditions of learning have been part of discussions about societal culture and identity throughout history. Within the European history of instruction it is a traditional and permanent issue, with examples such as:

- Plato's deliberations about prerequisites for a Socratic Dialogue (Platon, 1957; see also Prange, 1973; 1986), where choosing and asking questions works as a motivator within the course of understanding;
- Comenius' promise of the efficiency of his didactical method (Comenius, 1627/1910) which is based on learning as a natural function of unfolding in growth;
- Pestalozzi's reflections on "The Method of Basic Education (Elementarerziehung)", which include intellect ("the head"), skill ("the hand") and motivation ("the heart") with equal significance as the main targets (Pestalozzi, 1826/1979); or
- Herbart's lectures on structure and interaction of cognition and motivation in "Educating Instruction (Erzieherischer Unterricht)" (e.g., Herbart, 1806/1968), where a didactical theory is conceptualised in which efficient learning environments are proposed that explicitly take the correspondence between content (referring to practical philosophy) and learner characteristics (referring to psychological ideas about cognition and motivation) into consideration.

As for more recent contributions of the past century, within the different cultural approaches of the European continent, the Piagetian tradition in Hans Aebli's oeuvre (Aebli, 1997) should be mentioned, or — even closer to motivational arguments — Joachim Lompscher's work (Lompscher, 1966; 1999) having its anchors in the tradition of Galperin. From the North American continent we should not forget the controversy between David Ausubel (e.g., Ausubel, 1968) and Jerome Bruner (e.g., Bruner, 1961) and also Robert Gagné's Conditions of Learning (Gagné, 1965), where, even before the start of the most recent period of research on processes of cognition and motivation (Brown, 1994; Weinstein & Mayer, 1986), roles and structures of instructional environments were intensively

Motivation in Learning Contexts: Theoretical Advances and Methodological Implications, pages 171–187.
Copyright © 2001 by Elsevier Science Ltd.
All rights of reproduction in any form reserved.
ISBN: 0-08-043990-X

discussed. Following those itineraries it seems that learning, as an interaction between environment and personality, has also been subject to a pendulum phenomenon in its theoretical perspectives. The most recent contributions about concepts like Situated Learning (Anderson *et al.*, 1996; Brown *et al.*, 1989; Greeno, 1997) or Cognitive Apprenticeship (Collins *et al.*, 1989) are a vivid testimony in this respect. Furthermore, we should not forget research on social climate, school climate, class climate and the fact that many theoretical ideas about learning have led to a wide variety of instructional settings, materials and diagnostic instruments. Just think back to Comenius' Orbis Sensualium Pictus (Comenius, 1657/1777) or consider the impressive number of contexts and antecedents related to instruments which were developed, tested and validated both in Europe and the United States in the past century (c.f. Arter & Spandel, 1992; Dreesmann *et al.*, 1992; Pieters *et al.*, 1990). It seems that recent developments from research on the processes of cognition, emotion and motivation inside the learner quite paradoxically revitalised interest in the significance of contextual antecedents outside the learner (c.f. also Stallings, 1995; Sternberg & Horvath, 1995).

From a perspective that is also committed to the course of reflections in this field over the past centuries, the following ideas about the significance of learning environments might also be regarded as a necessary complement to research with special attention to the learners' motivational conditions (c.f. Boekaerts & Nenniger, 1999; Nenniger & Wosnitza, 1997). Therefore, the main focus of this chapter is to give insight into possible interactions coming from those external variables that can be expected to be significant within motivational components within the individual learning process. For this purpose, the influence of the subjective perception of a social learning environment on individual learning will be taken as an illustrative example, which is outlined, embedded in a frame of theoretical deliberations, and complemented with conclusions from a number of empirical findings.

Environmental Conditions of Learning and Motivation Processes

The first topic addresses the question of how to conceptualise learning environments. Two different levels of description have to be considered when conceptualising and then operationalising given aspects of learning contexts: the *perspective of reality*, and the *object of reality*. The above dichotonomy can be characterised as follows:

Perspective of Reality. From a systematic point of view based on sociological theories, reality may be understood as a sort of environment that is declared to be independent of its individual perception. However, within such realities it is possible to exert influence with the individuals' behaviour. Thus, learning environments can be regarded as a specific part of such reality that can be perceived and influenced by individual learning. The above view enables us to distinguish between two perspectives of reality. Reality can either be described from an *objective* or from a *subjective* point of view (c.f. Dreesmann, 1982). The *objective perspective* refers to a way of regarding reality which is least affected by individual perceptions (e.g., referring to class size, to supply of literature in a university library, to presence of textbooks, to provision of computers, to intensity of internet access, etc.). In contrast, the *subjective perspective* of reality refers to its individual perceptions (e.g., taking into consideration the individual learner's perceptions of the quality of his/her relationships to the teacher, the student's perceptions of the atmosphere of the classroom, etc.).

Object of Reality. Learning environments or learning conditions as objects of a study can be equally examined in terms of their content or nature, which may be *material* or *social*. *Material dimensions* of the environment in a university or in a school setting are represented, for example, by specific library resources or computer equipment available (which can also be described from an objective or a subjective perspective). In contrast, *social dimensions* are represented in terms of person (or role) dimensions, as for example by a student–teacher ratio (objective perspective) or the student's perceived quality of his/her relationship to the teacher or to fellow students (subjective perspective).

An intersection of the dichotomic "perspective" and "object" dimension of reality, as described above, provides a useful conceptual framework for the description and analysis of complex learning environments. The four different combinations arising from this intersection form a matrix of learning environments illustrated in Figure 1. The content of each combination (i.e., each cell of the matrix) can be the subject of a description and analysis of a concrete learning environment and is distinct from the remaining three combinations because of its respective specificity. Based on findings from research (c.f. Wosnitza & Hahl, 1998, Wosnitza, 2000), we would like to argue that each form of description contributes in a unique way to our overall understanding of the significance of contextual dimensions to learning and motivation.

		Perspective	
		Objective	Subjective
Object	Material	A	B
	Social	C	D

Figure 1: Matrix for the description of learning environments.

In this paragraph, each of the four combinations from the intersection between the dimensions object and perspective of reality (i.e., the cells A, B, C, D in Figure 1) will be introduced briefly. The rest of the chapter, however, will concentrate on the subjective perspective of social reality (cell D).

Objective Perspective of Material Reality (Cell A). The objective description of the material reality of learning environments requires a description of objects in the learning environment with objective methods such as counting, measuring, etc. The respective studies refer for example to effects of resource inputs on education where outcomes show rather heterogeneous results, even due partly to differences in research methodology (e.g., Hedges *et al.*, 1994). Further studies, with partly ambiguous results, refer to parameters like book size on a specific field in the university library, size of the classroom surface or quantity of available and functioning overhead projectors.

Subjective Perspective of Material Reality (Cell B). The subjective description of the material reality of learning environments consists of describing the material surroundings with subjective assessments. The general idea refers to the possible influence of material and institutional settings that may influence, in addition to characteristics of content, the frame or the perspective in which the individual's learning and motivation takes place. Research from the 70s and 80s of the last century about mainly positive effects of classroom design on pupils' and teachers' motivation (Gallimore & Tharp, 1974; Greet, 1984) serves as an illustrative example. Further issues in this field of research are effects of the subjective perceptions of present learning resources or of the course safety standards on student motivation and the learning process.

Objective Perspective of Social Reality (Cell C). The objective description of the social reality of learning environments refers to the social aspects of a learning environment by objective methods. A typical example is represented by research on the influence of the class size with the main result that smaller classes correlate with higher student motivation and that specific outcomes mostly depend on the subject (Chiu *et al.*, 1999; Glass & Smith, 1978; Wildberg & Rost, 1997). However, the respective studies — sometimes of doubtful quality (c.f. critique of von Saldern, 1992) — are mostly based on instructional methods design and rarely on longitudinal measures. Other research examples examine the number of student–teacher interactions during a lesson, the amount and manner of performance feedback by the teacher or the way the class is assembled.

Subjective Perspective of Social Reality (Cell D). The subjective description of the social reality of learning environments refers to a description of social aspects of the learning environment on an individual perception level. As explained in detail later on, it mainly encompasses the interaction between teacher, class and student characteristics in the context of motivation. An illustrative example is research on the influence of the individually perceived sense of autonomy on motivation that shows gradually differential effects on intrinsic motivation (Deci & Ryan, 1985). Further issues in this context relate to class climate or teacher behaviour.

Altogether, the results of the representative research examples cannot ensure a univocal tendency. They give a rather heterogeneous picture of research methods, research issues and resulting effects. As the most promising part, the subjective perspective of a social reality, insofar as research in this field is concerned, shows the strongest effects or at least the closest correspondence with motivation. In consequence, our detailed attention will be focused on this field. In order to be able to analyse the determining factors of subjective perception of the social components in a learning environment, and to comprehend their importance and their influence later on, one has to identify on the one hand the components of this complex social system, and on the other hand the relations between these components. In a real instructional situation such descriptors can be a) the teacher, b) the individual student and c) the class or the group of students which a student is part of.

These three descriptors have a direct systemic connection with each other, which can be described by an intersection between two descriptors which also defines their relation. This leads to the following three kinds of relations: d) student–teacher relations, e) student–class relations and f) class–teacher relations.

The complex correspondences between the system components and the three kinds of relations are elucidated in Figure 2. It presents the three social components of the learning environment as circles and the three kinds of relationships as their intersections. Altogether, the resulting six areas represent the aspects of a learning environment that have an influence on the individual learning motivation

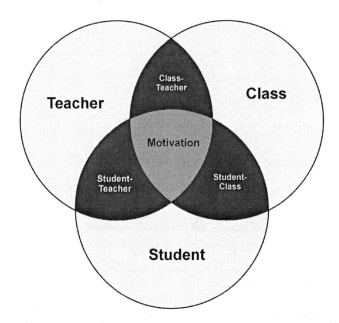

Figure 2: Areas of the social system "learning motivation".

and thus form the respective social system of learning motivation. The question referring to the significance of aspects of a subjectively perceived learning environment on motivation within schools and universities will be examined in the following. Each of the six areas described in Figure 2 (Descriptors "Student", "Class", "Teacher", and their intersections "Student–Class", "Student–Teacher", "Class–Teacher") will be illustrated separately.

Descriptor "Student"

When describing the component "student" in the social systems, *sense of autonomy* in a learning environment is extremely significant (Deci & Ryan, 1985; Prenzel *et al.*, 1998). Learning environments in which students' efforts to achieve autonomy are supported tend also to be conducive to developing motivation based on self-direction. This sense of autonomy refers to the entire process of learning in which individuals take the initiative and, with or without the help of others, ascertain their learning needs, formulate their learning goals, determine human and material resources, select and implement learning strategies and assess their learning outcomes (Knowles, 1975). By emphasising the sense of autonomy, a degree of freedom for the student is implicated which refers to various aspects of the learning process. This degree of freedom is based on the degree of self-direction with regard to the arrangement of individual learning (*learning arrangement*), on the degree of participation with regard to the *teaching arrangement* and on the extent to which students can show *initiative of their own* in a learning environment.

Descriptor "Class"

The component "class" denotes the subjective perception of the interaction structure that arises through given preconditions and interactions, which have taken place.

Schiefele (1978b) describes the "dynamic altogether" of group structure which, for the individual, is a complex emotional condition such as group atmosphere. It is influenced by the interaction between individual group members, by the teacher's leader behaviour, by the relationship between the students, by their needs and their fulfilment and by the degree of social difference and the group's integration in general. In institutionalised learning, the different interactions imprint upon shared forms of processing experiences. This experience contains an aspect which is shared by all students in a group (class) and in which the perceived atmosphere can be determined. For example, a favourable group atmosphere also has a positive effect on the students' motivation (Moos & Tricket, 1974; Schiefele, 1978b).

Descriptor "Teacher"

Because of their responsibility for the arrangement of learning environments, the part played by the system component "teacher" is not to be underestimated. It is up to the teacher's competence to direct the lessons in such a manner that the requirement of self-direction, namely supporting learning environments — connecting teaching and learning processes appropriately — is fulfilled. Three factors which relate to the structure of processes in teaching and learning arrangements play a crucial part in this context: first, the course of the lesson, second, the clarification of connections and third, the creation of transparency.

- The *course of the lesson* refers to the basic process or macro-structure of the lesson with content, tasks and methods as the main point of focus. Factors such as redundancy or varying the processes are significant in this context (Doyle, 1986).
- *Clarification of connections* in a lesson refers to integrating content and subjects within a course on the one hand, but on the other hand beyond the course boundaries (Jacobs, 1989; Klein, 1996).
- Whilst the aspect of connections concentrates on classifying subjects and content, the *creation of transparency* refers to understanding the material and to clarity of goals. Clarity of goals stands for clarity of learning goals and also for clarity of training goals. In this case, the main point of focus is in estimating how far the students can understand why certain contents are being conveyed. The transparency of what has to be learned is an important component on the path to helping the student to interweave new information with his/her own cognitions and understand its meaning so the information can be reprocessed and given a new meaning again and again (Doyle, 1986).

Intersection of Descriptors "Student" and "Class"

The extent to which a person feels able to act autonomously depends on the conditions of the learning environment, especially the extent to which the person feels socially involved (Deci & Ryan, 1985, Prenzel *et al.*, 1998). A positive sense of *social inclusion* is an important component of personality development, for social contact with others forms the basis of acquiring a realistic self-image. The appreciation offered by the classmates determines the feeling of our own value. This means that the type and extent of the "student–class" relationship is of great significance for supporting motivation (Krapp, 1996; Prenzel *et al*, 1998). Thus, conditions for education in which students can co-operate and compete have to be created in contrast to conditions in which they are isolated. In this context, *acceptance* or *rejection* of a "student" by the "class" is a point of focus.

Intersection of Descriptors "Student" and "Teacher"

The intersection between "Student" and "Teacher" forms a further important relation. At this point, teacher behaviour and acceptance converge. Two perspectives have to be considered here: On the one hand, the subjectively perceived teacher behaviour as a motivational component which refers to support of the students' self-concept, and, on the other hand, the level of demand which represents a performance oriented component.

Teacher Behaviour. This component is based on a personal dimension that concerns the teacher's behaviour towards the student. This relationship dimension includes two complexes: first, the co-operation between teacher and student and second, the individual extent to which the teacher attends to the student.

Whether a student feels disregarded or supported by the teacher or not affects the individual learning experience. If the teachers take little interest in the students or disregard them, the students in question experience this as negative (Brophy & Good, 1986).

Level of Demand. The assessment of one's own abilities is associated with self-estimate and its maintenance or even increase in various studies (c.f. in Möller & Köller, 1996). Whether students assess the demands made on them as fitting their own goal-related ability assessment as *optimal* or as *too high* or *too low* also depends on the subjectively perceived degree of difficulty of the subject. A level of demand the students deem optimal has a promotive effect on their intrinsic motivation and increases their motivation for work.

Intersection of Descriptors "Class" and "Teacher"

Similar to the intersection between "Student" and "Teacher", the motivational and the performance-oriented aspects also converge at this point. But, as opposed to the individual perspective of the "Student–Teacher" relationship, a collective perspective is taken in the "Class–Teacher" relationship. To take an example: *Teacher behaviour* or *level of demand* as characteristics perceived by the individual learners are now regarded as components of a social structure which affect in turn the social dynamics that may emerge in a class.

Motivation and the Subjective Perceptions of the Social Learning Environment

In our studies on self-directed learning at universities we analysed in which way such environmental conditions are related to the main motivational aspects that we identified in our former studies. These aspects are "Learning Needs" and "Motivational Control".

a) The notion of *Learning Needs* is defined by processes in which a subjective deficit of declarative and procedural knowledge is ascertained, assessed and linked with personal expectations, starting from an anticipated learning goal and the estimated individual learning conditions.

Identifying a learning goal or learning need is highly significant to individual self-directed learning processes because it initiates the learning process (Knowles, 1975; Nenniger, 1999; Straka, 2000). Only if the learner determines a learning need of certain importance to him/herself (i.e., either out of low interest because of an insignificant test or out of high interest because of a career related interview), the learning process will take place. One critical aspect that becomes evident is that motivational factors play a major part in the area of learning needs. Referring to Knowles' (1975) idea of learning needs and based on results from research domains of task motivation and interest, the motivational concept "Learning Needs" with the constituent subordinate constructs "Content-oriented Interest" and "Procedural Interest" becomes evident (c.f. Nenniger, 1999; Straka *et al.*, 1996; Straka & Nenniger, 1995). "Content-oriented Interest" describes the students' personal interest in the subject matter; "Procedural Interest" reflects the students' anticipation of learning strategies, which are indispensable when dealing with a task. Both, the "Procedural Interest" and the "Content-oriented Interest" determine a person's involvement in possible subsequent learning and are based on the general "Expectancy-x-Value Model" (Atkinson, 1964; McClelland, 1955; Nenniger, 1993). Hence, the action tendency of "Content-oriented Interest" results from the interaction between the perceived personal sense of a task's content (value component) and the expectancy of being able to explore this content, whereas the action tendency of "Procedural Interest" results from the interaction between the perceived usefulness of a procedure required for an adequate task treatment (value component) and the subjective competence which is required by the procedure (expectancy component).

b) The notion of *Motivational Control* addresses the fact that efficient learning demands strategies direct the learner's own learning process. This applies to the planning of, and to the selection of, learning strategies as well as to the control of the process of understanding and modifying procedures when learning difficulties arise. Those controlling strategies, which serve executive and self-regulatory purposes, are considered as keys to independent learning (c.f. Wright, 1992). One of these controlling strategies is conceived as "Motivational Control" because it refers to the individual motivation to reach an anticipated learning goal. On the one hand, it refers to judging the current significance of reaching an aspired goal, i.e., the subjective importance of a possible success or failure, and on the other hand to the specific goal orientation which can be oriented either towards the support of reaching goals (appetitive) or avoiding them (aversive) (Atkinson, 1964; Berlyne, 1960; Heckhausen, 1977; McClelland, 1955; Nenniger, 1988; 1993).

Some Additional Support from Empirical Findings

Despite the systematic arguments and results from research presented above, some additional support can also be reported from empirical findings of a project referring to self-directed learning at universities.[1] In particular, those hypotheses about the importance of social, cognitive and motivational conditions that reflect motivational aspects of academic learning will be taken into closer consideration.

The methodology of this project is based on an approach that has been pursued in a majority of studies about effects of emotional, motivational and social characteristics in the classroom. The instruments refer to situations which are remembered by the individual learners. Thus, they do not represent a particular frame of mind as it occurs in a specific moment of a learning situation (e.g., Schiefele & Csikszentmihalyi 1995; Krapp, 1996), but they reflect more lasting and perhaps more general perceptions or attitudes of learning and its environment (e.g., Pintrich et al., 1991; Nenniger & Wosnitza, 1999) and address in consequence the rather enduring peculiarities of motivation. The adequate forms of such instruments are preferably interviews or questionnaires.

The core of this project is based on interviews with 189 students of educational sciences and teaching at German universities.

The subjective perceptions of the social learning environment were measured by the "Multidimensional Instrument for the Study of Perceptions of Social learning Environments at Universities (MIPSE-UN)". The items of the MIPSE-UN were based on the "Instrument for the Study of Subjective Perceptions of Social Learning Environments in Initial Commercial Training" (ISSP-ICT) (Wosnitza & Hahl, 1998) and were adapted to the university context. All scales have reliabilities from 0.44 to 0.79 and explained variances as validity parameters from 53.7 percent to 70.8 percent (for details see Wosnitza, 2000).

In order to test different aspects of self-direction in academic learning, the "Questionnaire on Motivated Self-directed Learning at Universities" (QMSL-UN) was submitted to the students. The items of the QMSL-UN were adapted from the "Questionnaire on Motivated Self-directed Learning in Initial Commercial Training" (QMSL-ICT) (Nenniger, 1999; Nenniger et al., 1997). All scales have reliabilities from 0.41 to 0.89 and explained variances as validity parameters from 51.3 percent to 83.6 percent (for details see Wosnitza, 2000).

The outcomes of a detailed statistical analysis (for details see Wosnitza, 2000) refer to scales from the MIPSE-UN that can be summarised as *Environmental Conditions*, the composite scale *Motivational Control* from the QMSL-UN, and also from this questionnaire, *Content-oriented Interest* (referring to contents of the courses) and *Procedural Interest* (referring to the adequate use of selected learning strategies).

With respect to the preceding arguments, the following findings are suitable to additionally support the particular importance of environmental factors for motivated student learning.

Even at a first glance on a crude basis of correlational analysis, the results show that the environmental factors share only small amounts with the motivational control of the learning processes (see Table 1). Combining business with

---

[1] Grant of the "Ministerium für Bildung, Wissenschaft und Weiterbildung des Landes Rheinland-Pfalz", Mainz (Germany).

Table 1: Correlations between elements of instructional environment and motivational control of learning

	Environmental Conditions					
	Class Atmosphere	Sense of Autonomy	Class Management	Social Inclusion	Teacher Behaviour	Level of Demand
Motivational Control	**0.17**	0.09	0.13	0.14	0.08	**0.24**
	p = 0.04	p = 0.28	p = 0.12	p = 0.09	p = 0.32	**p = 0.00**

pleasure through the construction of a demanding (r = 0.24) and agreeable (r = 0.17) learning environment represents the most closely related factors to motivational control of the ongoing learning process. With respect to the concomitance between the environmental conditions and the interest concerned, the relative weight of the variables involved is clearly higher (c.f. Figures 3 and 4). The respective coefficients (R = 0.53 and R = 0.42) are at least of medium impor-

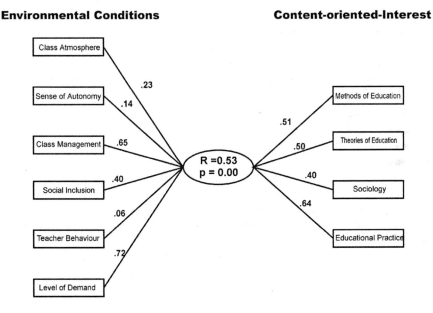

Figure 3: Canonical correlation between environmental conditions and content-oriented interest.

Environmental Conditions   **Procedural Interest**

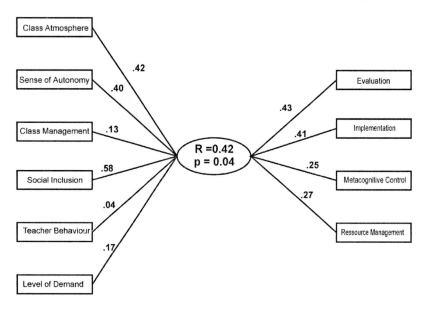

Figure 4: Canonical correlation between environmental conditions and procedural interest.

tance. Thus, if the relationship between Environmental Conditions and Interest is not regarded as an overall, but as a specific structure, the resulting covariation gains considerably in importance. However, specificity also means that the structures are different depending on the dimension of interest involved. With respect to Content-oriented Interest (c.f. Figure 3), Level of Demand, Class Management and Social Inclusion are the determining components of Environmental Conditions, whereas the content on the interest side (Methods of Education, Theories of Education, Sociology, Educational Practice) shows no particular specificity. Regarding the covariation between Environmental Conditions and Procedural Interest (c.f. Figure 4), the relative weights are different in two ways: On the one hand different, environmental conditions contribute to the relationship with significant weight. Social Inclusion, Class Atmosphere and Sense of Autonomy are the most characteristic variables. On the other hand, Procedural Interest is differentially concerned, Evaluation and Implementation are the variables of primary importance.

Summarising the main result we may therefore notice that Interests are primarily connected with the Environmental Conditions of Learning. However, the concern is in so far of a two-way specificity as the different aspects of the Learning Environment are affected depending on the kind of interest, and in a differential manner: Content-oriented Interest is rather holistically, but Procedural Interest rather specifically concerned.

Conclusions

Overal these results underline the importance of subjectively perceived learning environments for learning motivation in a global way.

The rather restricted significance of motivational components in classroom settings are already well known from other research (e.g., Eigler *et al.*, 1982; Nenniger *et al.*, 1993) on learning in instructional contexts. It is obvious that motivation is only part of the ongoing cognitive, content-related and social components of learning. Furthermore, Level of Demand and social aspects like Class Atmosphere are well known factors in this respect (Atkinson, 1957; Heckhausen, 1977; Nicholls, 1984; Schiefele, 1978a). More specifically interest seems to be a more differentiated object. On the one hand the general condition for arousing interest is embedded in good class management. Obviously, if learning in the classroom is not well structured, there is no way open to develop interest. On the other hand, interest has to be regarded from two independent perspectives: it includes the subject, the content to be learned and also the itinerary, the procedure that enables the learner to incorporate it. Thus, class management stands together with level of demand and social inclusion for the necessary boundaries that instigate and guide content orientation. The learner has to be assured that the content has to be, and can be, learned and that all emotional and social obstacles can be kept outside. However, class management also stands, together with sense of autonomy and class atmosphere, for freedom and autonomy given to the learner. This enables him/her to step towards the learning objective without being hindered in his/her actions.

What could be gathered from the results is, on the one hand, not surprisingly, the ratification of the traditional ideas which emphasise that motivation has to be understood as an embedded variable (c.f. in particular Pestalozzi's function of "the heart", Bruner's link of learning strategies with motivational antecedents). But on the other hand, the outcomes might also serve as a refined version of Herbart's "Erziehender Unterricht (Educating Instruction)", based on the recent findings of current research on learning and instruction and backed by results from empirical research. The main idea that instruction only meets its objectives if it can take place in a favourable environment and if the learner has a fascinating objective and an intriguing escort in the field — and two main components of this traditional concept, "Regierung", (i.e., government of learners to keep away bad influences in the instructional environment), and "Zucht", (i.e., cultivation of the learner to organise learning environments in a way that instigates and fosters learners to reach the end of the way and to reach the objective) — appear now more specifically as dimensions in the interaction between components of learning environments (e.g., as *class management* or *level of demand*) and antecedents of motivated learning (e.g., as *content-oriented interest*).

However, this refined interpretation of Herbart's concept is nevertheless a restricted one, insofar as it only addresses the subjective perception of the environment and mainly the motivational component of academic learning. For this reason, further research is needed that opens the door with regard to learning environments towards a more precise knowledge of the remaining cells of the interactions between the peculiarities of the object and the perspective of reality and combines it successfully with our growing knowledge about the mutual effects of cognition and motivation in learning.

References

Aebli, H. (1997), *Zwölf Grundformen des Lehrens* [Twelve Basic Forms of Instruction] (9th ed.). Stuttgart: Klett Cotta.

Anderson, J. R., Reder, L. M., & Simon, H. A. (1996), "Situated learning and education." *Educational Researcher 25* (4), 5–11.

Arter, J. A., & Spandel, V. (1992), "Using portfolios of student work in instruction and assessment." *Educational Measurement: Issues and Practice 11* (1), 36–44.

Atkinson, J. W. (1957), "Motivational determinants of risk-taking behaviour." *Psychological Review 64*, 359–372.

Atkinson, J. W. (1964), *An Introduction to Motivation*. New York: Van Nostrand.

Ausubel, D. P. (1968), *Educational Psychology: A Cognitive View*. New York: Holt, Rinehart/Winston.

Berlyne, D. E. (1960), *Conflict, Arousal, and Curiosity*. New York: McGraw-Hill.

Boekaerts, M., & Nenniger, P. (1999), Introduction. *European Journal of Psychology of Education 14* (1), 3–9.

Brophy, J. E., & Good, T. L. (1986), Teacher behavior and student achievement. In M. Wittrock (ed.), *Handbook of Research on Teaching* (pp. 328–375). New York: MacMillan.

Brown, A. L. (1994), "The advancement of learning." *Educational Researcher 23* (8), 4–12.

Brown, J. S., Collins, A., & Duguid, P. (1989), "Situated cognitions and the culture of learning." *Educational Researcher 18*, 32–42.

Bruner, J. S. (1961), "The act of discovery." *Harvard Educational Review 31*, 21–32.

Chiu, S., Wardrop J. L., & Ryan, K. E. (1999), Use of the Unbalanced Nested ANOVA to examine the Relationship of Class Size to Student Ratings of Instructional Quality (ED 432042).

Collins, A., Brown, J. S., & Newman, S. E. (1989), "Cognitive apprenticeship: Teaching the crafts of reading, writing, and mathematics." In L. B. Resnick (ed.) *Knowing, Learning and Instruction: Essays in Honour of Robert Glaser* (pp. 453–494). Hillsdale, New Jersey: Lawrence Erlbaum Associates.

Comenius, J. A. (1910), *The Great Didactic*. London: A. & C. Black (Original work published 1627).

Comenius, J. A. (1777), *Orbis Sensualium Pictus: J. A. Comenius's Visible World or a Nomenclature and Pictures of all the Chief Things that are in the World*. London: For S. Leacroft (Original work published 1657).

Deci, E. L., & Ryan, R. M. (1985), *Intrinsic Motivation and Self-Determination in Human Behavior*. New York: Plenum Press.

Doyle, W. (1986), "Classroom organization and management." In M. C. Wittrock (ed.) *Handbook of Research on Teaching* (3rd ed., pp. 392–431). New York: MacMillan Publishing Company.

Dreesmann, H. (1982), *Unterrichtsklima: Wie Schüler den Unterricht Wahrnehmen* [Classroom Climate: How Students Perceive Instruction]. Weinheim: Beltz Verlag.

Dreesmann, H., Eder, F., Fend, H., Pekrun, R., v. Saldern, M. *et al.* (1992), "Schulklima" [School climate]. In K. Ingenkamp, R. S. Jäger, H. Petillon & B. Wolf (eds) *Empirische*

Pädagogik 1970–1990 [Empirical Education 1970–1990] (Vol. 2, pp. 656–682). Weinheim: Deutscher Studienverlag.

Eigler, G., Macke, G., & Nenniger, P. (1982), "Entwicklung Kognitiver Strukturen — kognitive und motivationale komponenten" [Development of cognitive structures — Cognitive and motivational components]. In H. Mandl & L. Kötter (eds) *Kognitive Prozesse und Unterricht* [Cognitive Processes and Instruction] (pp. 169–206). Düsseldorf: Schwann.

Gagné, R. M. (1965), *The Conditions of Learning*. New York: Holt, Rinehart and Winston.

Gallimore, R., & Tharp, R. G. (1974), KEEP Motivational Research: Strategy and Results. Technical Report #24 (ED 158848).

Glass, G. V., & Smith, M. L. (1978), *Meta-Analysis of Research on the Relationship of Class-Size and Achievement*. Boulder/CO: Far West Laboratory for Educational Research.

Greeno, J. G. (1997), "On claims that answer the wrong questions." *Educational Researcher 26* (1), 5–17.

Greet, H. G. (1984), "Jazzing up your classroom." *Learning 13* (1), 68–71.

Heckhausen, H. (1977), "Achievement motivation and its constructs: A cognitive model." *Motivation and Emotion 1* (4), 283–329.

Hedges, L., Laine, R. D., & Greenwald, R. (1994), "Does money matter? A meta-analysis of studies of the effects of differential school inputs on student outcomes." *Educational Researcher 23*, 5–14.

Herbart, J. F. (1968), *Allgemeine Pädagogik aus dem Zweck der Erziehung abgeleitet* [General Pedagogies Derived from the Purpose of Education]. Paderborn: Schöningh (Original work published 1806).

Jacobs, H. H. (ed.). (1989), *Interdisciplinary Curriculum: Design and Implementation*. Alexandria: ASCD.

Klein, J. T. (1996), *Crossing Boundaries: Knowledge, Disciplinarities, and Interdisciplinarities*. Charlottesville: University Press of Virginia.

Knowles, M. S. (1975), *Self Directed Learning*. Chicago: Follet.

Krapp, A. (1996), *Interest Motivation and Learning — an Educational Psychological Perspective*. Paper presented at the International Conference on Motivation, Landau.

Lompscher, J. (1966), *Kenntniserwerb und Geistige Entwicklung in der Unterstufe* [Acquisition of Knowledge and Cognitive Development in Elementary Education]. Berlin: Volk und Wissen.

Lompscher, J. (1999), "Motivation and activity." *European Journal of Psychology of Education 14* (1), 11–22.

McClelland, D. C. (1955), "Notes for a revised theory of motivation." In D. C. McClelland (ed.) *Studies in Motivation* (pp. 226–234). New York: Appleton.

Möller, J., & Köller, O. (eds). (1996), *Emotionen, Kognition und Schulleistung* [Emotion, Cognition and School Achievement]. Weinheim: Beltz.

Moos, R. H., & Trickett, E. J. (1974), *Classroom Environment Scale Manual*. Palo Alto: Consulting Psychologists Press.

Nenniger, P. (1988), *Das Pädagogische Verhältnis als Motivationales Konstrukt: Ein Beitrag zur Lehr-Lern-Theoretischen Analyse eines Pädagogischen Paradigmas* [The Pedagogical Relationship as a Motivational Construct: An Analytical Contribution for a Pedagogical Paradigm from the Perspective of Learning and Instruction]. Weinheim: Deutscher Studien Verlag.

Nenniger, P. (1993), "Von der Summativen zur Strukturellen Betrachtung des Unterrichts: Zu den theoretischen Folgen des methodologischen Zugangs in der Unterrichtsforschung" [From the summative to the structural view of instruction: Theoretical consequences from a methodological approach to instructional research]. *Empirische Pädagogik 7* (1), 21–35.

Nenniger, P. (1999), "On the role of motivation in self-directed learning: The 'two-shells-model of motivated self-directed learning' as a structural explanatory concept." *European Journal of Psychology of Education 14* (1), 71–86.

Nenniger, P., Eigler, G., & Macke, G. (1993), *Studien zur Mehrdimensionalität von Lehr-Lern-Prozessen* [Research on the Multi-Dimensionality of Learning and Instruction]. Bern: Lang.

Nenniger, P., Straka, G. A., Spevacek, G., & Wosnitza, M. (1997), *Ein Instrument zur Erfassung von Bedingungen Motivierten Selbstgesteuerten Lernens in der Kaufmännischen Erstausbildung — in Schule und Betrieb* [Questionnaire on Motivated Self-Directed Learning in Initial Commercial Training (QMSL-ICT)]. Landau: ZepF.

Nenniger, P., & Wosnitza, M. (1997), "Motiviertes Selbstgesteuertes Lernen — eine Alternative zum methodischen angeleiteten unterricht?" [Is motivated self-directed learning an alternative of planfully induced instruction?]. In R. Dubs & R. Luzi (eds) *25 Jahre IWP: Schule in Wissenschaft, Politik und Praxis* [25 Years IWP: School in Science, Politics and Practice] (pp. 545–560). Universität St. Gallen: IWP.

Nenniger, P., & Wosnitza, M. (1999), *Interaction between Learning Environments and Learning Interests as Prerequisites for Self-Regulation in Learning.* Paper presented at the 8th Earli Conference — Gotenbourg.

Nicholls, J. G. (1984), "Conceptions of ability and achievement motivation." In R. Ames & C. Ames (eds) *Research on Motivation in Education: Student Motivation* (Vol. 1, pp. 39–73). New York: Academic.

Pestalozzi, J. H. (1979), *Schwanengesang.* Bern: Haupt (Original work published 1826).

Pieters, J. M., Breuer, K., & Simons, P. R. J. (1990), *Learning Environments: Contributions from Dutch and German Research.* Berlin: Springer.

Pintrich, P. R., Smith, D. A. F., Garcia, T., & McKeachie, W. J. (1991), *A Manual for the use of the Motivated Strategies for Learning Questionnaire (MSLQ).* Ann Arbor, MI: MCRIPTAL, The University of Michigan.

Platon (1957), *Menon. Sämtliche Werke* [Menon. Complete Works] (Vol. 2, pp. 7–70). Hamburg: rowohlt.

Prange, K. (1973), "Platos Lehre vom Lernen in 'Menon' und das Problem des Allgemeinen" [Plato's concept of learning in 'Menon' and the problem of the universal]. *Pädagogische Rundschau 27*, 675–689.

Prange, K. (1986), *Bauformen des Unterrichts: Eine Didaktik für Lehrer* [Models of Instruction: Didactics for Teachers] (2nd ed.). Bad Heilbronn/Obb.: Klinkhardt.

Prenzel, M., Kramer, K., & Drechsel, B. (1998), "Changes in learning motivation and interest in vocational education: Halfway through the study." In L. Hoffmann, A. Krapp, K. A. Renninger & J. Baumert (eds) *Interest and Learning: Proceedings of the Second Conference on Interest and Gender.* Kiel: IPN.

Schiefele, H. (1978a), *Lernmotivation und Motivlernen: Grundzüge einer Erziehungswissenschaftlichen Motivationslehre* [Learning Motivation and Learning of Motives: Basics of an Educational Theory of Motivation]. München: Ehrenwirth.

Schiefele, H. (1978b), "Sozialpsychologie der Schulklasse" [Social psychology of the classroom]. In H. J. Apel (ed.) *Die Schulklasse ein Pädagogisches Handlungsfeld?* [Is the Classroom a Field of Education?] (pp. 61–80). Ratingen: Aloys Henn Verlag.

Schiefele, U., & Csikszentmihalyi, M. (1995), "Interest and the quality of experience in classroom." *European Journal of Psychology of Education 3*, 251–270.

Stallings, J. A. (1995), "Ensuring teaching and learning in the 21st Century." *Educational Researcher 24* (6), 4–8.

Sternberg, R. J., & Horvath, J. A. (1995), "A prototype view of expert teaching." *Educational Researcher 24* (6), 9–18.

Straka, G. A. (2000), "Modeling a more-dimensional theory of self-directed learning." In G. A. Straka (ed.) *Conceptions of Self-Directed Learning: Theoretical and Conceptional Considerations* (pp. 171–190). Münster, New York: Waxmann.

Straka, G. A., & Nenniger, P. (1995), "A conceptual framework for self-directed-learning readiness." In H. B. Long & ass. (eds) *New Dimensions in Self Directed Learning* (pp. 243–255). Oklahoma: University of Oklahoma.

Straka, G. A., Nenniger, P., Spevacek, G., & Wosnitza, M. (1996), "A model for motivated self-directed learning." *Education 53*, 19–30.

von Saldern, M. (1992), "Metaanalyse zur klassengröße — eine Kritik" [Meta-analyses on class size — a critique]. *Empirische Pädagogik 6*, 293–314.

von Wright, J. (1992), "Reflections on reflection." *Learning and Instruction 2* (1), 59–68.

Weinstein, C., & Mayer, R. (1986), "The teaching of learning strategies." In M. Wittrock (ed.) *Handbook of Research on Teaching* (3rd ed., pp. 315–328). New York: Macmillan Publishing Company.

Wildberg, S. & Rost, D. H. (1997), "Klassengröße und Geschichtskenntnisse" [Class size and knowledge in history]. *Zeitschrift für Pädagogische Psychologie 11*, 65–68.

Wosnitza, M. (2000), *Motiviertes Selbstgesteuertes Lernen im Studium: Theoretischer Rahmen, Diagnostisches Instrumentarium und Bedingungsanalyse* [Motivated Self-Directed Learning at Universities: Theoretical Frame, Diagnostical Tools and Analysis of Conditions for Learning]. Landau: VEP

Wosnitza, M., & Hahl, A. (1998), "Die Mehrdimensionalität von Selbststeuerungsfördernden Lernumgebungen in der Kaufmännischen Erstausbildung: Theoretischer Rahmen und Diagnostisches Instrumentarium" [The multidimensionality of learning environments fostering self-direction in initial commercial training: Theoretical frame and diagnostical tool]. *Empirische Pädagogik 12* (1), 3–28.

Chapter 10

Towards a Multilayer Model of Context and its Impact on Motivation

Jean-Luc Gurtner, Isabelle Monnard & Philippe A. Genoud

How dispositional or situational factors influence student motivation has been investigated at length and given various interpretations. Perceptions, judgments and behaviors of high or low achievers (Atkinson, 1957), of external or internal attributors (Weiner, 1979), of children with adaptative or maladaptive patterns (Dweck & Leggett, 1988), or pursuing various achievement goals (Pintrich, 2000) are now well understood. Characteristics which make a text interesting (Hidi, 1990; Iran-Nejad, 1987), features of a task which can elicit intrinsic rather than extrinsic motivation (Ryan & Deci, 2000) or improve students' self-appraisals (Boekaerts, 1999), as well as the motivational effects of challenging students, boosting their self-confidence, heightening their curiosity or instilling in them a sense of control and self-efficacy (Malone, 1981), are nowadays well documented and have been given a place in most teacher-training programs or recommendations for building effective tutoring systems (Lepper *et al.*, 1993).

Contextual aspects, however, have been given much less attention with respect to motivation, although the importance of context on an individual's reactions and behaviors was acknowledged long ago (Anderman & Anderman, 2000; Turner & Meyer, 2000). Biologists always insisted that no behavior of any organism could ever be understood without considering the milieu in which it lives. Using these ideas in the field of psychology, Piaget (1936; 1937), showed that the interactions between an organism and its environment always result from two complementary processes which define and delineate what the organism can understand and take from its environment (assimilation), and what extension or revision of its current structures or schemes can be made for the organism to adapt to the characteristics of the environment (accommodation).

Another important contribution to our understanding of the interplay between an individual and its immediate environment is offered by Bronfenbrenner (1986) in his ecological systems theory. This model incorporates both the idea of bidirectional influence, which takes into account both the influence of the environment on the person and the reciprocal influence of the person on the environment, and the notion of indirect influence. In Bronfenbrenner's view, a relationship between two elements can be effected by the relationship that one of these elements holds with yet another element; the kind of relationship existing between a child's family

Motivation in Learning Contexts: Theoretical Advances and Methodological Implications, pages 189–208.
Copyright © 2001 by Elsevier Science Ltd.
ISBN: 0-08-043990-X

and his or her teacher, for instance, indirectly acts upon the teacher–pupil relationship. Using Bronfenbrenner's terminology: the various microsystems in which an individual is participating, together form a more global system called a "mesosystem". Even systems with no direct influence on the developing person can also have an indirect influence on his or her development; satisfaction or tensions experienced within the work environment of a child's father, for instance, will indirectly influence a child's developmental process, as will the political, economical or social environments in which all of these systems are embedded. Bronfenbrenner calls these systems "exosystem" and "macrosystem", respectively. The study of the complex entity built by all of these systems and their interactions forms what Bronfenbrenner has called the person–process–context paradigm.

Both Piaget and Bronfenbrenner have studied the impact that context has on a person in the long run, from a developmental perspective. As Bronfenbrenner puts it: "To be effective, the interaction must occur on a fairly regular basis over extended periods of time" (Bronfenbrenner, 1995, p. 620). Other authors have focussed on more temporary impacts of the context on an individual's behavior. According to Lewin (1935), for instance, tensions are created between a person's needs or wishes and the demands placed on him/her by the environment; the tension will only be released when the adopted behavior has enabled the person to attain his or her goal. The variables of the environment, taken into account to define behavior, constitute what Lewin labelled "the field". The selection of these variables depends on what the person currently knows, perceives or experiences from the environment, not on the objective aspects of this environment. Subjective appraisal of contextual factors is, in this sense, more decisive for the adoption of a specific behavior than is the objective reality of one's environment.

Is Context a Homogeneous Concept?

The concept of context has only recently spread into the field of motivation in education research, obviously with a certain diversity in its definition. As noted by Urdan in his foreword to Volume 11 of the "Advances in motivation and achievement" series, context includes features of the achievement environment (provided by classroom, school, or work), cultural factors (such as nationality or ethnicity) and the multiple social contexts in which individuals operate (mainly family, peers or teachers). If all of these features belong to context, they surely do not operate at the same level. We consider that the structure proposed by Bronfenbrenner to organize the various levels of influence of the environment on a person offers a good model with which the various sorts of context discussed in motivation research can appropriately be disentangled.

In our view, context refers to the specific configuration of variables used by a given person or student to recognize and index a particular task or learning situation. Included in this definition are proximal (for example, individual or group activity, school subject or instructional techniques) and more distal variables (such as the cultural significance of the activity, school policy or parental attitudes

Table 1: Levels of context and examples of contextual elements at school.

Level of context	"location"	examples
micro	lesson or type of work	school subject; type of lesson or work
meso	classroom or school year	Teacher attitudes; classroom environment; classroom goal structure; classroom norms and practices
exo	school	elementary vs. high-school organization and structure; streams or sections; special events
macro	outside school	familial; cultural; economic; political

regarding school and schoolwork, etc.). The impact of a given context on a particular student's performances, judgments, attitudes or motivation towards school and schoolwork remains constant, but two students placed in an apparently identical situation may react to it differently since the context in which each one will embed that situation might be quite different.

Building on Bronfenbrenner's typology, we propose to organize the elements of the context surrounding a pupil at school within a four-layer model with both direct and indirect influences on his or her reactions (Table 1). The nature and the "location" of the elements we attribute to the various levels, however, do not fully correspond to those considered by Bronfenbrenner. Whether a student likes or dislikes a particular school subject or a given type of work has a direct effect on his or her readiness to work; in this sense such features build a first level of context analogous to what Bronfenbrenner has called a microsystem. The specificity of the classroom in which a student sits, including the teachers' and classmates' attitudes and behaviors, classroom norms and practices, forms a second layer of context around the pupil and his or her relationship towards schoolwork. This level of context constitutes what Bronfenbrenner would have called a mesosystem. At these two levels, the influences are bi-directional, as Bronfenbrenner pointed out: students' willingness to work prompts teachers' attitudes surely as much as they are influenced by the teacher's behavior or by the classroom goal structure set up by the teacher.

For the other two levels, on the contrary, the influence of the contextual elements on the behavior of a student is unidirectional with generally no reciprocal effect. The way the school is structured, the kind of stream or setting a child is engaged in on the one hand (exo-level), familial or cultural relationship to education and schooling, and political or economical considerations on the other hand (macro-level), also influence a child's motivation to work hard at school. The influence of these last two levels, although weaker than that of the contextual elements of the previous two levels, can also be direct or indirect. Volet (1999) shows, for instance, that cultural differences interact with experience in group-work or feelings of self-efficacy for determining how much Australian and international students from Singapore appreciate this kind of work setting.

Levels of Context and their Influence on Students' Motivation

This section reviews important empirical work attesting to the nature, the direction and the strength of the influence exerted by variables from the four contextual levels on students' motivation at school.

Micro-Level Contextual Influences on Students' Motivation

Variables such as school subject and the type of lesson or work surely belong to the most critical elements of the learning context at the micro-level. Whether an activity is to be done in one's preferred or in a highly disliked subject, whether it is part of a test or simply an exercise, whether group work is suggested or not, will obviously act upon a student's disposition for, and outcome in, a given task.

Farmer *et al.* (1991) clearly show that students lacking achievement motivation at school might well have high achievement needs in other contexts such as sports, arts or social accomplishments. Duda and Nicholls (1992) also observe differences in high-school students' beliefs about the causes of success in school and sports. Intrinsic satisfaction is related to perceived ability in sports, but not in school-work, where the major predictor of satisfaction is task orientation. Comparing motivation and self-regulated learning in the various contexts of mathematics, English or social studies classrooms, Wolters and Pintrich (1998) conclude that differences in the motivational and in the cognitive components of learning can indeed be noticed, but that the relations among these components remain similar across contexts.

The type of lesson or setting also constitutes an important determinant of motivation and learning. Competitive structures tend to elicit more performance failure-avoiding strategies than individualistic or cooperative ones (Ames, 1981; Ames & Ames, 1984). Group work, however, will be positively appreciated by students only if they are convinced of the educational value of collaborating with peers (Gerlach, 1994) and if the assessment of the group performance will have no detrimental effect on their own grade point average (Volet, 1999).

Contextual Effects of Meso-Level Variables

Teachers' attitudes and behaviors, students' perception of the classroom climate or environment, as well as the classroom goal structure, norms and practices, belong to a second level of contextual variables.

Several researchers have already shown that teachers' attitudes play a role on children's and students' motivation (Fraser & Fisher, 1982; Pianta, 1992). Wentzel (1997), for instance, provides empirical evidence that perceived caring from teachers can predict current motivation even when performance level, control beliefs or previous motivation are taken into account.

Using the Academic Motivation Inventory scale (Moen & Doyle, 1977), Fry and Coe (1980) observe that classrooms perceived to be high in teacher support and involvement are associated with self-improvement and high motivation for academic success, as well as with an enjoyment of learning. Classrooms perceived as teacher-controlled or competition-oriented, by contrast, are associated with anti-school feelings and an absence of a desire for self-improvement or an enjoyment of learning. The way in which students are evaluated also constitutes an important factor that can influence their motivation (Ames, 1992). In classrooms characterized by frequent grading and public evaluations, for instance, children's interest for schoolwork drops, as does their perceptions of ability or their use of learning strategies (Boggiano *et al.*, 1987; Ames, 1984).

Finally, perceptions of the classroom goal structure also have a clear effect on motivation. Ames and Archer (1988) document how students who perceive performance goals as salient in their classroom tend to focus on their ability, evaluating it negatively, and thus making a lack of ability responsible for their failure. While a strong performance goal structure at school also leads students to use self-handicapping strategies (Urdan *et al.*, 1998) and to be more reluctant in seeking help when it is needed (Ryan *et al.*, 1998), the perception of a task-oriented goal structure, on the contrary, correlates with higher self-efficacy, greater use of cognitive learning strategies, positive affect and an enhanced sense of belonging (Roeser *et al.*, 1996).

Exo-Level Contextual Variables

Exo-level elements refer to the type of school or program in which a student is involved, mostly without having chosen it. Changes in the organization and structure of school, when moving from elementary to middle- or high-school, involvement in a special program or section, have been found to influence students' perceptions of school and attitudes towards schoolwork (Midgley, 1993), self-esteem or other psychological symptomatology (Hirsch & Rapkin, 1987). Midgley *et al.* (1991) argue that junior high-schools are developmentally inappropriate since they tend to reduce students' opportunities to make decisions exactly at the age where adolescents wish and express desires for more control over their lives. They also provide fewer opportunities for cooperation and more concern over one's relative performance compared to others. Finally, high-school students, as well as observers, generally see teachers as less friendly, supportive and caring than teachers at earlier levels; yet, on the contrary, those who perceive their high-school teachers as being more supportive than their previous teachers, consider, as Midgley *et al.* point out, mathematics as more useful and important in high-school than they did before.

The type of program or section can also have an impact on motivation and learning. Pintrich *et al.* (1995) find both positive and negative effects on student motivation and cognition with alternative, non-traditional chemistry or calculus courses, "stressing collaborative learning, mastery goals and deeper, more meaningful learning" (p. 2). Such courses produce more cognitive engagement, deeper processing of the material in the chemistry courses, but not in calculus. They also are associated with lower self-efficacy and higher student anxiety level, probably due to the students' lack of experience with that kind of work. It is also reasonable to assume that such programs influence motivation and cognition indirectly by improving students' perceptions of their classroom environment. Rentoul and Fraser (1980) show that both cognitive performances and enjoyment of the lessons are improved whenever there is congruence between the actual and the preferred climate in the classroom. Lens and Decruyenaere (1991) report that students attending a general education section are more motivated than those from technical sections, whatever scale is used to assess motivation; they have greater self-confidence, as well as what the authors call a more preferable attributional style, attributing their success more to internal and stable causes, and their failures to internal, but unstable variables. They also have a stronger belief that effort and study methods can modify school results and learning outcomes. Schools with a lower degree of segregation between low-achieving and higher-achieving students bring the low-achieving students to report higher motivation, especially with regard to school attraction and perceived utility of school, though at the cost of lowered self-esteem (Denicolà, 1999).

Another important contextual variable at the exo-level refers to special events or moments in the school year. We have all experienced such moments during our own schooling or in a sport club when everybody in the school or on the team has extra energy for practicing and working hard because of a forthcoming examination, selection or important game. In another paper (Gurtner *et al.*, 1999), we discuss how the preparation for an important examination, taken at the end of grade six, can temporarily boost students' motivation, especially regarding such variables as feelings of self-efficacy, learning intentions or test anxiety, or, at least, prevent motivation from declining with respect to other variables such as task orientation or school attraction.

Contextual Effects at a Macro-Level

Macro-level contexts refer to out-of-school environmental characteristics such as familial, cultural, economical or political variables. Studies conducted in various cultural or ethnic contexts provide much evidence of their effects, not only on student achievement, but also on motivation (Maehr, 1974), perception of school (Fuller & Clarke, 1994) or appraisal of the motivational and emotional aspects of various work situations (Volet, 1999). Observing that Japanese and Chinese mothers consider effort as more important than ability for a given performance at school, while American mothers stress ability over effort, Stevenson *et al.* (1986)

see this difference as a plausible reason for the higher willingness of Japanese and Chinese children to work hard in school. This difference in the attributional pattern is only weakly attenuated when Chinese mothers raise their children in the United States (Hess *et al.*, 1987).

The pressure to find a good job at the end of their schooling also introduces contextual elements in the way students value and use school. Lens and his colleagues (Lens & Gailly, 1980; De Volder & Lens, 1982; see also this volume) show, for instance, that the future time perspective of high-achieving students is more extended, due to the fact that they will stay in school longer and that the nature of their goals in life are broader, since more job possibilities remain open to them.

Evidence of Contextual Effects from a Semi-Longitudinal Project on the Evolution of Various Aspects of Motivation for School

Our own work has investigated the evolution of motivation for school during middle-school, using a semi-longitudinal approach. The study reported in this chapter was conducted during two entire school years over two cohorts, the first one involving 250 subjects from the beginning of grade six to the end of grade seven, the second composed of 271 students from grade eight to grade nine. In Switzerland, these grade levels cover the transition from elementary to middle-school for the first cohort and the last two years of compulsory school for the second one.

During these two years, various aspects of students' motivation were regularly tested, using adapted versions of Boekaert's (1987) *On-line motivation questionnaire*, Pintrich and De Groot's (1990) *Motivation and self-regulated learning questionnaire* and Nicholls *et al.*'s (1985) *Motivational orientation questionnaire*. Measures were taken during the first months of school in the first year, at the end of the first semester and at the end of the first year, at the beginning of the second year and at the end of the first semester of the second school year.

Two consecutive factor analyses (Ntamakiliro *et al.*, 2000) produced highly reliable dimensions, namely school attraction (mot-ATT: $\alpha = 0.86$), perceived utility of school (mot-PU: $\alpha = 0.76$), test anxiety (mot-ANX: $\alpha = 0.72$), task orientation (mot-TO: $\alpha = 0.53$), ego orientation (mot-EO: $\alpha = 0.76$), work avoidance (mot-WA: $\alpha = 0.57$), learning intentions and feelings of self-efficacy. For these last two dimensions, the analysis produced two separate factors, one for French and the other for mathematics. Cronbach alphas for these factors were also very high, with 0.94 for learning intention in French (mot-LI(F)) and 0.83 for learning intention in mathematics (mot-LI(M)), 0.91 for the feelings of self-efficacy in French (mot-Seff(F)) and 0.95 for the feelings of self-efficacy in mathematics (mot-Seff(M)).

Another important focus of this study was on students' perception of their social classroom environment or classroom climate. According to Moos and Trickett, social classroom environment encompasses three dimensions, a relationship dimension, a personal growth or goal orientation dimension and a system maintenance and change dimension. The first one relates to the intensity of teacher support, confidence and friendship prevailing in the classroom, as students perceive them; the second taps the degree of involvement, attention, interest and persistence that students feel among their classmates regarding schoolwork; the third one assesses "the extent to which the classroom functions in an organized and coherent manner, as well as the amount of variety and novelty in class activities" (Moos & Trickett, 1987, p. 3). This last dimension covers two variables, the impression of order and organization prevailing in the classroom on the one hand, and the level of interest the teacher seems to have for rules, norms and justice in the classroom on the other. An adaptation by Bennacer (1991) of Moos and Trickett's (1987) Classroom Environment Scale (CES) was used to assess students' perceptions of their social classroom environment. Since students stay in the same environment for a whole school year, with the same teachers and the same classmates, measures of their perceptions of the classroom environment were taken only once a year, together with the second and the fifth measurement of motivation. According to our classification, perception of one's classroom environment belongs to the second level of context (meso-level).

The Impact on Motivation of some Micro- and Meso-Level Contexts

The study reported here did not address the question of the effect of specific lessons or work formats on students' motivation. As already mentioned, only two variables on our motivation scale had to be considered separately for French and for mathematics, self-efficacy and learning intentions. We are therefore unable to gain much evidence of micro-level contextual influences from this study. In fact, no subject-specific effect appeared at grade six, where we started out our measurements. As one can see in Table 2, feelings of self-efficacy in mathematics and in French were highly correlated at the end of elementary school (r = 0.36), as were learning intentions (r = 0.38). A slight differentiation was visible at grade eight

Table 2: Across and within subject(s) correlations at grade six and eight.

	mot-Seff(F)	mot-LI(F)	mot-Seff(M)	mot-LI(M)
mot-Seff(F)		0.28**	–0.05	0.02
mot-LI(F)	0.20**		–0.10	0.37**
mot-Seff(M)	0.36**	0.08		0.48**
mot-LI(M)	0.16*	0.38**	0.36**	

** = $p < 0.01$;
* = $p > 0.05$.
Grade six correlations are under the diagonal, grade eight above.

where the feeling of self-efficacy was no longer correlated across the two contexts (r = –0.05). Learning intentions in French and in mathematics, however, remained significantly related at this level (r = 0.37). Like most studies dedicated to the impact of school subjects, with respect to students' self-concept (Marsh *et al.*, 1984) or to possible gender differences in mathematics (Friedman, 1994), this observation confirms that across school subjects differences often only begin to appear during secondary school.

Perceptions of one's classroom environment and one's motivation appear highly interdependent. In our study, 70 of the 160 correlations between variables of the classroom environment and those of motivation were significant, 57 of them beyond the 0.01 mark. School attraction was always significantly correlated with all the measures of classroom environment; perceived utility of school, learning intentions in French and in mathematics, as well as task orientation, also correlated with teacher support and with involvement, in every case between 0.15 and 0.39.

The impact of classroom environment variables on students' motivation can be captured in a causal path model (Figure 1). Presented here for French, the picture is also valid for mathematics; the model also appears rather stable between the end of elementary school (grade six) and middle-school (grade eight). Bold arrows indicate significant links for both grades, lighter ones only for one of the two grades.[1] The strengths of the links are indicated on the left of the slash for grade six and on the right for grade eight.

Fit indices of this model are χ^2 (12) = 10.724, p = 0.55, GFI = 0.99, Adjusted GFI = 0.97, Tucker-Lewis index = 1.02, RMSEA = 0.00 for grade six and χ^2 (11) = 8.882, p = 0.63, GFI = 0.99, Adjusted GFI = 0.97, Tucker–Lewis index = 1.00, RMSEA = 0.00 for grade eight.

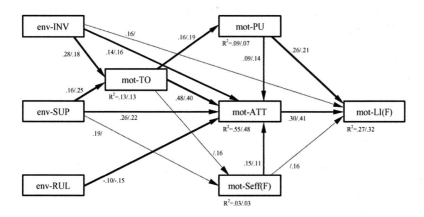

Figure 1: Causal links between classroom environment and motivation variables.

[1] Labels such as /.16 indicate that the corresponding link is only significant for grade eight, while .16/ indicates a link significant only at grade six.

In line with Seegers and Boekaerts' model (1993), our model emphasizes the important role played by task orientation (mot-TO), perceived utility (mot-PU), self-efficacy (mot-Seff(F)) and especially school attraction (mot-ATT) in raising students' learning intentions. It also clearly shows that three of the four classroom environment variables contribute significantly to the motivation of students in various ways. Involvement (env-INV) and teacher support (env-SUP) directly influence critical components of motivation such as task orientation and school attraction at both grades, self-efficacy and learning intention at grade six; they also have a strong, indirect impact on perceived utility of school. Rule clarity (env-RUL) plays a minor role; acting only upon school attraction while order and organization (env-ORG) never reaches a significant effect on any of the motivation variables.

Examples of Exo- and Macro-Level Contexts Influencing Motivation

As already mentioned, we repeatedly measured students' motivation and their perceptions of the classroom environment during the transition from elementary to middle-school. The decrease seen among most of the motivation components (except for anxiety and work avoidance) is also noticeable for perceptions of one's classroom environment. In fact, three of the variables of the Classroom Environment Scale (teacher support, involvement and order and organization), dropped between grade six (end of elementary school) and grade seven (first year of middle-school), while the fourth variable, namely rule clarity, increased. Figure 2 displays these evolutions, fully parallel with those observed by Ferguson and Fraser (1998) or by Midgley *et al.* (1991).

Perceptions of one's classroom environment and self-reported motivation do not evolve in the same way, however, for all students over this period of transition. If most students reported weaker teacher support and lower involvement in middle-school than in elementary school, others did not, or even reported higher teacher support and student involvement in middle-school. Students of the first group also reported an important decrease in all the motivation variables except for work

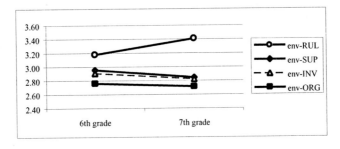

Figure 2: Evolution of classroom environment variables over the transition from elementary to middle-school.

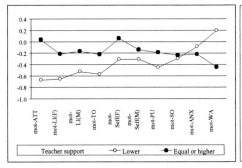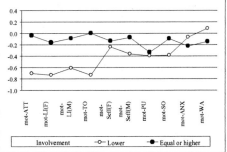

Figure 3: Differences in the perceptions of the components of motivation according to the evolution of two perceived classroom environment variables.

avoidance (mot-WA). In the second group of students, the decrease in motivation was only low to moderate (see Figure 3). This result, also replicating one of Midgley and co-authors' observations, constitutes clear evidence that perception of a high level of teacher support at the beginning of middle-school can prevent the drop of motivation regularly seen when children leave elementary school for higher grades. A similar protective effect can be played by students' involvement.

Yet another effect of the school structure on students' motivation can be seen in the following observation. Towards the end of grade six, pupils have to pass a special exam, the result of which is decisive for their future orientation in high-school. According to the results of this exam,[2] they are then oriented to complete their middle-school years (grades seven through nine) in one of three sections. The pre-college section gives access, after completion of the three years of middle-school, to what is called college or gymnasium, which ends after four years with the "baccalaureat". Each year this section accepts around one-fourth of all pupils. The general education section prepares students for vocational or technical schools or to begin an apprenticeship directly in a company. About half of all pupils enter this section at the end of grade six. The "practical education" section also receives one-fourth of all pupils and prepares them to enter manual or low-skill sectors of the job-market.

In our study, we asked students at the beginning of grade six which section they hoped to enter at the end of the year. At the beginning of grade seven, we compared students' desired and actual section. Three groups of students were compared: those who wanted to enter the pre-college section and actually managed to get there, those who wanted to enter the general education section and made it, and those who were hoping to enter the pre-college section but were not admitted. We found that students from this last group, at the beginning of

---

[2] In fact, four indications are considered for the pupils' orientations (exam results, GPA at the end of the school year, parental and teacher's wishes). Results of the exam, however, play an important role and, in many cases, overrule the other three.

grade six, displayed a specific pattern of motivation: this pattern consisted of stronger learning intentions, greater perceptions of school attraction and perceived utility and a stronger orientation towards the task; their feelings of self-efficacy were lower than those of the students who eventually made it to the pre-college section, attesting that these students had already realized that they were not quite as capable as those of the other group. It can be assumed that these students were hoping to overcome their perceived weaker competence through high effort and readiness to work hard. As their good dispositions were unfortunately not sufficient for them to end up in the desired section at the end of grade six, there was evidence that they rapidly lost most of their special motivation. Between grade six and the beginning of grade seven, their motivation showed a steeper drop than that of the students who were admitted to the pre-college section but also steeper than that of the students who wanted to be in the general section and actually got into that section. As a result, no significant differences were to be found between the three groups on any of the motivational variables at the beginning of grade seven. The boost in motivation observed at the beginning of grade six among students of the third group, due to the self-generated challenge, had interestingly no parallel in any of the classroom environment variables. The fact that motivation is highly personal while perceptions of one's classroom entail both an objective and a subjective component could explain this difference, as could the lower flexibility of contextual factors such as perceptions of classroom environment.

At the macro-level, our study did not explore the significance of familial or cultural contextual aspects; our data do, however, provide some evidence of the impact of societal or economic variables on specific aspects of students' motivation. The evolution throughout middle-school of test anxiety, perception of school attraction, involvement, teacher support or self-efficacy judgments among the students who were admitted to the "practical education" section attest to this influence. This section provides students with a lower level of competition, less pressure but also less ambitious objectives to reach. In recent years, however, pupils finishing this section have come to be considered by many companies, employers and entire professional sectors as insufficiently educated to start a professional education; consequently, they tend to experience considerable difficulties in finding a company with which to accomplish their apprenticeship after finishing their years of compulsory school.

In grade six, before entering the "practical education" section, and in grade nine, close to the completion of their studies, students expressed an especially high level of anxiety compared to that of the other students in our sample. During their middle-school years, however, in grade seven and eight, their anxiety remained lower, even lower than that of the students in the other two sections, as can be seen in Figure 4a. Conversely, the way students of this section perceived school attraction (Figure 4b), or evaluated their personal efficacy (Figure 4d) increased when they entered the section at grade seven, probably due to the satisfaction of being in a class whose pace is more adapted to their special needs and without high achieving students to compete with; these perceptions, however,

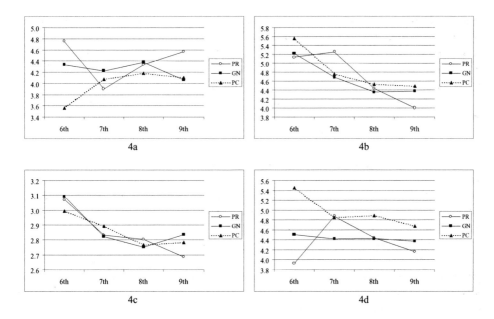

Figure 4: Evolution of anxiety (4a), school attraction (4b), students' involvement (4c) and self-efficacy judgments in French (4d) in the various sections (PR = "practical education", GN = general education, PC = pre-college section).

continuously dropped through grades eight and nine, more steeply than did those of the other two groups of students. We see the particular evolution of these motivational components among this group of subjects as influenced by the macro-level, socially-defined context, which turns the "practical education" section into a highly undesirable one when one enters or leaves it, but a quite comfortable and attractive one while one is in it.

Perceived utility of school (mot-PU) was also determined by out-of-school contexts. Students enrolled in the pre-college section consistently considered doing well at school as less important than did the students from the other two sections. Students heading for college and university obviously know that they will be granted many more opportunities to acquire relevant knowledge. This can explain why they do not attach much importance to what they are taught during middle-school.

The main goal of the study reported in this section is to deal with a specific aspect of context, namely that of students' perceptions of the psycho-social environment of their classroom and the effect of these perceptions on students' motivation and learning. The fact that little information was gained on other aspects of context does not, however, mean that those aspects are of less importance. Other contributions to this book powerfully demonstrate the impact on students' motivation of micro-, exo- or macro-level contextual variables. Our results simply show that meso-level aspects of context, principally perceived student involvement and perceived teacher support, can have a real impact on some of the more important determinants of motivation, such as task orientation and perceived utility of school and especially on school attraction and declared intentions to learn. Confirming other authors' claims (Fraser & Fisher, 1982; Pianta, 1992 or Wentzel, 1997), these observations are of high educational relevance. Given their strong influence on the psycho-social classroom environment, teachers should be made particularly attentive to the importance of establishing a positive, warm and open climate in their class. Teachers are not, however, the only contributors to a classroom's climate; their influence, although considerable, is moderated by factors coming from the students, the school system and the society. As the results of the present study clearly show, the evolution of students' motivation is only slighty touched by objective aspects of the classroom climate but more by students' perceptions of it, which proved as different among students of a same class as between students from different classes. Furthermore, students' motivation and their perceptions of the classroom psycho-social environment were sensitive to variables belonging to the exo- and even to the macro-level of context. In this sense, the results of this study globally confirm that revising the curriculum, improving teacher education or bettering classroom environment, all efforts made at the micro- or the meso-level, certainly can be part of a solution to prevent students' drop in motivation during adolescence (Eccles *et al.*, 1984); such measures are, however, insufficient per se, since life outside and after school can also contribute to a decrease in school attraction and perceived utility, as well as readiness to learn at school, in a teenager's mind.

Features of Contextual Effects in the Determination of Motivation

Variety and Globality

Under the label "context", a diversity of aspects are discussed in recent work on the determinants of motivation, including such diverse aspects as cultural (Volet, 1999), environmental and societal (Urdan, 1999), political (Ryan & La Guardia, 1999), or curricular features (Wolters & Pintrich, 1998). Our aim with this contribution is to try and disentangle the various kinds of contextual influences on students' motivation to learn and to articulate these various aspects in a more general and global framework. Bronfenbrenner's typology of four types of environmental systems shaping a child's development (micro-, meso-, exo- and macro-levels) proved a useful basis on which to construct a model of contextual influences on a student's perceptions and reactions at school, although the locations in which our levels of context are attached sometimes differ from those evoked in the developmental ecology theory (Bronfenbrenner, 1986). Such a model allows one to subsume the diverse and specific aspects of context under a unique and comprehensive entity.

Stability and Flexibility

In the discussion about the determinants of motivation, context offers a useful and needed contribution between the rigidness of influences coming from personality or development, and the all too flexible shaping of one's reactions by the specifics of the particular situation confronted with. Recognizing, in a given situation, aspects discovered and appreciated in analogous situations, that is, being able to insert it in a familiar context, allows the learner to confer upon it a given value, to build expectancies and to call up effective learning strategies. Conversely, negative feelings or learned helplessness developed against a specific school subject in a given context may not be elicited against this subject when it appears in another context. How strongly contextual aspects influence one's reactions can also vary from one situation to another; as Volet (1999) has shown, cultural dimensions, although stable and highly difficult to modify, only become salient in those situations including confrontation with people from another culture. For a teacher as well, both stability and flexibility of context can become of greater help when it comes to designing and setting up new learning situations. Knowing which kinds of contexts are likely to arouse students' willingness to work can provide good indications on how to present a new topic, choose new exercises or organize new activities. Conversely, if a given topic produced insufficient attention and curiosity among students, it is always possible to elicit deeper motivation for the same subject simply by inserting it into another, more challenging, competitive or playful context.

Objectivity or Subjectivity

Some aspects of context can be seen as objective. A person's cultural background or the structure of a given school system can be perceived in the same way by different people and therefore be conferred some sort of objectivity.

Other aspects are full of subjectivity. Features, like the variables building the classroom psycho-social environment, as our results clearly show, heavily depend on an individual's perceptions. Even when they are members of a same class and deal with the same teachers, students can report very different degrees of teacher support, student involvement or classroom organization and rule clarity. On this level, perceptions of context certainly exert a more decisive impact on motivation than objective ones (Wentzel, 1997).

Methodological Issues

In the project of which the study presented here is an element, we have adopted a longitudinal perspective. Taking the same measures several times among the same students has brought valuable contributions to our understanding of motivation in context, since it allowed us to detect both changes and regularities in the answers of the same students to the same set of questions. By keeping the number of items small and by rearranging them regularly in the test, it is possible to greatly reduce the detrimental effect of having to answer the same questionnaire several times. Longitudinal approaches can even lead to the detection of possible predictors of specific motivational states a few months or years later. In fact, as our data show, the evolution noticed along one variable has often proved a better predictor than simple, one-time measures. We expect to be able to detect specific profiles of motivational variables from the early measures of the study that are connected to severe decreases in motivation later on in the study. Knowing these patterns should also help parents and teachers act in an appropriate way in order to prevent demotivation while there is still time.

All the results discussed in this chapter come from quantitative analyses. Considering that more qualitative approaches might well bring interesting complementary insights into the effects of context on a student's motivation, we have started to try and understand the diversity in the evolution of motivation through middle-school using interviews of a small number of students selected on the basis of particularities observed in our data. With the help of a graphic representation displaying the values taken from all the motivation variables in the five consecutive measures, it was sometimes possible to get students to invoke more personal events or to explain a sudden drop in their perceptions of the utility of school, a steep increase in their feelings of anxiety or a reversal in the importance conferred to the various motivational goals.

Considering a shorter time period, there is no doubt that specifics of one's personal, day to day experiences, in school and out, during these difficult years of early adolescence, also act upon students' motivation for school in an even less regular manner. Increasing the frequency of the interviews or regularly asking for short descriptions of personal feelings or emotional states (Järvelä, 1995) might well prove of great help in getting a more fine-grained image of the specificity of a student's perception of context and its impact on his or her motivation for school. Specially programmed pocket computers (Perrez & Reicherts, 1996) could also be used to store this per diem or weekly evolution.

Obviously, taking into account contextual factors among the determinants of motivation will have methodological implications for motivation research. Developing new methodological approaches is now an inescapable task on the agenda of all researchers in the field.

Acknowledgements

This chapter is based on data from a research project funded by the Swiss national foundation for scientific research under contract # 1114-54159.98.
We are grateful to the editors for their comments on a first draft of this chapter.

References

Ames, C. (1981), "Competitive versus cooperative reward structures: The influence of individual and group performance factors on achievement, attributions and affect." *American Educational Research Journal 18*, 273–287.

Ames, C. (1984), "Achievement attributions and self-instructions under competitive and individualistic goal structures." *Journal of Educational Psychology 76*, 478–487.

Ames, C. (1992), "Classrooms: Goals, structures, and student motivation." *Journal of Educational Psychology 84*, 261–271.

Ames, C., & Ames, R. (1984), "Systems of student and teacher motivation: toward a qualitative definition." *Journal of Educational Psychology 76*, 535–556.

Ames, C., & Archer, J. (1988), "Achievement goals in the classroom: students' learning strategies and motivation processes." *Journal of Educational Psychology 80*, 260–267.

Anderman, L. H., & Anderman, E. M. (2000), "Considering contexts in educational psychology: Introduction to the special issue." *Educational Psychologist 35*, 67–68.

Atkinson, J. W. (1957), "Motivational determinants of risk-taking behavior." *Psychological Review 64*, 359–362.

Bennacer, H. (1991), "Echelle de l'environnement social de la classe (EEC)." *Revue de Psychologie et de Psychométrie 12*, 59–75.

Boekaerts, M. (1987), "Situation-specific judgements of a learning task versus overall measures of motivational orientation." In E. De Corte, H. Lodewijks, R. Parmentier & P. Span (eds) *Learning and Instruction: European Research in an International Context* (pp. 169–179). Oxford: Pergamon Press.

Boekaerts, M. (1999), "Motivated learning: Studying student * situation transactional units. *European Journal of Psychology of Education 14*, 41–55.

Boggiano, A. K., Main, D. S., & Katz, P. A. (1987), "Children's preference for challenge. The role of perceived competence and control." *Journal of Personality and Social Psychology 54*, 134–141.

Bronfenbrenner, U. (1986), "Ecology of the family as a context for human development: research perspectives." *Developmental Psychology 22*, 723–742.

Bronfenbrenner, U. (1995), "Developmental ecology through space and time: a future perspective." In P. Moen, G. H. Elder & K. Lüscher (eds) *Examining Lives in Context: Perspectives on the Ecology of Human Development* (pp. 619–647). Washington DC: APA.

Denicolà, M. (1999), *L'influence de la structure scolaire sur l'estime de soi et la motivation des élèves: analyse des effets d'un type de structure scolaire intégrative et d'un projet (SPAR) au cycle scolaire secondaire dans le canton des Grisons.* Unpublished Diploma's Work, University of Fribourg, Switzerland.

De Volder, M. L., & Lens, W. (1982), "Academic achievement and future time perspective as a cognitive–motivational concept." *Journal of Personality and Social Psychology 42*, 566–571.

Duda, J. L., & Nicholls, J. G. (1992), "Dimensions of achievement motivation in schoolwork and sport." *Journal of Educational Psychology 84*, 290–299.

Dunkin, M. J., & Biddle, B. J. (1974), *The Study of Teaching.* New York: Holt, Rinehart & Winston.

Dweck, C. S., & Leggett, E. L. (1988), "A social–cognitive approach to motivation and personality." *Psychological Review 95*, 256–273.

Eccles, J. S., Midgley, C., & Alder, T. F. (1984), "Grade-related changes in the school environment: effect on achievement motivation." In G. Nicholls (ed.) *The Development of Achievement Motivation* (pp. 283–331). Greenwich, CT: JAI.

Farmer, H. S., Vispoel, W., & Maehr, M. L. (1991), "Achievement context: Effects on achievement values and causal attributions." *Journal of Educational Research 85*, 26–38.

Ferguson, P. D., & Fraser, B. J. (1999), "Changes in learning environment during the transition from primary to secondary school." *Learning Environments Research 1*, 369–383.

Fraser, B. J., & Fisher, D. L. (1982), "Predicting students' outcomes from their perceptions of classroom psychosocial environment." *American Educational Research Journal 19* (4), 498–518.

Friedman, L. (1994), "Meta-analytic contribution to the study of gender differences in mathematics: The relationship of spatial and mathematical skills." *International Journal of Educational Research 21*, 361–371.

Fry, P. S., & Coe, K. J. (1980), "Interaction among dimensions of academic motivation and classroom social climate: a study of the perceptions of junior high and high school pupils." *British Journal of Educational Psychology 50*, 33–42.

Fuller, B., & Clarke, P. (1994), "Raising school effects while ignoring culture? Local conditions and the influence of classroom tools, rules and pedagogy." *Review of Educational Research 64*, 119–157.

Gerlach, J. M. (1994), "Is this collaboration?" *New Directions for Teaching and Learning 59*, 5–14.

Gurtner, J.-L., Ntamakiliro, L., & Monnard, I. (1999, August), *How Demotivation Finds its Way through High School*. Poster presented at the 8th EARLI Conference, Göteborg.

Hearn, J. C., & Moos, R. H. (1978), "Subject matter and classroom climate: a test of Holland's environmental propositions." *American Educational Research Journal 15*, 111–124.

Hess, R. D., Chih-Mei, C., & McDevitt, T. M. (1987), "Cultural variations in family beliefs about children's performance in mathematics: Comparisons among People's Republic of China, Chinese–American, and Caucasian–American Families." *Journal of Educational Psychology 79*, 179–188.

Hidi, S. (1990), "Interest and its contribution as a mental resource for learning." *Review of Educational Research 60*, 549–571.

Hirsch, B. J., & Rapkin, B. D. (1987), "The transition to junior high school: a longitudinal study of self-esteem, psychological symptomatology, school life, and social support." *Child Development 58*, 1235–1243.

Iran-Nejad, A. (1987), "Cognitive and affective causes of interest and liking." *Journal of Educational Psychology 79*, 120–130.

Järvelä, S. (1995), "The cognitive apprenticeship model in a technologically rich learning environment: Interpreting the learning interaction." *Learning and Instruction 5*, 237–259.

Lave, J. (1989), *Cognition in Practice: Mind and Culture in Everyday Life*. Cambridge, England: Cambridge University Press.

Lens, W., & Decruyenaere, M. (1991), "Motivation and de-motivation in secondary education: student characteristics." *Learning and Instruction 1*, 145–159.

Lens, W., & Gailly, A. (1980), "Extension of future time perspective in motivational goals for different age groups." *International Journal of Behavioral Development 3*, 1–17.

Lepper, M. R., Woolverton, M., Mumme, D., & Gurtner, J.-L. (1993), "Motivational techniques of expert human tutors: Lessons for the design of computer-based tutors." In S. P. Lajoie & S. J. Derry (eds) *Computers as Cognitive Tools*. Hillsdale, NJ: Erlbaum.

Lewin, K. (1935), *A Dynamic Theory of Personality*. New York: McGraw-Hill.

Maehr, M. L. (1974), "Culture and achievement motivation." *American Psychologist 29*, 887–896.

Malone, T. W. (1981), "Toward a theory of intrinsically motivating instruction." *Cognitive Science 4*, 333–369.

Marsh, H. W., Barnes, J., Cairns, L., & Tidman, M. (1984), "Age and sex effects in the structure and level of self-concept for preadolescent children." *Journal of Educational Psychology 76*, 940–956.

Marshall, H. H., & Weinstein, R. S. (1986), "Classroom context of student-perceived differential teacher treatment." *Journal of Educational Psychology 78*, 441–453.

Midgley, C. (1993), "Motivation and middle level schools." In M. L. Maehr & P. R. Pintrich (eds) *Advances in Motivation and Achievement: Motivation and Adolescence* (Vol. 8, pp. 217–274). Greenwich, CT: JAI Press.

Midgley, C., Eccles, J.S., & Feldlaufer, H. (1991), "Classroom environment and the transition to junior high school." In Fraser, B. J. & Walberg, H. J. (eds) *Educational Environments: Evaluation, Antecedents and Consequences*. Oxford: Pergamon Press.

Moen, R. E., & Doyle, K. O. (1977), "Construction and development of the Academic Motivations Inventory (AMI)." *Educational Psychological Measurement 13*, 509–512.

Monnard, I., Ntamakiliro, L., & Gurtner, J.-L. (1999), "Evaluation des composantes de la motivation pour les apprentissages scolaires." In C. Depover & B. Noël (eds) *L'évaluation des Compétences et des Processus Cognitifs* (pp. 197–210). Bruxelles: De Boeck.

Moos, R. H., & Trickett, E. J. (1987), *Classroom Environment Scale Manual*. Palo Alto, CA: Consulting Psychologists Press.

Murray, H. A. (1938), *Explorations in Personality*. Oxford: Oxford University Press.

Nicholls, J. G., Patashnick, M., & Nolen, S. B. (1985), "Adolescents' theories of education." *Journal of Educational Psychology 77*, 683–692.

Ntamakiliro, L., Monnard, I., & Gurtner, J.-L. (2000), "Mesure de la motivation scolaire des adolescents: Construction et validation de trois échelles complémentaires." *Orientation Scolaire et Professionnelle 29*, 673–693.

Perrez, M., & Reicherts, M. (1996), "Computer-assisted self-monitoring procedure for assessing stress-related behavior under real life conditions." In J. Fahrenberg & M. Myrtek (eds) *Ambulatory Assessment. Computer-Assisted Psychological and Psychophysiological Methods in Monitoring and Field Studies* (pp. 51–68). Seattle: Hogrefe & Huber Publishers.

Piaget, J. (1936), *La Naissance de L'intelligence*. Neuchâtel/Paris: Delachaux et Niestlé.

Piaget, J. (1937), *La Construction du Réel*. Neuchâtel/Paris: Delachaux et Niestlé.

Pianta, R. C. (1992), *Beyond the Parent: The Role of Other Adults in Children's Lives. New Directions in Child Development* (Vol. 57). San Francisco: Jossey-Bass.

Pintrich, P. R. (2000), "An achievement goal theory perspective on issues in motivation terminology, theory, and research." *Contemporary Educational Psychology 25*, 92–104.

Pintrich, P. R., & De Groot, E. V. (1990), "Motivational and self-regulated learning components of classroom academic performance. " *Journal of Educational Psychology 82*, 33–41.

Pintrich, P. R., Marx, R. W., & Boyle, R. A. (1993), "Beyond cold conceptual change: the role of motivational beliefs and classroom contextual factors in the process of conceptual change." *Review of Educational Research 63* (2), 167–199.

Pintrich, P. R., McKeachie, W. J., Yu, S. L., & Hofer, B. K. (1995), *The Role of Motivation and Self-Regulated Learning in Math and Science Classroom*. Paper presented at EARLI, Nijmegen, August 1995.

Rentoul, A. J., & Fraser, B. J. (1980), "Predicting learning from classroom individualization and actual-preferred congruence." *Studies in Educational Evaluation 6*, 256–277.

Roeser, R. W., Midgley, C., & Urdan, T. (1996), "Perceptions of the school psychological environment and early adolescents' psychological and behavioral functioning in school: The mediating role of goals and belonging." *Journal of Educational Psychology 88*, 408–422.

Ryan, R. M., & Deci, E. L. (2000), "Intrinsic and extrinsic motivations: Classic definitions and new directions." *Contemporary Educational Psychology 25*, 54–67.

Ryan, A. M., Gheen, M. H., & Midgley, C. (1998), "Why do some students avoid asking for help? An examination of the interplay among students' academic efficacy, teachers' social–emotional role, and the classroom goal structure." *Journal of Educational Psychology 90*, 528–535.

Ryan, R. M., & La Guardia, J. (1999), "Achievement motivation within a pressured society: Intrinsic and extrinsic motivations to learn and the politics of school reform." In M. L. Maehr & P. R. Pintrich (eds) *Advances in Motivation and Achievement: The Role of Context* (Vol. 11, pp. 45–85). Greenwich, CT: JAI Press.

Seegers, G., & Boekaerts, M. (1993), "Task motivation and mathematics achievement in actual task situations." *Learning and Instruction 3*, 133–150.

Stevenson, H. W, Lee, S. Y., & Stigler, J. W. (1986), "Mathematics achievement of Chinese, Japanese, and American children." *Science 231*, 693–699.

Turner, J. C., & Meyer, D. K. (2000), "Studying and understanding the instructional contexts of classrooms: Using our past to forge our future." *Educational Psychologist 35*, 69–85.

Urdan, T. (1999), "Foreword". In M. L. Maehr & P. R. Pintrich (eds) *Advances in Motivation and Achievement: The Role of Context* (Vol. 11, pp. IX–XI). Greenwich, CT: JAI Press.

Urdan, T., Midgley, C., & Anderman, E. M. (1998), "The role of classroom goal structure in students' use of self-handicapping strategies." *American Educational Research Journal 35*, 101–122.

Volet, S. (1999), "Motivation within and across cultural–educational contexts: A multidimensional perspective." In M. L. Maehr & P. R. Pintrich (eds) *Advances in Motivation and Achievement: The Role of Context* (Vol. 11, pp. 185–231). Greenwich, CT: JAI Press.

Weiner, B. (1979), "A theory of motivation for some classroom experiences." *Journal of Educational Psychology 71*, 3–25.

Wentzel, K. R. (1997), "Student motivation in middle school: the role of perceived pedagogical caring." *Journal of Educational Psychology 89*, 411–419.

Wolters, C. A., & Pintrich, P. R. (1998), "Contextual differences in student motivation and self-regulated learning in mathematics, English and social studies classrooms." *Instructional Science 26*, 27–47.

Chapter 11

Development of Interests and Interest-Based Motivational Orientations: A Longitudinal Study in Vocational School and Work Settings[1]

Andreas Krapp & Doris Lewalter

In modern theories of learning and knowledge acquisition, the problem of domain- or content-specificity plays an important role. For example, research on "the nature of expertise" (Chi *et al.*, 1988) has shown that the exceptional abilities of experts are based on a strongly content- and/or context-specific knowledge base (Hoffmann, 1992). In many empirical studies, it has emerged that the amount of prior knowledge or the quality of topic-related (cognitive) schemata determine, to a high degree, the learning outcomes in almost all educational settings. It is now widely accepted that research on teaching and learning has to take the fact of content- and context-specificity into account in order to be able to reconstruct the process of learning in an adequate way. However, when looking into the field of motivational research, the problem of content- or context-specificity is much less prominent (Renninger *et al.*, in press; see chapters from Järvelä, Hickey and Volet in the first section of this book). Two closely related reasons seem to be responsible for this deficit. On the one hand, there is a lack of theoretical concepts that provide an adequate theoretical background for both conceptualizing and analyzing content-specificity. On the other hand, there are severe methodological problems, because considering contents and situation-specific contextual conditions in analyzing motivational phenomena is complicated and requires more sophisticated methodical tools than the exploration of the development and effects of generalized motivational variables in the sense of motivational dispositions or "traits".

In this chapter, we will discuss some theoretical ideas and empirical results of an educational–psychological research approach that tries to overcome these problems. The theoretical background is a "person–object–conception" of interest (POI) that will be outlined in the first section. This approach interprets interest as a motivational component of learning and human development that is always related to a specific content or "object" of knowledge and competence acquisition.

[1] The research presented in this chapter was supported by a grant from the German Research Foundation DFG (Grant KR 715/5-1 to 5-3). Colleagues on this project were Klaus-Peter Wild and Inge Schreyer.

Motivation in Learning Contexts: Theoretical Advances and Methodological Implications, pages 209–232.

Besides more general aspects of this theory, central characteristics of the interest construct and hypotheses about the conditions and processes of interest development will be described.

The main part of the chapter is concerned with the theoretical framework, the methodology and selected results of a research project on "the conditions and effects of learning motivation in vocational education" (Lewalter *et al.*, in press).[2] More specifically, we will present results from a longitudinal study analyzing the development of vocation-related interests and motivational orientations in the area of *vocational education*. Beside school and academic education, vocational education (VE) plays an important role in a modern industrial society. In Germany, for example, Schober & Tessaring (1993) have shown that in 1990 about 67 percent of an age group completed a vocational education program while only about 13 percent completed an academic education; about 20 percent started professional life without any formal education.

The ultimate goal of our research approach is to provide empirically founded knowledge on how to foster the development of long-term effective motivational dispositions (e.g., interests and interest-related goal orientations). Since vocational education in Germany takes place in two different educational settings (vocational school and training on the job), research in this field inevitably has to deal with the problem of context-specificity of motivation (and learning). Methodical characteristics of our research approach are the combination of quantitative and qualitative methods of data collection and the explicit consideration of content- and context-specificity of motivation. Furthermore, we try to compare and integrate data from different research perspectives by analyzing developmental processes with respect to inter- and intra-individual changes. Besides questionnaires and tests, ESM-techniques (Experience-Sampling Method) and interviews have been used to gather a broad variety of data on conditions and effects of vocational education on the development of motivational variables including motivational orientations and content-specific interests.

Referring to the central topic of this book, we present results that demonstrate the importance and fruitfulness of considering context-specificity in motivational research.

1. A Person–Object Conception of Interest (POI)

Our theoretical conception, which has recently been outlined in more detail under the label "person–object theory of interest" (POI; c.f., Krapp, 1999a, 2000, in press), can be traced back to considerations of Hans Schiefele on the development of a genuinely educationally oriented theory of motivation (H. Schiefele, 1974). Such a theory was expected to be able to make explicit statements about how an individual develops enduring preferences for specific subjects or contents of

---

[2] This project was part of a rather extensive "research focus program" of the Deutsche Forschungsgemeinschaft (DFG) funding 18 projects concerned with teaching and learning processes within the setting of the German "Dual System" of vocational education (for an overview c.f. Beck, 2000).

learning, that is, how the development of content specific motivational dispositions (such as interests) can be explained.

1.1 Metatheoretical Premises

POI is based on explicit *metatheoretical premises*. One essential metatheoretical principle of POI is its readiness to respect educational ideas. From an educational point of view, for example, it is necessary to discuss motivational phenomena not only with respect to academic achievement and the prediction of inter-individual differences in learning, but also with respect to the emergence of content-specific motivational dispositions that are stabilized during the course of human development and may become an enduring or transitional component of a person's self-system. Other metatheoretical issues concern the question of which "model of man" should be used as the starting point for building a theory and which conception of the human personality is appropriate to describe and explain the role of interest-based motivation in learning and development.

In accordance with other theories (e.g., Deci & Ryan, 1985, 1991; Nuttin, 1984; Renninger, 2000), it has been suggested that a purely cognitive–rational model for describing the course of interest development is limited (Krapp, 1999a, in press). As a consequence, POI refers to a *personality–theoretic framework* that takes different levels of action control into account (c.f. below). Furthermore, POI suggests the use of an approach to personality that reconstructs motivational aspects of the developing person not only with respect to individual differences, but also with respect to functional relations and general "laws" of human development. In accordance with Deci and Ryan's "theory of self-determination" (SDT), it is postulated that such a theory has to take into account the fact that the person is aware of himself or herself, and that the "object" of this awareness is some sort of representation of the individual's personal "self". The self can be seen as the central area of an individual's structure of personality. During one's course of life, the psychological system that represents a person's self changes continually. Already existing components become more and more differentiated, others are reduced and finally excluded from the central area of a person's self. Since the person tries to create and maintain a coherent image, a "good Gestalt" of his/her sense of self, he or she cannot identify completely with all the thoughts, actions, tasks, and strivings, even if they are experienced as being important for the individual's wishes and future goals at that particular moment. As a consequence, only a rather limited selection of possible learning goals will become a longer-lasting integral part of a person's self-system.

1.2 Basic Characteristics of the Interest Construct

In accordance with ideas of Lewin (1951), Nuttin (1984), Deci & Ryan (1985, 1991), Renninger (2000) and many others, it is postulated that the individual, as a potential source of action, and the environment as the object of action, constitute a bipolar unit. Therefore, the interest-construct is conceptualized as a relational concept. An interest represents or describes a specific relationship between a person and an object of his or her "life-space" (Lebensraum; c.f. Lewin, 1951). It can be interpreted as a specific "person–object-relationship". An object of interest can refer to concrete things, a topic, subject-matter, an abstract idea, or any other content of the cognitively represented life-space.

The most important characteristics of an interest-specific relationship refer to one's values and feelings. From this point of view, an interest is composed of value-related and feeling-related valences (U. Schiefele, 1991; Krapp, 1993, 1999a, in press). *Value-related valences* refer to the assumption that any interest has a certain quality of personal significance. *Feeling-related valences* refer to a person's positive experiential state while being engaged in an interest-based activity, for example joy, optimal arousal or feelings of competence, autonomy and social relatedness. Thus, interest-based interactions with the environment are character-ized by optimal experiential modes that combine positive cognitive qualities (e.g., thoughts on meaningful goals) and positive affective qualities. Under extremely optimal conditions, *flow* may be experienced (Csikszentmihalyi, 1990). A further essential feature of interest is its intrinsic character. Interest-based activities meet the criterion of *self-intentionality* which means that an interest-related goal is com-patible with a person's actually preferred values and ideals. There is no gap between what a person has to do in a specific situation, and what the person wishes (or likes) to do (Dewey, 1913; Rathunde, 1993).

Conceptualizing interest as an interactive relation between an individual and certain aspects of his/her life-space makes it possible to study the conditions for, and effects of, interest from various research perspectives using different levels of analysis. On a first level, interest refers to current engagements. It describes a state or an ongoing process during an actual learning activity. This is the case when we observe the learning behavior of a student and characterize his or her motivational state as "being interested". On a second level, interest refers to the dispositional (or "habitual") structure of an individual. Here, interest is interpreted as a rela-tively stable tendency to occupy oneself with an object of interest. On this level, one usually speaks of *individual interest* (c.f. Krapp *et al.*, 1992; Renninger, 1990, 1992, 2000).

1.3 Development of Interest

From an educational point of view, it is important to know how an educationally desirable interest develops and which conditions are responsible for developmental change. This process is usually a multi-stage process. Therefore, one must consider a developmental continuum between the very beginning of a situational interest on the one hand, and a stabilized interest of a person who has totally identified with the related object of interest on the other hand. This idea has already been pointed out by Dewey (1913). In recent discussions on the role of interest in teaching and learning (e.g., Hidi, 2000; Hidi & Harackiewicz, 2000; Krapp, 1998, 1999b, Mitchell, 1993) the use of a developmental model that differentiates between three types of interest has been suggested. From an ontogenetic perspective they can be interpreted as three prototypical stages of interest development: (1) a situational interest awakened or triggered by external stimuli for the first time; (2) a situational interest that lasts during a certain learning phase and (3) an individual interest that represents a relatively enduring predisposition to concern oneself in a certain object-area of interest.

A developmental model that starts from such a conceptual differentiation has to describe and explain the occurrence of two qualitatively different "steps" of interest development (Krapp, 1998, 1999b): first, the shift from the transitional state of actual attraction to a more stable motivational state which is a necessary condition for deeper-level learning; and second, the shift from a rather stabilized situational interest to a more or less enduring individual interest.

The Role of Different Subsystems of Action Control. In order to be able to understand conditions and processes of interest development at the level of intra-individual changes, functional concepts and theories about the regulation of human behavior are needed. In accordance with theoretical models discussed in other fields of psychological research referring to developmental aspects in human motivation (e.g., Brunstein *et al.*, 1999; Epstein, 1990; McClelland *et al.*, 1989; Heckhausen, 2000), POI postulates a psychological system that operates at different levels of human experience and action control. A first subsystem is based on emotional states that remain mostly on a subconscious level of experience. It works rather autonomously and does not require reflective awareness in order to function in a proper way. A second subsystem seems to be typical for human beings and, thus, has been the main focus of modern cognitive psychology. Contrary to the control system at the first level, the second system is based mainly on decisions that a person consciously makes with respect to future goals and intentions. This cognitive subsystem requires the use of volitionally-directed strategies of action control.

With respect to conditions of interest development that can explain intra-individual changes on the basis of functional psychological principles, POI assumes that a person will only engage continuously in a certain area of tasks and/or topic-related objects if he or she assesses these engagements on the basis of rational considerations as sufficiently important (value-related valences), and if he or she experiences the course of interactions as positive and emotionally satisfactory on the whole (Krapp, 1999a, 2000; c.f. also Deci, 1992, 1998).

There is quite a number of theories and empirical research approaches that provide concepts and empirically tested models to describe and explain the regulation processes at the cognitive–rational level, for example concepts developed in the tradition of achievement motivation that describe the process of intention-formation (Heckhausen, 1991), theories about self-regulated learning (c.f. Boekaerts *et al.*, 2000) and personal goals (c.f., Brunstein & Maier, 1996; Elliott, & Dweck, 1988; Pervin 1989), or the broad variety of theoretical and empirical approaches that use the concept of self-efficacy (Schunk, 1991; Bandura, 1997). However, there is considerably less theoretical foundation for describing the processes that control the dynamics of motivated learning at the level of emotional experiences and situation-specific affects. Therefore, we have emphasized the role of affect-related experiences in our theoretical and empirical work.

The Role of Basic Psychological Needs in Interest Development. In the past few years, we have tried to specify those emotional experiences that are important to the course of interest development using the concept of basic psychological needs. Referring to Nuttin's (1984) "relational theory of behavioral dynamics" and Deci and Ryan's "theory of self-determination" (SDT; c.f., Deci & Ryan, 1985, 1991; Ryan, 1995), we assume that living organisms are naturally endowed not only with a system of innate basic *biological* needs (e.g., drives) but also with a system of basic *psychological* needs. During ontogenesis, these needs become more and more integrated into the increasingly complex systems of behavior control. Three qualitatively different basic needs can be distinguished within this system, namely, competence, autonomy, and social relatedness. Just as the fulfillment of basic biological needs is a natural necessity, sufficient fulfillment of the three psychological needs is a necessary requirement for optimal functioning of the psychological system.

It is important to notice that the meaning of "basic need" in these theories is not identical with the need-concept in everyday language or in traditional theories of motivation (c.f., Murray, 1938). They have to be understood as components of a holistically functioning system that provides continual signals about the functional efficiency of the current person–environment interactions on a mostly subconscious level of information processing (c.f., Nuttin, 1984). The conceptual separation into three specific needs is a theoretical construction in order to be able to investigate this phenomenon in a meaningful way in empirical approaches.

2. An Empirical Project to Explore the Development of Interests and Motivational Orientations in Dependence of Context

In our recent empirical research, developmental aspects have become a central focus. Besides the question of how interests and interest-based motivational orientations develop in dependence of context variables, we are mostly interested in exploring the functional principles of motivational development.

2.1 Theoretical Framework

In the theoretical framework which gives an overview of the kind of variables we are using in our empirical studies (see Figure 1), two motivational concepts form the main part of the *dependent variables*: vocation-related interests and motivational orientations. Whereas an interest is always directed to a more or less

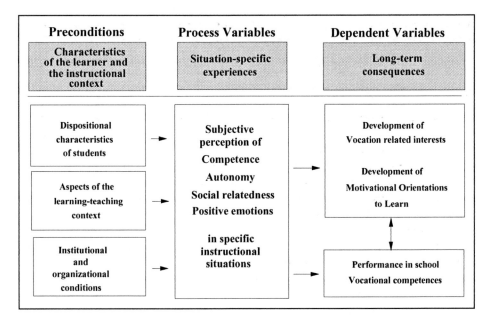

Figure 1: Theoretical framework of the research project.

specified content or object area (c.f. above), a motivational orientation refers to a person's generalized and relatively stable tendency to be motivated to learn by a specific category of incentives (Nolen, 1988; Pintrich, 2000; U. Schiefele, 1996). Recently, the concept of motivational orientation has been mostly discussed under the label *goal orientation* (e.g., Ames & Ames, 1989; Köller, 1998; Dweck, 1992; Pintrich, 2000). With respect to the concern of our study, "intrinsic goal orientations" are of special relevance. They are characterized by a person's motivational tendency to learn because instruction is enjoyable or because the content is experienced as "interesting". In the following presentation of results, we also take the opposite of these interest-related motivational orientations into account, namely "extrinsic goal orientations". They are characterized by the tendency to be motivated by external rewards and incentives (e.g., good marks, parental praise, or the wish to "be better" than others). The consideration of extrinsic orientations provides an opportunity to compare the effects of preconditions and process variables on the dependent variables used in our studies (c.f. Figure 1). In some of these studies, we have also taken cognitive outcome-criteria into account (e.g., performance in school or vocational competences).

Motivational development during vocational education can be analyzed under two different perspectives. First, the perspective of preconditions which can be located either in the person (dispositional characteristics of the students) or in different aspects of the context, including both institutional or organizational variables and specific conditions of the educational setting (e.g., curriculum, teaching strategies). Second, the perspective of process variables, especially situation-specific experiences and processes (e.g., the kind of emotional or cognitive experiences in specific learning and teaching situations). In accordance with the theoretical conceptualizations described above, we expect that the development of interest and intrinsic motivational orientations is a function of both the contextual and individual preconditions and the current situation-specific experiences (e.g., the opportunity to experienc competence, autonomy and social relatedness).

2.2 Design and Methods of the Longitudinal Study

As mentioned above, our research project consists of a series of separate but theoretically interrelated studies in the field of vocational education. VE in Germany is based on the so-called "dual system" and starts after students have accomplished either primary or secondary education. It extends over a period of two or two and a half years, respectively. Students who want to enter VE have to apply for a job in a company that is willing to provide professional training according to state-approved regulations. As a consequence, learning takes place in two rather different institutional contexts, the vocational school ("Berufsschule") and a "real" workplace in the companies (e.g., insurance companies). In the companies, VE includes periods of instruction at the place of work and formal in-house teaching. Twice a year, the students attend a vocational school for a period of six weeks. For the rest of the year, they work for the company.

Our research project concerns VE in the field of insurance business. In an initial longitudinal study, we wanted to obtain an overview of the kinds of observable motivational changes that might occur during the training period and the beginning of regular employment. Figure 2 provides an overview of the design and measurements of this study (for a detailed description of the procedures of data collection c.f. Wild *et al.*, 1994; Wild *et al.*, 1995).

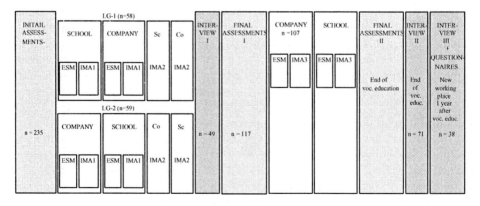

Figure 2: Design and methods of data collection.

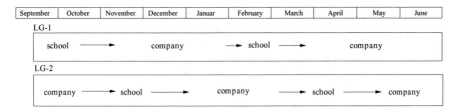

Figure 3: Rotation between instruction in school and in the workplace within the first year of vocational education for longitudinal group LG-1 and LG-2.

Sample. A total of 117 freshmen (apprentices) of insurance business participated in the study. In order to have a broader sample for statistical analyses referring to the measurement criteria of some scales, we gained data from 235 subjects at the first measurement point (initial assessments; see Figure 2). The students were drawn from 13 different companies. About half of the sample started their education in school (N = 58), while the other half started their education in the companies (N = 59). Thus, we have two longitudinal groups during the first year of training (LG-1 and LG-2; see Figures 2 and 3). At the end of the first year and at the end of the entire vocational training, two sub-samples of apprentices (n_1 = 49; n_2 = 71) were interviewed; one year after the end of the VE, an additional third interview together with a questionnaire-inquiry was realized with 38 subjects who were employed after having finished their training successfully.

Measures. Data collection was performed according to the following schedule:

Initial assessments: Questionnaires and tests were used to assess cognitive and motivational characteristics of the apprentices at the beginning of VE, including intelligence, prior knowledge; general interest towards the contents of the vocational education ("VE-interest"); intrinsic and extrinsic goal orientations; self-efficacy and the kind of preferred learning strategies. (A more detailed description of some of the scales will be given when we report on the results).

Experience Sampling Method (ESM): In the first and in the second year, ESM was used in each case during a one-week session in vocational school and another one-week session in the companies in which the apprentices were employed. The ESM-procedure requires the students to carry a signaling device with them while they are following their "normal" activities. As signaling and recording device we used a programmable pocket calculator. The calculator was programmed to give signals at random intervals. When being signaled, the respondent has to supply answers to a number of rating scales referring to his or her momentary external and internal situation. These scales are presented on a small sheet of paper attached to the pocket calculator. The answers, however, are directly typed into the calculator. The items of the Experience Sampling Form (ESF) contained questions on the students' perceptions of the actual situation and his or her subjective experiences ("psychological states") in the actual situation (e.g., quality of need-related emotional experiences, perceived "reasons to learn"). Furthermore, there were a number of items concerning the location, social context and content of thought (c.f. Wild *et al.*, 1994).

Intermediate assessments (IMA): Questionnaires were administered to subjects three times in each context including (a) scales to assess the perception of the learning and/or working context (e.g., the kind of teaching–learning situation; teaching objectives; perceived motivating techniques of teachers/instructors) and (b) scales to assess participants' motivational orientations and learning strategies.

Interview-study I and II: With two sub-samples, in-depth interviews were conducted to explore subjectively perceived changes of job-related content-specific interests during the past period of vocational training. The first interview with 49 students took place at the end of the first year; the second interview with 71 subjects was scheduled for the end of the entire vocational education.

Final assessments I and II: Questionnaires and tests that had been used at the initial and intermediate assessments were administered to participants once again at the end of the first year and at the end of the entire VE program.

Interview III: 38 subjects from the longitudinal sample who were employed after having finished their vocational training were interviewed one year after the transition from VE to a regular employment in the insurance company. Besides the interview, subjects were asked to fill in once more an "interest" questionnaire. In both inquiries, the same procedure and the same kind of questions were used as in the preceding stages of data collection.

3. Findings Specific to Context Specificity

In the following, we will present exemplary results from the longitudinal study. The first three sections refer to descriptive analyses of the course of the development in the area VE-interest, motivational orientations and content-specific interests. In a forth section, we will present results from explanatory analyses concerning the role of need-related emotional experiences in the observed courses of motivational development. In both kinds of analyses, we consider inter-individual as well as intra-individual differences and changes.

3.1 Developmental Trajectories of General Interest into the Topics and Contents of Vocational Education

VE-interest is supposed to measure the general interest into the topics, activities and learning tasks of VE and training in school and in the company. It was measured by the scale "Interest in Vocational Education" which is an adaptation of the "Study Interest Questionnaire" (SIQ; Schiefele *et al.*, 1993). The scale shows a high reliability at all times of the longitudinal study (scores reached from 0.88 to 0.92). Figure 4 shows two graphs representing the developmental trajectories of average VE-interest scores.

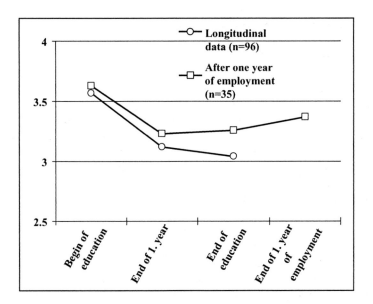

Figure 4: Developmental trajectories of VE-interest scores from the beginning of vocational education until the end of the first year of employment (From Lewalter, Wild & Krapp, 2001).

The lower line relates to data from those subjects of the longitudinal sample of whom we could raise a complete set of data (n = 96); the upper line relates to data from those 35 subjects that were employed after finishing their training. We can note a clear decline of general VE-interest during the whole time of training. The decline of the VE-interest scores from the first to the second measuring point is statistically significant $\eta^2 = 0.40$; p<0.01). The decline from the second to the third time of measuring cannot be statistically ensured $\eta^2 = 0.03$; p = 0.10). The curve of the sub-sample of those subjects that were employed after finishing the VE program is nearly identical. Here, too, a strong decline of the VE-interest scores can be noted from the beginning of the education to the end of the second year that is statistically significant $\eta^2 = 0.46$; p<0.01). In the second year, VE-interest scores remain stable $\eta^2 = 0.0$; ns). In the further course, a slight rise can be observed; the upwards trend after employment, however, cannot be ensured statistically $\eta^2 = 0.03$; ns).

3.2 Developmental Trajectories of Motivational Orientations

In contrast to VE-interest, motivational orientations were not only recorded at the beginning, middle and at the end of the training, but also during the intermediate assessments undertaken in the two training contexts: vocational school and company. In sum, data about motivational orientations are available from six measurement points (c.f. Figure 2). Furthermore, these motivational variables were measured with respect to the specific characteristics and contents of both teaching and learning contexts. Thus, it is possible to reconstruct the average course of development in dependence of the two different *institutional contexts*. The following data concern the analysis of developmental trajectories of two motivational orientations: intrinsic or interest orientation (IMO) and extrinsic orientation (EMO), which have been first reported in K.-P. Wild (2000). The intrinsic motivation scale (IMO) measures the extent to which students learn because they are interested in a certain topic at school or in the company and how far they assess the contents of instruction to be personally important (c.f., Wild *et al.*, 1995). The extrinsic motivational orientation scale (EMO) is captured by four items measuring "success orientation". They ask, for example, how far students learn primarily because they want to receive good marks (c.f. Wild *et al.*, 1995). The indices of internal consistency of both scales are at a satisfactory level (between $\alpha = 0.76$ and $\alpha = 0.94$).

Figure 5 shows the development trajectories of IMO- and EMO-scores over the entire period of the VE program. With exception of the first measure, all scores refer to "reasons to learn" during the *training periods in the insurance companies*. From the beginning to the end of the training we can find, in general, a negative trend in both cases. The negative trend is even clearer with EMO.

Developmental Trajectories in Dependence of the Institutional Context. In Figure 6, developmental trajectories of IMO- and EMO-scores are shown with respect to the repeated changes of the two contexts, school and company. Without going into detail, one can see a very strong dependence of both intrinsic and extrinsic learning goals from the institutional context: in the company, i.e., in the practical work

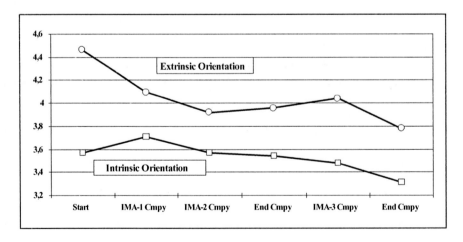

Figure 5: Intrinsic and extrinsic motivational orientations in the institutional context "company" (From K.-P. Wild, 2000, p. 84).

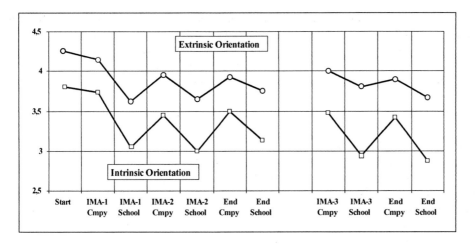

Figure 6: Intrinsic and extrinsic motivational orientations in dependence on the institutional contexts "school" and "company" (From Krapp & Wild, 1998).

area, higher values for IMO and EMO are registered than in school. The differences are more marked for IMO than for EMO. This is especially true for the second phase of the training.

3.3 Intra-Individual Reconstruction of the Development of Profession-Related Interests

The findings reported so far are from analyses of group-related data. They represent descriptions of average developmental trends in populations, and cannot directly be compared with the reconstruction of the developmental processes at the intra-individual level. According to Valsiner (1986) and others it is not justifiable, in principle, to draw conclusions from population data about the conditions and processes that govern an individual's course of development. Thus, the investigation of interest development from the perspective of intra-individual changes must be a research question of its own.

One possible methodical approach is the analysis of intra-individual changes of interests from the subjective perspective of the persons concerned. In order to test the efficiency of this approach, we carried out retrospective interviews at three different measuring points (c.f. Figure 2). In the following, we give a brief outline of the methods we used to achieve intra-individual reconstructions of vocation-related interests considering possible effects of the two different institutional contexts. (A more detailed description can be found in Lewalter *et al.*, 1998; Lewalter & Schreyer, 2000; Lewalter *et al.*, 2001).

The general goal of the interview-studies was to receive retrospective descriptions and explanations of the first occurrence and further development of specific

Table 1: Number of reported interests in interview I and II and subjectively recognized contextual source of interest development.

Sample		Total number of interests	Recognized source of development	
			School %	Company %
Interview I	All interests	111	19	81
(n = 49)	Most prominent interest	49	12	88
Interview II	All interests	181	15	85
(n = 71)	Most prominent interest	71	3	97

interests in the "object" area of VE. The trainees were asked which kind of topic- or action-specific interests they had acquired and maintained during the period of their education in the school and/or in the company as accurately as possible. Furthermore, they were asked to explain why they had developed this specific interest and to describe the subjectively experienced conditioning factors ("reasons" or "causes"). As a rule, this was done by using the most strongly developed interest. The interviewers did not ask for certain "possible" conditioning factors. The interviews were recorded on tape and transcribed completely. The findings for the first interview (end of first year) and the second year (end of entire training) are shown in Table 1.

During the first interview, 49 trainees mentioned 111 objects of interest that meet POI's criteria according to the definition explained above (Lewalter et al., 1998). The 71 students who were asked in the second interview mentioned 181 interests. With regard to the question of context-specificity of motivational development, the findings about the perceived contextual source of students' interests are important. As shown in Table 1, there are considerable differences between the two institutional contexts. Only relatively rarely the trainees state that they have developed new interests in the topic- and task-area of the vocational school (19 percent in the first and 15 percent in the second interview). The professional learning environment in the companies is far more important. In both interviews, more than 80 percent of the newly-developed interests have their origin in the context of the company. Looking at the strongest interests, the difference between both learning contexts becomes even more severe (see Table 1). Nearly all main interests (97 percent) at the end of the VE (interview II) were traced back to the learning context in the company.

3.4 The Role of Need-Related Emotional Experiences in Interest Development

Besides the description of developmental trajectories, our project aims to explain the observed inter- and intra-individual changes with respect to vocation-related interests and interest-related motivational orientations. One specific research question was directed to the exploration of *need-related emotional experiences* (n-Exp) in teaching and learning situations and their influence on the development of these motivational characteristics.

As with the analysis of the course of development, the question about the role of n-Exp can be answered from two different research perspectives: From a first perspective, data analysis aims to detect conditions or causes that are responsible for the occurrence of *inter-individual* differences during the process or at the end of a certain period of development. From a second perspective, the main aim of research is to identify the conditions or causes that can explain *intra-individual* changes during a certain period of development. Our data allow analyses from both perspectives.

a) HML Analyses Concerning the Role of Need-Related Emotional Experiences for the Development of Intrinsic and Extrinsic Motivational Orientations

K.-P. Wild (2000) has reported results based on HLM analyses (Bryk & Rauden-busch, 1992) using individual growth curves of IMO and EMO as dependent variables and indicators of need-related experiences as independent variables. The following results only refer to data from the workplace context. Empirical indicators of the quality of need-related experiences were drawn from scales of the MIZEBA-questionnaire (Zimmermann *et al.*, 1999) that was used in the three "Intermediate Assessments" (see Figure 2: IMA 1 to 3). The individual values in these scales which were compiled over the course of three measuring points serve as predictors in the HLM analyses (see Table 2).

All indicators of need-related experiences prove to be significant predictors of the individuals' growth curves of IMO. The results indicate concurrence with the theoretical assumption described above, i.e., that the subjectively-perceived degree of autonomy as well as the probability of experiencing positive achievement

Table 2: The influence of need-related experiences on the development of interest orientation and extrinsic orientation (HLM analyses based on questionnaire data; From K.-P. Wild, 2000. p. 87).

Indicators of need-related experiences	IMO			EMO		
	ß	t	p(t)	ß	t	p(t)
Autonomy	0.10	2.39	*	0.03	0.89	ns
Competence	0.15	3.62	**	0.09	2.40	*
Social relatedness						
Social climate	0.15	2.64	**	0.12	2.47	*
Integration in the culture of experts	0.12	3.11	**	0.04	1.19	ns

feedback as an indicator of the experience of competence goes along with a positive development of a motivational orientation based on interest. A positive social–emotional climate and the feeling of belonging to the "expert culture" at work — which can be interpreted as indicators of social relatedness — also appear to have a favorable influence on the development of IMO.

In our theoretical conception of interest, no explicit statements are made about the importance of the n-Exp for the development of *extrinsic* motivational orientations. At most it is assumed that they are on the whole of little importance and have an unspecific effect. K.-P. Wild's (2000) data agree with these general expectations: only two of the indicators included in the measurement of the n-Exp proved to be significant predictors of the EMO development (competence and social climate). For both values, the regression coefficients for EMO had lower values than for IMO.

The role of n-Exp was not only explored on the basis of questionnaire data but also on the basis of ESM data (Krapp & Wild, 1998). All of a person's individual ratings in the "Experience-Sampling-Forms" (see above) were aggregated over time separately for both institutional contexts. In a series of HLM-analyses, individual growth-curves of IMO and EMO were used as dependent variables and the aggregated ESM-measures of need-related experiences as independent variables. Students with a more positive development of interest orientation (IMO) reported a significantly higher level of feeling competent and self-determined (autonomous) in both contexts. However, we did not find a significant relation to social relatedness in these analyses. In HLM-analyses using the growth curves of EMO-scores as dependent variables, we found much lower coefficients in both contexts. And another result is remarkable: comparing the data for the two different time periods (first year vs. the rest of vocational education), there is a remarkable decline of predictive power after the first year of training.

b) Analyses of the Role of Need-Related Experiences for Development of Interests on the Basis of Intra-Individual Reconstructions

The results previously reported refer to the explanations of the genesis of motivational orientations. Contrary to the concept of interest, it deals with relatively general motivational dispositions not directed towards certain contents. The results about the importance of n-Exp for the development of motivational orientations thus can not be directly transferred to the question concerning the conditions necessary for developing specific topic-related interests in an individual's course of development. Indications about the importance of n-Exp in intra-individual development processes supply the results of our interview studies. With respect to the most prominent interest, the subjects were asked why they became involved in this specific topic and how they could explain the fact that they developed an interest in this specific area. Among other reasons, subjects spontaneously mentioned events and experiences that relate to the theoretically postulated basic needs. For a quantitative analysis for these need-related statements, we developed a system of categories that was based on both theoretical assumptions and empirical

Table 3: Percentage of subjects who refer to experiences of competence, autonomy or social relatedness in their explanations of the origins of their most prominent interest (From Lewalter *et al.*, 1998).

Need-related Experience	Interview I (n = 49) %	Interview II (n = 71) %
Competence	75	73
Autonomy	34	41
Relatedness	65	67

data. The system of categories takes the different facets of the particular need-related experience into account. For example, the statement "I became more and more interested because I could help the client, I had the experience of success" would have been interpreted as an indicator of the experience of competence (for a detailed description see Lewalter *et al.*, 1998).

The data show that subjects often mention need-related experiences when trying to explain the origins of their job-related interests (see Table 3). In the first year, 75 percent of the 49 subjects refer to competence and 65 percent refer to social relatedness as an important reason for interest development. However, only 34 percent mention the experience of autonomy. If we look at the results at the end of the second year (n = 71), we get almost the same picture. Only, the influence of autonomy seems to be a bit higher.

4. Discussion

At the outset of this chapter we have identified two closely related reasons why educational research in the field of motivation takes the fact of content- and/or context-specificity much less into consideration than cognitive-oriented research approaches, namely a lack of adequate theoretical concepts and methodical short-comings, such as the unbalanced usage of methods that are mainly suitable for exploring inter-individual differences and the generalized tendencies concerning the role of motivational dispositions in learning and development. The research approach we have outlined here is partly based on an educational–psychological theory of interest that explicitly refers to the fact that human motivation is, in principle, characterized by specific personal goals and more or less stable individual preferences. In accordance with other theoretical concepts developed in the area of recent interest research (c.f., Renninger *et al.*, 1992) the "person–object theory of interest" (POI) interprets interest as motivational category that is characterized to a great extent by its content or domain of "objects". Even though the aim of this chapter was not primarily directed to the problem of content specificity, we were able to demonstrate the fruitfulness of such a theoretical conceptualization. For example, it could be shown that the question of how interests and interest-related motivational characteristics develop during the period of vocation education lead to rather different answers when the related research approaches are more or less consequently based on the theoretical assumptions of the interest construct we have discussed in POI.

When analyzing developmental trends using either a totally content-unspecific concept like "motivational orientation" or a rather general interest concept like "VE-interest" that is supposed to represent the generalized interest of an individual into the totality of topics and activities offered in the vocational training program, we find definite *negative* developmental trajectories. In both cases our data show a marked decline, especially in the first months of the training. These results correspond with empirical findings in many other educational settings that have also found a negatively accelerated decline of subject interests over time (e.g., Anderman & Maehr, 1994; Baumert & Köller, 1998; Eccles & Wigfield, 1992; Fend, 2000; Gardner, 1985). We get, however, a qualitatively totally different picture when we use a research approach that reconstructs the process of interest development from a strictly intra-individual perspective. In our interview studies all students report that they developed new interests that relate to "objects" (contents, tasks, activities, knowledge areas) they studied during their vocational education. That is true for the first year as well as for the second year of vocational education. Not only in the sum of all individual cases but also for each single student, without exception, a *positive* developmental trend was found.

At first glance, these results seem to represent theoretically contradicting findings. But if we have a closer look at the theoretical meaning of the concepts used to operationalize "interest orientation" (IMO), "VE-interest" and "topic-related individual interest" this contradiction can easily be dissolved. Even though in all three cases the term interest is used to characterize the "content" of the theoretical concept, the meaning is not identical. On the contrary, the three concepts differ noticeably with respect to the degree of considering content-specificity of an individual's interests. Properly speaking, only the third research approach really takes care of the theoretically postulated fact that the contents of interests related to the same subject area vary remarkably between and within individuals when they are explored from a developmental research perspective. A related aspect is the kind of measures used to operationalize these concepts. IMO and VE-interest were measured by using questionnaires constructed according to common criteria of test construction that provide powerful instruments for measuring inter-individual differences. But these measures do not represent inter- or intra-individual differences with respect to specific contents or objects of vocation-related interests: IMO-measures do not ask for contents or topics at all, and the VE-interest-questionnaire only refers to contents of the vocational training program at a rather general level. A thorough reconstruction of the changing contents of an individual's pattern of interest was only achieved in the quantitative and qualitative reconstructions in the interview studies. Here we tried to gain data about the subjects' vocation-related interests, asking specifically about new individually shaped interest-topics the apprentices had learned to know in one of the contexts of their vocational training. Taken together, these findings show that it seems worthwhile to use different theoretical concepts and methodical approaches to explore interest-related phenomena.

The main concern of this chapter was to present empirical evidence for the importance of recognizing context-specificity in studies concerned with the development of motivational dispositions (motivational orientations; interests) and the functional conditions of motivational development. Our data did not allow context-specific analyses with respect to VE-interest. But we were able to analyze the developmental trends at the level of motivational orientations (IMO and EMO) and self-reported topic-related interests depending on the two institutional contexts that characterize the German "dual system", namely the vocational school and the work settings of the insurance companies, the trainees belonged to. In both cases the findings indicate a substantial influence of the context. The scores of both motivational orientations are much higher in the context of the company. This is especially true for the intrinsic orientation (IMO). In addition, the results show that there is no systematic connection between the kind of institutional context and the average degree of a particular motivational orientation. Combining these results with related findings of the interview studies we have a very good fit. Here, too, the results indicate a clear difference concerning the influence of the institutional context in favor of the educational setting in the company: According to the students' point of view the majority part of the interests were developed in the context of the work settings. This context seems to be more encouraging regarding the development of interest-related motivational dispositions by supporting the genesis of topic-specific individual interests respectively maintaining a somewhat higher intensity of intrinsic (and extrinsic) motivational orientations. In this connection we have to recognize that many of the topics of teaching and learning are quite similar in both contexts. Thus, the observed differential effects must be a matter of the quality of teaching and instruction in these contexts. In vocational school the topics are presented under a more theoretical perspective in a quite conservative fashion dominated by the "teacher talk". In the company the students are confronted with the same topics but the instructional situation is totally different. Here, a much broader variety of teaching methods is used, including discussions and hands-on activities. Furthermore, the contents are taught more often on the basis of authentic practical problems.

Thus, our results demonstrate very clearly that the (institutional) context plays an important role in vocational education when we try to describe and explain developmental conditions that are responsible for the development of content-specific motivational dispositions. Besides other aspects, the instructional design seems to be of special importance for fostering the development of enduring vocation-related interests.

According to POI, cognitive as well as affective experiential states in different learning situations (and learning contexts) can provide a functional explanation for the occurrence and maintenance of intrinsic motivational orientations and topic-specific interests. Referring to the concept of basic psychological needs, we have tried to explore the role of need-related experiences again using different measures and techniques of data analysis. In a first approach we used HLM-analyses in order to find out whether or not situation-specific ESM-measures of need-related experiences (n-Exp) can predict individuals' different growth-curves with respect to intrinsic and extrinsic motivational orientation. The results provide evidence that all three need-related experiential qualities are significant predictors of the individual growth curves of IMO. Concerning the EMO this is only true for the experience of competence and the aspect of social climate. Thus, these results seem to confirm our theoretical assumptions when using data from an inter-individual research perspective. The findings on the intra-individual access by interviews show that most of the students mention experiences related to basic needs when they describe spontaneously important conditions for the occurrence or mainte-nance of new topic-related interest in the area vocational education. However, we have noticed that not all students interviewed refer to all three need-related experi-ences; usually they only mention one or two. Thus, the findings do not completely confirm our theoretical assumptions.

Taken together, we can conclude from these data that in VE the need-related experiences play a substantial role for the development of both interests and interest-related motivational orientations. In many respects the results correspond with findings in other areas of research which also have shown, that situation-specific experiences related to the basic need (especially the need for experiencing competence) seem to have an important influence on the development of interest (Prenzel *et al.*, 1998; Kleinmann *et al.*, 1998; E. Wild, 2000) and intrinsic motiva-tion (Ryan, 1995). In our study we also found some evidence that the opportunity to fulfill basic psychological needs depends on a variety of content- and context-specific variables. A detailed exploration of these dependencies will be one of the next steps in the further analyses of our rather comprehensive database.

References

Ames, C., & Ames, R. (eds). (1989), *Research on Motivation in Education. Vol. 3: Goals and Cognitions*. San Diego: Academic Press.

Anderman, E. M., & Maehr, M. L. (1994), "Motivation and schooling in the middle grades." *Review of Educational Research 64*, 267–309.

Bandura, A. (1997), *Self-Efficacy: The Exercise of Control*. New York: Freeman.

Baumert, J., & Köller, O. (1998), "Interest research concerning secondary level I: An overview." In L. Hoffmann, A. Krapp, K. A. Renninger & J. Baumert (eds) *Interest and Learning. Proceedings of the Seeon-Conference on Interest and Gender* (pp. 241–256). Kiel: IPN.

Beck, K. (2000), *Lehr-Lern-Prozesse in der Kaufmännischen Erstausbildung — ein Schwerpunktprogramm der Deutschen Forschungsgemeinschaft. Kurzberichte und Bibliographie*. Landau: Verlag Empirische Pädagogik.

Boekaerts, M., Pintrich, P., & Zeidner, M. (2000), *Handbook of Self-Regulation*. London: Academic Press.

Brunstein, J. C., & Maier, G. W. (1996), "Persönliche Ziele: Ein Überblick zum Stand der Forschung." *Psychologische Rundschau 47*, 146–160.

Brunstein, J. C., Maier G. W., & Schultheiss, O. C. (1999), "Motivation und Persönlichkeit: Von der Analyse von Teilsystemen zur Analyse von Interaktion." In M. Jerusalem & R. Pekrun (eds) *Emotion, Motivation und Leistung* (pp. 147–167). Göttingen: Hogrefe.

Bryk, A. S., & Raudenbush, S. W. (1992), *Hierarchical Linear Models: Applications and Data Analysis Methods.* Newbury Park, CA: Sage Publications.

Chi, M. T. H., Glaser, R., & Farr, M. J. (eds). (1988), *The Nature of Expertise.* Hillsdale, NJ: Erlbaum.

Csikszentmihalyi, M. (1990), *Flow.* New York: Harper & Row.

Deci, E. L. (1992), "The relation of interest to the motivation of behavior: A self-determination theory perspective." In K. A. Renninger, S. Hidi & A. Krapp (eds) *The Role of Interest in Learning and Development* (pp. 43–47). Hillsdale, NJ.: Erlbaum.

Deci, E. L. (1998), "The relation of interest to motivation and human needs — the self-determination theory viewpoint." In L. Hoffmann, A. Krapp, K. A. Renninger & J. Baumert (eds) *Interest and Learning. Proceedings of the Seeon-Conference on Interest and Gender* (pp. 146–162). Kiel: IPN.

Deci, E. L., & Ryan, R. M. (1985), *Intrinsic Motivation and Self-Determination in Human Behavior.* New York: Plenum Press.

Deci, E. L., & Ryan, R. M. (1991), "A motivational approach to self: Integration in personality." In R. Dienstbier (ed.) *Nebraska Symposium on Motivation: Vol. 38, Perspectives on Motivation* (pp. 237–288). Lincoln, NE: University of Nebraska Press.

Dewey, J. (1913), *Interest and Effort in Education.* Boston: Riverside Press.

Dweck, C. S. (1992), "The study of goals in psychology." *Psychological Science 3,* 165–167.

Eccles, J. S., & Wigfield, A. (1992), "The development of achievement-task values: A theoretical analysis." *Developmental Review 12,* 256–273.

Elliott, E. S., & Dweck, C. S. (1988), "Goals: An approach to motivation and achievement." *Journal of Personality and Social Psychology 54,* 5–12.

Epstein, S. (1990), "Cognitive–experiential self theory: Implications for developmental psychology." In A. Gunnar & L. A. Sroufe (eds) *Minnesota Symposia on Child Psychology: Self Processes and Development* (Vol. 23, pp. 79–123). Hillsdale, NJ: Erlbaum.

Fend, H. (2000), *Entwicklungspsychologie.* Opladen: Leske & Budrich.

Gardner, P. L. (1985), "Students' interest in science and technology: an international overview." In M. Lehrke, L. Hoffmann & P. L. Gardner (eds) *Interests in Science and Technology Education* (pp. 15–34). Kiel: Institut für die Pädagogik der Naturwissenschaften.

Heckhausen, H. (1991), *Motivation and Action.* Berlin: Springer.

Heckhausen, J. (ed.). (2000), *Motivational Psychology of Human Development* (pp. 109–128). London: Elsevier.

Hidi, S. (2000), "An interest researcher's perspective on the effects of extrinsic and intrinsic factors on motivation." In C. Sansone & J. M. Harackiewicz (eds) *Intrinsic and Extrinsic Motivation. The Search for Optimal Motivation and Performance* (pp. 309–339). New York: Academic Press.

Hidi, S., & Harackiewicz, J. M. (2000), "Motivating the academically unmotivated: A critical issue for the 21st century." *Review of Educational Research 70,* No. 2, 154–179.

Hoffmann, R. R. (ed.). (1992), *The Psychology of Expertise.* New York: Springer.

Kleinmann, M., Straka, G. A., & Hinz, I. M. (1998), "Motivation und selbsgesteuertes Lernen im Beruf." In J. Abel & C. Tarnai (eds) *Pädagogisch-Psychologische Interessenforschung in Studium und Beruf* (pp. 95–109). Münster: Waxmann.

Köller, O. (1998), "Different aspects of learning motivation: The impact of interest and goal orientation on scholastic learning." In L. Hoffmann, A. Krapp, K. A. Renninger & J.

Baumert (eds) *Interest and Learning. Proceedings of the Seeon-Conference on Interest and Gender* (pp. 317–326). Kiel: IPN.

Krapp, A. (1993), *The Construct of Interest: Characteristics of Indvidual Interests and Interest-Related Actions from the Perspective of a Person–Object-Theory.* Studies in Educational Psychology. Munich: Institut für Empirische Pädagogik und Pädagogische Psychologie der Universität der Bundeswehr.

Krapp, A. (1998), "Entwicklung und Förderung von Interessen im Unterricht." *Psychologie in Erziehung und Unterricht 45*, 186–203.

Krapp, A. (1999a), "Interest, motivation and learning: An educational–psychological perspective." *European Journal of Psychology in Education 14*, 23–40.

Krapp, A. (1999b), *Structural and Dynamic Relations between Situational and Individual Interest — Theoretical Considerations and Empirical Results from a Developmental Perspective.* Paper presented at the 8th European Conference for Research on Learning and Teaching (EARLI) in Gothenburg, Sweden.

Krapp, A. (2000), "Interest and human development during adolescence: An educational–psychological approach." In J. Heckhausen (ed.) *Motivational Psychology of Human Development* (pp. 109–128). London: Elsevier.

Krapp, A. (in press), "The person–object-theory of interest and its relation to self-determination theory." In E. Deci & R. Ryan (eds) *New Perspectives in Self-Determination Theory.* Rochester: University of Rochester Press.

Krapp, A., Hidi, S., & Renninger, K. A. (1992), "Interest, learning and development." In K. A. Renninger, S. Hidi & A. Krapp (eds) *The Role of Interest in Learning and Development* (pp. 3–25). Hillsdale, NJ: Erlbaum.

Krapp, A., & Wild, K.-P. (1998), *The Development of Interest in School and Work Settings: A Longitudinal Study based on Experience-Sampling.* Paper presented at the 24th International Congress of the Association of Applied Psychology. August 9–14, 1998. San Francisco.

Lewalter, D., Krapp, A., Schreyer, I., & Wild, K.-P. (1998), "Die Bedeutsamkeit des Erlebens von Kompetenz, Autonomie und sozialer Eingebundenheit für die Entwicklung berufsspezifischer Interessen." In K. Beck & R. Dubs (eds) *Kompetenzentwicklung in der Berufserziehung — Kognitive, Motivationale und Moralische Dimensionen Kaufmännischer Qualifizierungsprozesse. Zeitschrift für Berufs- und Wirtschaftspädagogik, Beiheft 14*, 143–168. Stuttgart: Steiner.

Lewalter, D., & Schreyer, I. (2000), "Entwicklung von Interessen und Abneigungen — zwei Seiten einer Medaille." In U. Schiefele & K.-P. Wild (eds) *Interesse und Lernmotivation* (pp. 53–72). Münster: Waxmann.

Lewalter, D., Wild, K.-P., & Krapp, A. (in press), "Interessenentwicklung in der beruflichen Ausbildung." In. K. Beck & V. Krumm (eds) *Lehren und Lernen in der Beruflichen Erstausbildung. Grundlagen einer Modernen Kaufmännischen Berufsqualifizierung.* Opladen: Leske & Budrich.

Lewin, K. (1951), *Field Theory in Social Science.* New York: Harper & Row.

McClelland, D. C., Koestner, R., & Weinberger, J. (1989), "How do self-attributed and implicit motives differ?" *Psychological Review 96*, 690–702.

Mitchell, M. (1993), "Situational interest: Its multifaceted structure in the secondary school mathematics classroom." *Journal of Educational Psychology 85*, 424–436.

Murray, H. A. (1938), *Explorations in Personality.* New York: Oxford University Press.

Nolen, S. B. (1988), "Reasons for studying: Motivational orientations and study strategies." *Cognition and Instruction 5*, 269–287.

Nuttin, J. (1984), *Motivation, Planning, and Action.* Hillsdale, NJ: Erlbaum.

Pervin, L. A. (eds). (1989), *Goal Concepts in Personality and Social Psychology.* Hillsdale, NJ: Erlbaum.

Pintrich, P. R. (2000), "The role of goal orientation in self-regulated learning." In M. Boekaerts, P. R. Pintrich & M. Zeidner (eds) *Handbook of Self-Regulation: Theory, Research and Applications* (pp. 451–502). San Diego, CA: Academic Press.

Prenzel, M., Kramer, K., & Drechsel, B. (1998), "Changes in learning motivation and interest in vocational education: Halfway through the study." In L. Hoffmann, A. Krapp, K. A. Renninger & J. Baumert (eds) *Interest and Learning. Proceedings of the Seeon-Conference on Interest and Gender* (pp. 430–440). Kiel: IPN.

Rathunde, K. (1993), "The experience of interest: A theoretical and empirical look at its role in adolescent talent development." In M. Maehr & P. R. Pintrich (eds) *Advances in Motivation and Achievement* (Vol. 8, pp. 59–98). London: Jai Press Inc.

Renninger, K. A. (1990), "Children's play interests, representation, and activity." In R. Fivush & J. Hudson (eds) *Knowing and Remembering in Young Children* (Bd. III. Emory Cognition Series, pp. 127–147). Cambridge, MA: Cambridge University Press.

Renninger, K. A. (1992), "Individual interest and its implications for understanding of intrinsic motivation." In K. A. Renninger, S. Hidi & A. Krapp (eds) *The Role of Interest in Learning and Development* (pp. 361–395). Hillsdale, NJ.: Erlbaum.

Renninger, K. A. (2000), "Individual interest and its implications for understanding of intrinsic motivation." In C. Sansone & J. M. Harackiewicz (eds) *Intrinsic and Extrinsic Motivation. The Search for Optimal Motivation and Performance* (pp. 373–404). New York: Academic Press.

Renninger, K. A., Ewen, L., & Lasher, A. K. (in press), "Individual interest as context in expository text and mathematical word problems." *Learning and Instruction.*

Renninger, K. A., Hidi, S., & Krapp, A. (eds). (1992), *The Role of Interest in Learning and Development.* Hillsdale, NJ: Erlbaum.

Ryan, R. M. (1995), "Psychological needs and the facilitation of integrative process." *Journal of Personality 63* (3), 397–427.

Schiefele, H. (1974), *Lernmotivation und Motivlernen.* München: Ehrenwirth.

Schiefele, U. (1991), "Interest, learning and motivation." *Educational Psychologist 26* (2 & 3), 299–323.

Schiefele, U. (1996), *Motivation und Lernen mit Texten.* Göttingen: Hogrefe.

Schiefele, U., Krapp, A., Wild, K.-P., & Winteler, A. (1993), "Eine neue Version des 'Fragebogen zum Studieninteresse' (FSI). Untersuchungen zu Reliabiliät und Validiät." *Diagnostica 39*, 335–351.

Schober, K., & Tessaring, M. (1993), "Eine unendliche Geschichte. Vom Wandel im Bildungs- und Berufswahlverhalten Jugendlicher." *Materialien aus der Arbeitsmarkt- und Berufsforschung 3*, 1–19.

Schunk, D. H. (1991), "Self-efficacy and academic motivation." *Educational Psychologist 26*, 207–231.

Valsiner, J. (1986), "Between groups and individuals. Psychologists' and laypersons' interpretations of correlational findings." In J. Valsiner (ed.) *The Individual Subject and Scientific Psychology* (pp. 113–151). New York: Plenum Press.

Wild, E. (2000), *Elterliche Erziehung und Schulische Lernmotivation.* Münster: Waxmann.

Wild, K.-P. (2000), "Die Bedeutung betrieblicher Lernumgebungen für die langfristige Entwicklung intrinsischer und extrinsischer motivationaler Lernorientierungen." In U. Schiefele & K.-P. Wild (eds) *Interesse und Lernmotivation* (pp. 73–93). Münster: Waxmann.

Wild, K.-P., Krapp, A., Schiefele, U., Lewalter, D., & Schreyer, I. (1995), "Dokumentation und Analyse der Fragebogenverfahren und Tests." *Berichte aus dem DFG-Projekt "Bedingungen und Auswirkungen Berufsspezifischer Lernmotivation" Nr. 2.* Neubiberg: Universität der Bundeswehr München.

Wild, K.-P., Lewalter, D., & Schreyer, I. (1994), "Design und Untersuchungsmethoden des Projekts 'Bedingungen und Auswirkungen berufsspezifischer Lernmotivation'". *Berichte aus dem DFG-Projekt "Bedingungen und Auswirkungen Berufsspezifischer Lernmotivation" Nr. 1.* Neubiberg: Universität der Bundeswehr München.

Zimmermann, M., Wild, K.-P., & Müller, W. (1999), "Das 'Mannheimer Inventar zur Erfassung betrieblicher Ausbildungssituation' (MIZEBA)." *Zeitschrift für Berufs- und Wirtschaftspädagogik 95,* 373–402.

Chapter 12

Student Motivation and Self-Regulation as a Function of Future Time Perspective and Perceived Instrumentality

Willy Lens, Joke Simons & Siegfried Dewitte

"Do your best at school, it is so important for your future" was good advice, but many of us were tired of hearing it when we were in school. Being parents ourselves now — even the educational psychologist among us, doing research on student motivation, and knowing from the work by Locke and his collaborators (e.g., Locke & Latham, 1990) that such a vague and unspecified goal is not very motivating — we use that same advice to motivate our children. Also teachers very often refer to the future importance of education to motivate pupils and students.

By definition, schooling is future-oriented. Governments and also private institutions organize and finance schools to educate younger people for the future. Many students are indeed to a large extent motivated to study and to do their best at school by the educational and/or professional consequences in the future. People in the field realize very well that the future implications of education can be an important motivational resource for an individual. On the other hand however, this aspect of student motivation is almost totally neglected in educational psychology. Most chapters and handbooks on motivation in education discuss only different types of intrinsic motivation and the positive or negative effects of more or less immediate extrinsic rewards (Ames & Ames, 1984; Dweck, 1986; Pintrich & Schunk, 1996). They neglect the temporal context of education in pupils' life career.

In this chapter we will try to document theoretically, and with empirical data, the motivational role of perceived instrumentality, utility value and future time perspective. We will attempt to integrate it with commonly used motivational theories in educational psychology (i.e., achievement motivation, intrinsic–extrinsic motivation and self-determination, and goal theories). These are "process-theories", considering motivation as a psychological process in which personality dispositions (e.g., needs), and contextual characteristics, interact. Kurt Lewin's famous behavioral formula [B = f(P,E); B = behavior P = person E = environment] applies also to motivation as a process. The strength of the motivation or tendency to eat does not only depend on how hungry one is, but also on the characteristics of the food and the environment in which it is available. Intra- and inter-individual differences in student motivation result from interactions between

Motivation in Learning Contexts: Theoretical Advances and Methodological Implications, pages 233–248.
Copyright © 2001 by Elsevier Science Ltd.
All rights of reproduction in any form reserved.
ISBN: 0-08-043990-X

personal characteristics and those of the learning environment. This context can vary from very molar (e.g., family background, peers, school culture) to rather specific (e.g., the teacher's behavior, the content and difficulty of the learning task). In this chapter, we will focus on one particular feature of the learning context: the degree and the way in which a pupil is led to believe that the present behavior (learning or achieving) is instrumental for future goals. We discuss its motivational implications. Considering motivation as a psychological process implies that students' motivation can be affected by changing their needs, goals, expectations etc., but probably much easier by changing aspects of their learning context. However, due to the inter-individual differences among students, it is not possible to create a learning context on the class level that, from a motivational point of view, is most optimal for all pupils or students in that class.

Intrinsic versus Extrinsic Motivations

The first dimension on which students' goals can be situated is the intrinsic–extrinsic dimension. They are intrinsically motivated when learning and performing well at school are their final goals. Students then enjoy those activities as such; they are fun to do for their own sake. Until roughly the end of primary school most children have strong intrinsic interests to learn, to understand, to master. The need for knowledge (curiosity), the need to explore, to manipulate and the need for competence are inborn in animals and men. However, at the end of high-school there is not much left of the intrinsic motivation or interest in learning (Creten *et al.*, 2001; Harter & Jackson, 1992).

Students are extrinsically motivated to the extent that they learn and do their best at school because of material or immaterial rewards, punishments or pressures. Learning and performing are then instrumental activities; they are no longer "play" but "work". At each stage the total motivation is the sum of an intrinsic and an extrinsic component. This does not imply that the strength or intensity of these two components is independent. There is indeed empirical evidence showing that, over time, extrinsic motivation can negatively affect intrinsic motivation. In particular circumstances extrinsic rewards can undermine the intrinsic motivation (Deci & Ryan, 1985; Eisenberger *et al.*, 1999). We will argue that although instrumental motivation is (by definition) extrinsic, some types of instrumentality may rather enhance intrinsic motivation.

Secondly, students' goals can also be situated on the temporal scale. The goals of all types of intrinsically motivated behavior are (by definition) situated in the here and now. However, one might also have future goals for which a present intrinsically motivated task has instrumental value. The learning context may refer not only to the immediate, but also to the future relevance of the learning tasks. Contextual learning should not be limited to the present context as such. The anticipated individual future can create a meaningful context for learning and achieving, affecting student motivation, although the motivational role of the future may not have the same importance in different cultural contexts (Phalet &

Lens, 1995). The temporal localization of extrinsic goals can vary from the immediate to the very distant future.

By definition all intrinsic and extrinsic goals are personal goals. They may however differ very much regarding their origin. Some goals are self-set. Goal striving is then totally autonomous or self-determined (Deci & Ryan, 1985). But this is not the same as saying that individual and self-generated goals are formulated in isolation from the social and cultural context (Phalet & Lens, 1995). Further goals are imposed by others (parents, teachers, etc.) and may differ regarding the degree in which they are accepted as such. As we will discuss later, even these goals may differ in how much they are experienced as externally controlling one's behavior.

We first discuss briefly the role of the future in earlier theories of motivation. Moving to more recent developments of these theories, we observe that the motivational role of the future has been neglected. We further discuss the differential impact of several types of future goals on present motivation and goal orientation. We illustrate this impact with empirical evidence. In a final section, underlying hypothetical processes are discussed and relevant recent research is reviewed.

The Future in Achievement Motivation

Until recently, Atkinson's theory of resultant achievement motivation was widely used in research on student motivation (Atkinson & Feather, 1966; Atkinson & Raynor, 1974). It is a cognitive (expectancy × value) theory of intrinsic motivation to strive for success and to avoid failure in achievement tasks. To succeed and not to fail in the task is the goal related to the need for achievement and the fear of failure. Pride in accomplishment and being ashamed in the case of failure are the affective components of these motivational tendencies. The original theory of achievement motivation does not include the future as a motivational variable. The strength of the resultant intrinsic achievement motivation in a particular achievement task is a function of the need for achievement or motive to succeed, the motive to avoid failure, and the perceived difficulty of the achievement task or the subjective probability of success in that task, as the only contextual variable.

None of these components refers to the future. This does however not mean that the future has no motivational significance at all in the domain of achievement motivation. This should become clear when we look at how the strength of the need for achievement or the motive to succeed is measured in the McClelland–Atkinson tradition (McClelland *et al.*, 1953).

The clearest relationship to the future and to future time perspective is found in the second (unique accomplishment) and the third criterion (long-term involvement). Achievement imagery is scored when *"... one of the characters is involved in attainment of a long term achievement goal. Being a success in life, becoming a mechanic, a doctor, are all examples of careers which permit the inference of competition with a standard of excellence ... All types of career involvement permit the inference of competition with a standard of excellence unless it is made clear that another goal is primary, e.g., food for the kids, personal security"* (o.c., p. 184). The latter are indeed extrinsic goals.

Raynor (1969, 1974, 1981) elaborated Atkinson's theory to incorporate the concept of future time perspective (FTP). For Raynor, future time perspective is *"... the impact on motivation for some present activity of perceiving its instrumental relationship, as a step in a longer path, to more distant future goals and threatening consequences"* (Atkinson & Raynor, 1974, p. 5). He makes a distinction between isolated achievement tasks with no reference to the future (where the original theory of achievement motivation should be applied) and two types of future-oriented achievement tasks: contingent and non-contingent paths.

In a "non-contingent path" of achievement tasks, success in the foregoing task is not a prerequisite to strive for success in the next one (e.g., a series of exams at the end of a semester). There is no instrumental motivation.

In a "contingent path" of achievement tasks, success in the first task is a necessary condition to be allowed to try for success in the second task, and so on. Raynor's research on achievement motivation in contingent paths is relevant to our discussion of instrumental motivation. This type of future time perspective or instrumentality intensifies the achievement motivation in the first task. The longer a contingent path is (the more achievement tasks it includes) the stronger the resultant achievement motivation will be in the first task of that contingent path (positive for success-oriented and negative for test-anxious subjects).

In Raynor's theory, the immediate goal and the future goals that affect the present motivation, belong to the same motivational category, the intrinsic achievement motivation. The resultant achievement motivation in the first task in a contingent path has two components: the intrinsic achievement motivation for that task as such, plus a component that derives from the instrumentality of success in that task for future successes. Instrumental motivation is extrinsic motivation, but on the other hand, the two components are based on the same need system (the need for achievement and the fear of failure).

From the Theory of Achievement Motivation to Goal-Theory

In more recent research on motivation in educational settings, goal-theory replaced the theory of achievement motivation (Ames, 1992; Covington, 2000; Dweck, 1986, 1991; Maehr & Midgley, 1996). The traditional operational definition of the motive to succeed makes a distinction between two types of achievement goals, as a function of the social or individual criteria or standards of excellence that are used to evaluate a performance outcome as a success or as a failure. These two different types of achievement goals were understood as expressions of one and the same need for achievement (motive to succeed).

In goal-theory (-theories) these two different types of achievement goals are related to different types of motivation. Various labels are used to refer to these goal-orientations. We prefer the labels *learning-goals and task-oriented* versus *performance-goals and ego-oriented*.

These goals correspond to the two main activities that are expected from students in school: learning and performing. When pupils are involved in *learning activities*, their goal is to increase their knowledge and competencies, to understand, to master more and more complex issues. They are *task-oriented*. Understanding the problem at hand and finding how to solve it is the goal. This type of goal-orientation corresponds to the intrinsic motivation that derives from curiosity or the need for knowledge and information, and the need for mastery, competence, and efficiency in solving challenging tasks.

When students take tests or exams, their goal is to perform, to achieve academic success, or to avoid failure. Such tasks arouse an ego-orientation and performance-goals. One is less occupied with the task itself than with how well or how bad one will do, in comparison with others. Social norms or criteria are often used to evaluate the outcome.

Instrumentality and Goal-Theory

If we combine the new goal dimension "learning-goals versus performance-goals" and the temporal dimension (present versus future goals), we get eight different combinations (see Table 1). We will first briefly discuss the two cases were there is no future goal, and then we proceed with six cases where there is instrumentality.

Present Goal and No Future Goal

When learning, studying, taking a test or doing homework, students can either be task-oriented and have a learning-goal, or ego-oriented and have a performance-goal. These immediate goals are end-goals when the tasks have no utility value, no instrumentality (see the combinations one and five in Table 1). Atkinson's theory of achievement motivation and goal-theory both discuss these combinations.

Table 1: Eight different combinations of present and future goals in student motivation.

Present	Future
Task-oriented/Learning-goal	No future goal (1)
	Extrinsic goal (2)
	Task-goal (3)
	Performance goal (4)
Ego-oriented/Performance-goal	No future goal (5)
	Extrinsic goal (6)
	Task-goal (7)
	Performance-goal (8)

Present Goal and Future Goals

Based on daily contacts with students and on empirical data (Brickman *et al.*, 1997; De Volder & Lens, 1982; Eccles, 1984; Gorin *et al.*, 1998; Lens, 2001; Lens & Decruyenaere, 1991; Van Calster *et al.*, 1987; Zaleski, 1987), we doubt however the ecological validity of the combinations one and five for the school context. Most students, the majority of the time, have a multitude of motivational goals that they want to achieve in the present, the immediate, and even in the distant future by doing their best (more or less) at school. For youngsters education is not auto-telic, it is not pure play; it is hard work. The main question then becomes "How do(es) the future goal(s) for which the present learning or performance task is instrumental, affect the present motivation?" In order to gain some insight into the several types of relationships between future goals and present motivation, we distinguish two dimensions.

The first dimension concerns the relationship between a present task and a future task or goal. A present task and future task or goal can belong to the same motivational category (combinations three and eight). The relationship between both tasks is then endogenous (Husman & Lens, 1999, p. 122). *"... The same tasks, the same competencies ... are at stake in different phases ... The person's goals are, at the same time, inside and outside the immediate learning tasks, but they are all inside the broader task of becoming thoroughly skilled ...".* The present and the future task (and hence the skills they imply) are comparable. In contrast, the present and future task or goal can belong to different motivational categories (combinations two, four, six and seven). This type of relation is an exogenous one. The present task is carried out in order to achieve future consequences that are not inherently related to the present activity.

The second dimension refers to the kind of conditions that regulate behavior. Behavior can be externally or internally regulated (Deci & Ryan, 1985). Behavior is externally regulated when its underlying motives originate outside the person (e.g., the promise of a reward, an order, or the threat of a punishment). A behavior is internally regulated when its underlying motives are internal to the individual (e.g., own development, life projects). For some goals — such as making money or obtaining good grades — individuals may differ with respect to their position on the internal/external dimension. For instance, striving to become very rich can be internal (if it has developed out of one's own goal structure), as well as external (if the goal arises because others keep telling you how important money is). The combination of these dimensions results in three types of instrumentality for each kind of present goal.

Type 1. Present learning- or performance-goals and future extrinsic goals (combinations two and six)

Combination 2: Present learning goal (task-orientation) and future extrinsic goal
A high-school student is highly interested in, and motivated for, her courses in mathematics and science. She also wants to become a famous civil engineer and make a lot of money.

Combination 6: Present performance-goal (ego-orientation) and future extrinsic goal

A university student is highly motivated to outperform the others in his MBA-class because that will allow him to require a higher salary when negotiating a job.

In these examples, the present and the future goal belong to different motivational categories and the future task or goal externally regulates the present activities.

Type 2. Present learning- or performance-goals and future learning-goals (combinations three and seven)

Combination 3: task-oriented (learning-goal) in the present and in the future

A high-school student is highly motivated for her courses in mathematics and science. She also plans to go to the university to study engineering and to become a well-grounded civil engineer.

The relation between the present goal (learning mathematics) and the future goal (becoming an engineer) is endogenous. The same competencies are at stake at both moments (studying mathematics and using this knowledge as an engineer). The future task or goal internally regulates the present activities. Becoming a civil engineer is a life project for this student.

Combination 7: ego-oriented (performance-goal) in the present and learning-goal in the future

A high-school student is studying very hard to prepare for his final exams in compulsory courses like history, languages, and so forth. He wants to obtain the highest scores possible in those exams because that would help him a lot in getting admitted to a top university and becoming a researcher in biochemistry later on. That is what he really wants to become in his life.

The relation between the present goal (performing well in e.g., history) and the future goal (becoming a researcher in biochemistry) is exogenous. Different specific competencies are at stake at both moments. But the behavior is internally regulated. Becoming a researcher in biochemistry is his life project.

Type 3. Present task- or ego-orientation and future performance-goals (combinations four and eight)

Combination 4: task-oriented (learning-goal) in the present and performance-goals in the future

A high-school student is highly motivated for her courses in mathematics and science. She wants to understand those topics as much as possible because she knows that this is the way to prepare herself for the very competitive entrance examination at an elite technical engineering school.

In this example, the relationship between the present and the future goals is exogenous but the future task or goal internally regulates the present activities. Being accepted at an elite technical engineering school is not inherently related to being intrinsically motivated for mathematics and science (exogenous relation) but the acceptance (self-chosen goal) is important to the individual (e.g., the personal or professional development; internal regulation).

Combination 8: ego-oriented (performance-goal) in the present and in the future
A 12th grade student is highly motivated not to fail in his last year of high-school (negative performance goal) because he plans to succeed in a college entrance examination.
    The same types of goals are strived for in the present and the future. Also this future-goal is self-chosen, so the student's behavior is internally regulated.

Empirical Evidence

Goal-theory discusses the combinations one and five. It does not discuss the present motivational effects of future goals. The present learning- versus performance-goals influence how students approach and experience learning activities, how well they perform and primarily how much they enjoy the learning activity. Atkinson's theory of achievement motivation is also an example of combination five. It does not consider the instrumentality or utility value of success. The outcome of an achievement task can only be success or failure. Because failures are not possible when being task-oriented, the original theory of achievement motivation does not pertain to combination one (task-goal in the present and no future goal).
    Learning-goals and performance-goals are an expression of intrinsic motivation. To the extent that the present motivation is based on extrinsic goals in the future (e.g., money, status, . . .), the student is extrinsically motivated and externally controlled. That means that the findings from the extensive research on the effects of extrinsic rewards on intrinsic motivation (for a review, see Deci *et al.*, 1999a,b) also apply here. The facilitating versus debilitating effect of extrinsic rewards or goals on (intrinsic) motivation has not been studied as a function of their temporal localization. We do not see however why that effect would be different for delayed extrinsic goals than it is for immediate rewards, unless delayed extrinsic goals would be experienced as less controlling than more immediate extrinsic goals. They would then undermine the intrinsic motivation less (Manderlink & Harackiewicz, 1984).
    Concerning combination eight (performance-goal in the present and in the future), Raynor's (1981) research data are illustrative.
    The evidence that we recently collected pertains to the effects of future task- and performance goals on present motivation. In a first series of studies (Simons *et al.*, 2000a), we examined whether some of the combinations mentioned above exist in daily life and if they have a differential influence on an individual's goal-orientation. Participants were told that three possible relationships could exist between their present and future activities. Each relationship was illustrated with an example. Participants were asked to illustrate each relationship with an example

from their own life and to evaluate the task- and performance-orientation evoked by these self-generated activities. Participants received the following written examples:

> *Relationship 1*: "I am taking anti-skid driving lessons now in order to enhance my standing in my friend's eyes. In other words, I am doing this activity now only for the future consequences which are not directly related with the task itself such as having a good reputation, standing, higher status, ...".

This relationship reflects an exogenous link (extrinsic goals in the future and task goal in the present) and externally regulated behavior (called type Ex-E).

> *Relationship 2*: "I am taking anti-skid driving lessons now in order to become a good driver. The skills and knowledge that I am learning now are the same ones I will need later. Without these, I will never be a good driver."

This relationship reflects an endogenous link (same competencies at both moments) and internally regulated behavior (called type En-I).

> *Relationship 3*: "I am taking anti-skid driving lessons now in order to drive safely in the future. I feel very strongly about safety and safety measures. These are activities in which I persist because they are important to attain my full (personal or professional) development."

This relationship reflects an exogenous link and internally regulated behavior (called type Ex-I).

The data suggest that different types of instrumentality are related differentially to task- and performance-goals. An individual is more performance-oriented when performing an activity or task in order to reach extrinsic future consequences (Ex-E) than when the future consequences are inherently related to the present task (En-I) or when the task is important for an individual's personal or professional development (Ex-I). Furthermore, an individual is more task-oriented for tasks of type En-I and type Ex-I than for tasks of type Ex-E. Interestingly, goal-orientation accompanying type Ex-I was very similar to the goal-orientation following type En-I and very different from the goal-orientation following type Ex-E. Still, we repeatedly observed that performance-orientation was slightly higher for tasks of type Ex-I than for tasks of type En-I, although task-orientation did not differ.

In a second series of studies (Simons *et al.*, 2000b), these three types of instrumentality were experimentally manipulated to analyze their causal effects on goal-orientations, intrinsic motivation, level of information processing, and learning outcomes. Participants received written instructions that were manipulated to reflect the different types of instrumentality and a text of 1200 words. The following written instructions were given.

Instruction for type Ex-E:
"The text you will receive will be used as part of an experiment. This text will be only used today and will not be discussed any more during your training. You have to read the text because we will ask some questions about it. In other words, reading the text is necessary to complete the test at the end of this session."

Instructions for type En-I:
"The text you will receive will be used as part of an experiment. This text is not only used today, but you will discuss it again later this year. Reading the text will give you some information about 'communication', which is helpful in your future job and daily life. After reading the text, we will ask you some questions about it. In other words, reading this text is useful because you will discuss this and similar texts in the future and the content of this text can be personally helpful/beneficial."

Instructions for type Ex-I:
"The text you will receive will be used as part of an experiment. This text will be only used today and will not be discussed any more during your training. Reading the text will give you some information about 'communication' and can be helpful in your future life. After reading the text, we will ask you some questions about it. In other words, reading this text is not directly useful for your training, but the information in the text, can be helpful for your future life."

A fourth group of students (the baseline or *control condition*) received no instrumentality instructions at all.

After having studied the text for a maximum of 30 minutes, students had to take a test on the text. Three months later one of the questions of this test was repeated.

The data clearly suggested that different types of instructions were related differently to motivational and cognitive learning behavior. In comparison with no instructions, instructions of type En-I-instrumentality evoked more task-orientation and less negative ego-orientation. The students in this condition were more intrinsically motivated and received better marks. Moreover, they recalled the text better three months later. In contrast, students who received type Ex-E-instructions were more negative ego-oriented, less task-oriented and they received lower marks. Moreover, their less adaptive way of handling the material affects their free recall of the material three months later. Practically none of them could recall anything about the text. Interestingly, students who received type Ex-I-instructions fell in between and their behavior did not differ significantly from that of students in the baseline condition. These results nicely replicated the correlational findings by means of the experimental method. En-I-instrumentality is better than Ex-I-instrumentality, which is better than Ex-E-instrumentality, and these types of instrumentality can be quite easily induced in a learning context. Because there was a baseline condition in the experimental study, we could in addition interpret the position of Ex-I-instrumentality as a status quo in relation to the baseline condition.

Perceived Instrumentality in Action: The Role of Instrumentality in Self-Regulation

Hitherto, we have discussed various types of instrumentality as a contextual variable and their relation with present motivation (i.e., goal orientation). In this section, possible underlying mechanisms are addressed. We distinguish three processes: Perceived instrumentality may affect the initiation of behavior, its persistence, or its quality, and of course, it may affect a combination of those. For example, the awareness that studying now will enhance the likelihood of obtaining a future goal (such as mastering some valued skill) may merely motivate a student to start his/her activities leading to that goal. However, once the behavior has been started, the actor may temporarily forget about the instrumentality-relationship, which frees his or her mental resources that can then be allocated to the problem at hand. The instrumentality perception may, however, also remain cognitively available during the activities and in this way prevent early quitting due to fatigue, difficulties, or some other hindrance. In this case, perceiving instrumentality may reflect a form of self-regulation or volitional control, as far as it enhances persistence. Third, perceiving instrumentality may also affect the quality of the activity. That is, the effort exerted may become more intense when the task is perceived as instrumental for a future goal. This intensified effort may lead to qualitatively different information processing. We will now briefly discuss some findings that may throw some light on the three hypothesized processes just described.

Preliminary evidence for the first process (Dewitte & Lens, 2000c) showed marked individual differences in the subjective interpretation or definition of studying. For some people "Studying is making sure I pass the exams", which clearly refers to a future performance goal. Dewitte and Lens called this a high action identification level for studying, because this identification refers to a general goal or remote consequence of the present behavior (Vallacher & Wegner, 1987). Other students preferred short-term goals in their descriptions of studying behavior, such as "Studying is finding the core of this chapter", which refers to an intermediate action identification level. A third group of students preferred fairly low-level descriptions, which referred to some procedural subtask such as "studying is reading text". This type of action identification was considered as very low.

Dewitte and Lens (2000c) found that punctual students (in comparison with procrastinators), which were identified both by means of questionnaire and behavioral measures, seemed to prefer high action identifications for their study behaviors. These identifications (e.g., "studying is making sure I pass the exams") referred to instrumentality perceptions of the performance type. As the major feature of procrastinators is to postpone things that ought to be done in order to reach one's goals, these data support the hypothesis that perceiving the link between the present behavior and a future performance goal enhances the initiation of the relevant behavior. However, further evidence is required to find out whether all types of perceived instrumentality are equally conducive to the initiation of behavior. Presently, we do not think so, merely because the other types of instrumentality did not appear in the item generation phase. Students never favored identifications such as "studying is becoming good in the topic", which would reflect a future task goal.

The second hypothesized process refers to persistence enhancement and requires measurements of cognitive variables during ongoing activities. In a series of studies, Dewitte and Lens (2000a&b) measured the awareness of goals that were situated in the immediate future (i.e., at the end of the task). The findings suggested (at least for tasks requiring much effort) that being aware of a future task-goal during task engagement facilitated performance and persistence on solving anagrams or on writing texts (Dewitte & Lens, 2000a&b) in comparison with being aware of the procedural details of the task. It seems as if spontaneously perceiving the present task as instrumental for a future task-goal enhances motivation when it is initially low due to too great task difficulty. High action identifications that referred to performance-goals did not occur frequently (e.g., "writing a text of ten lines"). Dewitte and Lens (2000b, study 5) induced performance-goals as future goals, and found an effect on spontaneously arising task-goals (high action identifications, such as "finding words"), which enhanced persistence. However, they found no effect on spontaneously arising performance-goals (such as "showing my competence at this task"), which were again very uncommon. Similarly, when they (Dewitte & Lens, 2000d) let students study a text with the goal of doing a test on it afterwards, which is clearly a future performance-goal, they found no evidence of spontaneously arising awareness of performance-goals but in contrast, future task-goals were very common.

Apparently then, future performance-goals are not in awareness during an activity that is executed for the sake of those goals (even when they are explicitly stated), so it is unlikely that this type of instrumentality plays a major role *during* activities. In contrast, task-goals that are endogenously linked to the activity do occur frequently and seem to play a facilitating role. They interact with initial motivation to enhance persistence on difficult tasks. The question remains, however, whether task-goals that are in awareness during task performance but that are farther in the future, have similar effects on persistence.

The existence of the third postulated process was supported by recent evidence collected by Simons *et al.* (2000b, see also above). They asked students to study a text and to answer some exam-like questions on the text afterwards. As mentioned above, performance was highest after instrumentality instructions of the future task-goal type, lowest for instructions of the future extrinsic goal type, and intermediate after instructions of the future performance-goal type or after no instrumentality instructions. Moreover, these differences were found to be mediated by deep level learning strategies (as measured by questionnaires as well as by behavioral indices). This clearly suggests that perceiving the present task as instrumental for a future similar task goal (i.e., an endogenous link) affects the quality of the learning. This interpretation is supported by the finding that people in this condition performed much better on the same test question three months later than those in the other conditions.

Thus, perceiving endogenous instrumentality enhances motivation to the degree that the processing behavior becomes qualitatively superior. However, the striking finding that goal-orientation (that was strongly affected by instrumentality instruction) did not mediate the relationship between the instrumentality instructions and performance, suggests that this enhancing influence of instrumentality is no longer important after the initiation. It seems as if the awareness of future task-goals determines the extent of task engagement, and hence its quality right at the outset, but no longer afterwards. Comparing the findings pertaining to the second (i.e., persistence-enhancing) and third (i.e., quality-enhancing) postulated process by which perceived instrumentality affects behavior, we call for future research that helps to determine at which point in a task, future goals exert their influence.

Taken together, these three emerging lines of evidence suggest that the three hypothesized processes by which instrumentality might affect motivation play their role. Perceiving instrumentality may enhance behavioral initiation, may facilitate persistence when the task is hindered, and seems to facilitate superior information processing strategies. However, awareness of future task-goals and performance-goals may play differential roles. Possibly, awareness of future performance-goals may help initiating the relevant behavior, which is an aspect of volition but may then cease to influence the quality or the quantity of the behavior. When the activity starts, awareness of future task-goals seems to determine the commitment to the activity, and hence the quality of the engagement. Once the activity has been initiated, awareness of future task-goals seems to enhance persistence when smooth task progress is hindered, which is another aspect of self-regulation or volition.

Conclusion

The distinction between extrinsic and intrinsic motivation is very important to understand human motivated behavior. Educational psychology probably overestimates the importance of the intrinsic component. It certainly neglects too much the instrumental role of formal education for the student's future. This personal chronological context of learning has its motivational consequences. We argued that the future consequences of most activities play an irreducible role in determining the total motivation of almost any behavior. That is, people are aware that most of their behaviors, whether intrinsically or extrinsically motivated, have future consequences that may or may not be in congruence with the present motivation. A model was presented in which two present motivations (learning-goals vs. performance-goals) were combined with several types of future consequences or perceived instrumentality (none, extrinsic goals, task-goals, and performance-goals). Data that pertain to these combinations were reviewed. We showed that, in general, task-orientation tends to be higher for tasks that are perceived as instrumental for future task- or performance-goals and lower when they are instrumental for future extrinsic goals. Performance-orientation tends to be lowest for tasks that are instrumental for future task-goals, somewhat higher for tasks that are instrumental for future performance-goals, and much higher when they are instrumental for extrinsic goals.

Further, the analysis of the possible processes underlying the mechanisms suggested that future performance-goals might be important primarily in initiating the relevant behavior (and hence have no effect on performance itself). In contrast, task-goals may be helpful during the activity, because they may enhance the level of commitment at the outset (and hence the quality) and the behavioral persistence when the behavior is difficult. In other words, awareness of different aspects of instrumentality may be differentially related to several aspects of volitional control.

Acknowledgements

The third author's contribution was supported by a grant from the Fund for Scientific Research Flanders (Belgium)

References

Ames, C. (1992), "Classrooms: Goals, structures, and student motivation." *Journal of Educational Psychology 84*, 261–271.

Ames, R. E., & Ames, C. (eds). (1984), *Research on Motivation in Education. Vol. 1. Student Motivation*. Orlando: Academic Press.

Atkinson, J. W., & Feather, N. T. (eds). (1966), *A Theory of Achievement Motivation*. New York: Wiley.

Atkinson, J. W., & Raynor, J. O. (1974), "Introduction and overview." In J. W. Atkinson & J. O. Raynor (eds) *Motivation and Achievement* (pp. 3–11). Washington, DC: Winston & Sons.

Brickman, S., Miller, R. B., & Roedel, T. D. (1997, March), *Goal Valuing and Future Consequences as Predictors of Cognitive Engagement*. Paper presented at the annual meeting of the American Educational Research Association, Chicago.

Covington, M. (2000), "Goal theory, motivation, and school achievement: An integrative review." *Annual Review of Psychology 51*, 171–200.

Creten, H., Lens, W., & Simons, J. (2001), "The role of perceived instrumentality in student motivation." In A. Anastasia, J. Kuhl & A. Elliot (eds) *Trends and Prospects in Motivational Research*. Dordrecht, The Netherlands: Kluwer Academic Press.

Deci, E. L., Koestner, R., & Ryan, R. M. (1999a), "A meta-analytic review of experiments examining the effects of extrinsic rewards on intrinsic motivation." *Psychological Bulletin 125*, 627–668

Deci, E. L., Koestner, R., & Ryan, R. M. (1999b), "The undermining effect is a reality after all — Extrinsic rewards, task interest, and self-determination: reply to Eisenberger, Pierce, and Cameron (1999) and Lepper, Henderlong, and Gingras (1999)." *Psychological Bulletin 125*, 692–700.

Deci, E. L., & Ryan, R. M. (1985), *Intrinsic Motivation and Self Determination in Human Behavior*. New York: Plenum Press.

De Volder, M., & Lens, W. (1982), "Academic achievement and future time perspective as a cognitive-motivational concept." *Journal of Personality and Social Psychology 42*, 566–571.

Dewitte, S., & Lens, W. (2000a), *High and Low Action Identities Enhance Persistence in Different Conditions. The Moderating Role of Difficulty and Attractiveness of the Task.* Manuscript submitted for publication.

Dewitte, S., & Lens, W. (2000b), *Does Goal Awareness Enhance Self-Control? Required Effort Moderates the Relation between the Level of Action Identity and Persistence.* Manuscript submitted for publication.

Dewitte, S., & Lens, W. (2000c), "Procrastinators lack a broad action perspective." *European Journal of Personality 27*, 121–140.

Dewitte, S., & Lens, W. (2000d), "Exploring volitional problems in procrastinators." *The International Journal of Educational Research 133*, 733–750.

Dweck, C. S. (1986), "Motivational processes affecting learning." *American Psychologist 41*, 1040–1048.

Dweck, C. S. (1991), "Self-theories and goals: Their role in motivation, personality, and development." *Nebraska Symposium on Motivation 38*, 199–235.

Eccles, J. (1984), "Sex differences in achievement patterns." *Nebraska Symposium on Motivation 32*, 97–132.

Eisenberger, R., Pierce, W. D., & Cameron, J. (1999), "Effect of reward on intrinsic motivation — Negative, neutral, and positive: Comment on Deci, Koestner, and Ryan (1999)." *Psychological Bulletin 125*, 677–691.

Gorin, J. S., Husman, J., & Turner, J. E. (1998, April), *The Interaction of Extrinsic and Intrinsic Motivation on College Students' Use of Learning.* Paper presented at the annual meeting of the American Educational Research Association, San Diego, CA.

Harter, S., & Jackson, B. K. (1992), "Trait vs. nontrait conceptualizations of intrinsic/extrinsic motivational orientations." *Motivation and Emotion 16*, 209–230.

Husman, J., & Lens, W. (1999), "The role of the future in student motivation." *Educational Psychologist 34*, 113–125.

Lens, W. (2001), "How to combine intrinsic task-motivation with the motivational effects of the instrumentality of present tasks for future goals." In A. Efklides, J. Kuhl & A. Elliot (eds) *Trends and Prospects in Motivational Research.* Dordrecht, The Netherlands: Kluwer Academic Press.

Lens, W., & Decruyenaere, M. (1991), "Motivation and de-motivation in secondary education: Student characteristics." *Learning and Instruction 1*, 145–159.

Locke, E., & Latham, G. (1990), *A Theory of Motivation and Task Performance.* Englewood Cliffs, NJ: Prentice Hall.

Maehr, M. L., & Midgley, C. (1996), *Transforming School Cultures.* Boulder: Westview Press.

Manderlink, G., & Harackiewicz, J. M. (1984), "Proximal versus distal goal setting and intrinsic motivation." *Journal of Personality and Social Psychology 47*, 918–928.

McClelland, D. C., Atkinson, J. W., Clark, R. A., & Lowell, E. L. (1953), *The Achievement Motive.* New York: Appleton-Century-Crofts.

Phalet, K., & Lens, W. (1995), "Achievement motivation and group loyalty among Turkish and Belgian youngsters." In M. L. Maehr & P. R. Pintrich (eds) *Advances in Motivation and Achievement. Vol. 9. Culture, Motivation, and Achievement* (pp. 32–72). Greenwich, Conn.: Jai Press Inc.

Pintrich, P. R., & Schunk, D. H. (1996), *Motivation in Education: Theory, Research, and Applications.* Englewood Cliffs, NJ: Prentice Hall.

Raynor, J. O. (1969), "Future orientation and motivation of immediate activity: An elaboration of the theory of achievement motivation." *Psychological Review 76*, 606–610.

Raynor, J. O. (1974), "Future orientation in the study of achievement motivation." In J. W. Atkinson & J. O. Raynor (eds) *Motivation and Achievement* (pp. 121–154). Washington, DC: Winston.

Raynor, J. O. (1981), "Future orientation and achievement motivation: Toward a theory of personality functioning and change." In G. d'Ydewalle & W. Lens (eds) *Cognition in Human Motivation and Learning* (pp. 199–231). Leuven & Hillsdale, NJ: Leuven University Press & Erlbaum.

Simons, J., Dewitte, S., & Lens, W. (2000a), "Wanting to have versus wanting to be: The effect of perceived instrumentality on goal orientation." *British Journal of Psychology 91*, 335–351.

Simons, J., Dewitte, S., & Lens, W. (2000b), *The Future Motivates. Experimentally Manipulated Instrumentality Influences Performance through Motivated Behavior.* Manuscript submitted for publication.

Vallacher, R. R., & Wegner, D. M. (1987), "What do people think they're doing? Action identification and human behavior." *Psychological Review 94*, 3–15.

Van Calster, K., Lens, W., & Nuttin, J. (1987), "Affective attitude toward the personal future: Impact on motivation in high school boys." *American Journal of Psychology 100*, 1–13.

Zaleski, Z. (1987), "Behavioral effects of self-set goals for different time ranges." *International Journal of Psychology 22*, 17–38.

Part V

Situational Dynamics of Motivation and Cognition

Chapter 13

Multiple Goals, Multiple Contexts: The Dynamic Interplay between Personal Goals and Contextual Goal Stresses

Elizabeth A. Linnenbrink & Paul R. Pintrich

The investigation of the role of goals and goal orientation has been an important recent development in achievement motivation theory and research. In contrast to motivational theories that propose that personal needs or drives provide the source for behavior, goal theories suggest that goals are cognitive representations of what individuals are trying to attain and that these goals can guide and direct achievement behavior. In addition, another important aspect of goal orientation theory is the assumption that goals can arise not only from an individual's own personality or identity, but also from the goal stresses that are present in the context. Accordingly, the goal orientations that students adopt in classrooms may be a function of both individual and contextual characteristics.

Although goal theory does make the general assumption that there can be an interaction between personal and contextual goals, there has been very little empirical research that has examined how both personal and contextual goals may interact to influence subsequent motivation, cognition, and achievement. In fact, there has been little research that has even examined the interactions within different personal goals or within different contextual goal stresses. As Pintrich (2000a, b, c) has pointed out, goal theory has often conceptualized mastery and performance goals as opposite ends of a single continuum and not discussed the potential interactions. In addition, studies that use between-subjects experimental designs, where one group is induced to adopt mastery goals and another group induced to adopt performance goals, preclude the examination of the interaction of multiple goals. The purpose of this chapter is to discuss the potential interactions between multiple personal goals and multiple contextual goal stresses. We will discuss the general theoretical predictions that might be generated from a multiple goals perspective, summarize the limited empirical evidence bearing on the issues, and discuss the theoretical and methodological problems inherent in adopting a multiple goals perspective. We begin with a brief summary of the main effects of mastery and performance goals as well as recent developments within goal theory.

Motivation in Learning Contexts: Theoretical Advances and Methodological Implications, pages 251–269.
Copyright © 2001 by Elsevier Science Ltd.
ISBN: 0-08-043990-X

The Role of Mastery and Performance Goals in Learning and Achievement

Achievement goals refer to the purposes or reasons an individual is pursuing an achievement task (Pintrich & Schunk, 1996). This framework is typically applied to academic learning tasks, but can also be applied to other achievement contexts such as athletic or business settings. Classic achievement motivation research has been concerned with the energization and direction of competence-related behavior, which includes evaluation of competence relative to a standard of excellence (Elliot, 1997). Following this line of thinking, current achievement goal constructs consist of an organized pattern of beliefs that are comprised of both the purpose or reason underlying students' achievement behavior as well as the way in which competence or success is evaluated (Urdan, 1997). Although the achievement goal construct is similar to other representations of goals in the achievement motivation literature (c.f., the goals of mastery and superiority in Ford's 1992 taxonomy), they represent a combination of levels in that they also encompass specific criteria by which progress is judged. As such, achievement goal constructs can be thought of as integrating various levels of analysis to reflect an organized system for approaching, engaging, and evaluating performance in an achievement context.

Within the field of achievement goal theory, a number of different models of goal orientations have been suggested by different theorists (c.f., Ames, 1992b; Dweck & Leggett, 1988; Harackiewicz *et al.*, 1998; Maehr & Midgley, 1991; Nicholls, 1984; Pintrich, 2000a, b, c; Wolters *et al.*, 1996). These various models differ in terms of the labels used to identify achievement goals as well as the number of proposed goal orientations. However, two primary goal orientations, the first focusing on learning and improvement and the second focusing on demonstrating one's ability, often in relation to others, are represented in most models. These two goals have been labeled as *mastery* and *performance* (Ames, 1992b; Elliot, 1997; Harackiewicz *et al.*, 1997; Harackiewicz *et al.*, 1998), *learning* and *performance* (Dweck & Leggett, 1988), *task* and *performance* (e.g., Kaplan & Midgley, 1997; Maehr & Midgley, 1991, 1996; Middleton & Midgley, 1997; Midgley *et al.*, 1996), and *task-involved* and *ego-involved* (Nicholls, 1984, 1990; Nicholls *et al.*, 1989).

Normative goal theory has generally worked within a model of two general goal orientations, with mastery and performance goals being the labels we have adopted to refer to these orientations in this chapter. Given these two goals, theory and research within the normative model have focused on the adaptive benefits of adopting mastery goals and the maladaptive consequences of adopting performance goals (Ames b, 1992; Dweck & Elliott, 1983; Midgley *et al.*, 2001; Pintrich, 2000a, b, c). This research has shown that students that adopt a mastery goal orientation generally have better and more adaptive motivational and emotional profiles in terms of self-efficacy, task value, interest, and attributional responses to success and failure as well as more positive and less negative affect. In addition, this work has shown that mastery goals lead to more self-regulation and cognitive strategy use, and in some cases, better achievement or performance. Although there are some mixed findings, the research has also pointed to some problems for motivation, affect, cognition, and achievement that can result from the adoption of performance goals. The usual general conclusion drawn from this work is that mastery goals are "good" or adaptive and performance goals are "bad" or maladaptive for many different outcomes.

More recently, Elliot and his colleagues (Elliot, 1997; Elliot & Church, 1997; Elliot & Harackiewicz, 1996) have suggested that simply distinguishing between mastery and performance goals does not adequately describe students' motivation and that it is necessary to further differentiate between performance-approach and performance-avoid goals. Under a performance-approach goal, individuals are positively motivated to outperform others and demonstrate their competence (i.e., approach the goal of outperforming others and demonstrating ability). In contrast, a performance-avoid goal orientation reflects a negative motivation to avoid failure and to avoid looking stupid or incompetent. Other achievement goal theorists such as Midgley and her colleagues (e.g., Middleton & Midgley, 1997; Midgley *et al.*, 1998) have made this distinction as well. Skaalvik and his colleagues (Skaalvik, 1997; Skaalvik *et al.*, 1994) have proposed two similar dimensions of performance or ego goals, which they have labeled *self-enhancing ego orientation*, where the emphasis is on outperforming others and demonstrating superior ability similar to a performance-approach goal. They have labeled the other goal *self-defeating ego orientation*, where the goal is to avoid looking dumb or to avoid negative judgments, similar to a performance-avoid goal.

With the introduction of both approach and avoid goals as well as the various terms used to represent some similar and different features of goal orientations, a general framework to help classify and organize these goals seems useful. In developing this framework, we are not proposing a "new" model, but rather building on existing models to develop a way to integrate these various perspectives. Table 1 represents one attempt to organize achievement goals. The rows in Table 1 reflect the two general goals towards which students might be striving and parallel the two general goals of *mastery* and *performance*. The columns of Table 1 differentiate approach and avoid goal orientations.

Distinguishing between approach and avoid dimensions of motivation has been a hallmark of motivational research (Atkinson, 1957; Elliot, 1997; McClelland *et al.*, 1953). Furthermore, current social cognitive perspectives on regulating progress towards or away from a goal also reflect this distinction (e.g., Covington & Roberts, 1994; Elliot, 1997; Harackiewicz *et al.*, 1998; Higgins, 1997). In particular, Higgins (1997) emphasizes the importance of promotion (approach) and prevention (avoid) for understanding self-regulatory processes. That is, an individual with an approach or promotion focus will attempt to move towards positive or desired end-states while an individual with an avoidance or prevention focus will attempt to move away from negative or undesired end-states. This distinction between approach and avoidance goal orientations should have important implications for the types of learning and behavior that result based on the goals an individual adopts. For example, a promotion or approach orientation may have some generally positive relations with cognition, motivation, and behavior, while a prevention or avoidance orientation may be negatively related to these same outcomes.

Table 1: Two goal orientations and their approach and avoidance forms.

	Approach Focus	**Avoidance Focus**
Mastery Orientation	– Focus on mastering task, learning, understanding – Use of standards of self-improvement, progress, deep understanding of task (learning goal, task goal, task-involved goal)	– Focus on avoiding misunderstanding, avoiding not learning or not mastering task – Use of standards of not being wrong, not doing it incorrectly relative to task
Performance Orientation	– Focus on being superior, outperforming others, being the smartest, best at task in comparison to others – Use of normative standards such as getting best or highest grades, being top or best performer in class (performance goal, ego-involved goal, self-enhancing ego orientation, relative ability goal)	– Focus on avoiding inferiority, not looking stupid or dumb in comparison to others – Use of normative standards of not getting the worst grades, being lowest performer in class (performance goal, ego-involved goal, self-defeating ego orientation)

Each cell in Table 1 includes both the general-purpose goal and the specific evaluation standards for each particular goal orientation. For example, the cell for an approach mastery goal orientation reflects a focus on learning and understanding; progress towards this goal is evaluated in terms of self-set standards for improvement. This reflects the various models of mastery, task, and learning goals described previously. The approach and avoidance cells for performance goals reflect the distinction between a focus on outperforming others using comparative standards (approach performance goal) and a focus on trying to avoid looking stupid or incompetent using comparative standards (avoid performance goals).

Although previous models of achievement goal theory have not formally proposed the cell for avoid mastery goals, its existence seems possible based on logical grounds as well as theoretical symmetry (see Elliot, 1999; Elliot & McGregor, 2001; Pintrich, 2000 a, c). Additionally, there is preliminary empirical evidence to further justify the inclusion of this cell (Elliot & McGregor, 2001; Zusho & Pintrich, 2000). Previous models agree that mastery goals are represented by attempts to improve or promote competence, knowledge, skills, and learning, and that progress towards these goals are evaluated based on self-set standards. It seems possible that some individuals may want to avoid the demonstration of incompetence or misunderstanding relative to their own self-set standards. That is, approach mastery students may focus on getting it "correct" relative to the task or their own standards while avoid mastery students may try to avoid being "wrong" relative to their own standards. For instance, a student who is focused on being "perfectionistic" and never wants to be wrong relative to her own high self-standards may be operating under an avoid mastery goal orientation rather than an approach mastery goal orientation. Thus, avoid mastery goals can be contrasted to approach mastery goals in that avoid mastery-oriented students focus on avoiding doing their class work incorrectly or getting the wrong answer relative to the task while approach mastery-oriented students focus on learning and improving. Avoid mastery goals are also distinct from avoid performance goals in that the standards by which progress is evaluated are self-referenced rather than referenced in comparison to others.

Despite the relatively recent conceptualization of the mastery avoid goals, there are some recent empirical studies that have addressed the existence of this goal as well as its antecedents and consequences. For example, Elliot and McGregor (2001) have developed a self-report instrument to measure all four goals shown in Table 1. Their work with confirmatory factor analysis shows quite clearly that a four-factor model provides the best fit to the data and that the four goals can be separated, although they are related in theoretically meaningful ways. In terms of the antecedents, their work with college students shows that mastery avoid goals are predicted by a general set of negative antecedents such as high levels of fear of failure and low self-determination, similar to those of performance avoid goals, but mastery avoid goals are also positively related to self-reported class engagement, unlike performance avoid goals. In terms of consequences, mastery avoid goals predicted more disorganized studying and higher levels of anxiety, but they did not have as many negative consequences as performance avoid goals (Elliot & McGregor, 2001).

Zusho and Pintrich (2000), using a different self-report instrument, also found a similar pattern with mastery avoid goals being empirically separable from the other three goals in factor analyses, positively related to need for achievement, and positively related to performance on a math test in college students. In general, it appears that students do pursue mastery avoid goals and that these goals do have theoretically logical links to antecedent and consequence variables to make them worthwhile to include in our model of goals. Given this model of four goals, we now turn to how different goal stresses for the classroom context might promote these goals.

The Role of the Classroom Context in Promoting the Adoption of Achievement Goals

One of the strengths of achievement goal theory is the consideration of classroom context as an important precursor to the goals that students adopt. In particular, a number of achievement goal theorists have stressed how various features of the classroom environment may influence students' perceptions of the classroom goal structure, which in turn is thought to relate to students' own adoption of mastery versus performance goals (e.g., Ames, 1992a, b; Blumenfeld, 1992; Meece, 1991). When considering the impact of the environment, goal theory stresses the importance of examining both "objective" features of the classroom environment that can promote certain types of goals as well as more "subjective" and personal perceptions or construals of the context.

Although typically not applied to achievement goal theory, Murray's (1938) distinction between *alpha* and *beta* presses may be useful when examining the contextual features of the classroom (Middleton, 2000). In particular, Murray classified environmental demands as being either objective (alpha press) or subjective (beta press), which could result in either beneficial or harmful processes to the individual interacting within that environment. Although both types of environmental demands are important, Murray suggests that subjective perceptions are more likely to influence the types of actions an individual will take. We use this distinction between the alpha and beta presses as a framework for examining the relation of the classroom context to students' adoption of achievement goals.

The notion that students perceive differences in the classroom environment or school environment and that these beta presses relate to their own goal adoption has held up to empirical analysis, especially that using self-report data (e.g., Maehr & Anderman, 1993; Roeser *et al.*, 1996; Urdan *et al.*, 1998). It is important to note, however, that one aspect that may influence how students perceive the environment is their own existing goal orientation (Järvelä & Niemivirta, 1999).

In terms of alpha presses, results are mixed regarding the relation of objective environmental presses on students' goal adoption and learning. In particular, some studies suggest that various observable features of the classroom environment (alpha press) relate to students' perceptions of the classroom goal structure (beta press) and students' own personal goals (Anderman *et al.*, in press; Patrick *et al.*, in press). In contrast, there is evidence indicating that students' motivational orientations may be stable across typical classroom environments and that only extreme differences in the classroom context may have any real impact on the types of goals students adopt (Lemos, 1996). This suggests that although the alpha press may differ across a variety of contexts, students do not perceive differences in the environment. However, this may be due in part to real differences in teachers' interactions based on their perceptions of students' motivation (Lehtinen *et al.*, 1995). That is, the alpha press may differ for individual students within the same classroom. It seems plausible then that both alpha and beta presses may influence the types of goals that students adopt and subsequently their learning in school. Therefore, we now turn to a more detailed analysis of classroom context, focusing first on classroom structure and then classroom climate, using the distinction between alpha and beta presses as a framework.

Classroom Structure

Classroom structure refers to the way in which the teacher establishes routines, sets up rules, assigns tasks, and evaluates students (Ames 1992a, b). The classroom structure is often categorized along the dimensions of task, authority, and recognition or evaluation structures. A number of key articles have discussed in detail how these various structures of the classroom promote either a mastery or performance orientation (e.g., Ames, 1992a, b; Blumenfeld, 1992; Maehr & Anderman, 1993; Maehr & Midgley, 1991; Meece, 1991). However, these analyses have only considered the type of goal (mastery versus performance) and have not considered how classroom structures relate to whether or not students adopt approach or avoidance achievement goals (for an exception, see Church *et al.*, 2001). Therefore, our goal here is to discuss briefly the structure of the classroom based on previous descriptions and extend this analysis to consider how these various features might or might not influence the *direction* of the goal. We then extend this analysis to the classroom climate and consider how climate might relate to the adoption of approach versus avoidance achievement goals.

Task. The tasks used in the classroom convey important messages about what is valued there (i.e., learning or competition) and can thus play an important role in predicting students' achievement goals. Ames (1992b) suggests that tasks which are meaningful and appropriately challenging foster mastery goals. Using a variety of tasks in a given classroom also reduces performance goals because opportunities for social comparison are reduced. These three features of the task can be defined "objectively" in terms of the alpha press, or at least in terms of what the teacher or an outside observer sees as the meaningfulness, variety, and difficulty of the task. They can also be defined in terms of how students perceive these three features. In the first case, the implication is that the alpha press is consistent for all students and can be measured at a classroom level unit of analysis. The beta press for the classroom would show individual variation for students in the same classroom, albeit student perceptions in one classroom should be more correlated with each other than student perceptions of a different classroom with a different structure. It is important to keep in mind these different levels of analysis, conceptually as well as methodologically, as they have implications for measurement and data analysis. If a study is focusing on the alpha press of the classroom, then multi-level group analysis (within a program like hierarchical linear modeling-HLM), where classrooms and students are two different levels of analysis, would be appropriate. On the other hand, if the beta press of the classroom were the main focus, then typical individual student-level analyses would be appropriate. These issues apply to all the dimensions of the classroom we will discuss in this section on classroom structure.

To understand how classroom context fits in with a revised goal theory approach, it is important to consider how task structure relates to an approach or avoidance focus. It is unlikely that the first two dimensions of the task, meaningfulness and variety, relate to the adoption of approach versus avoidance goals. However, it seems plausible that the difficulty level of the task may predict whether students approach or avoid mastery or performance goals. In terms of the alpha press, if a teacher consistently gives very difficult tasks, then the whole class may focus on avoiding the tasks.

In terms of the beta press, students who perceive the task as extremely difficult should be more likely to adopt avoidance rather than approach goals. For instance, if a performance-oriented student is frequently faced with difficult tasks, he/she may realize that it is unlikely that he/she will excel and do better than others. Therefore, rather than adopting an unattainable goal of outperforming others (approach performance), he or she may instead focus on the more realistic goal of avoiding failure (avoid performance). This negative role of beta press perceived task difficulty might be especially salient in classrooms where students' capabilities vary substantially. In these classrooms, students who are low in skills or knowledge will confront more difficult tasks (relative to their own capabilities) than other students of average or high levels of expertise. These lower-achieving students might adopt an avoidance focus towards the classroom tasks much more readily than other students, even though the objective or alpha task structure is the same for everyone.

Authority. Another important component to the classroom structure is the teacher's use of authority. Classrooms where the teacher is controlling and grants little autonomy are generally thought to reduce a mastery goal orientation and promote the adoption of performance goals (Ames, 1992a, b). In contrast, classrooms where students are granted autonomy generally promote mastery goals. This may differ based on alpha or beta presses for authority structure. Some students may not find some classrooms controlling at all, while others might find the same classroom oppressive. For example, some of the same authority structures that are readily accepted in elementary school might be seen as very controlling by middle-school or high-school students who tend to have an increased developmental need for autonomy (Eccles *et al.*, 1998). It seems unlikely that the authority structure of the classroom relates to students' adoption of approach versus avoidance goals since the authority structure is not related to the perceived difficulty of the learning situation nor is it expected to influence students' beliefs about their own ability.

Recognition/Evaluation. Teachers' evaluation of students and their use of rewards and recognition in the classroom are also important for determining the types of goals students adopt (Ames, 1992a, b). In particular, evaluation practices focused on improvement and mastery tend to foster mastery goals, while those focused on performance relative to others or those that make performance public tend to foster performance goals. The way in which students are rewarded and evaluated should also influence whether or not students approach or avoid a mastery or performance goal.

In particular, Church *et al.* (2001) examined evaluation structures in college classrooms and found that when students perceived evaluation structures as harsh (beta press), they tended to adopt avoid performance goals. The criteria used for evaluation (alpha press) also may impact both the direction and type of goal adopted. For example, self-referenced criteria for evaluation may promote either approach or avoid mastery goals depending on the nature of the criteria used to evaluate learning. If a minimum criteria (such as developing an understanding of at least seven of the ten important science principles) is emphasized, students may adopt avoid mastery goals. Similarly, evaluation criteria that are other-referenced (i.e., based on a curve) may promote either approach or avoid performance goals. Evaluation criteria where only the top students are rewarded are more likely to promote approach performance goals while criteria punishing those who fail are more likely to promote avoid performance goals.

Furthermore, the use of punishment rather than rewards should also relate to students' adoption of avoidance versus approach goals. Students who are told that they must redo a poorly done assignment may focus more on being perfectionist (mastery avoid) than on trying to approach a goal of improving and learning (mastery approach). In contrast, students who are told that those scoring in the lower third on a test will have to do additional work may be more likely to adopt avoid rather than approach performance goals.

Classroom Climate

In addition to the way in which the classroom is structured, the classroom climate, which refers to teachers' expectations and beliefs, may be especially important in terms of promoting approach versus avoidance achievement goals. Teachers who expect that their students can do the work and are capable of learning may promote the adoption of either approach mastery or approach performance goals. That is, a teacher who conveys to his/her students that they are capable of completing assignments and who sets relatively high, but reachable expectations for student achievement should encourage students to adopt approach goals because they will feel capable of achieving them. In contrast, a teacher who conveys to his/her students that he/she does not think they can do well or really learn the material may be more likely to encourage the adoption of avoidance goals. Of course, the interpretation of these messages from teachers (the beta press) is crucial, as different students may perceive the statements in different ways, resulting in the adoption of different goals.

The overall affective climate of the classroom may also relate to students' adoption of approach versus avoidance goals. A negative classroom climate where students do not feel safe and secure may promote the adoption of avoidance rather than approach goals. In such a classroom, students may be more focused on not getting pointed out as a bad example or on not giving a wrong answer, especially when negative consequences follow, thus promoting avoid rather than approach goals. The traditional classroom climate literature (e.g., Moos, 1979) provides a good exemplar of research that has focused not just on the alpha press of climate, but also on the beta press of a classroom in terms of climate. This work has shown the importance of students' perceptions of the classroom climate as important mediators between the alpha press of a classroom and other important student motivational or achievement outcomes.

In summary, many of the features of the classroom context are related to the type of goals that students adopt (a mastery or performance orientation). However, it is also plausible that the classroom context can influence whether or not students adopt an approach or avoidance direction towards these goals. Therefore, in analyzing the classroom context, we must consider not only how the structure and climate relate to mastery and performance goals, but also how differences in both structure, such as rewards, evaluation, and difficulty in the tasks, as well as climate, such as teachers' beliefs and feedback and the overall affective tone of the classroom, relate to the direction (approach versus avoid) of students' achievement goals. In addition, most of the research has not fully addressed how alpha and beta presses may be related or interact to promote the four different types of goal orientations. Finally, there has been very little work on how classrooms that might show a mixed pattern of different features influence personal goal adoption. For example, what goals are promoted when the authority structure promotes a mastery goal, but the grading or evaluation criteria leads to a performance goal? There is a clear need for more research on how different contextual features interact to promote both personal mastery and performance goals and how individuals actually synthesize these divergent features into a coherent perception or beta press regarding the classroom context.

Exploring the Role of Multiple Personal and Contextual Goals

Given the diversity of four personal goals and both alpha and beta goal presses in the classroom context, there are many different possible interactions between personal and contextual goals. To simplify this discussion, we first examine the potential interactions among multiple personal goals, followed by a discussion of how multiple personal and contextual goals may interact to produce different outcomes.

Potential Interactions between Multiple Personal Goals

Normative goal theory and subsequent research have not fully developed or examined the potential interactions among multiple goals. This gap in the literature is partially due to the general theoretical assumption that mastery and performance goals are orthogonal or opposing endpoints on a single continuum, that students or classrooms would be either mastery- or performance-oriented. This assumption fits with general experimental between-subject designs that compare mastery and performance groups with each other. However, in much of the correlational research on these two goals using self-report questionnaires, the research is quite mixed in terms of their relations. Some studies find that the personal mastery and performance goals are moderately positively correlated, (r's in the 0.20s to 0.30s, e.g., Elliot & McGregor, 2001; Roeser *et al.*, 1996; Wolters *et al.*, 1996), while others find them unrelated (e.g., Anderman & Midgley, 1997). If the two goals are somewhat orthogonal or only moderately correlated, then it raises the possibility that students could endorse different levels of both goals at the same time. Furthermore, qualitative analyses of students' learning in classrooms suggests that they may adopt more than one goal orientation simultaneously and that it is essential to consider the pursuit of multiple goals in order to understand their behavior (Boekaerts, 1998). This suggests that different patterns in the levels of the two goals may lead to different motivational, cognitive, or achievement outcomes.

Normative goal theory would suggest that any concern with performance, even an approach performance orientation, could have negative effects on involvement due to distractions fostered by attention to comparisons with others or to negative judgments regarding the self. Under this dampening or reduction perspective, the overall level of involvement that would be fostered by a mastery goal would be reduced when students simultaneously endorse an approach performance goal, thus decreasing positive outcomes. Accordingly, under this normative model, it would be hypothesized that the most adaptive pattern of multiple goals would be a high mastery, low approach performance combination.

On the other hand, given the positive patterns found for the separate main effects of approach mastery goals and performance goals (c.f., Dweck & Leggett, 1988; Harackiewicz *et al.*, 1998; Pintrich, 2000a, b, c), it could be predicted that having high levels of both of these goals would be the most adaptive. In this case, following the logic of multiplicative interaction effects, if there are two positive main effects for mastery and approach performance goals, then it may be that a focus on mastery along with a focus on trying to outperform others at the same time (a high mastery-high performance pattern) would result in enhanced positive outcomes. This revised goal theory perspective promotes the idea that there can be interactions between multiple goals and that these goals can give rise to multiple pathways that result in similar levels of motivation, cognition, and achievement (Pintrich, 2000b, c). Although the revised goal theory model also includes avoidance goals, we do not discuss empirical findings regarding avoidance goals because there is very little evidence regarding multiple goal adoption that includes these goals.

In correlational classroom research regarding these issues, studies have used a variety of methodologies yielding mixed results. Variable-centered analyses examining the possibility of interaction effects tend to support a normative model with the high mastery–low performance group yielding the most adaptive pattern for self-efficacy, task-value, and strategy use (Wolters *et al.*, 1996). However main effects from variable-centered analyses are mixed with some studies finding positive effects of performance goals (Elliot & Church, 1997; Harackiewicz *et al.*, 1997; Wolters *et al.*, 1996) in support of a revised goal theory model and others showing that approach performance goals are maladaptive (Kaplan & Midgley, 1997; Middleton & Midgley, 1997), supporting a normative model. Similarly, person-centered analyses using median-splits or cluster analyses reveal a mixed pattern of results with some studies supporting a revised goal theory model (Bouffard *et al.*, 1995; Pintrich, 2000b) and others supporting a normative model (Meece & Holt, 1993; Pintrich & Garcia, 1991). There is very little experimental research examining the possibility of multiple goals. One exception is a recent study described by Barron and Harackiewicz (2000) in which three goal conditions were formed: mastery only, performance only, and both mastery and performance. Unfortunately, this study did not yield results clarifying whether a normative or revised goal theory model is more appropriate due to difficulties with separating personality variables from the goal manipulation itself. Accordingly, given the mixed results and conflicting theoretical interpretations, there is a need for more research that examines how multiple personal goals might interact.

In terms of all four goals, it is not clear that there is a need to examine all the two-way interactions between all four goals in Table 1 or the higher-order interactions that could be generated in a full model. It may be that multiple goal patterns that cross the approach-avoid distinction are not as likely to be operating, as it may be difficult to go towards a performance goal and at the same time avoid it. On the other hand, students that are trying to approach both mastery and performance goals at the same time may show some very interesting patterns relative to those who are only approaching mastery or performance goals, as suggested by the results of Pintrich (2000b). In the same manner, students who adopt both mastery and performance avoid goals may have some interesting profiles and pathways to different motivational, cognitive, and performance outcomes. As the results of more studies accumulate, it will become clear which interactions are the sites for more interesting and relevant motivational dynamics and our theoretical models will be less impoverished and more complex.

Beyond these conceptual issues, the search for interactions raises some important methodological issues, one of the key themes of this book. In terms of self-report correlational studies, there have been three basic data analysis strategies adopted in the extant studies. Some studies (e.g., Wolters *et al.*, 1996) have used multiple regression analysis to examine the interactions across the full range of the goal scales. This strategy provides a good estimate of the parameters of a variable and the relative importance of different constructs, but it does not really help us understand individuals who might show distinct patterns of goals.

In contrast, other studies (e.g., Bouffard *et al.*, 1995; Pintrich, 2000b) have used median-split analyses to form groups of students who show different patterns of mastery and performance goals. Median-split analyses are more in line with a person-centered analysis in contrast to the variable-centered analysis of regression. Magnusson (1998; Magnusson & Stattin, 1998) has suggested the importance of maintaining the integrity of a person-centered strategy because the effects of different constructs accrue to individuals, not to variables. In addition, persons move through different contexts, not variables, so if one is to examine person–context interactions, then it is important to find ways to measure the constructs at a person-centered level.

Of course, median splits are fairly crude and do result in the loss of some accuracy due to the truncation of the range of scores into a simple dichotomous variable. Other studies have used person-centered cluster analysis (e.g, Meece & Holt, 1993; Pintrich & Garcia, 1991, 1993) to form groups of students based on different profiles of goals. This technique takes advantage of the full range of scores as well as a multivariate perspective in contrast to simple median splits. On the other hand, given the diversity of algorithms and the sensitivity of cluster analysis algorithms to variance in scores, it is often difficult to replicate the cluster profiles across different samples. Furthermore, in some cases, the cluster solutions do not easily map on to theoretically meaningful groupings, making it difficult to test explicit interaction hypotheses. In addition, depending on the nature of the groupings formed by cluster analysis, it may be difficult to ascertain how the different variables in the cluster analysis actually contribute to the pattern of the results. In contrast, with a simple median split interaction analysis of two variables, it is usually clear how one variable conditionalizes the effects of the other variable. In any event, it is important to keep these methodological considerations in mind as one attempts to examine the interactions between multiple personal goal orientations.

Researchers using experimental rather than correlational methodologies to examine potential interactions need to carefully consider whether goal manipulations alter students' personal goals or merely change the context in which students are working. In our own work where we have tried to manipulate student goals we have had mixed success. We have used various inductions in an attempt to create a mastery or performance goal orientation, but in our manipulation checks, we find that some students do not adopt the goals of the condition to which they were assigned experimentally. Newman (1998) also notes a similar problem in his experimental study. Currently, we find that it is insufficient to use simple word changes (changing "doing better than others" for a performance induction to "trying to learn and improve" for a mastery induction) in a paragraph of text. One strategy that seems to be working is to describe a hypothetical student who is operating with a mastery or performance goal and then ask the participants to provide an example of when this happened to them.

Another issue with experimental methodologies is that the goal manipulation may interact with pre-existing differences in students' motivation. For instance, in the Barron and Harackiewicz (2000) study reported earlier, the authors found that the effect of the goal manipulation varied based on students' achievement motivation with those low in achievement motivation showing higher levels of interest under the mastery condition and those high in achievement motivation showing higher levels of interest under the performance condition. For the multiple goal condition, students reported moderate levels of interest. The authors suggest that this finding may be a result of those low in achievement motivation focusing on the mastery goal and those high in achievement motivation focusing on the performance goal in the multiple goal condition. Thus, rather than clarifying the issue regarding the possible benefits of adopting both approach mastery and approach performance goals, this study suggested that it is difficult to assign achievement goals and that effects of assigning the goals may vary based on individual differences (i.e., differences in achievement motivation) that students bring into the experimental setting. These problems with experimental inductions remind us of the importance of both personal goals as well as contextual goals as well as the difficulties of studying student motivation in the rather sterile environment of the laboratory.

Potential Interactions between Personal Goals and Contextual Goals

Although it is a common assumption that students can have personal goals that they bring with them to classrooms and that classrooms also can stress certain kinds of goals, there has been very little research that has examined the interaction of personal and contextual goals. Moreover, there is some disagreement about the potential directions of these interactive effects. On the one hand, from a normative goal theory perspective that stresses that adaptive nature of mastery goals and the maladaptive nature of performance goals, it would be expected that mastery goals (personal or contextual) would moderate any negative effects of performance goals (personal or contextual). For example, if a performance-oriented student came into a mastery context, then the positive mastery environment should reduce or "buffer" the negative effects of the personal performance goal. In the same manner, a mastery-oriented student in a performance-oriented context should be "buffered" by his or her own personal mastery goal from the negative effect of the performance context.

In contrast, in a revised goal theory perspective, performance goals are not necessarily seen as maladaptive, at least for some outcomes, for some students. In this case, a general congruence or synchrony hypothesis could be generated that suggests the importance of the "match" between personal goals and contextual goals. This general person–environment fit notion has quite a long history in educational and psychological research (e.g., Eccles & Midgley, 1989; Eccles *et al.*, 1998: Hunt, 1975). Under this hypothesis in goal theory, students who are personally mastery oriented and who are in a mastery-oriented classroom would show a positive pattern of outcomes, as would students who are performance oriented in a performance classroom context. This effect would be explained in terms of the fit between the affordances in the context and the personal goals and strivings of the individual. The approach performance goal student, who is oriented to trying to outperform others and is in a classroom context that provides the structure and climate that allows this goal to be met, may be successful and feel motivated as he or she can meet their personal goals.

There is little research that has tested these two general proposals, but one study by Newman (1998) has provided a very explicit test of the interaction between personal and contextual goals. He measured personal goals in terms of approach mastery and approach performance goals and then experimentally manipulated the contextual goals by assigning upper elementary students to either a performance condition or mastery condition in a microgenetic study. He then examined their problem-solving performance on a numerical inductive reasoning problem as well as their help-seeking behavior over two days. The results generally supported normative goal theory in terms of the main effects with personal mastery goals positively related to performance, personal performance goals negatively related to performance, and the mastery context condition being positively related to help seeking. In addition, in terms of the interactions between the personal and contextual goals, the results did not support a synchrony hypothesis, at least in terms of the help-seeking outcome. Students who had personal performance goals and were in the performance condition showed lower levels of help-seeking behavior. The person-by-context interactions were not significant for mathematical problem-solving performance. Although this one study was very well designed to address these types of interactions, it did not measure other outcomes of motivation or affect that may show a different pattern than help seeking. In addition, there is a need for the interactions to be examined in actual classrooms where the personal and contextual goals may have more time to unfold and be more meaningful to students than a short experiment.

To this point, we have only discussed the potential interactions between approach mastery and approach performance goals in terms of personal–contextual interactions. There are obviously a host of other potential interactions that could be tested. At the same time, the search for multiple interactions could lead researchers into a "hall of mirrors" in terms of an ever-expanding field of person-by-context interactions as Cronbach (1975) warned us about some time ago. It is important for future research on these interactions to proceed with theoretical caution and sense, rather than wholesale "data snooping".

We would suggest that although there may be four types of personal goals, at the classroom level there are probably two dominant alpha presses, a general mastery context and a general performance context. It seems likely that classrooms that stress a performance goal orientation might include messages about both looking smart as well as looking dumb. In this case, in terms of the confounding in the alpha press, it would be important to assess students' perceptions, or the beta presses of the context. It may be that students who perceive a performance-oriented classroom in terms of approach goals and have personal approach performance goals may show some positive outcomes. Tests of this type of interaction would be helpful in clarifying the utility of the normative and revised goal theory perspectives. Furthermore, considering multiple goals and how these emerge based on alpha and beta presses might provide a more nuanced view of students' motivation and subsequent learning.

Conclusions

Goal theory has progressed to a point where it seems fairly clear what the main goals are and how these goals can facilitate or constrain subsequent motivation, cognition, and achievement. In this chapter we have suggested the importance of a more complex and complicated perspective on goal theory. First, we have suggested that there is a need to move beyond a simple dichotomous view of two main goals, mastery and performance. We have proposed that there are really four main types of goals and that these goals may have different relations to various outcomes. More importantly, besides these four main goals, we have proposed that there is a need to move beyond a simple mastery–adaptive, performance–maladaptive assumption to concentrate on examining how different goals can give rise to multiple pathways to adaptive motivation, cognition, and achievement.

An important consideration in this proposal is that there is a need to examine how multiple personal goals may interact to influence various outcomes. Moreover, an examination of how both multiple personal goals and multiple contextual goals, including both alpha and beta versions of these contextual goals, interact in a dynamic manner to produce different outcomes is necessary. This multiple goals perspective certainly adds to the theoretical complexity of our scientific task in understanding student motivation in learning contexts and raises a number of methodological issues that must be addressed. However, given the complexity of contextual settings, a more nuanced view which goes beyond the mastery/performance goal dichotomy may better capture students' motivation and learning in complex classroom settings. Furthermore, this more complex view may also help to resolve some of the contradictory findings cited in this chapter. Although both these conceptual and methodological tasks are difficult, they are challenging and as we all grapple with them, we should come to a better understanding of student motivation and ways to improve education for all students.

References

Ames, C. (1992a), "Achievement goals and the classroom motivational climate." In D. H. Schunk & J. Meece (eds) *Student Perceptions in the Classroom* (pp. 327–348). Hillsdale, NJ: Erlbaum.

Ames, C. (1992b), "Classrooms: Goals, structures, and student motivation." *Journal of Educational Psychology 84*, 261–271.

Anderman, E., & Midgley, C. (1997), "Changes in achievement goal orientations, perceived academic competence, and grades across the transition to middle-level schools." *Contemporary Educational Psychology 22*, 269–298.

Anderman, L. H., Patrick, H., Hruda, L. Z., & Linnenbrink, E. A. (in press), "Observing classroom goal structures to clarify and expand goal theory." In C. Midgley, (ed.) *Goals, Goal Structures, and Patterns of Adaptive Learning*.

Atkinson, J. (1957), "Motivational determinants of risk-taking behavior." *Psychological Review 64*, 359–372.

Barron, K. E., & Harackiewicz, J. M. (2000), "Achievement goals and optimal motivation: A multiple goals approach." In C. Sansone & J. M. Harackiewicz (eds) *Intrinsic and Extrinsic Motivation: The Search for Optimal Motivation and Performance* (pp. 229–254). San Diego: Academic Press.

Blumenfeld, P. (1992), "Classroom learning and motivation: Clarifying and expanding goal theory." *Journal of Educational Psychology 84*, 272–281.

Boekaerts, M. (1998), "Boosting students' capacity to promote their own learning: A goal theory perspective." *Learning and Instruction 8*, 13–22.

Bouffard, T., Boisvert, J., Vezeau, C., & Larouche, C. (1995), "The impact of goal orientation on self-regulation and performance among college students." *British Journal of Educational Psychology 65*, 317–329.

Church, M. A., Elliot, A. J., & Gable, S. L. (2001), "Perceptions of classroom environment, achievement goals, and achievement outcomes." *Journal of Educational Psychology 93*, 45–54.

Covington, M., & Roberts, B. (1994), "Self-worth and college achievement: Motivational and personality correlates." In P. R. Pintrich, D. R. Brown & C. E. Weinstein (eds) *Student Motivation, Cognition, and Learning: Essays in Honor of Wilbert J. McKeachie* (pp. 157–187). Hillsdale, NJ: Lawrence Erlbaum Associates.

Cronbach, L. J. (1975), "Beyond the two disciplines of scientific psychology." *American Psychologist 30*, 116–127.

Dweck, C. S., & Elliott, E. S. (1983), "Achievement motivation." In P. H. Mussen (Ser. ed.) & E. M. Heatherington (Vol. ed.) *Handbook of Child Psychology: Vol. 4. Socialization, Personality, and Social Development* (4th ed., pp. 643–691). New York: Wiley.

Dweck, C., & Leggett, E. (1988), "A social cognitive approach to motivation and personality." *Psychological Review 95*, 256–273.

Eccles, J., & Midgley, C. (1989), "Stage–environment fit: Developmentally appropriate classrooms for young adolescents." In C. Ames & R. Ames (eds) *Research on Motivation in Education* (Vol. 3, pp. 139–186). San Diego: Academic Press.

Eccles, J., Wigfield, A., & Schiefele, U. (1998), "Motivation to succeed." In W. Damon (Ser. ed.) & N. Eisenberg (Vol. ed.) *Handbook of Child Psychology: Vol. 3. Social, Emotional, and Personality Development* (5th ed., pp. 1017–1095). New York: Wiley.

Elliot, A. (1997), "Integrating the 'classic' and 'contemporary' approaches to achievement motivation: A hierarchical model of approach and avoidance achievement motivation." In M. L. Maehr & P. R. Pintrich (eds) *Advances in Motivation and Achievement* (Vol. 10, pp. 143–179). Greenwich, CT: JAI Press.

Elliot, A. J. (1999), "Approach and avoidance motivation and achievement goals." *Educational Psychologist 34*, 169–189.

Elliot, A., & Church, M. (1997), "A hierarchical model of approach and avoidance achievement motivation." *Journal of Personality and Social Psychology 72*, 218–232.

Elliot, A., & Harackiewicz, J. (1996), "Approach and avoidance achievement goals and intrinsic motivation: A mediational analysis." *Journal of Personality and Social Psychology 70*, 968–980.

Elliot, A., & McGregor, H. (2001), "A 2 × 2 achievement goal framework." *Journal of Personality and Social Psychology 76*, 501–519.

Ford, M. (1992), *Motivating Humans: Goals, Emotions, and Personal Agency Beliefs.* Newbury Park, CA: Sage Publications.

Harackiewicz, J., Barron, K. E., Carter, S., Lehto, A., & Elliot, A. (1997), "Predictors and consequences of achievement goals in the college classroom: Maintaining interest and making the grade." *Journal of Personality and Social Psychology 73*, 1284–1295.

Harackiewicz, J., Barron, K. E., & Elliot, A. J. (1998), "Rethinking achievement goals: When are they adaptive for college students and why?" *Educational Psychologist 33*, 1–21.

Higgins, E. T. (1997), "Beyond pleasure and pain." *American Psychologist 52*, 1280–1300.

Hunt, D. E. (1975), "Person–environment interaction: A challenge found wanting before it was tried." *Review of Educational Research 45*, 209–230.

Järvelä, S., & Niemivirta, M. (1999), "The changes in learning theory and the topicality of the recent research on motivation." *Research Dialogue 2*, 57–65.

Kaplan, A., & Midgley, C. (1997), "The effect of achievement goals: Does level of perceived academic competence make a difference." *Contemporary Educational Psychology 22*, 415–435.

Lehtinen, E., Vauras, M., Salonen, P., Olkinuora, E., & Kinnunen, R. (1995), "Long-term development of learning activity: Motivational, cognitive, and social interaction." *Educational Psychologist 30*, 21–35.

Lemos, M. S. (1996), "Students' and teachers' goals in the classroom." *Learning and Instruction 6*, 151–171.

Maehr, M. L., & Anderman, E. A. (1993), "Reinventing schools for early adolescents: Emphasizing task goals." *The Elementary School Journal 93*, 593–610.

Maehr, M. L., & Midgley, C. (1991), "Enhancing student motivation: A schoolwide approach." *Educational Psychologist 26*, 399–427.

Maehr, M. L., & Midgley, C. (1996), *Transforming School Cultures*. Boulder, CO: Westview Press.

Magnusson, D. (1998), "The logic and implications of a person-oriented approach." In R. Cairns, L. Bergman & J. Kagan (eds) *Methods and Models for Studying the Individual: Essays in Honor of Marian Radke-Yarrow* (pp. 33–64). Thousand Oaks, CA: Sage.

Magnusson, D., & Stattin, H. (1998), "Person–context interaction theories." In W. Damon (Seri. ed.) & R. M. Lerner (Vol. ed.) *Handbook of Child Psychology: Vol. 1. Theoretical Models of Human Development* (5th ed., pp. 685–759). New York: Wiley.

McClelland, D., Atkinson, J., Clark, R., & Lowell, E. (1953), *The Achievement Motive*. New York: Appleton-Century-Crofts.

Meece, J. (1991), "The classroom context and students' motivational goals." In M. L. Maehr & P. R. Pintrich (eds) *Advances in Motivation and Achievement* (Vol. 7, pp. 261–286). Greenwich, CT: JAI Press.

Meece, J., & Holt, K. (1993), "A pattern analysis of students' achievement goals." *Journal of Educational Psychology 85*, 582–590.

Middleton, M. J. (2000), *Can Classrooms be Both Motivating and Demanding? The Role of Academic Press*. Unpublished doctoral dissertation, University of Michigan, Ann Arbor.

Middleton, M., & Midgley, C. (1997), "Avoiding the demonstration of lack of ability: An underexplored aspect of goal theory." *Journal of Educational Psychology 89*, 710–718.

Midgley, C., Arunkumar, R., & Urdan, T. (1996), "'If I don't do well tomorrow, there's a reason: Predictors of adolescents use of academic self-handicapping behavior." *Journal of Educational Psychology 88*, 423–434.

Midgley, M., Kaplan, A., & Middleton, M. (2001), "Performance-approach goals: Good for what, for whom, under what circumstances, and at what cost?" *Journal of Educational Psychology 93*, 77–86.

Midgley, M., Kaplan, A., Middleton, M., Maehr, M. L., Urdan, T. *et al.* (1998), "The development and validation of scales assessing students' achievement goal orientations." *Contemporary Educational Psychology 23*, 113–131.

Moos, R. (1979), *Evaluating Educational Environments*. San Francisco: Jossey-Bass.

Murray, H. A. (1938), *Explorations in Personality*. New York: Oxford University Press.

Newman, R. (1998), "Students' help-seeking during problem solving: Influences of personal and contextual goals." *Journal of Educational Psychology 90*, 644–658.

Nicholls, J. (1984), "Achievement motivation: Conceptions of ability, subjective experience, task choice, and performance." *Psychological Review 91*, 328–346.

Nicholls, J. (1990), "What is ability and why are we mindful of it? A developmental perspective." In R. Sternberg & J. Kolligian (eds) *Competence Considered* (pp. 11–40). New Haven, CT: Yale University Press.

Nicholls, J., Cheung, P., Lauer, J., & Patashnick, M. (1989), "Individual differences in academic motivation: Perceived ability, goals, beliefs, and values." *Learning and Individual Differences 1*, 63–84.

Patrick, H., Anderman, L. H., Ryan, A. M., Edelin, K., & Midgley, C. (in press), "Teachers' communication of goal orientations in four fifth-grade classrooms." *Elementary School Journal*.

Pintrich, P. R. (2000a), "An achievement goal theory perspective on issues in motivation terminology, theory, and research." *Contemporary Educational Psychology 25*, 92–104.

Pintrich, P. R. (2000b), "Multiple goals, multiple pathways: The role of goal orientation in learning and achievement." *Journal of Educational Psychology 92*, 544–555.

Pintrich, P. R. (2000c), "The role of goal orientation in self-regulated learning." In M. Boekaerts, P. R. Pintrich & M. Zeidner (eds) *Handbook of Self-Regulation* (pp. 451–502). San Diego, CA: Academic Press.

Pintrich, P. R., & Garcia, T. (1991), "Student goal orientation and self-regulation in the college classroom." In M. L. Maehr & P. R. Pintrich (eds) *Advances in Motivation and Achievement: Goals and Self-Regulatory Processes* (Vol. 7, pp. 371–402). Greenwich, CT: JAI Press.

Pintrich, P. R., & Garcia, T. (1993), "Motivation and self-regulation in the college classroom." *Zeitschrift für Pädagogische Psychologie 7*, 99–107.

Pintrich, P. R., & Schunk, D. H. (1996), *Motivation in Education: Theory, Research, and Applications.* Englewood Cliffs, NJ: Prentice Hall Merrill.

Roeser, R., Midgley, C., & Urdan, T. (1996), "Perceptions of the school psychological environment and early adolescents' psychological and behavioral functioning in school: The mediating role of goals and belonging." *Journal of Educational Psychology 88*, 408–422.

Skaalvik, E. (1997), "Self-enhancing and self-defeating ego orientation: Relations with task avoidance orientation, achievement, self-perceptions, and anxiety." *Journal of Educational Psychology 89*, 71–81.

Skaalvik, E., Valas, H., & Sletta, O. (1994), "Task involvement and ego involvement: Relations with academic achievement, academic self-concept and self-esteem." *Scandinavian Journal of Educational Research 38*, 231–243.

Urdan, T. (1997), "Achievement goal theory: Past results, future directions." In M. L. Maehr & P. R. Pintrich (eds) *Advances in Motivation and Achievement* (Vol. 10, pp. 99–141). Greenwich, CT: JAI Press.

Urdan, T. C., Midgley, C., & Anderman, E. M. (1998), "The role of classroom goal structure in students' use of self-handicapping." *American Educational Research Journal 35*, 101–122.

Wolters, C. A., Yu, S. L., & Pintrich, P. R. (1996), "The relation between goal orientation and students' motivational beliefs and self-regulated learning." *Learning and Individual Differences 6*, 211–238.

Zusho, A., & Pintrich, P. R. (2000, April), *Fear of Not Learning? The Role of Mastery Avoidance Goals in Asian American and European American College Students.* Paper presented at the Annual Meeting of the American Educational Research Association, New Orleans.

Chapter 14

Age and Gender Effects on Students' Evaluations Regarding the Self and Task-Related Experiences in Mathematics

Irini Dermitzaki & Anastasia Efklides

One of the features of current psychological research in educational settings is the emphasis on the dynamic interaction between the student and the learning context. Learning context can be defined in various ways: for example, in the school setting, we can talk about the *school context* (i.e., primary or secondary school), the *within-school context* (as exemplified in the various subject areas), the *social context* in school (i.e., the relationship of the students with teachers, peers, family, and school organization), and the *time-context* (namely, the first or second semester, or the beginning of learning in a domain vs. a more advanced stage) (MacCallum, 2001; von Rhoeneck *et al.*, 2001).

The broader sociocultural context, however, also affects students' learning through the values and community practices that involves (see Rogoff, 1990; Vygotsky, 1978). It influences the school context (particularly the social aspect of it), and also the family, community, and peers context outside school. Family and peers interact with the school and classroom context to determine student motivation.

At the opposite end of the sociocultural context, which is a general context, we can identify the very specific context of the task. This is related to the specific features of the task itself and its relationships with the rest of the learning material and testing conditions. Thus, the conceptualization of context may range from the general sociocultural milieu to the very specific features of the task and the learning situation in school or at home. It seems that student motivation changes as they move from one context to another, from one situation to the other.

In motivation research, existing theories usually stress motives as personality characteristics (e.g., need achievement, goal orientation, etc.) that predict performance across situations. However, in order to predict the exact effect of a motive one has to take into consideration the task and at least some of its features, namely difficulty or incentive value. In educational settings this is not enough, because both the difficulty and incentive value of the task change as the school, subject area, social and time context change. Thus, taking context into consideration provides an ecological approach to student motivation in learning context and a rich picture of the differentiation of student motivation as conditions change.

Yet, too much emphasis on context and situational effects on motivation may risk overlooking, on the one hand, of the more general or stable patterns of

Motivation in Learning Contexts: Theoretical Advances and Methodological Implications, pages 271–293.

motivation across contexts and, on the other, the interaction of context with cognitive or other individual difference factors that are known to affect student motivation. More importantly, one loses track of the individual and how they interpret the various contexts in light of their existing motivational tendencies or cognitive abilities. In other words, in order to have a complete picture of student motivation in learning context we need to take into consideration the perspective of the experiencing person, whose response to the learning situation is determined by general cognitive and affective characteristics, as well as by individual difference factors, and by the characteristics of the situation, that is, the task and its context, from the very narrow to the broader one. Turning to the experiencing person means that we include in our models the subjective experience of the person along with the objectively defined motivational tendencies and task/context features.

Furthermore, both cognitive abilities and motivation change along with age and increasing knowledge. This poses the question whether context influences the developmental process, and if motivational change can be explained in terms of changing context (see MacCallum, 2001; von Rhoeneck *et al.*, 2001) or by other age-related effects. Thus, although the developmental and individual difference approach to motivation represent the opposite pole of the situational or contextual approach, it is still a challenge to combine the two approaches in order to understand what is context-free or context-specific in motivational change. Our emphasis is, however, on the subjective experience of students because it summarizes the effects of general personal characteristics (which are affected by individual difference factors and age) and the task and/or context. Subjective experience expresses the outcome of the interaction of one's cognitive, metacognitive, and affective background with current task/context features (Efklides, 2001). It is how the person perceives the situation, its specific features and its demands through the filter of one's self. Therefore, the question is whether subjective experience is part of the mechanism that brings about motivational change.

To sum up, what we propose here is that in order to have a better understanding of student motivation in learning context, we need to consider three parameters: (a) the task and its context, such as home, school, individual or group learning, the time context, the presentation of the task, etc.; (b) the general personal characteristics, such as cognitive ability, personality, and individual difference factors, and (c) the subjective online experiences of the student (i.e., ideas, feelings, and judgments or estimates) as s/he is processing the task. These online subjective experiences are the expression of the resultant effect of the general and the specific person and task/context factors, the subjective and the objective features of the situation, the individual and the collective factors that come to bear in the particular situation.

Subjective Experience and Motivation

The advantage of including subjective experience in our studies is that it may give us insight into the mechanism through which context influences motivation, self-regulation, and performance. Specifically, context can exert its effects as an extrinsic variable that acts alongside the learning task and out of the person him/ herself. In such a case, context increases or decreases the task demands and through it the strength of motive(s). However, the sociocultural context may work independently of the specific task. It exerts its effects through the students' ideas, expectancies or attributions that shape the perception of and the attitudes towards the specific task. In this case context exerts its effects through a process of assimilation of social norms or stereotypes into one's existing self-concept, or through the effects of social comparison and external sources of feedback on students' sense of competence.

A third way through which context may affect students' motivation is subjective experience. Extrinsic or sociocultural context may affect (directly or indirectly) the online ideas, feelings, and judgments the student experiences as task processing goes on. In this case, it is the interaction of the student with the task that gives rise to an *intrinsic context* in which the student functions. This intrinsic context of feelings, ideas, and judgments is analogous to the state (physical or emotional) that affects learning and memory (Bower, 1981). However, what we are talking about here is not the non-conscious state in which the student functions while learning but the conscious experience of feelings, ideas, estimates, and judgments that exerts its effects through students' awareness of themselves and their subjective experience as they deal with learning tasks in various situations; for example, experiencing interest in the learning task in one context rather than another, when the task is familiar or not, when processing is fluent or not, experiencing interest at the beginning and boredom later on, etc. What we need to know is how this intrinsic context is being formed and how it affects students' motivation and self-regulation in a learning situation.

In this chapter we are dealing with students' self-concept and the intrinsic context, i.e., subjective, online experiences related to the task. Self-concept functions at a more general level than the task level. We could call it the *domain level* (for example, self-concept in maths). On the contrary, online subjective experience functions at the task level. Self-concept is influenced by social factors (for the formation of self-concept see Harter, 1988; Marsh, 1986), and at the same time interacts with performance as well as with students' feelings or subjective evaluations regarding themselves dealing with the task at hand (Dermitzaki, 1997; Efklides & Tsiora, 2000). Self-concept and its interaction with the feelings and subjective evaluations of the task is particularly important for self-regulation in the short and the long run, that is, during online task processing as well as future involvement with similar tasks (see Efklides & Tsiora, 2000; Metallidou & Efklides, 2001). This is so because they set the scene for the interpretation of the learning task. Thus, even if students have the capability to deal successfully with a task, their self-concept in the respective domain, or their experiences with a specific task (e.g., feeling of difficulty), may prevent them from getting engaged in it, or vice versa. From this point of view, in order to understand better the learner in context, we need to know their background in terms of abilities, personality traits or belief systems, their self-concept in the domain of interest, and their subjective experience with respect to the task at hand. Different combinations of the learner's background, the social situation, the educational environment and the task characteristics result in different cognitive and emotional interpretations in different individuals (Lehtinen *et al.*, 1995). This kind of interpretation is critical for the decision to go on with, e.g., the task at hand, and how much effort to invest in it.

Methodological Issues Regarding the Study of Intrinsic Context

Metacognitive Experiences. One way of studying students' intrinsic context is through their metacognitive experiences. *Metacognitive experiences* (ME) are defined as the online judgments/estimates, feelings, ideas and thoughts about the task at hand and reflect personal evaluations or inferences about one's own cognitive processing and the status of one's knowledge, understanding, or expectations (Clore & Parrott, 1994; Efklides, 1997; Efklides, 2001; Efklides & Vauras, 1999; Flavell, 1979). Examples of ME are feeling of knowing (FOK), feeling of familiarity (FOF), feeling of difficulty (FOD), feeling of confidence (FOC), or judgment of learning (JOL), estimate of effort expenditure (EOE), estimate of solution correctness (EOC) (Efklides, 2001). Metacognitive feelings and judgments, according to Nelson (1996), are the conscious product of the monitoring function of metacognition, and they provide the input for the control function of metacognition. Thus, ME are mediators of online self-regulation because they contribute to the person's awareness of online cognitive functioning and they influence the person's intention to deal with a task, his/her persistence, the strategies s/he will use, etc. (Efklides *et al.*, 1999).

Metacognitive experiences are influenced by factors such as one's ability to deal with the cognitive demands of the task, personality and affective factors, one's metacognitive knowledge, and task-related factors (Efklides, 1997; 2001; Efklides *et al.*, 1997, 1998). It has also been shown that ME are affected by students' self-concept and by their motivational orientation (Dermitzaki, 1997; Efklides & Tsiora, 2000; Hoge *et al.*, 1990). Domain-specific knowledge and previous experience with the task may also be important factors in determining students' self-awareness of their cognitive processing and performance (Efklides *et al.*, 1997, 1998; Newman, 1984). These findings imply that ME express the person's evaluation of the current situation vis-à-vis his/her previous encounters with the same or similar ones. Thus, although ME are task-specific, at the same time they reflect the person's history in similar situations and how s/he feels about it.

Measurement of Metacognitive Experiences. Metacognitive experiences, as they monitor online cognitive processing, are amenable to change as processing goes on. This implies that we need to measure them at least twice, once as soon as the student comes across the task and before starting to work on it, and once right after having completed the processing of the task. In the former case, the ME are *prospective* in nature whereas in the latter they are *retrospective* (Efklides, 1999; Nelson, 1996). One could also collect data of subjective evaluations (or behavioral data indicating feelings) during the processing of the task; for example, after the planning of the solution of the problem and before carrying out the computations, or at other points of task processing (see Efklides *et al.*, 1999). In this way we can have a more detailed picture of how the intrinsic context changes as new data (e.g., interruption of processing due to lack of available response) enter the scene.

A critical issue as regards subjective evaluations is how reliable they are (see Efklides, 1999; Nelson, 1996). Since metacognitive judgments are products of inferential processes (Efklides, 2001; Koriat & Levy-Sadot, 1999; Lories *et al.*, 1998; Nelson *et al.*, 1998) it is clear that measures of ME should be accompanied by performance measures and/or by other kinds of objective measures of the learning situation and the extrinsic context. In this way one can have a more precise conception of the interplay between the extrinsic and intrinsic context as they evolve.

Another issue regarding subjective evaluations is their generalizability. Subjective evaluations are tied to specific persons and specific tasks or situations. How then can they be generalized to other tasks or contexts or other people? A strategy adopted by Efklides and her collaborators, is to apply quantitative methods of analysis to measures of ME such as feeling of familiarity, feeling of difficulty, feeling of confidence, etc. What we do is measure ME with rating scales at various phases of problem solving for each of a number of tasks that differ in terms of content (e.g., subject area) or difficulty. Then with the use of correlational or confirmatory methods of analysis we identify the pattern of interrelations between ME at the various phases of problem solving and between ME and performance for each task (Efklides *et al.*, 1997, 1998, 1999). Following this, we compare the model(s) that fit the data of one task with the model(s) of a comparative task in order to identify what is common across tasks and what is task-specific. This kind of methodology allows us also to test hypotheses about differences between groups of students who differ in age, gender, expertise, etc. (Efklides *et al.*, 1997). Furthermore, we can study the effects of general personal characteristics, such as ability, personality or motivational orientation on ME (Efklides *et al.*, 1997, 1998) or of ME on motivation (for example, causal attributions; see Metallidou & Efklides, 2001). Finally, with longitudinal data of this type we could identify the long-term effects of online, subjective experience on more general personal characteristics such as self-concept (Efklides & Tsiora, 2000).

In what follows we are presenting empirical data showing that self-concept and ME interact with performance and between them, and these relations differ in both genders as well as in groups of different age. This kind of evidence may explain the different careers in mathematics both genders exhibit with advancing age.

Effects of Age and Gender on Metacognitive Experiences and Self-Concept

The focus of the present study was on students' feeling of difficulty (FOD), on the estimate of effort (EOE) required for task processing, and on the estimate of solution correctness (EOC). Feeling of difficulty makes the person aware of the lack of an immediate response to the task at hand and/or of the interruption of cognitive processing. It is a complex experience and not a mere reflection of task difficulty. Thus, there is no simple, direct relationship between objective task difficulty and FOD. Often objective task difficulty is not correctly perceived by the person (Efklides *et al.*, 1998), particularly when such a judgment is made before actual problem solving, that is, as a prospective judgment. According to Johnson, Saccuzo, and Larson (1995) FOD reflects a task by effort interaction. Efklides *et al.* (1999), on the other hand, found that FOD is influenced by the feeling of familiarity with the task. Feeling of familiarity signals the fluency of processing of the task unlike feeling of difficulty that signals the lack of fluency. The estimate of solution correctness is a judgment related to one's confidence to the solution produced (Efklides, 1999; Efklides *et al.*, 1999), whereas the estimate of effort reflects the person's response to task difficulty.

Age Effects on Metacognitive Experiences. Regarding the development of ME, the extant studies show that ME do change along with age but the various ME do not necessarily follow the same developmental course. For example, in a study by Saxe and Sicilian (1981, cited in Newman, 1984) cognitive monitoring, i.e., sensitivity to task difficulty on a quantitative task, was age-related. Efklides *et al.* (1996, 1999) found that age affected the reported FOD and estimate of solution correctness. As students become older they report less difficulty and increased solution correctness (when basic mathematics concepts are concerned). Increased estimate of solution correctness was also reported by older students, as compared to younger ones in a study of Metallidou & Efklides (1998), but this did not apply in the case of an objectively difficult task that continued to be judged difficult by older students. In another study, the main effect of school grade (or age) on FOD was not significant. Instead, grade interacted significantly with the testing wave and with objective task difficulty (Efklides *et al.*, 1998). Therefore, age may affect FOD and estimate of solution correctness but the strength of the effect depends on the type of the task and its objective difficulty.

Gender Effects on Metacognitive Experiences. Regarding the influence of gender on ME, there are few relevant studies and not enough evidence to come to a conclusion about gender effects on the various feelings and estimates. Newman (1984), for example, reported that although there was no effect of gender on actual performance there was an effect on feeling of confidence. Girls were less confident than boys and more realistic in their judgments of confidence. Similarly, Metallidou and Efklides (1998) found that boys reported significantly higher estimate of solution correctness in comparison to girls in quantitative and causal tasks. As regards FOD, Efklides *et al.* (1998) reported that gender did not have any significant effect on the difficulty reported in mathematics tasks. This implies that with similar objective and subjective difficulty, girls are less confident than boys in mathematics. The question is whether this difference in confidence is related to differences in the relations of ME with performance and with self-concept.

Self-Concept. Nowadays, there is general agreement that self-concept is a multidimensional, multifaceted dynamic structure (Byrne, 1996; Harter, 1990; Markus &

Wurf, 1987; Marsh, 1990; Marsh *et al.*, 1988). Different content areas or domains of self-concept have been identified such as social, physical or academic self-concept (Marsh, 1990). Self-concept in each of these domains represents one's subjective competence in the respective domain. Self-concept is also assumed to have different aspects, cognitively or affectively charged.

Four different components or aspects of students' academic self-concept can be identified: A cognitive component, namely *self-perception*, which involves beliefs about one's present state of abilities; an affective component, that is, *self-esteem*, which involves feelings of self-acceptance and self-liking; an expectancy component, which involves one's expectations about his/her abilities to perform specific tasks, namely *self-efficacy*, and, finally, a component that has to do with the role of significant others on the formation of self-concept. This last component has to do with how *one perceives the reaction of significant others towards his/her ability*. Research has documented the above different components of one's self (see Damon & Hart, 1982; Dermitzaki, 1997; Dermitzaki & Efklides, 2000; Geen, 1995; Harter, 1990; Markus & Wurf, 1987; Pajares & Miller, 1994).

Age Effects on Self-Concept. It has been shown in the past that, during adolescence, academic self-concept goes through major changes insofar as students' ideas about their abilities are concerned. However, there is no consistent pattern of age effects in studies of self-concept in early and middle adolescence. Some studies suggest that there may be a curvilinear effect in which ratings of self-concept decline during pre-adolescence and early adolescence, level out in middle adolescence, and then increase in late adolescence and early adulthood (e.g., Marsh, 1989). Other studies have found systematic increases or systematic decreases in self-concept during this age period. An important reason for such developmental changes in self-concept is that, as students move through changing environments and evaluation systems, they start using more external criteria for judging their abilities (Dweck, 1999; Nicholls, 1989; Stipek & MacIver, 1989). By the years of junior high-school, students' perceptions of their competence may be affected by school competition and other indicators of their achievement in relation to certain norms. A shift towards use of such criteria in evaluating competence often brings about decreases in perceptions of ability (Stipek & MacIver, 1989).

Gender Effects on Self-Concept. Gender has been found to influence students' motivation, self-perceptions and enjoyment of school subjects along the lines of traditional sex stereotyping (Evans *et al.*, 1995; Lightbody *et al.*, 1996; Meece & Courtney, 1992). Research in maths education, for example, has provided evidence that females display less confidence than males in their ability to do mathematics (Fennema, 1989).

The above-mentioned differences in students' academic self-concept seem to persist despite the fact that often there may be no significant gender differences in achievement in the respective domains. Some researchers have suggested a self-fulfilling prophecy according to which sex stereotypes influence self-concept, which in turn influences achievement indirectly (Marsh *et al.*, 1988). In general, it seems that girls, especially during adolescence, hold less stable self-concept, lower self-confidence and self-esteem, and more anxiety than boys even if their performance is the same or better than that of boys (Leondari *et al.*, 1998; McLeod, 1989). But there are also findings showing no differences between boys' and girls' academic self-concept in maths (e.g., Skaalvik & Rankin, 1990).

Recently, it has been claimed that gender effects do not produce such large differences in self-concept as it has been previously maintained (Marsh, 1993). In general, gender differences in academic motivation are less marked than they were in the past (Lightbody *et al.*, 1996). Furthermore, some researchers argue that gender by itself does not adequately explain differences in students' achievement patterns (Meece & Courtney, 1992) and age effects should be taken into consideration because age seems to strengthen the differences between genders (Marsh, 1993; see also Eccles *et al.*, 1993). The question, therefore, is what is the mechanism that produces this growing gender effect on self-concept in the developing person and if ME are part of this mechanism.

Self-Concept and Metacognitive Experiences. It is known that cognitive abilities along with academic performance influence students' self-perceptions (Fontaine, 1993; Helmke, 1989; Marsh. 1990; Weinert & Helmke, 1998), and the relationship of academic performance with self-concept becomes stronger with increasing age (Weinert & Helmke, 1998). The question is why and how this happens. One explanation is the growing awareness of external criteria for judging one's performance in adolescence, which leads to a more realistic conception of one's self dealing with task in a specific domain. However, one cannot rule out the effects of growing awareness of one's own capabilities, which is based on subjective feedback offered by ME (Efklides & Tsiora, 2000). This subjective feedback provides data for an internal comparison process that informs the person that s/he is more competent in one domain than in another (for the internal/external comparison model see Marsh, 1986). This growing metacognitive awareness of one's self as problem-solver along with better awareness of the criteria for judging one's own performance probably make one's self-concept more realistic as time passes and experience in a knowledge domain accumulates. Yet, the awareness of one's performance and ME may vary in the two genders.

In what follows we shall present empirical evidence on how self-concept, ME and performance are related, and how these relations vary in the two genders and different age groups. In this way we can identify the intrinsic context that accompanies mathematics learning and the factors that contribute to it.

The Study

Our study aimed at testing the following hypotheses:

Age Effects. Taking into consideration that age is related to increased knowledge and skill in basic mathematical concepts, older students were expected to have better performance on tasks tapping such concepts than younger ones. Better performance should be related to lower feeling of difficulty and estimate of effort expenditure and higher estimate of solution correctness. Students should also exhibit more accurate perception of themselves as mathematics problem-solvers, that is, less optimistic self-reports along with increasing age. This should lead to a differentiation of the effects of self-concept on ME, with older students relying for their metacognitive inferences more on their own perception of their capability and efficiency in dealing with mathematics tasks rather than the younger ones (Hypothesis 1).

Gender Effects. Extant data suggest that self-concept affects ME and boys have a more positive self-concept in mathematics than girls, despite the lack of significant performance differences. Consequently, boys should be affected in their reports of ME and they should report less difficulty and effort and higher solution correctness than girls. However, it was not clear which aspect of self-concept affects ME and if the pattern of relations between self-concept and ME is differentiated in the two genders (Hypothesis 2).

Method

The participants were 512 students from different schools of a Greek city. The students were of 7th, 9th (junior high-school) and 11th grade (high-school) with 159, 168, and 185 participants in the respective groups. There were 261 girls and 251 boys of predominantly middle-class population, according to parental educational background.

The students were tested with a set of ten mathematics problems, which were developed by the authors to assess *performance in school maths*. The problems represented basic concepts of the Greek curriculum concerning maths classes in junior high-school. They required participants to solve two fractions tasks, two algebraic operations tasks, two percentages tasks, two tasks of VAT calculation, and two geometry tasks.

Three kinds of students' *metacognitive experiences* were recorded when solving the mathematics problems. The participants were asked to rate twice, before and after the solution of each maths task, the difficulty of the task, the effort required to solve it, and the correctness of the solution. The ratings were on four-point scales.

A questionnaire tapping the students' *academic self-concept in maths* was developed by the authors for the purposes of the present study. The questionnaire comprised 22 items regarding four different aspects of self-concept: *self-perception, self-esteem, self-efficacy,* and the *perceived image that significant others have about one's own abilities* (i.e., how the student thinks the teacher and classmates perceive him/her with respect to mathematics). The Self-Concept Questionnaire was always administered before the mathematics tasks and the ME questions. The structural validity of the questionnaire was confirmed (Dermitzaki & Efklides, 2000). The internal consistency of the questionnaire was very satisfactory, with Cronbach's alpha for the whole questionnaire being 0.96. Participants gave their answers on a five-point scale. Examples of items for each different aspect of self-concept are shown below:

Self-perception (Cronbach's *alpha* = 0.91): "I believe that my ability in the maths course is high."

Self-esteem (Cronbach's *alpha* = 0.92): "I am happy with my ability in the maths course."

Self-efficacy (Cronbach's *alpha* = 0.90): "I am sure I will do very well in tests in the current maths course."

Others' perception of one's own abilities (Cronbach's *alpha* = 0.89): "My peers acknowledge my ability in the maths course."

Results

With a series of MANOVAs we firstly tested the effects of age and gender on performance, ME, and academic self-concept in maths. Path analysis was then applied for the testing of models regarding the relations between maths performance, ME, and self-concept in different age and gender groups.

Age Effects. The MANOVAs showed significant age effect on performance and self-concept as predicted. The older the students the better their performance in the mathematics test was (see Table 1). Also, younger students as compared to older ones had more favorable self-perception and self-esteem in mathematics, more optimistic expectations about their future performance (self-efficacy), and they attributed to significant others a more positive perception of themselves. Overall, only the self-evaluations of the 7th graders differed significantly from the self-evaluations of the other two age groups in all aspects of the academic self-concept in maths (see Table 1).

However, there was an interesting interaction of age with aspect of academic self-concept. This indicates that the different aspects of self-concept in maths did not change in the same way along with increasing age. The most stable aspect of self-concept was others' perception of one's own abilities whereas the most changeable aspect, especially from 7th to 9th grade, was self-efficacy.

The MANOVAs testing the age effect on the three ME showed that the older the students the less difficult they found the maths tasks, the less effort they reported they invested in order to solve them and the more correct they estimated the solution of the problems. These findings were consistent with Hypothesis 1.

Gender Effects. As predicted, there was no significant gender effect on maths performance, although gender did affect the self-concept in mathematics. It was found that boys had significantly more positive academic self-concept about their maths abilities than girls. This finding is consistent with the gender stereotype and it applied to all aspects of the academic self-concept in maths, namely, self-perception, self-esteem, self-efficacy, and others' perception of their ability (see Table 1).

Table 1: Mean ratings (and standard deviations) of the variables of the study as a function of grade and gender.

	7th Grade		9th Grade		11th Grade	
	Girls	**Boys**	**Girls**	**Boys**	**Girls**	**Boys**
Maths performance	15.667	11.750	11.852	12.467	16.629	17.246
	(9.292)	(5.120)	(5.395)	(5.416)	(5.003)	(4.960)
Self-concept						
Self-perception	3.000	3.396	2.632	2.918	2.521	3.080
	(1.481)	(1.061)	(0.911)	(0.977)	(0.882)	(1.053)
Self-esteem	3.556	3.187	2.702	2.951	2.581	3.065
	(1.602)	(0.897)	(0.997)	(1.114)	(0.887)	(1.071)
Self-efficacy	4.200	3.200	2.736	2.995	2.635	3.206
	(0.600)	(0.855)	(0.988)	(1.003)	(0.882)	(1.073)
Others' perception	3.667	2.700	2.541	2.643	2.365	2.838
	(0.945)	(0.894)	(0.909)	(1.084)	(0.985)	(1.071)
Metacognitive experiences						
Difficulty before	2.433	2.564	2.228	2.054	2.015	1.758
	(1.124)	(0.677)	(0.495)	(0.555)	(0.504)	(0.545)
Difficulty after	2.300	2.350	1.978	1.976	1.740	1.601
	(1.054)	(0.588)	(0.353)	(0.426)	(0.384)	(0.413)
Effort before	2.433	2.566	2.328	2.141	2.155	1.794
	(1.124)	(0.701)	(0.517)	(0.565)	(0.545)	(0.561)
Effort after	2.267	2.300	2.103	1.926	1.873	1.683
	(1.002)	(0.641)	(0.373)	(0.416)	(0.385)	(0.440)
Correctness before	2.600	2.712	2.692	3.012	2.953	3.371
	(1.082)	(0.618)	(0.500)	(0.559)	(0.525)	(0.541)
Correctness after	2.433	2.825	2.993	3.230	3.214	3.553
	(1.102)	(0.587)	(0.399)	(0.408)	(0.428)	(0.404)

Furthermore, an interaction of gender with aspect of self-concept was found. Table 1 shows that the two genders differed more in the case of self-perception and less in the case of others' perception of their maths abilities and of self-efficacy.

A significant interaction was also found between age, gender and aspects of self-concept. Seventh grade girls reported more optimistic others' perception of their maths abilities than boys, but from 9th grade on this difference was reversed in favor of boys. In general, as students grow up the difference between the two genders as regards their academic self-concept in maths is becoming larger, in favor of boys.

Of the various ME studied, gender significantly differentiated only the estimate of solution correctness. In both problem-solving phases, boys estimated that they would solve or had solved the maths tasks more correctly than girls did. There was no significant difference in the case of feeling of difficulty or estimate of effort, which means that the two genders do not differ in their perception of the difficulty of the task or the effort needed for solving the problem, but only in their confidence in the solution produced.

In the case of estimate of effort (EOE), a significant interaction was found between age, gender and phase (i.e., before–after problem solving). As students grow older, the EOE needed to solve the mathematical tasks decreased more abruptly in boys than in girls. Furthermore, as girls grew older, they reported more EOE after the solution of the problem in comparison with the EOE before the solution of the problems. The opposite pattern was found in the case of boys. This means that girls tend to overestimate the effort they invest for solving maths problems. Finally, it was found that only in 7th grade did boys estimate that they needed more effort to solve the maths tasks in comparison with girls' respective estimates. This applied to estimates both before and after problem solving. From 9th grade on, boys estimated that they needed less effort than girls.

Relations between Performance, Self-Concept, and Metacognitive Experiences

Age. Having established that age did have an effect on all three dependent variables of the study, we applied a path analysis (Bentler, 1993) in order to test the hypothesis regarding the possible differentiation of the relations between performance, self-concept, and ME along with age. The same pattern of relationships between the variables, based on the literature review, was tested for the different age groups. According to this model, maths performance explained part of the variance of students' evaluations regarding their self (i.e., their self-concept) and task-related ME. Academic self-concept in maths was also assumed to affect ME. Relationships between the various aspects of academic self-concept and between the various ME were also added to the model.

With regard to age, we decided to test one model in the case of 7th graders and one model regarding the 9th and 11th graders. This decision was made because the Scheffe multiple comparisons tests had shown that the significant age differences were systematically found between 7th graders and the other two age groups. Moreover, in the model regarding 7th graders, the variables measuring ME *after* the solution of the problems were dropped due to a large amount of missing data.

The first model tested concerned the data of 7th graders and was found to have an excellent fit. The model's indices were the following: $x^2(14) = 13.164$, $p = 0.513$, *BBNFI* = 0.986, *BBNNFI* = 1.002, *CFI* = 1.000. The fit of the model regarding 9th and 11th graders was: $x^2(30) = 38.826$, $p = 0.129$, *BBNFI* = 0.990, *BBNNFI* = 0.996, *CFI* = 0.998, which is also a very good fit. The two models are presented in Figures 1 and 2 respectively.

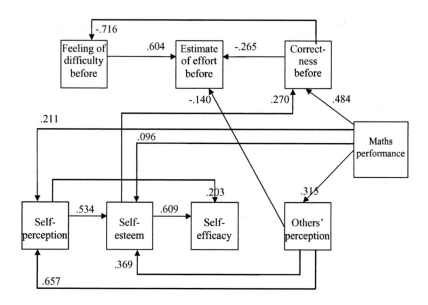

Figure 1: The relations between the variables of the study in grade 7.

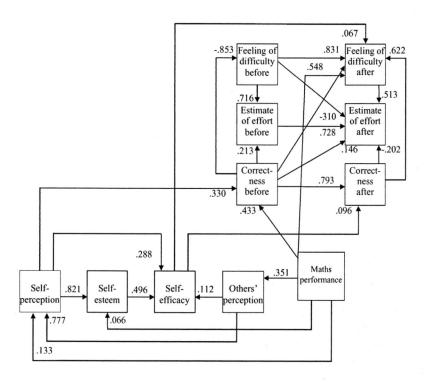

Figure 2: The relations of the variables of the study in grades 9 and 11.

The two models had significant similarities. Maths performance explained directly or indirectly a significant part of the variance of the different aspects of academic self-concept in maths, but mainly of others' perception of students' ability. Performance also explained a significant part of the variance of the estimate of solution correctness (EOC). Academic self-concept in maths, in its turn, affected students' online ME, and particularly EOC. We noticed, however, a number of differences between the two models at the following points. First, 7th grade students' reports of EOC (before actual problem solving) were influenced by their self-esteem, whereas the estimate of effort (EOE) was influenced by others' perception of one's own abilities in maths. In the case of older students, there was only an effect of self-perception on EOC. This implies a change in the pattern of relations between self-concept and ME from 7th to 9th–11th grade: EOC in younger students was not based on their perception of their own ability but on their affective reaction to themselves; in older students EOC was more closely related to self-perception which means a more realistic conception of the situation, that is, of themselves solving mathematics problems. Furthermore, younger students' report of EOE was based on significant others' response to them. This suggests external regulation of effort rather than regulation based on self-perception of their capability to deal with the tasks.

Moreover, in younger students, others' perception of their abilities affected their self-perception and self-esteem, whereas in older students, it affected self-perception and self-efficacy. This again indicates a shift in the way students perceive the response of others towards them. Older students adopt the criteria used by others in order to judge their performance and this influences their self-perception but not their self-esteem that is based mainly on their own perception of themselves.

Gender. With regard to the relations between performance, self-concept and ME, path analysis was applied, firstly, on the data of girls and, secondly, on the data of boys. The path model already identified in the case of age groups was also tested in the case of gender.

The model that best fit the data as regards boys had the following indices: $x^2(32) = 42.556$, $p = 0.100$, $BBNFI = 0.978$, $BBNNFI = 0.990$, $CFI = 0.994$. The fit of the model regarding girls was: $x^2(31) = 30.952$, $p = 0.468$, $BBNFI = 0.986$, $BBNNFI = 1.000$, $CFI = 1.000$, which is an excellent fit. The two models are presented in Figures 3 and 4.

The two models showed that all aspects of girls' academic self-concept in mathematics were influenced by others' perception of their own abilities whereas in the case of boys only self-perception was influenced. This means that girls relied heavily on others' perception of themselves in order to judge their abilities, self-esteem, and self-efficacy in mathematics. Boys relied more on their own self-perception and indirectly on other's perception of them.

Furthermore, girls' reports regarding their self and their ME were affected more by their respective performance as compared to boys. Girls' estimate of solution correctness (which reflects their confidence in themselves as maths problem solvers) was also related to their performance in both phases of problem solving

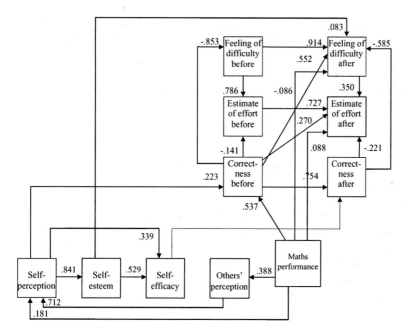

Figure 3: The relations of the variables of the study in boys.

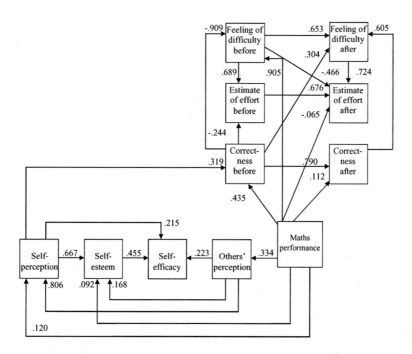

Figure 4: The relations of the variables of the study in girls.

whereas in boys performance was mainly related to EOC in the phase before the solution. Finally, it was shown that, in boys, academic self-concept in maths was related more to their ME than in girls.

The above findings suggest that gender, although it did not differentiate performance, did affect self-concept and ME.

General Discussion

This chapter focused on the effects of age and individual difference factors on the relationships between self-concept, metacognitive experiences (ME), and performance. The guiding assumption was that when the student is solving a problem (maths problems in our study) there is an intrinsic context that accompanies the processing of the task. This is the context of subjective experience or ME, which changes with growing age and varies in the two genders.

Our data showed that age was related to changes in the estimate of solution correctness (EOC) and the estimate of effort expenditure (EOE). The change was not only in the magnitude of the judgment but also in the source of the judgment. In grade seven, EOC was based on students' self-esteem whereas in grades nine and eleven on self-perception of ability. The estimate of effort in younger students was directly related to others' perception of themselves; in older students EOE was directly related to EOC and indirectly to self-perception through its effect on EOC.

Gender also affected students' intrinsic context and particularly EOC and EOE. In general, girls' ME were more closely related to actual performance than boys'. Furthermore, as girls grow up they report less EOC and more effort expenditure than boys. Also girls' maths self-concept continues to be influenced by others' perception of themselves whereas in boys this effect is absent. This implies that girls' ME are formed in the light of significant others' response toward them and their performance whereas boys' ME are formed by their self-perception and self-esteem. The question is if these age and gender effects are related to learning context or other developmental factors and if they have implications on students' motivation.

Age and gender presumably contribute to the formation of the self-concept and ME in different ways. Age is associated with increases in capability (see Demetriou *et al.*, 1991) and students' knowledge base or expertise and, therefore, with changes in the fluency with which students deal with specific problems; this fluency results in better performance outcome. Increased capability and better performance entails changes in the students' ME regarding the task at hand and also in the perception of their competence in the respective domain of knowledge, that is, in their domain-specific self-concept (Efklides, 2001; Efklides & Tsiora, 2000).

Our data confirmed that with increasing age, performance on basic mathematics notions in general became better, feeling of difficulty (FOD) and estimate of effort (EOE) expenditure decreased, and estimate of solution correctness (EOC) increased. These findings denote that subjective evaluations reflect performance changes. Yet, performance change does not fully explain how ME change along with age. Our data showed that performance directly affected EOC but not the feeling of difficulty and estimate of effort. Moreover, the change of EOC was also mediated by self-concept changes. This implies that there were other effects on ME besides developmental ones.

Age is also related to changes in the school, time, and social context. In our study, school context did not differ in students of grade seven and nine (that is, it was junior high-school). It differed in the case of grade eleven (senior high-school). However, participants' self-concept and ME did not differ in the students of 9th and 11th grade. Significant differences were found mainly between 7th graders, on the one hand, and 9th and 11th graders, on the other. This suggests that it was not the transition from junior to senior high-school that made a difference, but probably the transition from primary school to junior high, as was the case of the 7th graders. It is also plausible that time context had an effect on ME, because the concepts we included in the maths tasks are being taught only in grade seven and eight and not later on. Students of grade seven were at an early stage of learning the concepts whereas older students had already mastered them. Our study, however, was cross-sectional and we cannot make any inferences about time context effects. For such a hypothesis longitudinal data should be available. Therefore, what seems a more plausible explanation of our findings is the change of knowledge base or developmental effects on performance along with social (or classroom) effects on self-concept.

The social context effects, although speculative, because we did not include such measures in our study, can be inferred from the effect of performance on self-concept and on EOC. It seems that students learn the criteria of assessment of their performance and use these criteria to judge the correctness of the solution they produced. Also, through school marks, which are related to performance, and social comparison processes, they infer their own level of competence in maths. Indeed, in 7th grade others' perception of their ability was the main source of information for students' self-perception. However, it was self-esteem that also effected students' EOC. This means that 7th graders use partly the criteria of others (who are also the ones that provide the assessment of performance) and partly self-based sources, that is, how well they feel about themselves with respect to mathematics. Their self-perception and self-efficacy in mathematics are not so strong yet as to influence their estimate of solution correctness, as it happens in 9th and 11th grade. How can we explain this change from self-esteem to self-perception effect on EOC?

Young students of junior high-school already have a maths self-concept based on their experiences with mathematics in primary school. This self-concept is gradually being changed during the transition to junior high-school because in junior high-school the criteria used for the assessment of performance change, and therefore students have to revise their personal views regarding their competence in maths or their ranking in their classroom. Thus, early junior high-school students, being in a state of transition (see Ruble's phase model of transition; Ruble, 1994), rely on upward social comparison processes for attaining criteria for their personal assessment of their performance. The same reliance on external feedback explains the finding that students' estimate of effort needed for solving mathematics problems was affected by other's perception of their ability besides the subjective difficulty of the task.

The situation, however, is different for 9th and 11th grade students who are in a different phase of transition and have already formed a more accurate perception of themselves in mathematics. They have a less favorable self-concept than 7th graders, despite better maths performance, which means that they have bridged the discrepancy between the subjective and objective criteria of performance and self-competence evaluation. They achieve it by assimilating the objective or external criteria of evaluation and by building their own self-perception and self-efficacy beliefs. Therefore they need not rely exclusively on others' feedback in order to judge their capability or to an undifferentiated affect.

It is noteworthy that although others' perception of students' abilities was relatively stable across the three age groups studied, self-efficacy was the most changeable. Self-efficacy is related to the students' confidence in themselves to deal with specific learning situations. Self-efficacy then mediates the expectation of success in specific tasks. Thus, 9th and 11th graders base their estimate of solution correctness on their self-perception and self-efficacy beliefs. Emotional aspects of self-concept, i.e., self-esteem, cease to influence students' estimate of solution correctness or other ME as they grow older. These findings suggest a turn in students' self-regulation process from an externally guided regulation in 7th grade to an internal regulation in 9th–11th grade, according to one's perception of one's self and of the task situation, which becomes more precise as evidenced in the differences in FOD between age groups.

In conclusion, the present study showed that intrinsic context in students of junior high-school and high-school, as exemplified in ME, undergoes changes that are related not only to performance changes but also to changes in self-concept. The changes of self-concept are presumably due to changes in school context (primary vs. junior high-school) and social context of the classroom. This change of intrinsic context has implications for students' motivation and self-regulation. Self-regulation is moving from being based mainly on external sources of feedback to internal ones, and specifically, to self-perception and self-efficacy beliefs in specific learning situations.

Gender. Gender does not seem to directly influence performance as age did, because there were no gender differences in basic mathematics concepts at least in early high-school years. On the contrary, there were differences in maths self-concept. Therefore, the source of gender effects should be sought in the social and sociocultural context. It seems that social stereotyping influences girls' self-concept and expectations of success in the maths, and these, in their turn, influence girls' ME, and particularly EOC. These findings are in agreement with Hypothesis 2 and previous studies showing girls to be less confident in maths than boys. How can these findings be explained?

Girls more than boys seem to base their estimates of ME on performance criteria and on self-perception of their capability (which is highly correlated with others' perception of them). Boys, unlike girls, were influenced in their reports of feeling of difficulty and estimate of solution correctness (after problem solving) by their self-esteem and self-efficacy beliefs. Although the effects of self-esteem were small they are worth noting because boys' self-esteem and self-efficacy reports were not influenced by others' perception of their capability as it happened with girls. This means that boys, having adopted the stereotype of male superiority in maths, have higher self-esteem and sense of self-efficacy than girls and interpret their experiences in the light of this optimistic perspective. This self-reliance limits the role of the external feedback provided by significant others, such as teachers, or by social comparison processes. Thus, based on higher self-esteem and self-efficacy boys relatively to girls "underestimate" the effort they invest and "overestimate" the correctness of the solution they produce in tasks of similar subjective difficulty, and this provides the subjective feedback and motivation for continuing to get involved in maths. Therefore, ME, by being influenced by students' existing self-concept, provide the subjective feedback that maintains the stereotypic views already incorporated into their self-concept. This helps boys get all the more engaged in maths and girls to get disengaged because maths for them is something requiring effort. Having in mind that effort in relatively easy tasks (as shown by their mean estimate of effort reports) denotes lack of ability (Nicholls, 1989), girls by overestimating effort reinforce the stereotype of lack of ability in maths in females.

In conclusion, the findings of this study along with those of Efklides and Tsiora (2000), which show the effect of self-concept on ME and vice versa, and Metallidou and Efklides (2001), which show the effect of ME on causal attributions, provide a good account of the mechanism that underlies the progressively growing dissociation of girls from mathematics in high-school. The extent to which external feedback, that is, teachers' behavior, adds to the strengthening of the male maths superiority stereotype is an issue to be investigated in the future.

However, it is not only teachers' behavior or social comparison processes that are responsible for female students' growing disinterest in maths. There is developmental evidence that girls are less efficient than boys when it comes to ratio concepts (Demetriou *et al.*, 1991). Since girls are more sensitive than boys to performance factors, it seems that girls are highly aware of even small variations in their performance and this affects their self-concept and ME. Therefore, even if teachers' behavior changed as to eliminate possible stereotypic effects on it, it is not certain that female students' lack of self-confidence in maths will be totally eliminated.

It is important to know the cognitive as well as the affective and sociocultural factors that determine female students' response to maths. It may be the case that girls use insufficient cognitive strategies for processing maths and this causes mental load that leads to heightened awareness of the exerted effort in relation to a specific performance outcome in maths. This leads to attributions of lower ability. Therefore, future research should look at the learning context in a more holistic way that should include intrinsic context besides the other kinds of context already identified. This will show how students' feelings, self-evaluations, and self-related ideas interact with the task and learning context to determine their motivation and self-regulation.

References

Bentler, P. M. (1993), *EQS: Structural Equations Program Manual* (2nd ed.). Los Angeles, CA: BMDP Statistical Software.

Bower, G. H. (1981), "Mood and memory." *American Psychologist 36*, 129–148.

Byrne, B. M. (1996), *Measuring Self-Concept Across the Life Span: Issues and Instrumentation*. Washington, DC: The American Psychological Association.

Clore, G. L., & Parrott, W. G. (1994), "Cognitive feelings and metacognitive judgements." *European Journal of Social Psychology 24*, 101–115.

Damon, W., & Hart, D. (1982), "The development of self-understanding from infancy through adolescence." *Child Development 53*, 841–864.

Demetriou, A., Platsidou, M., Efklides A., Metallidou, Y., & Shayer, M. (1991), "Structure and sequence of the quantitative–relational abilities and processing potential from childhood to adolescence." *Learning and Instruction 1*, 19–44.

Dermitzaki, I. (1997), *The Relations of the Dimensions of Self-Concept and Level of Cognitive Development with School Performance* (in Greek). Unpublished doctoral dissertation, Department of Psychology, School of Philosophy, Aristotle University of Thessaloniki, Thessaloniki, Greece.

Dermitzaki, I., & Efklides, A. (2000), "Aspects of self-concept and their relationship to language performance and verbal reasoning ability." *The American Journal of Psychology 113* (4), 643–659.

Dweck, C. S. (1999), *Self-Theories: Their Role in Motivation, Personality, and Development*. Ann Arbor, MI: Psychology Press.

Eccles, J., Wigfield, A., Harold, R. D., & Blumenfeld, P. (1993), "Age and gender differences in children's self- and task perceptions during elementary school." *Child Development 64*, 830–847.

Efklides, A. (1997), "Brain and mind: The case of subjective experience." *Psychology: The Journal of the Hellenic Psychological Society 4*, 106–117.

Efklides, A. (1999, August), *Feelings as Subjective Evaluations of Cognitive Processing: How Reliable are They?* Keynote address at the 5th European Conference on Psychological Assessment, Patras, Greece.

Efklides, A. (2001), "Metacognitive experiences in problem solving: Metacognition, motivation, and self-regulation." In A. Efklides, J. Kuhl & R. Sorrentino (eds) *Trends and Prospects in Motivation Research* (pp. 297–323). Dordrecht, The Netherlands: Kluwer.

Efklides, A., Papadaki, M., Papantoniou, G., & Kiosseoglou, G. (1997), "The effects of cognitive ability and affect on school mathematics performance and feelings of difficulty." *The American Journal of Psychology 110*, 225–258.

Efklides, A., Papadaki, M., Papantoniou, G., & Kiosseoglou, G. (1998), "Individual differences in feelings of difficulty: The case of school mathematics." *European Journal of Psychology of Education XIII*, 207–226.

Efklides, A., Petropoulou, M., & Samara, A. (1999, September), *The Systemic Nature of Metacognitive Experiences: How are Feelings of Familiarity, Difficulty, Confidence, and*

Satisfaction Interrelated in Problem Solving? Paper presented at the Scientific Meeting: Metacognition. Process, Function, and Use, Clermont-Ferrand, France.

Efklides, A., Samara, A., & Petropoulou, M. (1996), "The micro- and macro-development of metacognitive experiences: The effect of problem-solving phases and individual factors" (in Greek). *Psychology: The Journal of the Hellenic Psychological Society 3* (2), 1–20.

Efklides, A., Samara, A., & Petropoulou, M. (1999), "Feeling of difficulty: An aspect of monitoring that influences control." *European Journal of Psychology of Education XIV*, 461–476.

Efklides, A., & Tsiora, A. (2000, May), *Effects of Metacognitive Experiences on Self-Concept.* Paper presented at the International Conference on Motivation: 7th Workshop on Achievement and Task Motivation (7th WATM), Leuven, Belgium.

Efklides, A., & Vauras, M. (Guest eds). (1999), "Metacognitive experiences and their role in cognition" (Special issue). *European Journal of Psychology of Education XIV* (4).

Evans, R. H., Baumert, J., & Geiser, H. (1995), *Gender and Nature of Out-of-School Experiences, Motivation and Science Learning in School.* Paper presented at the 6th EARLI Conference, Nijmegen, The Netherlands.

Fennema, E. (1989), "The study of affect and mathematics: A proposed generic model." In D. B. McLeod & V. M. Adams (eds) *Affect and Mathematical Problem-Solving: A New Perspective* (pp. 205–219). New York: Springer.

Flavell, J. H. (1979), "Metacognition and cognitive monitoring: A new area of cognitive developmental inquiry." *American Psychologist 34*, 906–911.

Fontaine, A. M. (1993), *Motivational Variables and School Achievement: Their Relationships During Adolescence.* Paper presented at the 5th EARLI Conference, Aix en Provence, France.

Geen, R. (1995), *Human Motivation: A Social Psychological Approach.* Pacific Grove, CA: Brooks/Cole.

Johnson, N. E., Saccuzzo, D. P., & Larson, G. E. (1995), "Self-reported effort versus actual performance in information processing paradigms." *The Journal of General Psychology 122*, 195–210.

Harter, S. (1988), "The construction and conservation of the self: James and Cooley revisited." In D. K. Lapsley & F. C. Power (eds) *Self, Ego, and Identity: Integrative Approaches* (pp. 43–70). New York: Springer.

Harter, S. (1990), "Cause, correlates, and the functional role of global self-worth." In R. Sternberg & J. Kolligian, Jr. (eds) *Perceptions of Competence and Incompetence Across the Life-Span* (pp. 67–97). New-Haven, CT: Yale University Press.

Helmke, A. (1989), "Affective student characteristics and cognitive development: Problems, pitfalls, perspectives." *International Journal of Educational Research 13* (8), 915–932.

Hoge, D. R., Smit, E. K., & Hanson, S. L. (1990), "School experiences predicting changes in self-esteem of sixth- and seventh-grade students." *Journal of Educational Psychology 82*, 117–127.

Koriat, A., & Levy-Sadot, R. (1999), "Processes underlying metacognitive judgments. Information-based and experience-based monitoring of one's own knowledge." In S. Chaiken & Y. Trope (eds) *Dual Process Theories in Social Psychology* (pp. 483–502). New York: Guilford.

Lehtinen, E., Vauras, M., Salonen, P., Olkinuora, E., & Kinnunen, R. (1995), "Long-term development of learning activity: Motivational, cognitive and social interaction." *Educational Psychologist 30*, 21–35.

Leondari, A., Syngollitou, E., & Kiosseoglou, G. (1998), "Academic achievement, motivation and future selves." *Educational Studies 24* (2), 153–163.

Lightbody, P., Siann, G., Stocks, R., & Walsh, D. (1996), "Motivation and attribution at secondary school: The role of gender." *Educational Studies 22*, 13–25.

Lories, G., Dardenne, B., & Yzerbyt, V. Y. (1998), "From social cognition to metacognition." In V. Y.Yzerbyt, G. Lories & B. Dardenne (eds) *Metacognition: Cognitive and Social Dimensions* (pp. 1–15). London: Sage.

MacCallum, J. (2001), "Motivational change in transition contexts." In A. Efklides, J. Kuhl & R. M. Sorrentino (eds) *Trends and Prospects in Motivation Research* (pp. 121–143). Dordrecht, The Netherlands: Kluwer.

Markus, H., & Wurf, E. (1987), "The dynamic self-concept: A social–psychological perspective." *Annual Review of Psychology 38*, 299–337.

Marsh, H. W. (1986), "Verbal and math self-concepts: An internal/external frame of reference model." *American Educational Research Journal 23*, 129–149.

Marsh, H. W. (1989), "Age and sex effects in multiple dimensions of self-concept: Preadolescence to early childhood." *Journal of Educational Psychology 81*, 417–430.

Marsh, H. W. (1990), "The structure of academic self-concept: The Marsh/Shavelson model." *Journal of Educational Psychology 82*, 623–636.

Marsh, H. W. (1993), "The multidimensional structure of academic self-concept: Invariance over gender and age." *American Educational Research Journal 30*, 841–860.

Marsh, H. W., Byrne, B. M., & Shavelson, R. J. (1988), "A multifaceted academic self-concept: Its hierarchical structure and its relation to academic achievement." *Journal of Educational Psychology 80*, 366–380.

McLeod, D. B. (1989), "The role of affect in mathematical problem-solving." In D. B. McLeod & V. M. Adams (eds) *Affect and Mathematical Problem-Solving: A New Perspective* (pp. 19–36). New York: Springer.

Meece, J. L., & Courtney, D. P. (1992), "Gender differences in students' perceptions: Consequences for achievement-related choices." In D. H. Schunk & J. L. Meece (eds) *Students' Perceptions in the Classroom* (pp. 209–227). Hillsdale, NJ: Erlbaum.

Metallidou, P., & Efklides, A. (1998), "Affective, cognitive, and metamemory effects on the estimation of the solution correctness and the feeling of satisfaction from it" (in Greek). *Psychology: The Journal of the Hellenic Psychological Society 5*, 53–70.

Metallidou, P., & Efklides, A. (2001), "The effects of general success-related beliefs and specific metacognitive experiences on causal attributions following performance on mathematical tasks. In A. Efklides, J. Kuhl & R. Sorrentino (eds) *Trends and Prospects in Motivation Research* (pp. 325–347). Dordrecht, The Netherlands: Kluwer.

Nelson, T. O. (1996), "Consciousness and metacognition." *American Psychologist 51*, 102–116.

Nelson, T. O., Kruglanski, A. W., & Jost, J. T. (1998), "Knowing thyself and others: Progress in metacognitive social psychology." In V. Y. Yzerbyt, G. Lories & B. Dardenne (eds) *Metacognition: Cognitive and Social Dimensions* (pp. 69–89). London: Sage.

Newman, R. S. (1984), "Children's numerical skill and judgements of confidence in estimation." *Journal of Experimental Child Psychology 37*, 107–123.

Nicholls, J. G. (1989), *The Competitive Ethos and Democratic Education.* Cambridge, MA: Harvard University Press.

Pajares, F., & Miller, D. M. (1994), "The role of self-efficacy and self-concept beliefs in mathematical problem-solving: A path analysis." *Journal of Educational Psychology 86*, 193–203.

Rogoff, B. (1990), *Apprenticeship in Thinking: Cognitive Development in Social Context.* New York: Oxford University Press.

Ruble, D. N. (1994), "A phase model of transitions: Cognitive and motivational consequences." *Advances in Experimental Social Psychology 26*, 163–214.

Skaalvik, E. M., & Rankin, R. (1990), "Math, verbal and general academic self-concept: The Marsh's model and gender differences in self-concept." *Journal of Educational Psychology 82*, 546–554.

Stipek, D., & MacIver, D. (1989), "Developmental change in children's assessment of intellectual competence." *Child Development 60*, 521–538.

von Rhoeneck, Ch., Grob, K., Schnaitmann, G. W., & Voelker, B. (2001), "Learning in basic electricity: How do motivation, cognitive factors, and classroom climate influence achievement in physics." In A. Efklides, J. Kuhl & R. M. Sorrentino (eds) *Trends and Prospects in Motivation Research* (pp. 145–161). Dordrecht, The Netherlands: Kluwer.

Vygotsky, L. S. (1978), *Mind in Society: The Development of Higher Psychological Processes.* Cambridge, MA: Harvard University Press.

Weinert, F. E., & Helmke, A. (1998), "The neglected role of individual differences in theoretical models of cognitive development." *Learning and Instruction 8* (4), 309–323.

Chapter 15

Long-term Development of Motivation and Cognition in Family and School Contexts

Marja Vauras, Pekka Salonen, Erno Lehtinen & Janne Lepola

Introduction

Increasingly, the limitations of pure cognitive, individual and decontextualised approaches to cognition and motivation have been recognised, as witnessed by this whole volume. Individuals learn and develop in a social and cultural context, and it is obvious that they share very fundamental experiences and learning outcomes (e.g., Lave & Wenger, 1991). However, they also have unique roles, perspectives, and interpretations in these situations that cannot be reduced to socially shared cultural experiences. In order to understand the complex development of individuals' cognitive and motivational interpretations and behaviour, a combination of the individual, social situation and educational environment factors must be understood. Our view of cognition and motivation is strongly based on the systemic view of human development. Systemic approaches, e.g., to classroom learning, help us to understand the manifold interactions of the learning environment, the behaviour of significant others (like teachers and peers) in the situation, and a student's cognitive and motivational interpretations. However, even research and discussions from this perspective are often focused mainly on short-term changes in these interactions. Contrary to this, we have emphasised (Lehtinen *et al.*, 1995; Salonen *et al.*, 1998) the interactive, *long-term* development of cognition and motivation in multidirectional social interactions, embedded in complex institutional–cultural contexts.

Our main interest has been in the educational polarisation phenomenon (Berends, 1995) in school, that is, in progressing and retarded learning careers. Vastly diverging developmental trajectories have been recognised not only within tracked (segregated) school environments, but also in mainstream school settings (see e.g., Salonen *et al.*, 1998, for a detailed discussion). Using an industrial allegory, one could say that the "educational factory" produces end products with the utmost variability in quality. From the main production-line emerge not only top-achieving students showing, e.g., well-automated decoding skills and sophisticated learning strategies, but also extremely low-achieving students manifesting severely impaired learning skills. The achievement differences between the extreme groups are even more profound if one considers the dropouts and the output of

Motivation in Learning Contexts: Theoretical Advances and Methodological Implications, pages 295–315.
Copyright © 2001 by Elsevier Science Ltd.
ISBN: 0-08-043990-X

segregated special education production-lines. We have been forced to realise that without a systemic analysis of a combination of individual, social interaction and educational environment factors, it is impossible even to begin to understand, on the one hand, the vast individual differences in learning careers, and, on the other hand, the striking similarities of cognitive and motivational outcomes in different student groups. Since fully-fledged systemic research on the development of cognition and motivation that seriously considers both the role of the individual and the developmental environment is only now slowly emerging, diverging learning careers form a real, still unconquered, challenge for educational psychology.

This chapter will focus on four main issues. The methodologies used in research mirror the underlying conceptual notions of cognition and motivation (c.f. Volet, this volume). Therefore, it is important to make transparent the notions and methodology underlying the research enterprises. For this reason, we first, briefly, discuss different motivational notions of achievement differences and our theoretical model of situational and developmental dynamics of cognitive–motivational interpretations and social interactions on which the actual research methods are based. Second, although our own empirical research has focused on long-term development of cognition and motivation in school, we recognise in our interpretations that the origins of individual cognition and motivation are to be traced back to early social interaction within the home and family context. Therefore, we outline the current research that helps us to understand early family interactions that contribute to later progressing or retarded cognitive and motivational development, before we turn to discussing this development in conventional school contexts in the light of the studies on reading and motivation. In the final section, we contrast and discuss conventional and emerging learning contexts as motivational constraints.

Motivational Notions of Achievement Differences

Goal Orientation Dichotomies

A variety of motivational and socio-emotional orientation or goal dichotomies, such as intrinsically vs. extrinsically oriented, task-involved vs. ego-involved, mastery vs. performance oriented, learning vs. performance oriented, and task- vs. ability-focused, have been used to depict differences between high- and low-achieving children (see, for reviews, Urdan & Maehr, 1995; Switzky, in press). There are two general motivational constructs inherent in these conceptualisations: (1) *personal reasons* why individuals behave in the way they do, that is, their goals, and (2) *belief systems* which influence the degree to which these goals are pursued. Although these dichotomies are not consistently operationalised in the same manner, they seem to accentuate the basic distinction between *task-focused* (or task intrinsic) and *non-task-focused* (or task extrinsic) goal orientation.

Students with a *task-focused* goal orientation are pursuing task–intrinsic goals, such as gaining task-related understanding, insight or skill. Because of their strong belief in personal control (or self-efficacy), these students try hard, persist in the face of difficulty, make more positive self-statements, and express less negative affect (Diener & Dweck, 1978; Elliott & Dweck, 1988). *Problem-focused coping*, aimed at attacking a problem and doing something to alter the conditions causing the difficulty, similarly, implies principally task-oriented goal setting and the belief in task-related personal control or self-efficacy (Endler & Parker, 1990, 846). Task-focused goal orientation and the quality of cognitive performance, as a tendency to use deeper level cognitive and self-regulatory strategies, are strongly interrelated (Graham & Golan 1991; Nolen 1988; Pintrich & DeGroot, 1990; Pintrich *et al.*, 1994).

Performance (or ability) oriented students have been characterised as striving for outcomes derived from social expectations associated with task engagement: they fight to receive positive judgements or to avoid negative judgements of the self. These students have been characterised in at least three different ways. They wish either (1) to gain a favourable judgement of their ability and avoid an unfavourable judgement of ability, (2) to be superior to others or outperform others, or (3) to receive extrinsic rewards, such as good grades (Seifert, 1995). Seifert (1995) states that although each of these definitions may be correlational (i.e., coexisting within an individual), they all treat performance behaviours as defensive mechanisms designed to avoid failure. Studies indicate that performance-oriented students tend to believe that success and failure are not under their personal control, the lack of ability explains failures, and difficult problems suggest failure (Dweck & Leggett, 1988; Urdan & Maehr, 1995). Moreover, these students have been found to show lack of effort and persistence, to express more negative self-statements and affects during the performance, and to withdraw in response to failure (Diener & Dweck, 1978; Seifert, 1995).

Motivational constructs referring to various forms of *non-task-focused goal orientation* (extrinsic, performance- or ability-focused orientation, or helplessness) seem to be more incoherent than constructs of task-focused orientation (see Wolters, Yu & Pintrich, 1996). Non-task-focused goal orientation has been characterised by a variety of partly overlapping, partly incompatible social and emotional behaviours and goal-descriptions. We argue that conceptual and operational vagueness is based on simplified dichotomizations of goal orientations, the undifferentiated inclusion of social and emotional goal components, insufficient analysis of the role of emotional processes in goal setting, insufficient differentiation between efficacy-beliefs within task and social dimensions of personal control, and loose ties to contextual conditions.

First, non-task focused goals have been associated with students' *strivings to alleviate intra-psychic states of emotional distress and restore their emotional well being* (see, e.g., Boekaerts, 1993; Dweck & Leggett, 1988). Particularly, if the learner's belief in personal control is low both in task and social dimensions, his/her goals will be directed rather toward altering his/her self-system than transforming the environment. Instead of task- or socially-directed problem-solving efforts, the learner is likely to alleviate distress through emotion-focused coping strategies, such as self-preoccupation, disengagement, avoidance, and denial (Boekaerts,

1993; Carver *et al.*, 1989). Emotion-focused coping strategies, aimed at reducing or managing the emotional distress, bear a close resemblance to ego-involved, ability-focused, or helplessness-type motivational goal orientations (Endler & Parker, 1990, 846).

Second, non-task-focused goals have been connected with a variety of students' *social efforts*, such as striving for good grades, outperforming others, complying with classroom rules, co-operating with others, and seeking social approval, support and rewards (e.g., Dweck & Leggett, 1988; Wentzel, 1992). Among these social efforts, however, we can find distinguishable subgroups with differing goals and self-efficacy beliefs. Outperforming others or striving for the best grades may indicate one's goal to show relative ability, i.e., to win in competition and enjoy the resulting feelings of pride, which implies a relatively strong sense of task- and social-self-efficacy and high expectations of success. One may also strive for good grades or rewards to avoid the emotional consequences of failure and loss of social esteem, which implies a relatively weak sense of task- and social self-efficacy and low expectations of success. Or, a learner may try to comply rather passively with social rules and demands, which implies a weak sense of task-related and a relatively weak sense of social self-efficacy. Finally, the learner may actively try to manipulate the social environment to accept his social strivings, which implies a weak sense of task-related, but a strong sense of social, self-efficacy.

Although the relationships between cognitive outcomes and non-task-focused goals are not as unequivocal as in the case of task-focused goal orientation, there is still considerable evidence for the association of non-task goal orientation and immature cognitive strategies, such as shallow level processing, lack of self-regulation and insufficient comprehension monitoring (Graham & Golan, 1991; Nolen, 1988; Pintrich *et al.*, 1994). The findings from *process-focused learned helplessness* research are particularly striking and indicate marked differences in the motivational vulnerability vs. resilience of students with mastery and helplessness orientations. Cumulative failures and successive failure feedback induce, in helpless students, not only an increase in negative expectations and ego-related emotional expressions, and self-deprecatory causal attributions during subsequent performances, but also profound deterioration of cognitive strategies. In contrast, mastery-oriented students show greater immunity to the deteriorating effects of cumulative failures. They not only maintain their positive attitudes, expectations and self-encouraging causal attributions, but also keep up or even improve their cognitive strategic level and strategy monitoring during cumulative failure feedback. (Boggiano & Barrett, 1985; Diener & Dweck, 1978.).

Intentionally or unintentionally, these dichotomised conceptualisations are easily interpreted and treated as trait-like entities, and, thus, the contextual factors contributing to the emergence, shaping, and stabilising of these orientations become imprecise or remain merely as vague background variables (see, for a more in-depth discussion, Volet, this volume). The research methodology preferred in goal orientation research, that is, the use of often decontextualised inventories, strongly supports an individualistic, trait-like interpretation of human motivation as well as the notion of stability of motivational coping and orientations.

A Three-part Model of Motivational Orientation and Coping in Learning Contexts

Our analysis of the situational and developmental transactions between a child's adaptive efforts and significant others' guidance, control or reward strategies led us to conceptualise a three-part, integrated model comprising basic motivational orientation dimensions and corresponding sets of coping strategies: (1) Task orientation, (2) Ego-defensive orientation, and (3) Social dependence orientation (Olkinuora & Salonen, 1992; Lehtinen *et al.*, 1995; Salonen *et al.*, 1998; Salonen, 2000). These orientations were derived from three adaptive goal dimensions, which are established during children's learning and social reward or control histories. Each orientation dimension can be characterised by its paramount adaptive focus (task, guiding other, self) and the constellation of self-efficacy beliefs a person assigns either to situational task or social features. The activating or inhibiting motivational valence is associated with a child's self-efficacy beliefs.

Task Orientation. Earlier learning experiences may lead a child to develop a high initial task-related sense of self-efficacy and intrinsic motivation as regards many kinds of new environmental challenges. The challenging elements of a new task thus represent for the child the most substantial positive valence of all the situational elements. The child has usually also developed a strong belief in his self-efficacy within the social dimension (i.e., the belief in getting instrumental help or rewards from others when needed), but, due to his/her strong task-related pursuits, his coping activity will not be focused on the guiding other. Even if the child is confronted with obstacles, a high task-related sense of self-efficacy keeps his coping activity task-focused. Due to strong intrinsic motivation, the student is fully concentrated on the task, ignores incidental stimuli, and thus the integrity of action is maintained. Sustained effort, intense task-related manipulations, as well as cognitive elaboration and self-corrections are characteristic of task-orientation. Any inconsistencies, obstacles, or teacher prompts and criticism are interpreted as challenges to be coped with growing persistence and more sophisticated task-related strategies (Salonen *et al.*, 1998).

Ego-Defensive Orientation. A learning history, with experiences of "doing wrong", deprecatory feedback, and/or strict social constraints (e.g., parental over-control) predominating, may often result in a weak belief in self-efficacy both in task and social dimensions. Instead of assigning a positive valence to new tasks or guiding adults, the child is sensitised to contextual elements suggesting an ego-related threat, such as task difficulty and signs of others' negative responses. Novelties and ambiguities are interpreted as discomforting obstacles that suggest failure or loss of personal control. Since the primary adaptive goal is self-protection or restoration of personal well-being, the child is likely to use emotion-focused coping strategies. These are indicated by various forms of behaviour tending to reduce the tension or threat, such as avoidance, substitute actions, justifying the failure beforehand, or social manipulation and reaction. Ego-defensive coping behaviours are often accompanied by signs of emotional conflict, as well as by expressions of negative emotions and self-deprecatory thoughts (Salonen, 2000). Ego-defensive coping may comprise some "active" scanning of environmental cues, such as seeking familiar (or "safe") perceptual features of the task or social environment, but this usually leads to superficial, fragmented association trials and arbitrary short-cut activities. The extent of the child's sense of self-efficacy in the social dimension determines how *approaching* vs. *inhibited* or *avoiding* his social coping behaviour will be.

Social Dependence Orientation. The child with a social dependence orientation has been over-guided, over-helped and excessively rewarded during his learning history. Consequently, his or her performance may become exclusively directed toward fulfilling the guiding others' momentary wishes, getting social cues, acceptance, and rewards. Since the child shifts the intellectual responsibility and control to a significant other, the objective task requirements do not represent a major positive valence, and the child's sense of self-efficacy in the task dimension is not remarkable. He/she does not experience even successive failures as threatening as he/she has a very strong sense of self-efficacy in the social dimension. The child relies on others' help, and cumulative failure feedback only enhances his/her persistent efforts in the social domain. The guiding adult represents almost an "almighty" positively-charged social agent who continuously asks, helps, prompts, and finally rewards the child's attempts. With regard to task requirements, the child's responses usually remain random and inconsistent. When confronted with a learning task, he/she engages in various forms of social cue-tracking, feedback-hunting, or explicit help-seeking (Salonen, 2000).

Despite our effort to avoid a too simplistic and conceptually unclear notion of motivational orientation, we have, for good reasons, faced criticisms similar to those expressed earlier (p. 288). Therefore, in our recent writings, we have tried to link motivational coping and orientations more carefully to long-term developmental, situational interaction dynamics (i.e., the microgenesis) and contextual and institutional–cultural (macro-level) factors (e.g., Lehtinen *et al.*, 1995; Salonen, 2000; Salonen *et al.*, 1998). Nevertheless, a combination of partly subsequent and partly simultaneous experiences in home and traditional school environments seems to result in a limited set of more or less generalised and stabilised motivational tendencies, which are increasingly manifested in a similar manner in succeeding situations with similar cues (we return to this issue in the final section). This does not mean, however, that motivational orientations are considered as trait-like in nature but as essentially *interactionist constructs*, that is, as a dynamic typology (Harter & Jackson, 1992). As we have also stressed (e.g., Salonen *et al.*, 1998) environmental influence is not unidirectional, but drifts among all participants in the situation.

Origins of Children's Resilience and Vulnerability in Home Context

Most developmental theories presuppose that the growth of the infant's adaptive capacity is based on increasing organisation and differentiation of mental and behavioural structures, progressively leading to growing self-regulation and independence of action from immediate external stimuli. The development of self-regulation is accompanied by a growing sense of self-efficacy and motivation to initiate and maintain task-focused activities related to new environmental challenges. There is, however, evidence of maladaptive developmental transactions. Such developmental cycles increase infants' motivational vulnerability in the sense that they begin to respond to environmental demands with growing externally-imposed regulation, or with emotional–behavioural dysregulation, accompanied by a decreasing sense of self-efficacy and strengthened non-task-focused motivation (Cherkes-Julkowski & Mitlina, 1999; Crittenden & DiLalla, 1988; Jacobsen *et al.*, 1997; Sansbury & Wahler, 1992).

Previous research has identified several maladaptive parenting styles or early interaction patterns that seem to have an influence on the development of children's motivational and emotional vulnerability and later learning and behavioural problems (Crittenden & DiLalla, 1988; Gardner, 1989; Sansbury & Whaler, 1992). These styles can be grouped into two main categories: inconsistent and over-controlling behaviours. *Inconsistent responses* include parental over-compliance (i.e., extreme compliance with the child's momentary demands and refusals), "asynchronous" feedback (i.e., responses lacking reciprocity and co-ordination in relation to the joint task or the infant's activity), randomly given aversive and positive responses (e.g., punishing and rewarding based on parents' current mood), as well as unresponsiveness. Parental inconsistency is likely to bring threatening elements into the socially-mediated construction of the task, to hinder the child from forming contingencies between his behaviour and its consequences, to bias the child's task-directness, and deteriorate his sense of self-efficacy both in social and task dimensions (see, e.g., Cherkes-Julkowski & Mitlina, 1999; Sansbury & Wahler, 1992).

Over-controlling parenting style comprises overprotecting, excessive use of extrinsic incentives, repeated helping and rewarding, frequent "positive" interfering as well as directive behaviours and harsh forms of discipline, often charged with negative affect (Barrett & Boggiano, 1988; Sansbury & Wahler, 1992). Parental over-control, such as superfluous use of rewards, undermines the infant's intrinsic or task-focused orientation in learning situations. The infant's extrinsic goal-orientation or social dependence will be reinforced as his attention becomes biased towards the anticipating of social incentives (Barrett & Boggiano, 1988). Since the responsibility of the activity-control is shifted to the adult delivering rewards, the infant's sense of self-efficacy will not grow in the task dimension. The more the parental over-controlling behaviour takes directive and coercive forms, the more inhibited but also emotion- and conflict-charged compliant behaviour can be expected.

Crittenden and DiLalla (1988) found that abused infants who were exposed to the coercive control and harshness of the mother, responded before one year of age with general *passivity* and from one to two-and-a-half years of age with increasing *compulsive compliance* or "frozen watchfulness" (i.e., waiting warily for demands, responding quickly and compliantly, and then returning to the previous vigilant state). Infants who were merely neglected, encountered maternal unresponsiveness first with passivity and later with increasing anger and resistance. All of these patterns may be seen as adaptive in immediate situational terms (see, Crittenden & DiLalla, 1988). Even though the above patterns temporarily increase the infant's resilience, in the long run they heighten his/her vulnerability through disturbing the spontaneous task-related activities and social mediation processes necessary for the learning of complex skills. Originally, in situ, adaptive strategies may generalise into rigid dispositions that are unresponsive to changes in environmental conditions. For instance, elementary-school-aged abused children have been found to show over-compliance, vigilance and wariness toward all adults they interact with (Martin & Beezley, 1977).

The origins of early motivational and socio-emotional adaptations leading to diverging developmental pathways characterised by increasing vulnerability vs. resilience can be traced to the mutuality and reciprocity of social transactions (Sameroff, 1975). Just as parents and other adults influence the course of socialisation during childhood, an infant participating in the transaction can be viewed as a source of influence over his/her own development. Here too, we see a multidirectional path. Self-reinforcing transactional cycles seem to be essential for the early development of motivational and socio-emotional dispositions. Parents tend to reinforce certain child behaviour dominant at one time and shift their interactional styles according to the type of child behaviour (Marcus, 1975). For example, dependent behaviour in children has been found to elicit greater encouragement of dependence from parents, whereas independent conduct elicits the opposite (Osofsky & O'Connell, 1972; Yarrow *et al.*, 1971).

There are several possible starting points for maladaptive developmental cycles. (1) The child has a congenital characteristic (e.g., inert or irritable temperament) that elicits from adults a uniform response (e.g., directiveness, coerciveness). (2) The parents, for instance because of their educational attitudes or unfavourable life situation (e.g., unemployment, family problems), tend to experience even the infant's normal environment-related activity as disturbing and attempt to inhibit this tendency through over-control. Both of these lead to increasing passivity, withdrawal, compulsive compliance, or defiance. (3) The parents, because of their own personal and social problems, are unresponsive or respond ambiguously or compliantly to the infant's defiant activities, which in turn increases the child's further tendency toward uninhibited behaviour, such as coercion. Favourable cognitive–motivational development presupposes an adequate amount of parental control while "scaffolding" the infants' mastery of tasks. Additionally, parental guidance and feedback should be well-synchronised with the infant's social and task-related efforts (Cherkes-Julkowski & Mitlina, 1999; Harrist & Pettit, 1994). Scaffolding implies the growth of the child's self-regulation through gradual internalisation of socially-supported mediation processes (Rogoff & Gardner, 1984). The parent should adjust the external support according to the child's developing capability to function independently.

Long-Term Development of Cognition and Motivation in Conventional Classroom Contexts

Learning to read and write forms the core learning and achievement context for a school beginner. Several longitudinal studies focusing on early reading skills (e.g., Francis, 1992; Juel, 1988) and more advanced text-processing strategies (e.g., Vauras *et al.*, 1994), yield evidence for strikingly diverging reading trajectories. For example, advantaged beginning readers, due to their previous linguistic experiences, have important prerequisites for reading. They rapidly learn to utilise new reading experiences, to widen their linguistic knowledge base, and to develop the automatics of the decoding development, which increases their sense of competence and motivation to seek exposure to more demanding texts. The opposite is true for disadvantaged beginning readers, and they tend to fall behind in the progress of rapid and accurate decoding processes, which decreases their sense of competence, weakens their motivation to read, and leads to insufficient exposure to more demanding reading materials. (Crijnen *et al.*, 1998.) Studies consistently indicate the existence of "long-term backward" readers who are likely to fall further and further behind their accelerating peers. However, straightforward linear–causal inferences are often unwarranted. Longitudinal studies indicate that certain linguistically advantaged and disadvantaged individuals may show developmental trajectories, which are non-linear or even contrary to predictions, for example, "slow starters" with curvilinear acceleration patterns (see, Cox, 1987; McGee *et al.*, 1988; Francis, 1992), or children with "unforeseeable" developmental courses (see, Salonen *et al.*, 1988). In the following, we present some empirical evidence for both linear and non-linear developmental trajectories in reading and for their inter-relatedness to motivational and socio-emotional co-determinants in conventional school context. So far, little work has been done to understand how motivational orientations develop in conventional classroom contexts. Even more, longitudinal research on the early interplay between motivational orientations and reading skills has been virtually non-existent (c.f. Wigfield, Eccles & Rodriguez, 1998).

Turku Studies on Reading and Motivation as Examples

Over the past years, we have examined the long-term development of children's motivational and reading competencies in pre-school and elementary school contexts. Here, we discuss findings from longitudinal studies focusing on the situational formation of word reading skill as a function of pre-school motivational orientation and reading prerequisites (Salonen *et al.*, 1998), and on the developmental inter-relatedness of motivational patterns and diverging reading careers (Lepola *et al.*, 2000). The follow-up data for these two studies were gathered from kindergarten to the fourth grade in elementary school.

We prefer the multimethod approach to assess children's motivational tendencies (like teacher- and experimenter-reports and on-line coping behaviour). In this

Table 1: Examples of items in the motivational orientation scales.

TASK ORIENTATION item examples
- a child's verbal behaviour indicates task-involvement (e.g., explains what he or she is doing or planning) and willingness to think in a problem-solving situation
- a child displays persistent effort and willingness to complete a task

EGO-DEFENSIVE ORIENTATION item examples
- a child's behaviours in a task are characterised by passivity and inhibition of action such as freezing (e.g., desperate staring while questioning, empty gaze)
- a child expresses anticipation of failure or unwillingness toward a task situation (e.g., expressions from anxiety-related emotions to anger, from threats to irritation-related reactions)

SOCIAL DEPENDENCE ORIENTATION item examples
- a child asks help immediately in a task either by means of verbal help-seeking or by being helpless (e.g., looks inquiringly or helplessly at the teacher, tactical inhibition of activity in order to be assisted)
- a child imitates the peer's or teacher's activity or changes easily (without thinking) his/her own behaviour in order to comply with the other's wishes

---

way, we aim to overcome the limitations related to the use of only self-report measures: lack of developmental and contextual appropriateness, specificity and validity. In our example studies here, children's motivational orientations were annually rated by the teachers and experimenters, with the help of the Motivational Orientation Scale (see Table 1; e.g., Salonen *et al.*, 1998). The more alike the features of the rating contexts, such as allowing self-guided activity, were, the stronger was the relationship, e.g., between teacher and experimenter ratings. In addition, ego-defensiveness was detected most congruently across situations.

Children's on-line *coping behaviour* was observed in pre-school and school in *play-like construction* tasks involving three induced pressure situations, one competition and two obstacle tasks. Task-oriented, ego-defensive, and social dependence type coping strategies were classified from transcribed videotapes according to a pre-described category system (see, Salonen *et al.*, 1998). The duration of different coping behaviour episodes was computed across the whole situation as well as across the pressure episodes.

In the study by Salonen *et al.* (1998) we concentrated on whether learning to read fluently is a direct reflection of linguistic prerequisites such as phonemic awareness and letter knowledge (Adams, 1991; Juel, 1988), or whether the early progress in reading is also influenced by motivational tendencies. Furthermore, the situational dynamics of children's coping efforts were analysed in order to examine how situation-specific motivational vulnerability differences may be related to the formation of diverging reading trajectories. The participants (n = 32) were selected from 151 kindergarten children on the basis of teachers' and experimenters' orientation ratings. They were assigned according to their dominating motivational disposition to one of the four orientation *extreme* groups: (1) Task Orientation (TO), (2) Social Dependence Orientation (SDO), (3) Ego-Defensive Orientation (EDO), and (4) Social Dependence plus Ego Defensive Orientation, i.e., "multiple non-task-orientation" (SEO).

Although children's pre-school phonemic awareness predicted their word reading skill at the end of the first grade, regression analyses showed that task orientation was a significant explanatory factor of first grade reading skill, independent of phonemic awareness. Children rated as task-oriented at pre-school level outperformed both ego-defensive and multiple non-task-oriented children, while the reading skill of ego-defensive children was the poorest of all groups. Task-oriented and ego-defensive children differed already with regard to pre-school phonemic awareness. In addition, on-line analysis of pre-school children's coping behaviour confirmed greater motivational–emotional vulnerability in children rated high in ego-defensiveness. Situational ego-defensive coping increased and task-oriented coping decreased significantly under a pressure situation in children rated high in ego-defensiveness, but not in children rated low in ego-defensiveness. This study underscored the individual and transactional influences on diverging reading trajectories. Furthermore, the above results, as well as our more recent analyses (Lepola *et al.*, 2000), suggest that differing *reading trajectories* have their origins in both cognitive–linguistic and motivational factors that are formed interactively before the formal reading instruction, already in day-care and familial practices.

In the second study by Lepola *et al.* (2000), we examined the parallel developmental patterns of motivational orientations, coping behaviour and reading skills among non-readers (n = 48) from pre-school to the end of the 2nd grade. We focused on the long-term development of children's motivation as a function of progressive and regressive (relative to others) reading trajectories. Four groups with distinctive reading trajectories were formed: (1) low phonemic awareness — regressive word reading achievement (n = 14), (2) low phonemic awareness — progressive word reading achievement (n = 9), (3) high phonemic awareness — regressive word reading achievement (n = 12), and (4) high phonemic awareness — progressive reading achievement (n = 13). In order to control for confounding effects of verbal ability and reading, only children who could be matched pair-wise in terms of pre-school phonemic awareness and verbal ability (WISC-R) were included.

Although we did not find any clear differences in motivational orientation at pre-school level between the progressive and regressive readers with matching cognitive starting-points, progressive readers seemed to display more favourable motivational orientation patterns (i.e., stronger dominance of task orientation) than regressive readers. In addition, children with low phonemic awareness showed less task-oriented and more ego-defensive coping behaviour under pressure settings than children with high phonemic awareness. In terms of the coping development, we found that an increase in task-oriented and a decrease in social dependence behaviour were related to reading progress. This finding supported our assumption of the situation-based formation of diverging reading trajectories.

Further analyses revealed significant motivational–developmental differences in the 1st and 2nd grades as a function of reading trajectories. Progression in reading was related to increased task orientation and decreased non-task orientation, whereas regression was associated with decreased task and increased non-task orientation, especially growing social dependence. At the end of the 2nd grade, these motivational–developmental patterns distinguished most clearly the regressive and progressive readers with low pre-school phonemic awareness, although similar trends existed in the reading career groups with high phonemic awareness (see Figure 1). Finally, our results showed that the progressive word reading groups outperformed the regressive groups also in the development of *reading comprehension*. In particular, the low-progressive readers scored higher than the high regressive and the low-regressive readers, suggesting a more generalised progress in learning.

Our studies give evidence for both linear and non-linear learning trajectories, which cannot be predicted in a straightforward manner from cognitive–linguistic prerequisites. The predictions seem to become more accurate, if not precise, when

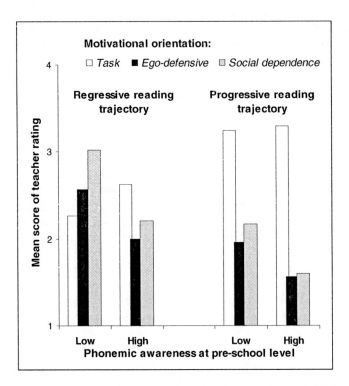

Figure 1: The second grade teachers' motivational ratings of children with progressive and regressive reading trajectories.

motivational factors are also taken into account. Our several case analyses have further depicted the interaction and developmental dynamics of motivation and cognition in the classroom context (see e.g., Lepola, 2000, Lepola *et al.* 2000, Salonen *et al.* 1998). These results indicate that increasing motivational vulnerability tends to be mutually reinforced in teacher–student interaction (c.f. also, Poskiparta *et al.*, 2000). Our most recent analyses (Lepola *et al.*, 2000) indicate, especially, that extreme learning trajectories and motivational orientations rapidly stabilise after the school start, and can be traced even to the end of the 8th grade. In sum, our studies indicate that in a conventional school context, cumulative retarding learning experiences and transactions lead very rapidly to a certain level of achievement and relatively stable student motivational dispositions. Thus, this underscores the critical role of teaching–learning-transactions and contextual factors in this development (c.f. also Lehtinen *et al.*, 1995; Salonen *et al.*, 1998).

Long-term Cyclical Developmental Processes in Classroom Interaction

Recent research and theoretical reflections on beginning reading have clearly shown that the developmental interactions of pre-reading linguistic competencies and early reading experiences contribute to the formation of learning careers in general. When compared to disadvantaged children, linguistically advantaged children can be said to profit more from early "reading to learn" activities (McGill-Franzen & Allington, 1991). Adequate development of reading skills in the early grades is crucial for later school success in all academic areas since these skills have generalised effects on a broad range of other learning skills (Baker *et al.*, 1994; Juel, 1988). Thus, it can be argued that the diverging developmental patterns of early reading skills essentially contribute to the widening gap between high- and low-performing students' general learning skills and attitudes.

Although early linguistic skills and pre-reading competencies are important determinants of later academic achievement, cyclical developmental processes comprise essential motivational, socio-emotional, and institutional–contextual co-determinants (Deci & Ryan, 1996; Howard-Rose & Rose, 1994; Kaplan *et al.*, 1994; Lehtinen *et al.*, 1995; Schultz & Switzky, 1990; Young, 1997; Yair, 2000). High-achieving children, because of their more self-regulated and less disruptive behaviour, meet better the autonomy expectancies of the teachers, and are thus likely to receive more autonomy-inducing or informational feedback (Deci & Ryan, 1996). They tend to become increasingly sensitised to task-intrinsic incentives, experience growing personal control, enjoy the feelings of mastery, and seek new self-imposed challenges (Boggiano & Katz, 1991; Switzky, in press).

Instruction in inclusive settings is rarely sufficiently accommodated to the special needs of low-achieving students. As these children confront the rapid introduction of new skills, they begin to fall increasingly behind their normally-achieving classmates (Crijnen *et al.*, 1998). They feel they are being compared to their accelerating peers, regularly experience loss of personal control, feelings of inferiority and, consequently, fall into maladaptive motivational and socio-emotional behaviours, such as passivity, task-avoidance, acting-out, or dependency (see Boggiano *et al.*, 1987; Boggiano & Katz, 1991; Schultz & Switzky, 1990). When compared to "normal" children, children at risk are given more help and incentives, but also more direction, criticism, reprimands, and rejection (Barker & Graham, 1987; Boggiano & Katz, 1991; Bryan, 1979; Jordan *et al.*, 1997; McNaughton, 1981). Teachers seemingly try to normalise the "deviant" behaviours of low-achieving children, particularly through increasing the amount of social incentives and control (see Olkinuora & Salonen, 1993; Salonen *et al.*, 1998). Although children at risk receive more attention and feedback than their "normal" counterparts, the controlling nature of the feedback may make them more sensitised to task-extrinsic incentives, external control and social threats (see Boggiano & Katz, 1991; Deci & Ryan, 1996).

Stabilising maladaptive student dispositions is likely to contribute to children's profound resistance to teaching and treatment. This holds not only for conventional, inclusive classrooms, but even for sophisticated small-group remedial instruction settings, in which instruction is much more accommodating and optimised to the special needs of the children at risk (e.g., Vauras *et al.*, 1999). This may result from new, still largely unanalysed, motivational constraints in new learning environments, or from an unfavourable mixture of various motivational constraints, when a child, simultaneously, has to adapt to both conventional (classroom) and new (remedial instruction) learning contexts. We now conclude our chapter by discussing motivational constraints of conventional and emerging learning contexts at a more general level, anticipating, we hope, the necessary future developments in motivation research.

Conventional and Emerging Learning Environments as Motivational Constraints

Many of the theories of motivation aim at describing it as a distinct factor, which can be applied to explain an individual's readiness to act or learn. In these theories, motivational concepts can refer to individual traits, rewarding features in the environment, social comparison, or qualities of the tasks. Motivation as a distinct factor suits conventional traditional models of teaching–learning situations very well. Particularly, didactical models originating from the behaviourist tradition conceptualise teaching and learning as a sequence of distinct acts carried out by the teacher and the learner. In its simplest form, this model includes (1) a task given by the teacher, the student's interpretation of the task as a stimulus (including the evaluation of the pleasantness of the task, and the estimation of the task difficulty in relation to the student's own ability), (2) the student's performance as a direct response to the task, feedback given by the teacher (including possible reward, punishment, or social comparison), and (3) the student's interpretation of the feedback (including causal attributions of success or failure).

From a motivational point of view, this way of organising and conceptualising teaching–learning processes is very clear. There are certain episodes deliberately intended for motivational interpretations. The type of evaluation involved in this model also influences motivational experiences. In the conventional didactical model, achievement is assessed on the basis of fixed criteria, and the unit of evaluation is an individual student's performance on externally defined test tasks. When social group is considered, it is mainly used as a comparison standard for the performance of an individual. Different motivation theories focus on the different phases of the activity sequence. For example, interest and goal orientation theories, as well as self-efficacy and expectancy value theories describe students' interpretation of the tasks. Correspondingly, attribution theory and self-worth theories focus on the interpretation of the feedback (Ford, 1992). The conventional didactical model makes success and failure obvious, and highlights achievement differences among students. It also maintains a culture of competition in the classroom. As discussed above, empirical studies show that traditional teacher-centered classrooms tend to increase motivational and cognitive differences among students. Some students benefit motivationally from the features of conventional teaching, whereas in others it leads to a regressive motivational circle (Covington, 1998; Lehtinen *et al.*, 1995; Salonen *et al.*, 1998).

During the last two decades learning scientists have proposed several innovative learning environment designs. These models are consequences of the deep changes in the epistemological and theoretical foundations of learning (Brown & Campione, 1996). The changes in theories of learning can be characterised by two major paradigm shifts. First, empirical epistemology and the notions of various direct forms of constructivism have replaced knowledge transmission. Second, the "learning as knowledge acquisition" metaphor has been supplemented by the "learning as participation" metaphor (Sfard, 1998).

At the end of the 1980s, Alan Collins and his collaborators proposed a learning environment design they called cognitive apprenticeship, in which they applied several principles developed in various innovative educational experiments (Collins *et al.*, 1989). This model emphasises learners' active problem solving and collaboration, as well as apprenticeship-like and reciprocal interaction between students and teachers. Two new terms, *scaffolding* and *fading*, were used to describe the teacher's role in the teaching–learning process. From the point of view of motivational analyses, this means that the teacher's role as the task giver and the evaluator of students' competence is no longer so clear. In the conventional didactic model, the termination of a teaching–learning episode was the teacher's evaluative feedback, in which he/she told the student whether the performance was a success or a failure. In the apprenticeship type of learning environment, it is no longer possible to find any clear end-points of didactical events. In the ideal case, there is only a gradual fading of teachers' guidance and an increase of students' self-regulated activity. There is much less explicit information to make causal attributions than in a conventional educational setting.

Since then, more advanced models have been developed in which these ideas have been elaborated further. Distinct from conventional schooling, these learning environments are aimed at supporting students in coping with open, complex, ill-defined, and consequential tasks (Brown & Campione, 1996; Bransford *et al.*,

1999). This may have important motivational effects as well. Open and complex tasks, typical of innovative learning environments, are not strictly defined and presented to the students beforehand, instead the problems are clarified and redefined several times during the teaching–learning process. It is very difficult to anticipate the difficulty of the task and to estimate the success probability from the student's point of view. It seems obvious that it is exactly this uncertainty of complex and ill-defined tasks that is interpreted as threatening by many students. When open-ended tasks are redefined during the teaching–learning process, and when very many different solutions are seemingly possible, it is difficult for the student to know what the teacher's expectations are and how to fulfil them.

New forms of collaboration are introduced in many of the innovative models. The notion of distributed expertise is important in modern working life. Many learning environment developers have tried to apply it in classrooms. In the ideal case, this means that the diverse strengths of different students are valued and cultivated. Many learning environment designs also emphasise the value of joint products created by a group of students instead of an individual student's separate contribution. It is not clear whether these learning environments would avoid inter-individual competition and ability comparison. However, the explicit information about the ability and achievement levels of the individual students is far less coherent than it is in a conventional educational situation.

The use of a variety of tools and information resources like computers and networks has an important role in these models. The new learning environments also try to expand learning out of the traditional circles of the school by making use of more authentic learning tasks and students' participation in various cultures of expertise. All this somehow breaks the conventional forms of classroom life and may have deep systemic effects on the activity as a whole and the interaction structures of the classroom (Salomon, 1996). This is a challenge for motivation research; there are still few models describing these changes in motivational terms.

Generally speaking, many new models have proved to be very successful. They have resulted in more adequate ways to organise teacher–student and student–student interaction, new ways to connect school learning with the activities of the external world, and to develop social co-operation in a more meaningful way. Moreover, progress in students' academic knowledge, learning skills and motivation has been reported (Bruer, 1993; Lamon et al., 1996; McGilly, 1994). Despite the generally positive results of these learning environments, there are reasons to doubt that individual differences are not adequately considered in these models. In our opinion, the instructional designers have applied the learning theory-based principles, believing in their possibilities to create an optimal learning environment for all students (Järvelä et al., 2000). There are valid reasons to suppose that the new learning environment will solve some of the motivational problems caused by the conventional classroom teaching conventions but, at the same time, they may lead to new undesirable, motivational, consequences. Some features of the innovative learning environments would increase inter-individual motivational and cognitive differences. For example, more challenging and authentic tasks, a shift from direct teaching towards coaching and scaffolding, and an increasing emphasis on autonomous learning, may result in more adequate motivation and higher order cognitive processes in some students, whereas these learning environment features may be counterproductive in others.

The shift from traditional to emerging learning environments has also demonstrated the limitations of current theoretical models of motivation. There is a need to move towards more integrated theoretical models, in which motivation is no longer dealt with as separate variable but as an inherent part of a socially and culturally embedded activity system.

References

Adams, M. J. (1991), *Beginning to Read. Thinking and Learning about Print*. Cambridge, MA: The MIT Press.

Baker, S. K., Kameenui, E. J., Simmons, D., & Stahl, S. (1994), "Beginning reading: Educational tools for diverse learners." *School Psychology Review 23*, 372–391.

Barker, G. P., & S. Graham. (1987), "A developmental study of praise and blame as attributional cues." *Journal of Educational Psychology 79*, 62–66.

Barrett, M., & Boggiano, A. K. (1988), "Fostering extrinsic orientations: Use of reward strategies to motivate children." *Journal of Social and Clinical Psychology 6*, 293–309.

Berends, M. (1995), "Educational stratification and students' social bonding to school." *British Journal of Sociology of Education 16*, 327–351.

Boekaerts, M. (1993), "Being concerned with well-being and with learning." *Educational Psychologist 28*, 149–167.

Boggiano, A. K., & Barrett, M. (1985), "Performance and motivational deficits of helplessness: The role of motivational orientations." *Journal of Personality and Social Psychology 49*, 1753–1761.

Boggiano, A. K., Barrett, M., Weiher, A. W., McClelland, G. H., & Lusk, C. M. (1987), "Use of the maximal-operant principle to motivate children's intrinsic interest." *Journal of Personality and Social Psychology 53*, 866–879.

Boggiano, A. K., & Katz, P. (1991), "Maladaptive achievement patterns in students: The role of teachers' controlling strategies." *Journal of Social Issues 47*, 35–51.

Bransford, J. D., Brown, A. L., & Cocking, R. R. (1999), *How people learn. Brain, Mind, Experience, and School*. Washington: National Academy Press.

Brown, A. L., & Campione, J. C. (1996), "Psychological theory and the design of innovative learning environments: On procedures, principles and systems." In L. Shauble & R. Glaser (eds) *Innovations in Learning: New Environments for Education* (pp. 289–325). Mahwah, NJ: Erlbaum.

Bruer, J. T. (1993), *Schools for Thought. A Science of Learning in the Classroom*. Cambridge, MA: MIT Press.

Bryan, T. S. (1979), "Learning disabled children's classroom behaviors and teacher–child interactions." *Journal of Pediatric Psychology 4*, 233–246.

Carver, C. S., Scheier, M. F., & Weintraub, J. K. (1989), "Assessing coping strategies: A theoretically based approach." *Journal of Personality and Social Psychology 56*, 267–283.

Cherkes-Julkowski, M., & Mitlina, N. (1999), "Self-organization of mother–child instructional dyads and later attention disorder." *Journal of Learning Disabilities 32*, 6–21.

Collins, A., Brown, J. S., & Newman, S. E. (1989), "Cognitive Apprenticeship: Teaching the

Craft of Reading, Writing, and Mathematics." In L. B. Resnick (ed.) *Knowing, Learning and Instruction: Essays in Honor of Robert Glaser* (pp. 453–494). Hillsdale, NJ: Erlbaum.

Covington, M. V. (1998), The will to learn: A guide for motivating young people. Cambridge: Cambridge University Press.

Cox, T. (1987), "Slow starters versus long term backward readers." *British Journal of Educational Psychology 57*, 73–86.

Crijnen, A. M., Feehan, M., & Kellam, S. G. (1998), "The course and malleability of reading achievement in elementary school: The application of growth curve modeling in the evaluation of a mastery learning intervention." *Learning & Individual Differences 10*, 137–157.

Crittenden, P. M., & Di Lalla, D. L. (1988), "Compulsive compliance: The development of an inhibitory coping strategy in infancy." *Journal of Abnormal Child Psychology 16*, 585–599.

Deci, E. L., & Ryan, R. M. (1996), "Need satisfaction and the self-regulation of learning." *Learning & Individual Differences 8*, 165–183.

Diener, C., & Dweck, C. (1978), "An analysis of learned helplessness: Continuous changes in performance, strategy, and achievement cognitions following failure." *Journal of Personality and Social Psychology 36*, 451–462.

Dweck, C., & Leggett, E. (1988), "A social–cognitive approach to motivation and personality." *Psychological Review 95*, 256–273.

Elliott, E. S., & Dweck, C. S. (1988), "Goals: An approach to motivation and achievement." *Journal of Personality and Social Psychology 54*, 5–12.

Endler, N. S., & Parker, J. D. (1990), "Multidimensional assessment of coping: A critical evaluation." *Journal of Personality and Social Psychology 58*, 844–854.

Ford, M. E. (1992), *Motivating Humans.* Newbury Park, CA: Sage.

Francis, H. (1992), "Patterns of reading development in the first school." *British Journal of Educational Psychology 62*, 225–232.

Gardner, F. E. (1989), "Inconsistent parenting: Is there evidence for a link with children's conduct problems?" *Journal of Abnormal Psychology 17*, 223–233.

Graham, S., & Golan, S. (1991), "Motivational influences on cognition: Task involvement, ego involvement, and depth of information processing." *Journal of Educational Psychology 83*, 187–194.

Harrist, A. W., & Pettit, G. S. (1994), "Dyadic synchrony in mother–child interaction." *Family Relations 43*, 417–424.

Harter, S., & Jackson, B. K. (1992), "Trait vs. nontrait conceptualizations of intrinsic/extrinsic motivational orientation." *Motivation and Emotion 16*, 209–229.

Howard-Rose, D., & Rose, C. (1994), "Students' adaptation to task environments in resource room and regular class settings." *Journal of Special Education 28*, 3–26.

Jacobsen, T., Huss, M., Fendrich, M., Kruesi, M., & Ziegenhain, U. (1997), "Children's ability to delay gratification: Longitudinal relations to mother–child attachment." *Journal of Genetic Psychology 158*, 411–426.

Järvela, S., Lehtinen, E., & Salonen, P. (2000), "Socio-emotional orientation as a mediating variable in teaching learning interaction: implications for instructional design." *Scandinavian Journal of Educational Research 44*, 293–307.

Jordan, A., Lindsay, L., & Stanovich, P. (1997), "Classroom teachers' instructional interactions with students who are exceptional, at risk, and typically achieving." *Remedial & Special Education 18*, 82–93.

Juel, C. (1988), "Learning to read and write: A longitudinal study of 54 children from first through fourth grades." *Journal of Educational Psychology 80*, 437–447.

Kaplan, D. S., Peck, B. M., & Kaplan, H. B. (1994), "Structural relations model of self-rejection, disposition to deviance, and academic failure." *The Journal of Educational Research 87*, 166–173.

Lamon, M., Secules, T., Petrosino, A., Hackett, R., Bransford, J. *et al.* (1996), "Schools for thought: Overview of the international project and lessons learned from one of the sites." In L. Schauble & R. Glases (eds) *Innovations in Learning. New Environments for Education.* Mahwah, NJ: Erlbaum.

Lave, J., & Wenger, E. (1991), *Situated Learning: Legitimate Peripheral Participation.* Cambridge: Cambridge University Press.

Lehtinen, E., Vauras, M., Salonen, P., Olkinuora, E., & Kinnunen, R. (1995), "Long-term development of learning activity: motivational, cognitive, and social interaction." *Educational Psychologist 30*, 21–35.

Lepola, J. (2000), *Motivation in Early School years: Developmental Patterns and Cognitive Consequences.* Annales Universitatis Turkuensis B, 236. Turku: University of Turku.

Lepola, J., Salonen, P., & Vauras, M. (2000), "The development of motivational orientations as a function of divergent reading careers from pre-school to the second grade." *Learning and Instruction 10*, 153–177.

Lepola, J., Vauras, M., & Poskiparta, E. (2000), Unpublished data.

Magnusson, D. (1985), "Implications of an interactional paradigm for research on human development." *International Journal of Behavioral Development 8*, 115–137.

Marcus, R. F. (1975), "The child as elicitor of parental sanctions for independent and dependent behavior: A simulation of parent–child interaction." *Developmental Psychology 11*, 443–452.

Martin, H. P., & Beezley, P. (1977), "Behavioral observations of abused children." *Developmental Medicine and Child Neurology 19*, 373–387.

McGee, R., Williams, S., & Silva, P. A. (1988), "Slow starters and long-term backward readers. A replication and extension." *British Journal of Educational Psychology 58*, 330–337.

McGill-Franzen, A., & Allington, R. L. (1991), "Every child's right: Literacy." *The Reading Teacher 45*, 86–90.

McGilly, K. (ed.) (1994), *Classroom Lessons: Integrating Cognitive Theory & Classroom Practice.* Cambridge, MA: MIT Press.

McNaughton, S. (1981), "Low progress readers and teacher instructional behavior during oral reading: The risk of maintaining instructional dependence." *Exceptional Child 28*, 167–176.

Nolen, S. B. (1988), "Reasons for studying: Motivational orientations and study strategies." *Cognition and Instruction 5*, 269–287.

Olkinuora, E., & Salonen, P. (1992), "Adaptation, motivational orientation, and cognition in a subnormally-performing child: A systemic perspective for training." In B. Wong (ed.) *Intervention Research in Learning Disabilities: An International Perspective* (pp. 190–213). New York: Springer Verlag.

Osofsky, J. D., & O'Connell, E. (1972), "Parent–child interaction: Daughters' effects upon mothers' and fathers' behaviors." *Developmental Psychology 7*, 157–168.

Pintrich, P. R., & DeGroot, E. V. (1990), "Motivational and self-regulated learning components of classroom academic performance." *Journal of Educational Psychology 82*, 33–40.

Pintrich, P. R., Roeser, R. W., & DeGroot, A. M. (1994), "Classroom and individual differences in early adolescents' motivation and self-regulated learning." *Journal of Early Adolescence 14*, 139–161.

Poskiparta, E., Niemi, P., Lepola, J., Ahtola, A., & Laine, P-L. (2000), "Development of motivational–emotional vulnerability from pre-school to grade 2 among children diagnosed as poor, average or good readers in grade 2." (Submitted)

Rogoff, B., & Gardner, W. (1984), "Adult guidance of cognitive development." In B. Rogoff & J. Lave (eds) *Everyday Cognition: Its Development in Social Context* (pp. 95–116). Cambridge, MA: Harvard University Press.

Salomon, G. (1996), "Studying novel learning environments as patterns of change." In S. Vosniadou, E. De Corte, R. Glaser & H. Mandl (eds) *International Perspectives on the Psychological Foundations of Technology-Based Learning Environments*. Hillsdale, NJ: Erlbaum.

Salonen, P. (2000), *Subnormally Performing Children's Coping Strategies in Situational Context: Field-Theoretical Foundations, Taxonomy, and Case Analysis*. Centre for Learning Research, University of Turku. (Unpublished manuscript)

Salonen, P., Lehtinen, E., & Olkinuora, E. (1998), "Expectations and beyond: The development of motivation and learning in a classroom context." In J. Brophy (ed.) *Advances in Research on Teaching. Vol. 7: Expectations in the Classroom* (pp. 111–150). Greenwich, Conn.: JAI Press.

Salonen, P., Lepola, J., & Niemi, P. (1998), "The development of first graders' reading skill as a function of pre-school motivational orientation and phonemic awareness." *European Journal of Psychology of Education 13*, 155–174.

Sameroff, A. J. (1975), "Early influences on development: Fact or fancy." *Merrill-Palmer Quarterly 21*, 267–294.

Sansbury, L. L., & Wahler, R. G. (1992), "Pathways to maladaptive parenting with mothers and their conduct disordered children." *Behavior Modification 16*, 574–592.

Schultz, G., & Switzky, H. N. (1990), "The development of intrinsic motivation in students with learning problems." *Preventing School Failure 34*, 14–20.

Seifert, T. L. (1995), "Academic goals and emotions: A test of two models." *Journal of Psychology Interdisciplinary & Applied 129*, 543–552.

Sfard, A. (1998), "On two metaphors for learning and the dangers of choosing just one." *Educational Researcher 27*, 4–13.

Switzky, H. N. (in press), "Personality and motivational self-system processes in persons with mental retardation: Old memories and new perspectives." In H. Switzky (ed.) *Personality and Motivational Differences in Persons with Mental Retardation*. Mahwah, NJ: Erlbaum.

Urdan, T. C., & Maehr, M. L. (1995), "Beyond a two-goal theory of motivation and achievement: A case for social goals." *Review of Educational Research 65*, 213–244.

Vauras, M., Kinnunen, R., & Kuusela, L. (1994), "Development of text-processing skills in high-, average-, and low-achieving primary school children." *Journal of Reading Behavior 26*, 361–389.

Vauras, M., Rauhanummi, T., Kinnunen, R., & Lepola, J. (1999), "Motivational vulnerability as a challenge for educational interventions." *International Journal of Educational Research 31*, 515–531.

Wentzel, K. R. (1992), "Motivation and achievement in adolescence: A multiple goals perspective." In D. Schunk & J. Meece (eds) *Student Perceptions in the Classroom* (pp. 287–306). Hillsdale, NJ: Erlbaum.

Wigfield, A., Eccles, J. S., & Rodriguez, D. (1998), "The development of children's motivation in school context." In P. D. Pearson & A. Iran-Nejad (eds) *Review of Research in Education 23*, 73–118.

Wolters, C. A., Yu, S. L., & Pintrich, P. L. (1996), "The relation between goal orientation and students' motivational beliefs and self-regulated learning." *Learning & Individual Differences 8*, 211–238.

Yair, G. (2000), "Reforming motivation: how the structure of instruction affects students' learning experiences." *British Educational Research Journal 26*, 191–210.

Yarrow, M., Waxler, C., & Scott, P. (1971), "Child effects on adult behavior." *Developmental Psychology 5*, 300–311.

Young, A. J. (1997), "I think, therefore I'm motivated: The relations among cognitive strategy use, motivational orientation and classroom perceptions over time." *Learning & Individual Differences 9*, 249–283.

Part VI

Conclusion

Chapter 16

Emerging Trends in Recent Research on Motivation in Learning Contexts

Simone Volet

At the conclusion of this book, it becomes clear that the case for understanding and researching motivation in learning contexts is strong. Overall, and despite different theoretical underpinnings, units of analysis and research foci, a number of common trends emerge across the fourteen chapters. Six conceptual shifts in the way research seems to be evolving, and eight methodological implications are discussed in turn, with reference to material from the different chapters. Given the richness of the contributions, referencing is obviously limited and illustrative.

Conceptual Shifts

From a Decontextualised to a Situated and Experiential Approach

There is growing support for the view that productive engagement in learning activities (assumed to provide evidence of motivation) has to be understood in relation to the context in which it is embedded — since context is assumed to give meaning to task-oriented actions. Situated and experiential approaches to the study of motivation are therefore prioritised at the expense of decontextualised investigations of general motivational beliefs and orientations, or both approaches are combined. Rather than treating context as a 'vague' background variable (Vauras) which produces 'effects on motivation' (Boekaerts), it is now conceived as 'a major constituent of motivation' (Turner) to which learners are sensitive (Boekaerts). Many contributors stress the complexity of conceptualising and operationalising motivation in natural learning contexts, a task viewed as 'much more complicated and requiring more sophisticated methodological tools than the exploration of generalised motivational variables (Krapp & Lewalter). Researching situated motivation implies locating goals and engagement in the dynamic activities of social systems or communities of learners, where individuals mutually influence each other and where the construction of motivational meanings reflects individuals' motivational beliefs, prior experience and subjective appraisals of the affordances and constraints of the current situation (whether elicited in self-reports or inferred from observations).

Motivation in Learning Contexts: Theoretical Advances and Methodological Implications, pages 319–334.

Wosnitza & Nenniger propose a conceptual distinction between contexts as material or social objects of reality and between objective and subjective perspectives of this social or material reality. The latter distinction is similar to Linnenbrick & Pintrich's notions of alpha and beta presses of the context. Examining contextual influences on motivation from a subjective perspective has traditionally received less attention than its objective counterpart. This volume, therefore, fills in a gap by examining how students' current emotional state, goals, motivation, commitment and involvement are related to, for example, their appraisals of social relatedness in their vocational learning context (Krapp & Lewalter), their perceptions of future instrumentality of current learning activities (Lens, Simons & Dewitte), their anticipation of future job prospects depending on whether they attend an academic or practical education section (Gurtner *et al.*), their understanding of what is appropriate in an unfamiliar learning situation (Volet), or their interpretations of the immediate learning environment (Järvelä & Niemivirta), in particular their perceptions of teachers' goal orientations (Lemos, Turner). Treating learners as actors (Op't Eynde, DeCorte & Verschaffel) with appraisals, feelings, metacognitive experiences (Dermitzaki & Efklides) and subjective interpretations of situations is viewed as critical to identify the extent of congruence between learners and teachers' expectations (Volet) or between multiple personal and contextual goals (Linnenbrick & Pintrich).

These examples highlight the multiplicity of ways in which contexts are conceptualised and operationalised, including different perspectives and objects of reality (Wosnitza & Nenniger), time perspectives (Krapp & Lewalter; Lens *et al.*), levels of specificity (Gurtner *et al.*; Volet) and self-context relationships (Hickey & McCaslin). The complexity of conceptualising and researching situated motivation may contribute to explaining why the study of general motivational beliefs and goal orientations in a decontextualised way has dominated mainstream motivation research for so long. Taking trait-like constructs of motivation in the experiential domain, incorporating them into the network of concepts needed to capture the reality of real-life learning, and examining their dynamic interactions with situational dimensions, is expected to provide a more fine-grained and richer understanding of their relative and conditional significance.

The growing importance given to the situated nature of motivation is also related to fundamental changes over the last decade in the theoretical foundations of learning and instruction. Social–constructivist and sociocultural perspectives on learning have led to the design of new learning environments and the development of innovative pedagogical practices, where active and social forms of learning are emphasised. These so-called communities of learners capitalise upon distributed expertise and promote the design of 'communal, open, complex and meaningful inquiry-based activities' (Järvelä & Niemivirta). According to Vauras *et al.*, such challenging environments break the conventional forms of classrooms that value individual learning, motivation and achievement. Inevitably, the new social practices challenge traditional motivation research. Situated and experiential approaches are viewed as best suited to investigate how these new learning environments support the development of adaptive motivation and engagement, and the extent to which 'undesirable motivational consequences' may emerge in some students (Vauras *et al.*).

From Stable Motivational Traits to Dynamic Conceptualisations of Motivation

Consistent with the move towards studying motivation in real-life learning contexts is the emergence of dynamic conceptualisations of motivation which challenge traditionally trait-based conceptualisations investigated in one-off surveys. The majority of contributors reporting empirical work have investigated the dynamic aspects of motivation in their own research. This may involve in-depth analyses of individuals' online appraisals of specific learning situations as they unfold and interact with their motivational beliefs, or the close monitoring of a group of learners' on-going social interactions and engagement in a specific classroom activity with stimulated retrospective reports by multiple participants (e.g., Boekaerts, Järvelä & Niemivirta; Lemos, Op't Eynde *et al.*; Turner & McCaslin; Vauras *et al.*) or alternatively comparative studies of groups of learners across contexts and over time (e.g., Gurtner *et al.*; Krapp & Lewalter; Volet).

The fine-grained studies of the dynamics of natural classroom activities provide useful indicators of the extent to which students' participation, interpretations of situations and appraisal processes are consistent with their motivational beliefs and tendencies to engage in such activities. They also highlight some of the conditions under which students' appraisals of specific local circumstances trigger affective responses and consequently alternative, rather than 'habitualised' (Boekaerts), forms of engagement and commitment. Regardless of the theoretical grounding of those studies, there is convergence in research purpose — i.e., to understand the dynamics of motivation in real-life situations — and consensus on at least one theoretical assumption – i.e., that individual and social dimensions are dynamic constructs which mutually interact.

Although studies grounded in sociocultural perspectives (e.g., Turner) take a learning activity as the unit of analysis and those based on socio-cognitive perspectives (e.g., Boekaerts) focus on the individual engaged in a particular learning task and context, researchers from both intellectual traditions highlight the importance of combining the two perspectives. For Turner, although these theories can be interpreted as conflicting and incompatible views of reality, 'their triangulation offers an opportunity to explore the phenomenon of person-in-situation'. Similarly, Op't Eynde *et al.* highlight the importance of adopting a multilevel approach and a range of units of analysis. Like Anderson, Greeno, Reder & Simon (2000), with reference to educational psychology research in general, they argue that examining motivation in the context of real-life activities does not mean that the activity should be the only level of analysis. In addition to observations and discourse analysis, recent research has used online questionnaires, online interviews, experience sampling methods, and video-based stimulated recall interviews with multiple participants. In combination, these different methodological approaches are assumed to provide rich information on the interplay of individual and social dimensions in the construction of motivation in situation. According to Boekaerts, although relatively similar learning situations tend to activate habitualised domain-specific motivational orientations, learners remain constantly alert to cues in their immediate environment that may be emotionally arousing. These specific environmental conditions need to be of high personal importance (Boekaerts) or represent exceptional conditions (Lemos) for students to display motivated behaviours which are not consistent with their domain-specific motivational beliefs. Op't Eynde *et al.*'s research found that students' interpretations and appraisals can reflect their general task-specific competence. Boekaerts, Lemos and Op't Eynde *et al.*'s research, along with the work of Järvelä & Niemirvirta, Krapp & Lewalter and Turner highlights how learners' appraisals of their current learning activity can play a mediating role between their domain-specific motivational beliefs and tendencies and their learning intentions and commitment to engage in that activity — and thus contribute to explaining why general motivational beliefs are not very good predictors of actual motivated behaviour.

Like their colleagues involved in micro-level naturalistic studies, researchers examining the dynamics of motivation at a more macro level also work from hybrid conceptual frameworks and use mixed methods (e.g., Gurtner *et al.*; Krapp & Lewalter; Volet). In order to build up the detailed descriptions of settings valued by researchers working on case studies, they use longitudinal research design, multi-level approaches, comparisons of groups of learners across contexts, and combine quantitative and qualitative data with additional sources of information about contexts from both objective and subjective perspectives. Such data may include, for example, curriculum documents, assessment practices, various information on school cultures and sub-cultures, on education systems in relation to the world of work, and on political or economic indicators of the value of education in society. The overall purpose of such research is to understand the socio-cultural conditions which foster continuity, adaptability or responsiveness in motivational beliefs and goals over time and across contexts. Such contexts may be different high-school sections (Gurtner *et al.*), on the job vs. institutional vocational education settings (Krapp & Lewalter) or different cultural–educational learning settings (Volet). Overall, this research reveals that while broad socio-cultural contexts have an enduring influence on individuals' motivational orientations, which trait-based studies had documented and emphasised, once activated in a real learning situation, this influence is mediated by subjective appraisals and interpretations of personally important aspects of the immediate learning situation. The differentiated patterns of stability and change which emerge in macro level studies are consistent with the evidence of habitualised, or alternatively context-sensitive, behaviours in micro-level studies The macro-level studies of the dynamics of motivation also highlight how, at the group level, some forms of motivation seem to be sensitive to contextual aspects while others appear more stable across contexts and over time.

Overall, our understanding of the dynamic conditions under which general motivational beliefs and values and local contextual circumstances affect students' appraisals, emotions and engagement in real-life learning situations remains fragmented and speculative. More research is needed to understand the interactive contextual and psychological conditions under which stability and change in motivation and engagement can be found, whether at the micro or the macro level of analysis. There is a need to combine perspectives, levels of analysis and methods of investigation in order to accumulate converging evidence, interpret puzzling situations (Turner) and contradictory cases (Järvelä & Niemivirta), and eventually uncover paradoxes and contradictions (Turner) which reveal unexamined assumptions.

From a Dominance on Cognitive Aspects to Multi-Dimensional Aspects

Another implication of entering the experiential domain of motivation in context is the recognition that neither motivational traits, nor cognitive constructions of motivation, nor qualitative features of tasks and context are sufficient on their own to understand the complex, multidimensional and interactive nature of motivation and engagement in learning. Emotional and social aspects are given increased attention in this volume.

Emotions can be conceptualised as negative, for example, feelings of anxiety, worry, unhappiness, frustration and boredom, or positive, for example, feelings of happiness, eagerness, fun or excitement. The relationship of emotions to motivation and learning is discussed in length by Boekaerts and Op't Eynde *et al.* Boekaerts stresses the emotional arousal experienced by students when they perceive a mismatch between their own goals and those of others in the classroom. Her research shows how unfavourable domain-specific motivational beliefs directly affect emotional arousal vis-à-vis a learning task, and when those beliefs are favourable how their impact is mediated by cognitive appraisals of the task. She raises the critical issue, for educators, of the conditions under which optimistic appraisals of a learning situation may 'buffer negative attitudes/feelings about a subject-matter domain' and the extent to which 'perceived availability of social support' may act as such a buffer. Op't Eynde *et al.* also highlight the impact of negative emotions experienced in the process of learning and problem solving. Like Boekaerts, they stress how affect forms an integral part of the 'act of participating' in a learning activity, and thus cannot be dissociated from the cognitive and social aspects. Op't Eynde *et al.*'s call for a holistic approach to the study of emotional experience in learning is echoed in Volet's university students' accounts of their lack of motivation to engage in intercultural learning activities due a feeling that their emotional needs would not be met if they studied with peers from a different cultural–educational background.

Op't Eynde *et al.*'s in-depth study of a few students' on-going (meta)cognitive processes and emotions during a problem-solving task, combined with video-based stimulated accounts of their behaviours, feelings and subjective rationale, unveiled the flow of negative emotions which arose from their appraisals of inadequacy in their problem-solving strategies. Yet, although those subjective appraisals and emotional experiences appeared to be context-sensitive, they also reflected students' underlying belief systems. Understanding the environmental conditions that, despite unfavourable motivational beliefs, trigger positive situational appraisals and emotions and in turn increased task-focused activities should be a priority of any study of 'new powerful learning environments' (Järvelä & Niemivirta). This issue is also stressed by Vauras *et al.* who argue that while new learning environments may solve some of the motivational problems of conventional classroom teaching, they may also have 'undesirable motivational consequences', some of their features being 'counterproductive' for some students. The role of context on the development of emotions suggests that their importance should not only be examined in context but also across contexts. The work of Krapp & Lewalter is a step in this direction. Their comparative and longitudinal study of vocational education students taught either in an on-the-job or institutional learning setting illustrates how the predictive power of needs-related emotional experiences on the development of content interest, can vary across contexts. Furthermore, the cross-cultural literature provides indications that emotions are also culturally-bound (Markus & Kitayama, 1991), an issue under-examined in the context of multicultural learning environments.

A major challenge in studying the significance and function of emotions is methodological. Physiological measures are inadequate to provide information on the nature of arousal, one-off questionnaires are not suited to monitor change in emotions during learning, repeated experience sampling methods may have an interfering effect, and retrospective accounts of feelings provide subjectively perceived and incomplete information on the flow of emotions. Mixed methods and triangulation approaches, therefore, appear useful to provide the best possible approximation of the role of emotions in motivation and learning.

The social aspects of motivation in context are also paramount and have been addressed explicitly or implicitly in all chapters. Depending on the theoretical grounding, they become either the main object of attention, as in the studies of micro-systems of learning framed within a sociocultural perspective, or they form an integral part of the study of the interplay between individual and situational influences on appraisals, emotions and goals, typically framed within a socio cognitive conceptual perspective.

A number of chapters examine the social aspects of motivation in context from a socio-cognitive perspective. The focus is on the dynamic interactions, in real-life situations, between self-related motivational dimensions, various aspects of the broader socio-cultural context and subjective appraisals of the immediate social setting. Wosnitza & Nenniger's empirical work, grounded in their framework for conceptualising and operationalising the social aspects of learning contexts, reveals the influence of subjective perceptions of the social learning environment on an individual's content or procedural interest. Further empirical support for the significance of subjective perceptions of macro aspects of the social environment on engagement in learning can be found in Krapp & Lewalter and Gurtner *et al.*'s chapters. Krapp & Lewalter report how vocational students' interest is influenced by their perception of (lack of) social relatedness in their vocational learning setting. Similarly, Gurtner *et al.*'s data shows how high-school students' motivation is affected by their perceived lack of attractiveness of completing their schooling in a practical section. The impact of future time perspective, emerging in Gurtner *et al.*'s findings, is examined in depth by Lens *et al.* Lens *et al.* argue that prior motivation research has neglected the instrumental role of future goals — whether extrinsic, performance or learning goals — or of no future goals on students' current motivation. In their research, future goals are linked to students' representations of their future study or profession and its socio-economic status.

The significance of social dimensions of motivation is particularly critical in Boekaerts' work, which combines the general, the domain-specific and the more micro task-level of analysis. Boekaerts' research stresses the significance of individuals' online appraisals of the local social conditions in which learning takes place. Her empirical work reveals that habitualised domain-specific behaviours can be altered in the presence of 'salient contextual information [typically of a social nature] ... consequential in nature' to the person. Boekaerts argues that investigating the effect of local context sensitivity and related emotional experience is critical to a full understanding of how students' engagement in learning changes 'as a function of their current concerns'.

Researchers working from a sociocultural or situative perspective also emphasise the importance of investigating motivation at the micro-level of analysis. Unlike Boekaerts, however, they tend to play down the importance of appraisals and self-related cognitions at the expense of social dimensions. In other words, while Boekaerts stresses the importance of understanding motivation from a learner-in-context perspective, researchers working from a sociocultural or situative perspective conceptualise motivation as a socially embedded interactive experience that is best understood through analyses of a learning activity conceptualised as a dynamic micro-system. Yet, despite the possible conflicting interpretations that could be made from focusing on the self or the social aspects of motivation, some situative researchers, such as Turner, point to the value of triangulating theoretical perspectives. Turner sees the 'fruitful tension between and among deductive and inductive approaches' and the benefits of a more 'stringent test of motivation theories in classrooms'.

According to Hickey & McCaslin, focusing on social issues and participants' engagement in learning is essential for understanding the dynamics of motivation and learning in classrooms which operate under new pedagogical approaches. In the case of communities of learning, there has been a significant change in the cognitive division of labour between the teacher and the students, a major reconceptualisation of learning tasks which tend to be ill-defined and constantly evolving, and a new focus on joint products rather than separate contributions. In such cases, individuals' appraisals of the difficulty of a task relative to perceptions of self-competence may become difficult, and even irrelevant, and so is a students' estimation of the probability of success (Vauras *et al.*). According to Järvelä & Niemivirta, Vauras *et al.*, Turner and Lemos, the study of motivated learning in new powerful learning environments has an inherently social focus. The research methodologies used by motivation researchers (a label no longer appropriate) who situate their work in a situative perspective reflect this conceptual shift. They prioritise the documentation of context-bound manifestations of motivation (Lemos) through observations of groups of students and discourse analysis where participants' social interactions can be closely examined. Interestingly, however, all these researchers use complementary methods conceptually grounded in cognitive approaches, such as questionnaires (online, semi-online) and interviews (online, confronted, video-based recall) in order to elicit individuals' subjective appraisals and interpretations. The importance given to both social and individual dimensions in situated motivation may reflect a concern that some new pedagogical practices may increase motivational and cognitive differences among students (Vauras *et al.*). According to Dermitzaki & Efklides, researchers should not lose track of the individual and, in particular, how people interpret contexts in light of their motivational tendencies and in relation to their cognitive ability, gender and age. These individual characteristics clearly have a social dimension in the way they are experienced.

From Single-Level to Multi-Level Conceptualisations and Analyses

Focusing on the dynamics of motivation in context does not imply that only situation-specific dimensions affect current motivation and engagement. The significance of individuals' prior experience, history of motivation and learning, as well as the importance of broad contextual dimensions outside the classroom are widely acknowledged even by researchers working at the micro-level of a specific task. Most contributors in this volume mention the need for multi-level conceptualisations and multi-level analyses of motivation in context.

Two chapters (Gurtner *et al.* and Volet) present a multi-level conceptual framework for understanding and researching motivation in context. Building on Bronfenbrenner's ecological systems theory, Gurtner *et al.*'s four layers model of learning contexts incorporates micro, meso, exo and macro levels. They argue that at the micro (e.g., school subject and type of lessons) and meso (school climate, classroom goal orientations, norms and practices) levels, students and contexts exercise mutual, bi-directional influences on each other. These mutual influences could be seen as instrumental in the revision of personal goals to match contextual ones (Linnenbrink & Pintrich) and re-establish congruence (Volet). At the exo (school structure, streaming) and macro (familial, cultural, political or economic aspects as they relate to education and schooling) levels, Gurtner *et al.* postulate that individual–context influences are uni-directional and relatively weaker. While the issue of directionality has not received much empirical attention, Volet's findings suggest that the strength of contextual influences may not systematically be linked to proximity since some fundamental societal values related to education

— and which have been internalised by individuals as their own — are enduring and seem relatively unaffected by participation in a community of practice which does not share the same values. Which aspects of motivation are more sensitive to local affordances or alternatively macro level influences is still not well understood, nor are the conditions under which engagement in learning reflect beta presses of macro or micro level of the context.

Like Gurtner *et al.*, Volet's multi-level model acknowledges a range of levels of context but it also incorporates the individual in the multi-level conceptualisation. The centre part of her model highlights the experiential domain where the individual and the context merge in the here and now of learning. Although recognising the difficulty of conceptualising and representing motivation in context from a combined cognitive and situative perspective, Volet stresses the value of complementarity of perspectives. She argues that a multi-level conceptualisation of the learner in context is necessary to fully understand the dynamic interplay between individuals' motivational beliefs and values for typical learning situations, the significant socio-cultural influences related to education beyond the classroom, and the specific situational affordances in the current learning setting. Her empirical work supports the usefulness of a multi-level approach to capture the complex network of mutual influences and in particular to understand stability and change in motivation over time and across contexts. Vauras *et al.*, in their attempt to link motivational orientations to long-term developmental aspects and situational interaction dynamics, and to contextual and institutional-cultural macro level factors reflect a similar multi-level approach.

A number of contributors investigating the dynamics of motivation at the micro level of the classroom have also adopted a multi-level perspective in their work. Boekaerts' dual focus involves examining the stable aspects of motivation as well as a student's sensitivity to local conditions in situation. She argues that a focus on context sensitivity is not sufficient since 'students have to infer the meaning of learning opportunities from indirect cues, bringing their self-efficacy, beliefs expectations and attributions into the picture'. Järvelä & Niemivirta, Op't Eynde *et al.*, and Boekaerts provide empirical support for this contention. There is converging evidence of the need to take into account the dynamic interplay of multi-level elements in research on motivation in context. Järvelä & Niemivirta combine overall goal orientations and observed engagement in actual classroom behaviours with interpretations of learning situations on several occasions. This provides an opportunity to explore micro-level change in appraisals. Op't Eynde *et al.* include domain-specific motivational beliefs, subjective appraisals of a problem and thinking processes during its resolution, and compare these with video-based stimulated reflections aimed at clarifying the relation between underlying beliefs and problem-solving behaviours. Consistent across studies is the recognised criticality of distinguishing between general motivational tendencies and habitualised behaviours (usually at the domain-specific level), and context-sensitive motivational appraisals and behaviours (at the task or activity level). Exploring further their development and demonstration across macro and micro level contexts and over time is likely to be high on the agenda of future research on motivation in context.

From Uni-Directional to Bi- or Multi-Directional Individual and Contextual Influences

As discussed earlier, a major conceptual shift in research on motivation in learning contexts is towards recognition of the dynamics of motivation in context. Consistent with this shift is a move away from research that focuses on the uni-directional influences of either individual characteristics (whether traits, general beliefs or orientations) or context characteristics (whether distal or proximal, social or material), and ignores the mediating impact of situation-specific appraisals and affordances on current motivation and engagement. Motivation is conceived as located at the heart of a dynamic and complex system of interactions and mutual influences.

The importance of systemic, dynamic and reciprocal influences of individuals' effectivities and contextual affordances (Volet) at the experiential or micro level of analysis is widely acknowledged. The reciprocity of bi-directional interactions between individual and context is stressed particularly strongly by researchers who work from a situative perspective. For example, Lemos argues that motivational processes and goals in particular develop within this reciprocal relationship. Similarly, Vauras *et al.* highlight the interactionist nature of motivational orientation constructs and claim that environmental influences are not unidirectional but 'drift between all participants in the situation'. This view is echoed in Turner's contention that the environment is 'multidirectional and is constituted by group members in their activities'.

Overall, however, empirical evidence of the reciprocal nature of influences remains limited and fragmented, which reflects the complexity of operationalising and investigating interactive constructs. Linnenbrick & Pintrich argue that the limited research examining the interaction of personal and contextual goals shows disagreement about the potential directions of the interactive effects. Finally, while the importance of micro-level bi-directional and reciprocal influences of individual and context is widely recognised, conceptualising bi-directional influences at the more macro level is more complex, and their existence has even been questioned (Gurtner *et al.*).

From Single to Integrated or Multidimensional Theoretical Perspectives

As stressed throughout this volume, motivation in learning contexts is socially situated, dynamic, interactive and multi-dimensional. Demonstration of motivated behaviour — or engagement in learning — can be traced to relatively stable individual characteristics which are mediated by appraisals, affordances and emotions in specific situations, and to broader socio-cultural influences outside the classroom, in the school system, at home, in the community and society at large. It is therefore not surprising that the shift towards conceptualising motivation in context has stretched traditional theories of motivation. It has revealed their limitations (Vauras *et al.*; Dermitzaki & Efklides), and in particular their difficulty in conceptualising motivation as both a psychological and social phenomenon at the same time (Volet). As encapsulated by Turner's statement, 'the present challenge to motivational research is to integrate the notions of self and context'.

In their analysis of different epistemological perspectives on the study of engagement in learning, Hickey & McCaslin argue that both the behavioural and the cognitive are inadequate, on their own, to form the basis of a contextual and dynamic conceptualisation of motivation. They reject the case for an aggregation approach to reconciliation — which would attribute different levels of analysis to the different theoretical perspectives (behaviourist–individual behaviour — cognitive–patterns of activities across individuals — and situative — broader social groups) — on the grounds that the behaviourist and cognitivist perspectives are fundamentally incompatible. Instead, Hickey & McCaslin propose a dialectical approach to reconciliation which subsumes the behavioural and the cognitive approaches under a contextualist sociocultural world view. Locating the individual in context, rather than emphasising the individual or the context, makes it possible to 'interpret individuals' specific behaviours in context as well as the patterns of activity across individuals within a broader historical and sociocultural perspective'.

Many studies in this volume are framed within a sociocultural, situative perspective but it is remarkable to note that most incorporate some concepts and methods grounded in a cognitive perspective (such as motivational beliefs, goal orientations, or subjective appraisals and interpretations). Conversely, a number of studies investigating the interactive influences of self-related motivational constructs, situational appraisals and affordances complement individually-oriented constructs with a study of classroom observations in order to enrich their understanding of motivation in context. Integrated conceptual perspectives and cross-references to alternative explanatory perspectives to complement the weakness of the main perspective are frequent in this volume.

Grounding research in multidimensional conceptual perspectives, and choosing units of analysis and methodologies for pragmatic reasons rather than theory–method consistency, highlights the fact that contextual motivation theory is still in development. Turner argues that 'until our theoretical understandings of motivation and persons in contexts develop further it may be fruitful to integrate two powerful theories and use one to complement the other'. For her, 'triangulating theory (such as goal theory and discourse analysis) provides an opportunity to explore the phenomenon of person-in-situation' — one explicating individual construction and the other social construction of reality. Like Volet, Järvelä & Niemivirta explicitly locate their research in a combination of sociocultural and sociocognitive perspectives. Alternatively, Vauras *et al.* and Dermitzaki & Efklides try to integrate concepts and methodologies from cognitive, sociocultural and developmental theory. The importance of adopting multiple levels of analysis (personal, interpersonal and community processes) is also stressed by Op't Eynde *et al.* but they observe that most studies of emotional experiences in the classroom are in fact 'limited to one level of analysis, due to limited resources and practical reasons'. Finally, adopting a multi-dimensional conceptual perspective can also involve the combination of a theory driven approach and inductive content analysis (Lemos).

Overall, triangulating conceptual perspectives seems promising in enriching our understanding of motivation in real-life classroom contexts. Yet, since different perspectives may be based on conflicting assumptions about learning, motivation and engagement, there is always a risk of reaching unreconcilable interpretations of the same psychological and social phenomena. Dermitzaki & Efklides point to the challenge of combining developmental and individual difference approaches to motivation with the situational or contextual approach 'in order to understand what is context-free or context-specific in motivational change'. Maintaining theoretical clarity and coherence, perhaps via a dialectical approach (Hickey & McCaslin), presents a major challenge for the future of research on motivation in learning contexts.

Methodological Implications of the Conceptual Shifts

The conceptual shifts emerging from recent research on motivation in learning contexts have challenged traditional research methodologies. New innovative approaches have been developed. The major methodological implications of those conceptual shifts are summarised below.

From Quantitative or Qualitative to Mixed Methods

The general trend across studies is for mixed, rather than mono-methods and a combination of quantitative and qualitative analyses, even if these are grounded in different — essentially cognitive/rationalist and situative/sociocultural — epistemological traditions. Complementarity of angles, perspectives, sources of data and analyses is valued at the expense of single theory–method consistency. Several researchers suggest that the choice of methodology and level of analysis be pragmatic (e.g., Hickey & McCaslin; Turner, Op't Eynde *et al.*) and dependent on the research purpose. Overall, there is widespread agreement across chapters on the view that since the reality of motivation in context is complex, dynamic multi-dimensional, multi-level, and constantly changing, a variety of methods of inquiry, sources of information and analytical tools is required. The value of combining quantitative and qualitative, deductive and inductive methods of analysis is not confined to research on motivation in learning contexts. It is part of a growing trend in educational psychology research (Anderman & Anderman, 2000). Combining methods of inquiry grounded in different conceptual perspectives, however, can provide major challenges for researchers, since data obtained with different methods may lead to conflicting interpretations of the target phenomenon, and lack of conceptual clarity.

From Single to Multiple Data Sources

Most researchers exploring motivation in learning contexts use multiple rather than single data sources. Traditional one-off surveys are still common but new types of questionnaires are being developed (e.g., online) and these are combined with data obtained in observations, repeated experience sampling, videos of classroom interactions, and various types of interviews (e.g., online, confronting, video-based). The influence of ethnography, anthropology and sociology research methodologies is noticeable. Complementary information on norms and practices that characterise classroom activities, school systems or community values about education are also sought — for example, curricula or policy documents related to education.

From Positivist to a Combination of Positivist and Experiential Approaches

Exploring motivation and engagement in learning as it unfolds requires methodologies that can reveal the experiential, the subjective and the emotional, in addition to the externally observed and interpreted. Emphasing the experiential represents an acknowledgment that situations are subjectively perceived and thus can vary across individuals. A range of innovative methodologies has been developed to elicit individuals' (as actors) subjective experience and interpretations of tasks, classrooms and broader contexts. Examples of such methodologies are online questionnaires, online interviews, experience sampling methods, confronting or stimulated recall interviews immediately after a target activity, in addition to discourse analysis and inductive content analysis. Furthermore, objective measures are not well suited to reveal 'hot' cognitions and emotional experiences. Understanding the flow of emotions during a learning activity can be approximated by combining multiple sources of data, including thinking aloud to access online problem-solving processes, (semi)online questionnaire to reveal emotional appraisals, and video-based stimulated recall interviews to elicit individuals' recollection of feelings at critical times and their interpretations and clarifications of the relation between their emotions and problem-solving behaviour (Op't Eynde *et al.*).

From One-Off to Longitudinal and Online Data Collection

The conceptual shift towards understanding the dynamics of motivation and engagement in context has created a move away from studies with a single data point towards longitudinal, repeated measure designs and online data collection. Research at the more macro level of analysis tends to use combined longitudinal and comparative research designs in order to explore stability and change in motivation over time. In contrast, the most popular methods used by those interested in tracing the dynamics of motivation in real time are semi or online questionnaires, repeated online interviews, observations and discourse analysis. The value of combining a developmental approach (with a longitudinal design) with micro-level studies of the dynamics of motivation in real time, and for the same individuals, is mentioned as worth exploring in future research (Vauras *et al.*). The think aloud method, extensively used by cognitive psychologists to obtain data on online thinking processes, was used in one study (Op't Eynde *et al.*) but to assist interpreting the emerging flow of emotional experiences during a problem solving task rather than to provide data on motivational processes.

From Single to Multiple Perspectives

In line with the focus on motivation as an individual characteristic, mainstream prior research has naturally concentrated on the individual learner, and underestimated the significance of socially distributed and jointly constructed motivation. The research reported in this volume stresses the importance of seeking multiple perspectives to understand motivation and engagement in learning. This is viewed as critical to examine the extent of congruence in expectations, goals and interpretations of situations between students and teachers, and among students (Volet). The possibility that maladaptive motivational beliefs, goal orientations and engagement reflect a lack of synchrony among participants has been examined (e.g., Vauras *et al.*). Typical methodologies involve interviews with students and teachers, or matched questionnaires given to students, teachers and sometimes parents in order to systematically compare their interpretations of individual, situation and task dimensions. At the micro-level, stimulated recall interviews with different participants are being used to elicit and then compare participants' interpretations of situations (e.g., Turner). The overall aim of those studies is to develop a more holistic and systemic picture of motivation in context, where participants represent each other's social context.

From Single to Multiple Contexts

An alternative and complementary way of exploring the dynamics of motivation in context is to investigate evidence of consistency and variability across learning contexts and over time. A number of researchers have included multiple contexts in their research designs in order to trace the evolution of motivation in relation to context. Krapp & Lewalter and Gurtner *et al.*, for example, carried out longitudinal studies of groups of students in different (but related) learning contexts. Another distinct feature of these studies is the inclusion of subjective perceptions of each social learning environment in addition to external information about the characteristics of those environments. A few studies at the micro-level also included multiple contexts (e.g., Järvelä & Niemivirta and Lemos). These researchers monitored the online classroom engagement of the same students in different classes and, like the studies at the macro level, included students' subjective interpretations of the context. Such methodologies provide rich data sets to explore inter and intra-individual patterns of stability and change over time, consistency and variability across learning contexts, as well as the possibility of relating these patterns to individual and contextual dimensions.

From Variable to Person-Centred Analyses

Some researchers have promoted the view that the study of motivation in learning contexts should go beyond traditional variable centred approaches and move towards person centred analyses and patterning of motivational functioning. According to Linnenbrick & Pintrich (and Magnusson, 1998), person-centred approaches (e.g., cluster analysis or median-splits) are more appropriate since 'persons move through different contexts, not variables so if one is to examine person–context interactions, it becomes important to find ways to measure the constructs at a person-centred level'. A person-centred approach can lead to the identification of patterns or profiles of motivational functioning that incorporate various motivational dimensions (Lemos). Lemos's research revealed the conceptual usefulness of patterning over the use of 'discrete, mutually exclusive categories of dimensions' for understanding coping strategies in the classroom. She argues that a combination of variable and patterning approaches is useful to capture 'the phenomena under study in terms of the several relevant attributes'. Consistent with these views, and the importance given to mixed methods in this volume, is Murdock's (2000) claim that cluster analysis techniques and qualitative methods of inquiry represent two alternatives to a variable approach since these focus on, or identify people 'who share common contexts of niches' (p. 122).

From Single-Level to Multi-Level Designs and Analyses

The emerging interest in studying the interactive effects of different levels of contexts requires a re-thinking of quantitative methods of analysis. Linnenbrick & Pintrich propose hierarchical linear modelling as an appropriate method to examine the interactive influences of structural aspects of the classroom (alpha press) and students' perceptions of those structures (beta press), since two levels of analysis are involved. This raises the issue of the nested nature of multi-level contexts, and the need for multilevel designs when different levels of contexts are included in a single study. A comprehensive discussion of the methodological implications of the nested nature of educational contexts, and of addressing contextual research questions — by nature multilevel questions since individuals are nested in these contexts — can be found in Murdock (2000) and Lee (2000). Interestingly, and consistent with the research emphases promoted in this volume, Murdock points to the value of collaboration across disciplines on the ground that anthropologists' detailed qualitative descriptions may complement psychologists' sophisticated quantitative analyses and ultimately produce a better understanding of the complexity of social contexts.

In conclusion, this volume makes a significant contribution to the development of a theory of motivation in learning contexts. Together, the fourteen chapters illustrate the conceptual advances made in the late 90s and the variety of innovative research methodologies that have been developed to address new and challenging research questions. The proposed integrative, holistic and systemic approaches to the study of motivation and engagement during the process of learning highlight that motivation research is reaching out beyond its own traditional domain of study and is now taking a leading role in the overall study of learning and instruction. The combination of sociocultural, situative and socio-cognitive epistemological traditions underlying the different contributions, complement each other and together have the potential to substantially enhance our understanding of individual and social dimensions in the construction of motivation, engagement and learning. A major challenge, however, is how to capitalise on the conceptual enrichment provided by the triangulation of different perspectives, without compromising on overall theoretical coherence and meaningful interpretations of motivational phenomena.

References

Anderman, L. H. Y., & Anderman, E. M. (eds). (2000), "Considering contexts in educational psychology: Introduction to the Special Issue." *Educational Psychologist 35* (2), 67–68.

Anderson, J. R., Greeno, J. G., Reder, L. M., & Simon, H. A., (2000), "Perspectives on learning, thinking and activity." *Educational Researcher 29* (4), 11–13.

Lee, V. E. (2000), "Using hierarchical linear modelling to study social contexts: The case of school effects." *Educational Psychologist 35* (2), 125–141.

Magnusson, D. (1998), "The logic and implications of a person-oriented approach." In R. Cairns, L. Bergman & J. Kagan (eds) *Methods and Models for Studying the Individual: Essays in Honor of Marian Radke-Yarrow* (pp. 33–64). Thousand Oaks, CA: Sage.

Markus, H. R., & Kitayama, S. (1991), "Culture and the self: Implications for cognition, emotion and motivation." *Psychological Review 98* (2), 224–253.

Murdock, T. B. (2000), "Incorporating economic context into educational psychology: Methodological and conceptual challenges." *Educational Psychologist 35* (2), 113–124.

Index